Living with Africa

Living with Africa

Jan Vansina

The University of Wisconsin Press

The University of Wisconsin Press
114 North Murray Street
Madison, Wisconsin 53715

2   4   6   8   10   9   7   5   3   1

Printed in the United States of America

Library of Congress Cataloging-in-Publication Data
Vansina, Jan.
Living with Africa / Jan Vansina.
328 p.   cm.
Includes bibliographical references and index.
ISBN 0-299-14320-1   ISBN 0-299-14324-4 (pbk.)
1. Vansina, Jan. 2. Africanists—United States—Biography.
3. Africa—Historiography. I. Title.
DT19.7.V36A3   1994
960'.07202—dc20
[B]   94-588

In celebration of
all my students everywhere

Contents

Preface

I LIVED in Africa for only a decade or so, yet I have lived with a certain "Africa" ever since. Claudine, my wife, was born in Rwanda. By now even she has lived longer outside the continent than on it. But she too has lived all her life with Africa. We know that we belong in "Africa." The Tio of the Republic of Congo believe in a *mpiini*, an unknown object kept in a distant place that holds one's personal life force: our *mpiini* is something somewhere in Africa. This belonging to Africa is so compelling that it seems to us as if our common experience of belonging to this place where we are not but with which we constantly remain in contact has forged our common destiny. I studied the history of Africa, and now in the autumn of life the urge to look back at my itinerary has caught me. The moment has come, perhaps, to discover what kind of object our *mpiini* is. As it happens, the urge has caught me just at a moment when the historiography of Africa is also going through an introspective phase. Out of this confluence flows this book.

The academic study of the history of Africa is almost half a century old, and it is useful to reflect on the enterprise's past, which is little known by most younger practitioners today. No book has been devoted to this subject so far, although a number of accounts dealing either with the history of major ideas in the field or with "the state of the field" have been written. But they leave me unsatisfied, because all too often they tell a disembodied tale of ideas traveling along their appointed celestial spheres as if the present state of affairs had always been a foregone conclusion. Where are the doubts and hesitations, the false starts and the fascinating byways of yore? Have we historiographers really been merely faceless robots at the service of social forces or abstract ideas? Where in all of this is the flesh and blood of the adventure that African history was and is? Where is the elation, the sense of struggle, the ups of dazzling insight, or the downs of frustrating dead ends?

I have always disliked the conventional genre of historiography because it is too bloodless, too faceless, and too likely to praise predestina-
tion. It occurred to me that as a participant in the study of African history,
almost from its inception, I might try my hand at a different sort of historiography, by providing a contrast between an account of the general
development of African history and an account of the personal experience
of one researcher. Such a comparison would make it clear that, when all
is said and done, the practice of African history, with its fieldwork, its
unusual source materials, and its imperious demands on health and com-
fort, often bears only a faint resemblance to the work of most other historians. Surely such differences must also produce differences in the products of historical research about Africa and about other parts of the world.
Moreover, such a contrast should show why the conventional genre of
historiography is often so frustrating. To put the tale of one person's experience next to one about a body of history writing can only lead one to
query the validity of many of the generalizations which the authors of
general historiographies are compelled to make. The contrast between the
two tales should arouse curiosity about the links between the role of
"forces" or "ideas" and actual people. Hence, this book was written, first,
to show how the practice of African history often differs from others, and
then to argue that there can be no such thing as a definitive historiography.
Rather, many historiographies are possible. The glorious disorder generated by the vicissitudes of a researcher's life, in which all the themes are
constantly brewing together, nicely illustrates this point.

The writing of history is the sediment from much dynamic action,
including the accident of individual temperament and talent, the serendipity of events, the vicissitudes of individual research and other experience, the cumulative growth of relevant institutions, the vagaries of
financing, technological change—think of microfilm, tape recorders, photo-
copiers, computers—networks created by family, age, school, neighbor-
hood, and friendship, and also the power of ideas, insights, and methods,
as well as the flights of fancy of the collective imagination of individuals,
communities, societies, and even the nations in which historians operate
and which themselves express prevalent cultural and social trends. Moreover, not one of these factors is wholly independent of the others. Such,
then, is the complexity of what lies behind the writing of history, a complexity which explains why so many potential historiographies of history
can be written.

This book is just one among those many possible essays. It tells the
history of the writing of African history from the point of view of one

practitioner who also tells his own story. Thus the reader can evaluate something of the subjective experience that created his points of view. What this work definitely is not is either a slice of autobiography or even a genuine memoir. It does not chronicle a personal life, nor does it subscribe to the rhetorical rules for that genre. It is at best a truncated professional memoir, truncated because I have chosen to talk about my own activities only insofar as they are relevant to the writing of African history. That means suppressing most of the anecdotes and omitting details of other endeavors, such as the study and teaching of anthropology. The link between the sections that deal with personal experience and the others, which present general developments in the field, therefore runs far deeper than the occasional cross-references indicate.

With regard to sources, I must both warn the readers and crave their indulgence. The chapters dealing with personal experience are well documented, while the ones which discuss the general historiography are not. All studies about the writing of history in Africa have relied on a fraction of the available publications in the field. As Carolyn Neale, in *Writing "Independent" History: African Historiography, 1960–1980*, writes, "In a work on historiography everything is grist for the mill" (197). She relied on publications. A wealth of archival material is available as well, not to speak of a vast reservoir of oral reminiscences. Potentially the sources for a work on historiography are exceptionally vast, so vast that they seem to be endless. Among the more obvious written sources are a mass of academic writings about African history; archival material held by publishers or major journals, such as reader's reports and draft manuscripts; newspaper and other media files; reports and records of conferences; the papers held by scholars or administrators in the field; proposals and reports of progress to foundations or research institutes; documents such as curricula and syllabi, matriculation records, reports on seminars or doctorates, and personnel files generated by various educational institutions; proposals, accounts, and correspondence held by financial establishments; personal correspondence; and more. So one may well ask which of these sources were used in this book. The candid answer is that while the notes indicate what backs up specific assertions in the chapters dealing with general historiography (almost always publications), those assertions rest on a foundation of wide readings in the field, although I was not always reading for that purpose. Hence, to a certain extent the sources are haphazard, and it would be misleading to provide something labeled "bibliography" at the end. Moreover, I consulted unpublished records to answer a few questions, and in a handful of cases I sought information from fellow scholars. While this information suffices for the general outline provided by the relevant chapters here, the reader should know that I am just skimming the surface. The topic could easily sustain a score of researchers for a score of years, and perhaps in the future it will.

The situation is almost the opposite when it comes to the personal part. These chapters rest on a wealth of records. Being familiar with the vagaries of oral reminiscences, I have only relied on my own memory diffidently. Whenever possible I have also followed a paper trail. This consists of personal correspondence, mostly letters to my parents before 1978, full fieldwork records, full correspondence files (comprising about five hundred letters a year) from 1973 onward, my personnel file in the department of history at the University of Wisconsin–Madison (1960 onward), a few documents such as annual reports for that department, some group photographs, and some published items, including reviews of my books. These documents have helped to recall circumstances or to enhance pertinent memories, sometimes altering their significance by placing them in a fuller context. In the notes I distinguish between correspondence, the personnel file, files about particular books, and "activities reports." For the moment I keep all these documents at home.

Acknowledgments

T HIS BOOK was written with financial support from the John D. and Catherine T. MacArthur Foundation. Although in many ways similar to the grants the foundation itself makes, this fellowship was in fact awarded by the University of Wisconsin–Madison, with funding provided by the foundation. Nevertheless, the particular philosophy underlying the MacArthur program encouraged me to try my hand at an unorthodox genre, while the funding itself freed me of formal teaching obligations for the time required to compose the book. For this I am grateful to both institutions. I am also grateful to the William F. Vilas Trust for its long-term support.

The task of writing a work which touches on such a large portion of my life has constantly reminded me of how much I owe to colleagues and students, and even more to kinsfolk and friends on three continents. Their gifts can never be repaid—it would be obscene even to attempt to do so. But I do rejoice in the gifts and remember the givers. If my thought dwells a little longer on the Africans among them, it is because their lives have been or still are so hard, and their giving of themselves has been so generous. And are they not both the heirs and the creators of a genuine history of Africa? Most of them will not read this work, and a roll call of their names would only sound bombastic or meaningless to others. But I do not forget them.

Let me mention then by name only those who have actively given me advice about the writing of this book. Even though I did not always accept their suggestions, they saved me from many an error, contributed information, and forced me to think more clearly about some issues. They are professors such as Willy De Craemer, Renée Fox, Michele Wagner, and Carolyn Keyes (she is not quite a professor yet) and the two readers for the press, who read the whole first draft, as well as professors Allan Isaacman and Jean Hay, who read a portion of it. Of all my critics, however, the

Acknowledgments

most influential and the best-informed one certainly is Claudine. Collectively they may be more responsible for the outcome than they are willing to admit. Therefore, reader, give them credit for the good points, but never blame them.

Barbara Hanrahan—may she be blessed—until recently the senior editor at the University of Wisconsin Press, forcefully encouraged me both when I first adumbrated the idea of this book and later when I diffidently sent her a few chapters. My gratitude also goes to Cathy Skidmore Hess, who helped me with some of the references, and to Kathy McKeegan and Lois Corcoran, who undertook the final preparation of the manuscript. May they be blessed as well.

Abbreviations

CICIBA	Centre International des Civilisations Bantu
CNRS	Centre National de la Recherche Scientifique
IFAN	Institut Français de l'Afrique Noire, later
	Institut Fondamental de l'Afrique Noire
IRSAC	Institut pour la Recherche Scientifique en
	Afrique Centrale
ORSTROM	Office de la Recherche Scientifique et Technique
	d'Outre-Mer
SOAS	School of Oriental and African Studies, London

Living with Africa

1

Before

We . . . president, secretary and members of the committee, charged by order of the Rector Magnificus with the examinations of licenciate in Philosophy and Letters, considering that he has submitted and defended with great distinction a thesis, *The Historical Value of Latin Dirges (797–1313)* . . . have conferred and confer the degree of licenciate in Philosophy and Letters, group B: History, to Jan Vansina . . . Enacted at Leuven, June 20, 1951.

A "FINAL" diploma of this sort is an aspiration fulfilled, an end and a beginning, the launching of a specific career. No one reveres the concept of a career more than Belgians did then and even do now. The word conjures up not just a lifelong activity but a permanent social status. A diploma slots its bearer into a precise spot in the social hierarchy. It tells strangers as well as one's family and the parents of any prospective spouse what to expect, and in everything they do people are supposed to "further their careers." In my case, though, the choice of a practical aspiration had been neither obvious nor easy to begin with, and as to the launching of the appropriate career . . . it did not happen. Better let me tell the tale.

Born on September 14, 1929, in the city of Antwerp, Belgium, I was the seventh living child in a Roman Catholic family that would eventually have twelve children. That was unremarkable. Catholicism was the dominant religion then in Belgium, and large families were not unusual, although few were quite as large as ours. Both parents were professional artists. At the time of my birth my father was a writer, a painter, an art historian, and a well-known figure in Flemish nationalist circles. Mother was a painter. He ran a business, making and selling liturgical vestments and associated objects as well as richly decorated flags. He had inherited the store from his mother, who had embroidered the field of glittering diamonds on the great coat of the statue of the Virgin Mary in Antwerp's cathedral. But the depression gradually ruined the demand for such fine work, and in 1940 the business was closed. We were lucky that my mother was well-off. Her father, starting out as a country boy, made good and became a major force in the tobacco industry. He left her with business acumen, a sense of frugality, and a practical socialism.

Such artistic parents were unusual, and after the war their system of education became even more unusual. Pressured by the vagaries of life in wartime, after 1940 the family became a self-regulating community in which parents were the managers and the ultimate authority but in which daily aspirations, norms, and rules were set by the children, the elder ones ordering the younger ones around and the latter resisting. We had "fought ourselves free," to use a colorful Dutch expression, and we felt both suspicious of the outside world and rebellious toward all outside authority. In consequence, many of us were regularly thrown out of school, a feat that would usually elicit admiration from our siblings. Nevertheless, we learned a lot at home. No one in the region knew more about woods, wastelands, and wild animals than we did. We loved to read literature—I recall competition over who was to read Dostoyevsky's *Brothers Karamazov* next—and we learned a good deal about painting, drawing, and other interesting things that were not taught at school.

The times were unusual indeed. We grew up in the fear and clamor of war, first in Antwerp, later in the woods at Gooreind, near the military proving grounds north of the city. I was used to the sound of incoming artillery by the time I was seven or eight. Then the war broke out. Antwerp was one of the major fortified places in the country, so my father, a veteran of the First World War, decided to move to Bruges, further away from Germany, a place which he felt would be a safe haven. Yet, ironically, it was in Bruges that the Belgian army and Allied contingents were encircled and had to surrender. At that time my mother had just found a new school for me. She enrolled me in a Benedictine boarding school at nearby Zevenkerken. The school was small, an adjunct to a large abbey, and it was steeped in the serene spirit of St. Benedict's rule, with its emphasis on regulated work and contemplation. But Zevenkerken was unlike other Benedictine monasteries, because its monks and pupils came from the French-speaking lower nobility in the Flemish provinces. In my class, for instance, I was the only plebeian in a company of French-speaking nobles, albeit mostly nobles of lower rank. I hated their snobbishness, and I was always fighting my elitist "betters," who made snide remarks about "Flemish primitives." But their vainglory and my pugnacity both faded somewhat, because soon we were half starved. I remember dinners consisting of a single potato, which one had to defend from the older boys.

I managed to hold out mainly because the school's misfortune became my luck when the abbey was commandeered by the Germans in March 1942. The school broke up in small groups of twenty pupils or so, each with their teacher, and roamed about West and East Flanders, from one temporary site to another and from one food supply to another. At times we lodged and studied in a fancy castle, at times in the back room of a shoe factory working full blast, and lastly in a forbidding Jesuit novitiate. At times there were books, and at times there were none. Every semester was different, and the impersonality of school discipline became impossible to uphold. I thrived in those circumstances. Meanwhile, the family returned to Gooreind, where food was easier to find. Traveling from school to home for the holidays now became more and more of an adventure, as the war dragged on and planes strafed trains, roads, and sometimes even pedestrians. At school we always feared massive bombing carried out at night by huge fleets of planes. Then came the invasion of Normandy, and the school was closed. We returned home and took our examinations by mail. Liberation came September 3, 1944, to Antwerp, but the Allied advance was halted north of the city. As a result, in Gooreind we lived in the cellar, coming out for fresh air and food only when the artillery duels abated. Finally, six or eight weeks later, the Canadians came.

That day I roamed through the woods again and stumbled on a scene of recent fighting at the edge of a remote pond. A cloying smell overpowered me, more than the absolute silence of the scene. Sap was oozing from the shrapnel wounds of every tree and shrub, like lifeblood running out. Here and there lay a few rolled-away helmets, and the crushed grass preserved the memory of the bodies that had lain there. I had just turned fifteen. Suddenly I recoiled: here had been strapping young men, full of the rising sap of life, only three years older than I was, perhaps, now inexorably mowed down. What for, by what? By the intolerance of deadly ideologies: they had all succumbed to poisonous ideals, whether nationalist, socialist, populist, democratic, or whatever, ideals promoted by a few strident voices far away in safety. The poison had killed them. Staring at the scene, I realized both the power and the abjectness of all ideologies which required sacrifices of young life. Ever since, I have hated the intolerance of any orthodoxy with an undying passion.

Back I went to school at the abbey, and back to revolt against the resurgent elitism of my schoolmates. At the end of the war and of that school year my mother was convinced that I would not be able to hold out for another year in that snobbish sepulchre. (I liked the monks; it was just the pupils I could have thrown in boiling oil.) She encouraged me to take the state examinations for a high school diploma in Brussels. This was a grand gamble. The examinations lasted for days, covering the substance of six years of high school, and only a few of the hopeful candidates ever made it. I was among them. Free at last!

Then the trouble began. I could go to university, but I had just turned sixteen, so I was too young to choose a destiny, a "career." I wanted to become a writer, but my father, influenced by his conventional bourgeois sisters, had me matriculate in the school of medicine at the Catholic University in Leuven, to join my cousins who were busy becoming physicians.[1] The next two years proved to be miserable. I only liked gymnastics and the bit on genetics in the botany course, and I was too young to have friends. In retrospect, it is evident that I learned the basics of chemistry and physics, but at the time all I knew was that I was becoming a good gymnast. What profession does that lead to?

The crisis was resolved when my parents allowed me to change over to law. But in secret I also enrolled in history. After two years I had a bachelor's degree in both, and my parents reluctantly let me continue in history. Why history? I liked the subject because it was "real fiction" and because one learned about cultures different from one's own. At that time the whole history department numbered fewer than a dozen students, mostly women, and we formed a close-knit community with its own social life.

Nearly all of us studied medieval history. The bulk of our training took place in a large seminar room, furnished with very long, wide tables, high up in the phony Renaissance library. There the comedy and the drama of turning us into historians occurred, presided over by Canon Albert De Meyer and his assistant, Jozef Desmet. We were under the gaze of the portrait of Ernest Cauchie, the founder of the seminar, who himself had been a pupil in the seminar of the great methodologist Ernst Bernheim at the end of the nineteenth century and who had transplanted Bernheim's seminar to Leuven.[2] We wrote and presented papers, or research for the M.A., in turn, usually to see them shredded to pieces by the lords of the manor. But we also subtly satirized these masters of method even as we discoursed before the unsuspecting(?) lordships, and we enjoyed the weekly drama. In that same room we also became professionals, as we mastered medieval Latin, economic history, the fine points of medieval paleography, and other recondite subjects.

We became, without ever being aware of it, thorough historical positivists, albeit devotees of the Marc Bloch who wrote *The Craft of the Historian.* A historical positivist holds that there is but one Truth, one correct reconstruction of the past. The truth could be found by a scrupulous application of the rules of historical critique to the sources. These then supposedly yielded a picture of the past in the most objective way possible. When Fernand Braudel, the future titan of French history, visited us in 1948 or 1949 and spoke about the *longue durée,* we were fascinated, but it was oh so daring. The panorama he evoked was so much wider than our preoccupations with the minutiae of medieval history, and he jumped so much further than his sources seemed to allow. In the last two years we traveled to the Netherlands for joint history meetings with students and some faculty there. We were disconcerted by the pessimistic insights of Pieter Gheyl, who saw no progress at all in historiography but only endless revisionism inspired by the present, and elated at the daring of Jan Romein, who worked on the most recent past, a past which sometimes spilled over in predictions about the future.[3] For their part, the Dutch admired our mastery of textual criticism.

In my first year as a student of history, Desmet decided that a long paper about the Viking raid on Leuven suited my adventurous spirit. The next year my literary inclinations were put to use in the analysis and translation of a long satirical poem in medieval Latin, accompanied by the appropriate grammatical, literary, and historical commentary as an exercise in textual editing. Then came the M.A. topic. This was to be a discussion of the value of a certain type of medieval dirge as a source for history. Such dirges were created for rulers or other prominent persons and sung shortly after the funeral at their gravesites. Many of these were oral compositions, but a few had been written down as *probatio pennae,* that is, as samples of writing in trying out a new pen. Thus I first met the voice of oral history accidentally preserved on paper. It was a Latin voice, often poetic and strikingly appealing. Yet I learned not to linger over the beauty of the songs. My job was to discover what those dirges told us about the deeds and reputations of the deceased and how honest they were. Literary sensitivity merely dealt with the wrappings; hard-headed application of the rules of evidence with the substance.

I enjoyed these years, but nevertheless there was a shadow. My down-to-earth friend Jos once shook me up by stating that life after the diploma consisted of teaching so many thousand hours of high school and then of retiring on a pension of such and such. As a curriculum vitae this sounded a bit anemic. Then just at the time of the final examinations, Jos struck again. He told me about an advertisement in the newspaper. The director of the Royal Museum of the Belgian Congo at Tervuren, Frans Olbrechts, invited candidates to apply for a research position as anthropologist in Belgian Africa. Now here was high adventure, compared with the endless hours of high school teaching that were awaiting me. I applied right away and received information about a scheduled interview by return mail. There was not much time to prepare for the interview, so I carefully read Olbrechts' *Ethnologie* and learned the practical bibliography it contained by heart.[4] The plan was to duck any question asked with "It all depends. One should read X and Y." The tactic worked splendidly. So on the eve of the proclamation of the diploma at Leuven, my goal for so many years and the gate to a chosen career, I received a letter appointing me as anthropologist at the Institute for Research in Central Africa (IRSAC). At the very moment that I became a certified historian, I turned my back on the profession. A week later I was at work in Tervuren.

Tervuren was a sumptuous palace converted into a museum, and it was known all over Belgium for its magnificent park. Inside on ground level the great marble halls and majestic state rooms housed collections of all sorts, from forestry to zoology, including household and art objects from what was then the Belgian Congo. What the visitors did not see was even more exotic. The cavernous cellars, crammed with stuff, linked by long dark tunnels, also half filled with "material culture," with the cellars of outlying pavilions offered a setting worthy of any ghost story. They were also an ideal place to try out throwing knives during lunch break when there were not too many people around! Above the grand ground floor, the rooms were long and narrow, with low ceilings and a musty smell. They were lined with endless rows of tall wooden closets. The light from half obscured skylights threw a diffuse gleam on the wide wooden tables in the center, where the staff silently worked. In the "ethnology section" the landscape on the tables varied almost as often as the array of clouds in the sky. Yesterday warm colored masks were strewn around in piles of raffia; today a few huge spearheads lie silent and menacing. Tomorrow it will be surly-looking statuettes with mirrors in their bellies. A few people in laboratory coats milled around, opening closets full of sculpture or pulling huge files from somewhere, searching for objects that were in demand, or to be repaired, or to be compared with reproductions in a jumble of art books. It was at one of those tables that I was given a ringside seat to observe and learn about curating.

I arrived with some notions about ancient Egypt and China, topics which had intrigued me since I was ten. I harbored recollections of thrilling travel accounts, mostly about Central Asia or Siberia, and an uneasy memory of Leo Frobenius' *Kulturgeschichte Afrikas*, which I had not understood, although I had liked the reproductions of various artworks. Now Albert Maesen, the curator of the department of ethnology and an expert on African art, gave me E. E. Evans Pritchard's book *Witchcraft, Oracles and*

Magic among the Azande to read.[5] As I only knew a smattering of English (it had not been taught at school), the going was slow. Luck was with me, however, for this was the most literary and perhaps the most original work by one of the great British anthropologists. A portion of the summer passed, and I began slowly to wonder how I was to tackle fieldwork if I was suddenly packed off to "the Congo." Then I was called before the director to be told, almost apologetically, that I was to repair to University College, London, in early September, where I would attend the courses for the third and last year of anthropology study and take the final exams. Given my autodidactic knowledge, this would be easy. What could I say? Hoisted with my own petard, I kept mum and prepared to go. Then, in the last days before my departure, Olbrechts called me once again to his pavilion and announced that I would do fieldwork among the Kuba, a people in the Belgian Congo famous for their art. No doubt he wished me to collect more of that, but the main goal was to provide "the social context" for the many silent art objects that populated the closets of the museum.

Thus I arrived in Kensington. My mother, who had lived in Britain in 1912–13 and was fluent in English, helped me to find lodgings and to start the process of getting food coupons, since food was still rationed. Then I was by myself. In my memory the next months are hazy still. I understood very little and said even less. But somehow I introduced myself to Daryll Forde, the head of the anthropology department and director of the International African Institute, and even found his house in one of those crazily numbered crescents. During our first meeting he mentioned something about "this fellow Roland Oliver," who was supposed to be over at the School of Oriental and African Languages (SOAS) and who was launching an odd new specialty, African history. I was in London to become an anthropologist, and therefore I hardly took notice—I had understood only half of what Forde said anyway. As Oliver was on leave that year and was never mentioned again, even the notice faded away. At first all my time was absorbed by finding my way around London and picking up some practical English, much of it Cockney off the street. The opaque lectures in the department of anthropology rolled over me like clouds, broken here and there when the blue sky of understanding peeked through. Time passed, and the days grew darker and foggier while Christmas was nearing. Then one morning, incredibly, the scales fell, and the English language became as clear as a bell. Finally I could begin to learn social anthropology.

Daryll Forde, a wiry, gentle, no-nonsense Welshman, the only senior academic in Great Britain not to be conquered by the doctrine of structural functionalism, ruled over the department in the dungeons of Gower Street, and his secretary ruled us, the students.[6] He taught us only one course on West Africa, but he influenced me deeply because of his interest in geography and his openness to other schools of anthropology, especially American schools. I also saw him at work at the International African Institute, where he had me write abstracts of articles in Afrikaans.

Functionalism was the creed of all the other teachers. It held that societies were like organisms (strict functionalism) or like watches (structural functionalism). Society consisted of a set of institutions accompanied by practices and beliefs pertaining to each of them. Every institution was like an organ in the body, or a gear in a watch, built and working in such a way that it fulfilled a function for the whole social organism. All parts of society were perfectly integrated with each other, so that change brought to any part affected all others. In fact, the integration was deemed to be so perfect by the structural functionalists that change could not be generated internally. Only outside influences could bring it about. In order to study societies in the contemporary colonial world, one needed to participate in the life of the people studied. One needed to observe, rather than to ask questions, because function was often unconscious anyway, and one needed to analyze in a synchronic way, as if the data had been gathered at a single moment in time. Any consideration of history muddied the analysis by introducing extraneous factors.[7]

We were taught this doctrine by Phyllis Kaberry, Michael G. Smith, and Mary Douglas. Phyllis was a presence, a woman exuding pluck and common sense, with a wealth of experience.[8] Michael G. Smith, a listener rather than a talker, reminded one of the popular image of an engineer. Indeed, for him the most abstruse abstractions of kinship were but blocks in a playpen.[9] Mary Douglas was then the youngest faculty member. She radiated efficient energy, disciplined enthusiasm, and a taste for awkward issues.[10] To Mary I owe a special debt. She was special because she was my tutor and because not long before she had done fieldwork among the Lele, the neighbors of the Kuba. Moreover, she really guided me. She found me better lodgings, vetted my papers, and pounded into my head the idea that social anthropology was a genuine science, whose laws were on the verge of discovery. Mary, like all social anthropologists then, was as much a positivist as anybody in Leuven had ever been. Like her colleagues, she swore by "participant observation" and a strictly synchronic approach, albeit one that erased all traces of colonial influence from the field record. She did not then like history. Once I found a large red accusation in the margin of a paper on Central Africa: "History!" All British social anthropologists then dismissed history as conjectural, a phrase coined by the great ancestor Radcliffe-Brown, who was still alive. I remember a lecture in the spring of 1952 at Burlington Gardens. We students sat reverently in the back rows of the elegant room, waiting and craning our necks. Then he strode out of the wings, a living legend, and began to talk about cockatoos and their different hues.[11] It was an appropriate lecture: so learned that it went right over my head. Yet that was precisely what was expected, and therefore the occasion was a perfect happening.

University College was not the only place where I took courses. I also attended classes at SOAS to get a smattering of linguistics. One course was phonetics, where we learned to hear what sounded like different leaky faucets. By the time I gave up on it, these had turned out to be pharyngeals in some Burmese language. The other course was taught to me by the famous Bantuist Malcolm Guthrie himself, who tutored me in the Kuba language.[12] Guthrie then still cultivated his image as a stern Baptist missionary endowed with Scottish thrift and empiricism who happened to be a professor of languages. I would present myself in his office, gliding between shelves loaded with books and pieces of paper classified by Bantu language from *A* to *T*. He'd look up, surprised to see me there, remember, and then pick up a missionary grammar and teach from it, stopping from time to time to warn me that this or that was certainly not right.[13] As he did not know a word of Bushong (as its speakers call their language) himself, but knew enough to see that something was seriously wrong with the book, his tutoring was surrealistic. Still, it gave me an inkling of what a Bantu language was like, although I learned no Bushong. Indeed, I never even managed to acquire the book and take it with me. The other anthropology students thought that this learning of a language beforehand was weird: Did one not pick up the language during one's fieldwork? So why bother with linguists? They also disliked the lectures in physical anthropology, and they despised the ones on material culture and technology, even when the famous art historian William Fagg of the British Museum taught them.[14] We all hated the incomprehensible diagrams on weaving. But I enjoyed parts of that course, especially the day when we learned to sail a creaky Polynesian outrigger canoe on the floor of one of the basements of the museum, or the day when Fagg had us peer at the insides of a Benin brass head to show how it had been made.

After Christmas the school year flowed on faster and faster until the examinations came, to be passed with flying colors—Olbrechts would never know how little I knew when I first met him. Soon I was on the ferry, plowing through the North Sea toward Ostend, ready for the "Africa" of anthropologists, a mental world that included tropical Africa, which was inhabited by myriad "tribes," with endlessly varying kinship systems. Indeed, anthropology had converted me. I stood in awe of the way in which anthropologists made sense of whole societies by using "function" to integrate the most diverse-looking customs and beliefs, like buttresses shoring up the cathedral of a social structure. Clearly, ethnologists such as Emil Torday, who had collected so much art and written so much about the Kuba, had missed the boat.[15] It was up to my generation to discover and describe the cathedrals as a whole. And anthropology was more fun than history. The tales of Mary Douglas about her life as a participant observer among the Lele clinched that matter. Historians, after all, only pore over dead papers in archives, while anthropologists interact with living people.

Back at Tervuren I was put to work writing an ethnographic monograph about the Kuba "and related peoples" from known material, whether published or culled from administrative records in the files of the museum.[16] It was a job well suited to the technical skills of historian, and I liked the challenge of digging up obscure and oblique references. I also was to be coached on Bantu languages by Emiel Meeussen, the resident linguist and the foremost Bantuist of the era.[17] When I first arrived in his office, he began to test the accuracy of my ear for tones. Then he gave me a tape and told me to transcribe it. Every day I listened for a few hours, wrote, and showed the results. Every day something was wrong. Patiently Meeussen pointed out the errors and sent me back to correct them. When finally, after weeks of work, I succeeded in correctly transcribing a page or two, he declared: "Enough. Take this and find the grammar!" "How can I do that?" I replied, astonished. "Look for regularities of any kind, and sort them out," he replied matter-of-factly. So I went and looked for regularities. Thus I found the main principles of the concordance system and the outline of the verbal system. When this was correctly done, as far as the texts allowed one to do it, he finally relented, told me which language it was, and gave me a grammar. Now I could compare my "grammar" with the real thing and find the application of other rules in my texts. By the time I left, I had thoroughly internalized the structure of a Bantu language, and I knew how to tackle a hitherto unknown language. Moreover, I now also revered Meeussen, even though I was told later that he thought that I was a waste of his time: I was too flighty and superficial.

The summer came and went. I hoped to leave in September with Jean-Jacques Maquet, a veteran anthropologist and the head of IRSAC for the social sciences, who was returning to Rwanda by car.[18] One day Maquet appeared in the ethnographic section to interview me for this task. Here then was the man who would be my boss: a look-alike of V. I. Lenin, without the beard. This Lenin, though, would never have stood on any barricade: his perfect, albeit unctuous, manners and his natty bow tie (an Americanism at that time) would not have allowed it. But I failed my test: I could not drive. He chose to go with the other new recruit, Luc de Heusch, who had studied in Paris with the "sacred monster," as an eminent scholar is called in France, Claude Lévi-Strauss. So I was to stay and leave later by ship, traveling as convoying officer to a load of many tons destined for the IRSAC station in Kivu on the eastern edge of the Belgian Congo. The woods had turned a glorious red by the time I went for medical examinations and visited the headquarters of IRSAC in Brussels to meet its secretary general, Jean-Paul Harroy, later governor of Ruanda-Urundi.[19] Seated before a round table with a big map of the Congo under glass, he radiated benevolence and confidently asserted that I would have no problems with the itinerary. Between a car from the IRSAC fleet, buses, and trains, I would travel from one dot on the map to the next one just as smoothly as he pushed his pudgy finger from point to point over the tabletop. Little did I know!

Finally the long-coveted day came, and I boarded the *Copacabana*, a mixed passenger and freight ship. It was a bitterly cold day, December 17, 1952, when we glided out of the harbor of Antwerp. The desolate frozen wastes of Zeeland passed by, framed by the rigging covered with hoarfrost. Off the estuary of the Scheldt, the ship turned around for the captain to gauge its gyroscopes and then headed south into unruly seas. It was night when we rounded Dover. The spray of the waves was hitting the bridge, and below we only glimpsed a ghostly chalky whiteness between the crash of waves on the portholes. In the middle of the night I found myself flung from bed onto the floor, ducking malevolent objects of all sorts and weights which were flying to and fro in the midst of a cacophony of sound, as everything breakable was being broken. The ship had lost steerage and was laying broadside to the waves, rudderless, helplessly wallowing in a major storm. We drifted toward the distant shoals off the coasts of Brittany.

2

In the Field: Kuba Country

T H E *Copacabana* did not founder on the rocks of Brittany. As it drifted, the engineers frantically attempted makeshift repairs to get its propellers turning again. Eventually they succeeded, and the ship regained steerage, albeit at very low speed. The next day the storm began to abate. We now limped southward into sunnier climes and quieter seas toward Santa Cruz de Tenerife, in the Canary Islands, where we put in for repairs. For a few days the white and pastel town, nestled between a high barren peak and the bluest of seas, offered an idyllic interlude for us, being neither the Europe I knew nor yet Africa: a dream-like experience. Then we limped on. One after the other, passengers began to shed their familiar clothing. Officials donned their khaki or white colonial outfits, helmet and all, nuns and male missionaries shifted from black to white robes, the other women sprouted flowery dresses and floppy hats, while the male settlers loafed around in somewhat disreputable beachwear. As I had read it would, one day the sea turned brown, laden with clumps of vegetable material. The next morning we turned into the estuary of the Congo River. All the novices, including me, stood at the railing to spot the first "ethnographic" houses on the Angolan shore, the first "natives," the first palm trees, while the old timers were busy in the bar. Gradually the mountains grew wider and wider, the river narrower and narrower, and late that day we docked under the red-brown rocks of Matadi. We disembarked amid an official fuss about passports, and inspection of luggage, and tips or no tips for porters. We waited a while longer on the pier and then went off along a steep slope to a fortress on a rocky spur: the hotel. So this was Africa.

The next morning as the cocks crowed, we, sleepy and solemn, were stowed aboard the white painted coaches of what was called the White Train, while a joyous bustling crowd of Congolese, mostly women with

14

huge basins on their heads, settled in the other coaches, which, as I was told in no uncertain terms, were off-limits to us. Finally off we went, ever so slowly at first as the train negotiated steep inclines on the edges of precipices, then at greater speed as the mountains ceased to loom around us. All day we traveled through the landscapes of lower Zaire, stopping for long disorderly halts at stations where African crowds got on or off, food sellers cried their wares, and local Europeans on the quay loudly gossiped with white passengers leaning out of the windows. Late in the afternoon we pulled in at Léopoldville. On that quay I was met by an official with new marching orders. The freight I was convoying for IRSAC—and my own luggage with it—was to be put on board a river steamer and then forwarded by road to Kivu. I was to fly first to Luluaburg, the capital of Kasai, then travel by train to Mweka, the administrative center of Kuba country, and from there to Nsheng, residence of the Bushong king. The next days were hectic, and my memory of them now is a series of snapshots: trying to pry quinine out of its capsules (until I knew better), seeking my way over the oil slicks in the warehouses at the port, boarding a plane and then being stuck for nearly a week at the airport in Luluaburg, many miles from town, until a train came. Again landscapes, stops, the search for the "first" authentic Kuba—and I arrived in the dead of the night amid palm trees at Mweka.

He must have been an odd sight, this boy wearing a sun helmet at midnight, trudging from the station to the local motel with two aluminum suitcases and high hopes. There everything fell apart. There was no public transportation to Nsheng. So much for Harroy's effortless moving from spot to spot. I was stuck without equipment, funds, or letters of introduction for the authorities, and I remained stranded for nearly three long months. When IRSAC officials had rerouted me in Léopoldville, they had thought only about their freight, not about my fate, and now they ignored telegrams and letters. So I lived on credit and waited. At long last I received instructions to proceed to the IRSAC station in Kivu, but no funds to do so. Somehow I managed to travel by train and plane on credit, and I caught a ride from Bukavu to the research station forty-eight kilometers away, to find a grand gate in *Bonanza* ranch style and, a kilometer or two further, sprawling buildings, all empty of directors or scholars. They had gone to a conference in Uganda. There was only one other penniless new IRSAC recruit, the linguist John Jacobs. We scrounged around as best we could until finally the bevy of savants returned from their conference. The logistics were now straightened out, I was given a lesson or two in the art of driving a jeep on steep mountain roads, the jeep was loaded with equipment, and I was packed off on a more than sixteen-hundred-kilometer journey to Mweka, with an African driver to teach me to drive as we went. Jacobs was sent off at the same time. Once in Mweka, the driver left me on my own for the final stretch to Nsheng.[1]

The first few days there I roomed with a European medical assistant until I was allowed to settle in a tiny, decrepit, but still inhabitable mud house in the ruins of a former administrative post at a place called the Tail of the Parrot, a good hour's walk from the capital. On arrival, the jeep shuddered and gave up the ghost. I stayed at the Tail of the Parrot for nearly two months, spending all day with Mikwepy Anaclet, an unemployed young man I had first met during my enforced stay in Mweka. I learned the language all day long and in the evening walked over to watch a religious revival in progress at the small Bushong village nearby, from which the place derived its name.[2] At long last, a month later, I felt confident enough to venture out, on foot, naturally, to town, and there I appeared one day, the first European ever to speak some Bushong, a person whose existence was known by gossip but who nevertheless suddenly walked out of nowhere one day, someone who was neither government official, missionary, or trader: in one word, a conundrum. For a while people furiously speculated about my real identity. Some held that I was a Bushong soul reborn by a dreadful accident in a white body, and one day some women offered me condolences about that. Others rejected this explanation, but they had no other. So everyone just followed my every deed and word with Argus eyes to gather further clues. Soon people realized that I was neither a danger nor a profit to them. Gradually they accepted me in the compounds, reluctantly began to believe that I was there to record their culture, and set about to educate me. Finally I was doing fieldwork.

May 8, 1953, was a warm, sunny day. The fierce sunlight shimmered off the pale sands in the courtyard. It was peaceful there in the open space, surrounded by a high wall of plaited and dried leaves, while the crowns of raffia palms gently swayed to and fro. Three men were sitting, conversing, on mats in front of the little thatched cottage. One of them, dressed in a skirt, was Mbop Louis, a mature man and the householder of the compound. He was patiently giving well-considered answers in sonorous Bushong to the questions of his sister's son, Mikwepy Anaclet, a youth in shorts and shirt. The third person, an obvious stranger, was exotic-looking in his odd cavalry boots, shorts, and a sun helmet topping a yellowish sweating face. He was taking notes, stopping only to ask a question in halting Bushong when the conversation languished. Or again he inter-

rupted Mbop and his nephew when he did not follow them, so that Anaclet could translate the conversation to him in basic French. It was a
peaceful scene. They were discussing genesis.

Suddenly Mbop interrupted the leisurely pace of his speech and exclaimed rhetorically as he addressed me, the stranger: "We too we know
the past, because we carry our newspapers in our heads." Full of enthusiasm, he recited as proof, a number of short poems. This one was the first:

Mbe lashey bakong,	If I quarrel with the Kongo,
Mbe lanan ibamboon	If I fight with the Mboon
Kolakal adia ashey mubaan.	I will not eat their salt.[3]

In a burst of insight, half-forgotten dirges such as *Laxis fibris,* "With loos-
ened strings," or *A solis ortu,* "Whence the sun rises," surged through my
mind. Those Bushong poems were just like these medieval dirges. They
were texts, and hence just as amenable to the canons of historical method.
Once one could assess the value of a tradition, it could be used as a source
like any other: one could then use such poems to reconstruct aspects at
least of a "real" Kuba history. That would mean a significant advance in
anthropology. Hitherto one used only descriptions of cultures and societies, slices of dead tissue frozen in time, adequate for a dissection of social
organs, structures, and institutions, but not for an observation of their
physiology, their functioning. Now one might hope to watch living tissue
pulsing with life, to document how institutions actually functioned and
changed over time. Only much later was I to realize that this made all the
difference between the notions of function and process.

In a flash Mbop Louis's comment about newspapers awakened the
historian in me. What I had learned about anthropology and history
fused. From then on, as my notes show, I was mesmerized by this poetry,
called *shoosh* by the Bushong.[4] In subsequent days I recorded all the poems
Mbop Louis could remember and in their wake also whatever tales about
the past he knew. Mbop was a *bulaam*, a local community historian, that is,
a curious person obsessed with history, and he knew a great deal, but not
everything. So I went to other *bulaam* for more poems and more tales.
Despite my own attraction to such people, I was to argue in my first work
about oral tradition that they were the worst informants because one could
not clearly trace the sources of their assertions.[5] It would take many years
for me to realize that these were my confreres, historians just as I was, only
community historians, not academics like me. Only recently have I fully
come to appreciate their crucial role in the fashioning of the historical
consciousness of their communities.

17

Bushong attitudes toward such *bulaam* were ambivalent. They enjoyed public prestige, but they were also frowned upon as reckless people. The telling of oral traditions and the building of histories were not harmless activities. Traditions were used to bolster or to attack political preroga- tives, and hence the king claimed the right to proclaim the official tradi- tion, a claim disputed by the senior patricians, who put forth their own versions. Telling traditions could therefore be a sensitive political activity. According to the gossips, it could be fatal: had not the best *bulaam* in the country been poisoned by the king in 1951 for citing traditions to the European district commissioner that were harmful to the royal interest? In relating this episode, public rumor illustrated why these stories were so sensitive. The kingdom was administered by indirect rule based on its "historical constitution" as recorded by the European administration around 1920. From 1949 to 1951, however, a new round of inquiries had been started by administrators to "reform" the structure—that is, to find excuses to streamline the administration and make it more efficient from the European point of view—and they kept tinkering with it from then onward. The incident had taken place in that context. But there were other reasons also to limit the diffusion of oral tradition. According to a bit of gossip recorded in 1954, Shep Mathias, who suddenly died in October 1953, had been poisoned on orders of the king with acid from a car battery, "because he had told the European [me] too many secrets."[6]

So I was soon steered toward the king and told by others that they could not speak to me as long as he had not laid down an official record. Therefore, whenever the king had time to hear me out, which was not very often, I pressed him to tell the official story as he had related it during the rituals of his accession. At this juncture, as it happened, the linguist John Jacobs came to the rescue, armed with the first tape recorder ever seen in the area. It was an impressive sight to watch this machine set up and operated. Being powered by electricity, it needed its own generator. To avoid getting a recording of its throbbing hum, the generator needed to be dug in downwind, hundreds of meters away, and then wired by cable to the recorder. Once the machine was turned on, a fluttering green light, indicating the varying sound level, appeared. Everyone was intrigued by the animated bursts of green "flames" whenever a person spoke into the microphone. It did look as if some struggling living thing was entrapped there. Both Jacobs and I had to record our own voices first to show that the machine was harmless and did not imprison our inner selves. Naturally the king heard about this tape recorder, and this induced him to put the official history on perpetual record.

On July 8, 1953, the whole court crowded into the council square *yoot* within the palace. The king, preceded by a medicine man carrying his charm of rule covered with a white cloth, by another medicine man bearing his throne, and by his official speaker, made his entrance when all were seated on mats. He was dressed for war, eagle feathers in his hat, a great sword in one hand, a war bell in the other. All fell silent when he sat down on his throne, which a crouching medicine man held behind him. His speaker squatted on a mat in front of him, and the Keeper of the charm of rule on one side. He then hit the bell three times with his sword, and the crowd roared its greeting: *"Yiiii."* The king then shouted a slogan: "The crowd is powerful." The crowd echoed, "Powerful." Other slogans followed: "The Bushong are strong," "The king has burning authority," "When your national nature spirit will roar, listen," "We and that spirit are a single person!" Each time the crowd echoed his last word. There followed a brief exposition explaining why the ceremony was taking place, and then he began: "And we here, we came from the ocean."

The performance consisted mainly of a recitation of the names of rivers, capitals, and kings, often with their *shoosh*. When he came to the slogan of his own capital, "The search for money," he digressed to explain its *shoosh* and stress the importance of earning money. Then followed a peroration in which he emphasized his status as the lieutenant of God, whereupon a final public acclamation signaled the end of the ceremony. This performance was much more than a lesson in history. It stressed the unassailable position of kingship in a public display of allegiance to the king by Bushong and foreign Africans alike.

The king had not foreseen that we would replay the tape countless times, day after day, while transcribing, translating, and annotating it with a minimum of explanatory notes.[7] Many people came to our workplace to listen to it again and again, and even I learned it almost by heart. In this way the tape "demystified" the official record. It also gave me access to the knowledge of everyone else. I could now ask any knowledgeable person to elaborate or comment on it. Thus, rather than being a conclusion to the collection of oral traditions, this performance initiated a further phase of that process.

It was easy to find out how and on which points the official royal version had been doctored, but that did not tell me "what had really happened." I had to rely on what officials or others at court and *bulaam* would tell me. The search inevitably led me to the tiny court of the *muyum*, the antiking who lived in the small village of Kosh, not far from the sacred lake But aPwoong. He was the man who crowned kings and who kept the

19

national charm. After his enthronement, the king could never again meet the *muyum* face to face. If kings became tyrants, the *muyum* had the magical means to kill them. In a sense, he was the conscience of the nation.

One day the *muyum* agreed to lead me to his shrine. He indicated the mouth of a tiny path that disappeared in the deep forest on the side of his village. He told my assistant Evariste Shyaam aNce and me that when we were called, we were to follow that path until we met him. Late one evening, August 8, 1953, the call came.[8] The night was partly cloudy with a fitful, weak moon, and we set out by the feeble light of a small smoky lantern. As soon as we were by ourselves on the narrow path, the forest swallowed whatever moonlight there was, and we proceeded step by step along the tiny, twisting trail. The forest was alive with the reassuring sounds of nocturnal animals moving around: this was reassuring because the absence of such noise meant that a leopard was prowling in the vicinity. As we proceeded, the muted screeches and scufflings abated from time to time, and our hearts leapt to our throats until the noises resumed. After ages, it seemed to us, suddenly the dark path in front of me was blocked off by the even darker shadow of a man. We had arrived. The man made us leave the trail, and a few meters away our light revealed the *muyum* and his main official squatting in a small clearing, next to a tiny doll-sized house, a shrine. As soon as we entered the clearing and sat down, invisible people suddenly erected tall fences of mats and shut the *muyum* and us off.

The official told us first in a low voice about early kingship and about King Lashyaang, who had been killed in war, and about a certain Ngol aWoot who had found his "relic." After a moment of silence, the *muyum* then drew a package wrapped in rags from the shrine and began to unwrap it. As he undid one rag, he called it by the name of a king, and thus he mentioned a series of kings until the packet was undone. Each of these rags had been part of the shroud of the king the *muyum* named. The last to die was the first to be unwrapped. Finally the rags were peeled off to leave a core, a skullcap. That was the relic of the first of the kings kept here: Lashyaang. The *muyum* then drew other venerated objects from the shrine: first a war bell, and then a huge double bell half rusted away, but still over a meter high, the bell of rule brought by the first mythical ruler. Then followed a small earthenware pot decorated with the same kind of scarifications women wear on their abdomens and a paddle on which were carved sets of scarifications representing all the ethnic groups which make up the kingdom. The paddle referred to the unity of the kingdom and recalled the emigration of the first kings by boat from the primeval waters.

20

The small pot contained pure white kaolin, the substance with which kings are anointed on their coronation. This had come from far away, outside the country, from the spot where the Bushong chief had lived before he entered this land. Beside it appeared an egg of kaolin, representing the heart of an anthill (society), an egg that the Bushong Adam had brought from the primeval waters. It had later been found inside the skull of Lashyaang and was believed to have the power to move by itself. It sallied forth to go and kill any ruling monarch who was a tyrant, once the *muyum* told it to do so. Finally there also was a big tusk, but we were not told what it represented.

Then the *muyum* told us what happened when a king arrived to be crowned. They would meet here during the night, and the initiation ritual began:

King: My father.
Muyum: Son.
King: I came to fetch life.

The King then showed his gifts for the *muyum* whereupon the latter showed him the contents of the shrine, the objects we had just seen.

When this tale was told to us, the *muyum's* official turned to the shrine and addressed Lashyaang again, singing his praise names:

> Lashyaang, son of Ming [his mother], the fearless one
> Lashyaang, son of Ming, with the cloth
> I am the one who takes the basket [of rule] of the ancestors
> I am the one who takes the post of the oldest of people
> It is not forbidden for me to sit on the trap [the basket of rule]
> You, the elder of King Kwet aMbweeky,
> the elder of King Mboongaleeng, Miko miMbul, Kot a Mbul.

Then he concluded by addressing Lashyaang at the shrine in his conversational voice: "Your clan brothers came to see you; I did not come to take you without reason. The children of your mother, who have come from downstream [the ocean], have come to visit you."[9] The ceremony was thus finished.[10]

From then on I collected many more accounts about the past of the realm, but none more authoritative for the Bushong than this one. The blessing of the *muyum*, for that is what I had received, meant that all Bushong could now tell me what they knew without fear. Still, I had to go even beyond this point, because the official tradition, however authoritative, was still stamped by all the biases of its status. From then on, therefore, I began systematically to collect unofficial traditions and set up the means to do so.

21

* * *

There had not been a boy's initiation since the early thirties in Kuba lands. Yet two months after my visit to the shrine of the *muyum*, I participated in an initiation in the village of Mapey. It came about as follows: Shep Mathias, one of my teachers in the Bushong way of life, had told me something about the initiation wall. Soon after that he died. He was born in the village of Mapey, and according to custom he was to be buried there. I was told that on that occasion the initiation masks would come out. Therefore, I attended the funeral with the firm intention of organizing an initiation session. Indeed, some masks came out, and people danced in front of the house where the corpse was lying in state. The elders of Mapey were keen on holding an initiation, but they told me that it could not be done without the explicit permission of the king. So I went back to Nsheng, where I found a very busy king pacing the ground, surveying and laying out a new quarter for his capital. Having already been informed before I arrived, he listened to my request, and a day later he agreed to the initiation. In due course I was to learn that he had conferred with the local European administrative resident, Makupkup, who had agreed to the venture.[11]

Once I was back in Mapey, the preparations began.[12] I gathered a large number of bottles of beer, to replace the customary gifts of palm wine, while a local carver began to choose wood and whittle away at masks and sculptures in the bush, far from the prying eyes in the village. There people talked about nothing else, and terrifying stories circulated about the ordeals ahead. During the day a masked person clad in raffia fibers ran around chasing the women away and frightening the children. In the evening the initiated men danced and sang to express their aggressive masculinity and their contempt for women. At nightfall a village official went on his rounds, chanting: "Stay in your houses, the leopard is coming, the dead are coming, initiation is coming!" In one night a shelter was erected on the village plaza, and four days later the boys to be initiated and I were inducted. We became novices as small raffia ropes were laid around our necks. The next day we entered the shelter. We stayed there for some days, to be taught riddles and songs. At night we would come out to dance on the village square to the sound of horns, drums, and a xylophone. One early dawn we all woke up as the shelter was taken away from over our heads. After a sequence of ritual events, the boys and I were driven to the east end of the village, where the sun was rising, to behold the initiation wall, a huge construction of poles and raffia topped by masks and other objects. One by one we went through the raffia curtain to meet a ferocious masked man waving a wicked sword. We dove between his legs into the mouth of a tunnel, where we were frightened by the growl of a leopard. Then we emerged, again between the legs of a standing figure, this one the mother of initiation. We had been reborn, acting like crybabies. We waited until all the boys had appeared and then were led off into the bush.

There followed a few weeks in initiation camp, where the boys of each clan section built shelters with the help of the elders and spent most of their time being taught ethics and "social structure." I was not in good shape to follow it all, for I was felled by such an attack of malaria that I remained semiconscious for days. Yet somehow I still kept notes on what was going on. Days passed, until one night we left camp for the next phase of the initiation, a roaming life near the village that culminated in a trip to "foreign lands." We were to make salt from reeds in a faraway village. In fact, we simply went to buy salt at a shopping center many kilometers away. One day during this period we were warned that a government agronomist was heading toward Mapey to check on the progress of work in the fields of "educational crops."[13] That was perhaps the facet of colonial rule which the Kuba resented most. They hated the agronomists, who, unlike the territorial administrators, cared nothing about customs and culture and were only concerned with ordering people about or fining them. When the news broke, the men and the boys happened to be quite close to the village. There was no time to flee, yet we all had to vanish if initiation was to continue. So I hid in a ditch with the boys. Through the long grass we saw the helmeted khaki bully ride past us, unaware that hundreds of eyes stared at him at almost spitting distance. Finding no men in the village, he ranted, railed, and rode off.

Then came the last phase of the rituals, the reinduction into village life. After a symbolic dance on the square, in which the men were reunited with their mothers (somebody found me an old mother), and a joyful reunion, we were again all herded at night into the middle of the square and surrounded by hunting nets, while we slept on the bare earth. The next morning the whole village gathered about the nets. We now had to exhibit our male ferocity by killing live rats with our teeth and eating bits of them raw. Then the nets were opened, we were sent behind the initiation wall, whose symbolism we had studied for weeks, and after a short final rite initiation was over. Its paraphernalia were to be destroyed. But the men agreed to give them to me, including the most spectacular sculpture, the tall statue of the mother of initiation. The objects were wrapped up before dawn in rough matting of plaited leaves of the sort used for roofing, so that the women would not suspect anything but building materials. I

23

then conveyed them right away to the railway station in Mweka. Now the statue, shorn of all its meaning, is on display in the museum at Tervuren. It is no longer the same object, but just a carved bit of art, alienated from its culture and obediently resonating to whatever symbolic universe the viewer brings to it.

At the time of this initiation, the process called participant observation in anthropology was well under way, but not as the textbooks foresaw. I learned much more from being taught than from watching, and the experience was altering me: I was becoming partly Bushong. That was not surprising. I was a young man, barely twenty-four years old, living day in, day out with Bushong who continuously and patiently were teaching me how to behave, how to speak, what to think. My earlier familiarity with woods and wastelands at home made life here much easier than it might have been for another person. Even severe food shortages—at one time I literally ate crow—were not novel for one who had been a war child.

By the time I went off to initiation, my resolve to study Kuba history forced me to abandon the then-recommended pattern of participant observation anyway. To begin with, the pursuit of oral traditions meant that I was granting much more weight to what people said than was then usual. Moreover, participant observation was clearly inadequate for the goal I was pursuing. It would not do to study one or a few places in depth and generalize from this to the whole of Kuba lands. For historical research one had to gather all the relevant oral traditions, not just some representative specimens. One could not apply sampling procedures to this subject matter because traditions were not similar and interchangeable units. So I needed help. I began to hire and train young men to help me systematically collect all the traditions about families, villages, clan sections, and chiefdoms everywhere in the country. As it turned out, these usually dealt with settlement and population movement and only rarely included stories affecting central government. Thus to cross-check most of the official versions, I needed to track down *bulaam* and "wise people" for months and years to come.

Eventually half a dozen of us formed a close-knit group. I had begun in 1953 with Mikwepy Anaclet, but by the fall of that year he had left me for an appointment as a clerk of the European court in Mweka.[14] A month or two after my arrival I also hired Evariste Shyaam aNce, who had gone to teacher's training school but fell out with the missionaries there and did not complete the course. Evariste, a brilliant mind and a born intellectual, was a slender person, more spontaneous and less reserved than most

Bushong are, a great joker who perpetually carried the somewhat disreputable air of a gentle sarcasm about him, directed especially toward the pompous patricians of the capital. Kuba history, culture, language, and artwork soon became his passion, and he learned with exceptional facility. By the summer we were trusting friends. We discussed his dreams about an independent country, and he confided his denunciations of racism and the petty outrages of the color bar in Mweka to me.[15] By fall we were fast becoming the leaders of a little group of young men who traveled from village to village recording all the *shoosh*, village and family traditions, and whatever else they were told.[16] By 1990 several members of this club had achieved high status in the country, and today they are influential in shaping the contemporary historical consciousness of the Bushong.

But where in all this were the distinctions between scholarly observer and the objects of study? Bushong elders, especially *bulaam* such as Mbop Louis, were teaching me, Shyaam aNce was a friend, and so-called ordinary informants became neighbors with whom one swapped stories, me telling about Belgian customs and they about theirs. Within a year Kuba culture had marked me in obvious ways. For years my speech, whatever the language spoken, was shot through with Bushong tones and occasional turns of speech. At one point when I had to go to Luluaburg, the "white town," I was so attuned to Bushong mores that I was unsettled by such sights as the then fashionable short shorts of young European girls on bicycles, or the surreal-looking rows of yellowish ghostly shapes, seated under the garish neon lights of a segregated restaurant. How weird, and . . . was I really that ugly too? The Bushong educated me so thoroughly in their way of life that I was permanently marked by it. By the time I left in 1956, I had partly become what they said I was, a *mwaan Bushong*, "a child of the Bushong."

No one in London had taught me about these effects of participant observation. Nor had much been said about other drawbacks such as ill health. In the arrogance of youth I shrugged them off. Nevertheless, living in the disease-ridden environment of the Kuba, yet without the resistance they had built up, I collected malaria, dysenteries, filariasis, typhoid fever, a local scabies, and sundry sores, although I mercifully escaped tropical ulcers, sleeping sickness, and leprosy, still endemic in parts of Kuba country. As a result of these afflictions I was reduced to a state of perpetual torpor by April 1954, induced by general anemia. When I arrived in Luluaburg for a scheduled seminar meeting, I was checked in at the hospital there as an outpatient and walked around by the physicians, who were proud to show a specimen apparently lacking all vitamins!

No one had taught me either that the vaunted method of participant observation was so interwoven with the colonial situation. That troubled me as soon as I set foot on shore in the Congo. When I boarded the train for Léopoldville in that carriage "for whites only," I was inevitably reminded of the German occupation. Then, too, the best coaches had borne placards, marked "Nur für Wehrmacht," that is, reserved for the occupying forces. So was I one of the *Wehrmacht* in the Congo? In the field the colonial situation influenced everything, for instance, the initiation. In 1957 a Belgian journalist praised the gracious behavior of the Kuba king who had so magnaminously allowed me to attend it.[17] Nothing of it. He had been prevented for over twenty years from holding any initiation. The missionaries had used all their influence ever since 1904 to ban them, and the government agents had effectively outlawed them by 1930 on the grounds that the time passed in the rituals and festivities was time lost on "useful" pursuits like gathering palm fruit for the Compagnie du Kasai or cultivating maize for the hated agronomists. Unwittingly I had given the king a chance. He had conferred with Makupkup for permission to hold an initiation and for reassurance that if anything happened to me, he would not be blamed. Indeed, my initiation set a precedent. These rituals have been practiced until today.[18]

I did not know it, but I was very lucky in that Makupkup genuinely cared for the Kuba and hence did not object to any of my activities. Yet he was just as paternalistic as most colonial officials were. He too tried to raise economic productivity, and the king was his ally in this endeavor. But unlike many other officials, Makupkup genuinely wanted to preserve Kuba cultural values and to raise productivity for the benefit of the Kuba's own living standards, be it by selling their maize to the mining areas of Shaba or their carvings to tourists.

The king himself was deeply enmeshed in the colonial system. He earned a substantial income both through the provision of labor to the Compagnie du Kasai, for which he received commissions, and by levying taxes for the government, which provided him with some 15 percent of the money raised. With his official salary, his income was apparently higher than that of any regional official, including the district commissioner. His revenues were the foundation of his power, for they allowed him to reward his dignitaries and to threaten the unruly. He had named his capital "The search for money" for good reason. Yet no one had told me what the name and his comments about it actually referred to. I was then still too innocent to suspect any of this. So I was taught by the Kuba, but not taught everything. Thus I often chatted with Jules Lyeen, the leading carver of the town, but he never told me that he collected taxes in the countryside for the king.[19] Also I never heard any comment about undue influence in the local courts, although now I am certain that they were not totally impartial.

On the other hand, I was well aware of the ignorance and arrogance of the Europeans in Mweka. I knew of the color bar—and got into mild scrapes about it—and the Kuba did not hide their feelings about agronomists, missionaries, and traders. By the end of 1953 I heard occasional talk among the young people about what would happen when the people of the Congo were independent once again; this was years before these ideas openly cropped up among the urban elites. Everyone dreaded the Force Publique, the army, but I did not see this myself until 1956, when I unexpectedly ran into a "military walk" destined to cower the inhabitants of a more remote area. Yet I heard nothing, not even fleeting gossip about the arrangements by which the colonial goals and interests were yoked to further the opportunities of local Kuba leaders, especially at the court where I lived. Everyone carefully refrained from showing me exactly how Kuba lives were affected by this situation.

Thus participant observation and even being educated did not yield completely unbiased evidence. It was a selective process that protected vested interests. It is easy now to see that a description of Kuba institutions and ways of life really made little sense without its colonial context. But even though I myself, like everyone else, was involved all the time in negotiating colonial situations, I simply missed the point. I was blinded by the social anthropology of the day and its emphasis on an atemporal ethnographic present. I was collecting data by listening to people and observing what they did, as if the passing of time was affecting neither their behavior nor their thought, despite the fact that the changes in the public climate over time, especially between 1954 and 1956, were quite obvious to me. It would take fifteen years for me to realize fully how efficiently this fiction of an ethnographic present had hidden the workings of the colonial situation. The colonial environment and my own position and status at the time precluded me from fully becoming a Bushong, from being a genuine *participant* observer. I could never truly become a *mwaan Bushong* after all.

Even while this process of socialization as a Bushong was going on, a countervailing force was molding me in the role of academic researcher. After all, I was a research officer of IRSAC. That institution had been founded in 1947 and endowed with a portion of the price the United States had paid for the uranium purchased to build the first atomic bombs which devastated Japan.[20] Its director was Louis van den Berghe, a specialist in tropical medicine, especially parasitology, who was nicknamed Louis le magnifique for his stature, his demeanor, his grand views about the development of science (some said his megalomania), and his taste for show.[21] The institute was the child of his brilliant and unconventional mind: a place where interdisciplinary research was to be conducted around topics of major scientific importance to the health, the environment, the societies, and the cultures of Central Africa.[22] He had succeeded in creating an institute that was almost completely free of Belgian academic interference and interference from the colonial authorities. Despite its office in Brussels, which was presided over by the secretary general, Jean-Paul Harroy, IRSAC was actually run by van den Berghe from its Lwiro station near Bukavu. In 1953 IRSAC's two main stations were Lwiro and Astrida (now Butare) in Rwanda. Researchers were recruited in Belgium under two-year contracts. Each person was given a topic of research and the means to achieve the set goals. After two years van den Berghe evaluated the results and decided whether to renew the contracts or not. If the solution to the research problem had been substantially advanced, the fellowship was renewed, even if no major publication had yet resulted from the research. Because such research opportunities clashed with the usual track toward a university career in Belgium, most of those who joined IRSAC were highly motivated by research interests. The irony of it is that so many of them became leading authorities in their fields and that all of them eventually were absorbed by universities.

From the start van den Berghe saw the goals of science less in building theory than in solving problems. Consequently he deplored the negative effects of the conventional barriers between the disciplines. The scholars at IRSAC were at first divided in two groups: natural scientists were stationed at Lwiro, and scholars in the humanities and social sciences were stationed at Astrida. Within each of these groups interdisciplinary seminars were held frequently, and once a year or so a general meeting of all researchers took place at Lwiro.[23] This approach proved quite fruitful. The seminars contributed to the quality of individual research by raising questions and opening avenues that were new for one discipline but common in others and by building strong personal ties between researchers in different fields.

In 1953 the group at Astrida comprised five social anthropologists, one physical anthropologist, and two linguists, to be joined soon by an economist, a sociologist, and a demographer. These were my colleagues, most of whom were to influence me in some way, perhaps because I was the Benjamin of the group, at least half a decade younger than any of the others. Our leader was Jean-Jacques Maquet. In 1953 his *Le système,* about the society of late precolonial Rwanda, was in press. It was to become famous and hotly disputed because he argued that a status of inequality between the three hierarchical categories of society in Rwanda (Tuutsi, Hutu, and Twa) was accepted as right and natural by the exploited groups as well as by their overlords.

The other veteran researcher in residence was a bear of a man, Jean Hiernaux. Trained in Brussels as a physician and a physical anthropologist, he also had developed competence as an archaeologist.[24] Locally he was infamous for his categorical rejection of the notion of race and his advocacy of miscegenation. He was the archetypal Belgian anticlerical. If anyone ever believed that science held all the answers to the future but first had to chase away the obscurantist mists of religion, it was he. But the precise mind of this scientist coexisted with an adventurous imagination. Later he gained fame through his studies of the biological characteristics of the various populations of tropical Africa. He was also the first, in 1958, to establish a link between a certain type of pottery, now called Urewe ware, and the huge immigration of Bantu speakers in eastern and southern Africa. Hiernaux was then working in Rwanda, Burundi, and the area around Bukavu and Lwiro. I had met him six months earlier in Kuba country, where he had come to take biological samples and measurements. We had then traveled to Cwa (so-called pygmy) lands in the east of the Kuba kingdom, where he diagnosed severe malnutrition on a large scale induced by compulsory sedentarization. Then we had gone on a wild goose chase to dig up early archaeological sites related to the foundation of the Kuba kingdom, only to find ourselves, with a small caravan carrying shovels, trowels, and measuring rods, finally knee-deep in a "holy" marsh, being told that crocodiles were still prowling around there! From Hiernaux I learned a great deal about population genetics and a little about the practical aspects of digging up a small site.

Then there was Luc de Heusch, slender and vivacious as a dragonfly, who had been recruited when I was. Also a graduate of Brussels, he had later studied in Paris with Lévi-Strauss, whose most ardent disciple he became. He was the most unconventional of us all: a convinced anarchist and an inspired artist.[25] He was then studying the Tetela people, northeast of the Kuba country in Kasai. Unlike the other anthropologists who had been educated in London, he had little interest for social structure as such, but rather wanted to discover the expressions of the unconscious workings of the untutored mind in myth. In March–April 1954 he would visit the Kuba capital, with a plan to shoot a film there. By then he was tired of living in the deep rainforests and frustrated because his Tetela did not seem to thrive on intricate myths such as those one could find among the Kuba and in Rwanda.

André Coupez, an angular, wiry, but reserved person who oozed calm, was the senior linguist. He was a relentlessly rationalist logician endowed with mordant wit and extraordinary tenacity. He valued linguistics for its quasi mathematical approach and for the precision of its results, while he seemed to bear a grudge against spontaneous enthusiasm as the source of all academic follies. Trained in Brussels, he had taught in a prestigious high school in that city before studying with Meeussen at Tervuren.[26] In Astrida he lived at the station and had begun a study of Kinyarwanda, on which he is still working today. He was also involved with the comparative study of Bantu languages, and in 1953 he set out to gather data about them for the use of lexicostatistics, a technique just then pioneered by Morris Swadesh and publicized by Meeussen. The clarity of his thought and his technical skills were to be of considerable assistance to me when I was composing a grammatical sketch of Bushong in 1954. We became good friends, and we have collaborated on historical linguistics ever since I met him at the 1953 seminar.

The only person who did not influence me very much was John Jacobs, the other linguist. He was a sturdy and dignified person and such an urban product that I imagined that he knew the outdoors only from school outings and books. He was the only one among us with a burning ambition to become a professor at his alma mater, Ghent, and he knew all about the proper connections necessary to achieve this lofty goal.[27] By the time of the seminar he was an old acquaintance. We had first met briefly in Antwerp, we had been stranded together at Lwiro, we traveled in convoy from there to his research area in Tetela country, whence I had proceeded to Nsheng further west, and we had taped and transcribed the Kuba king's performance together.

In December 1953, just when Bushong values and worldviews were having their greatest impact on me following the initiation, I was summoned to Astrida to participate in the sixth interdisciplinary seminar there.[28] I found Rwanda to be utterly different from the Congo. The country was mountainous, and the temperate climate seemed cold to anyone from Kasai. The density of the population was astonishing. Wherever one looked there were fields, beehives hidden under banana trees, and long-horned cattle, and bush was nowhere to be seen. Even the rows of eucalyptus trees seemed artificial, as they provided only filtered light rather than genuine shade. The spacious IRSAC station, consisting of scattered buildings surrounded by lawns on a hillside below the hospital, well beyond the European town of Astrida, also struck me as artificial. It reflected the uneasy position of an institution totally out of place either in the Rwandan countryside or in the colonial town.

I felt myself totally alien here too and quite disoriented. The sizable European population of Astrida disconcerted me. It was different in manners and raiment from the colonials of the Congo. It recalled Belgium, except that everyone dressed in the same meticulous metropolitan summer dress and behaved as if they all belonged to the same class. The people here seemed dedicated to upholding the stifling standards of living and decorum beloved by retired middle-class persons in Belgian provincial towns. I felt trapped. When I was called on to attend social functions, I felt cornered. The worst of these occasions promised to be a christening party held on the station. It could not be escaped, so I arrived late, with a heavy heart beating under a borrowed pullover, and entered a room where a noisy party was in full swing. But I did not see the revelers. I saw only a very attractive young delicate girl with jet black hair and instantly fell in love. From that moment Astrida changed. I spent all my time scheming to meet her again, first by accident, and later by appointment. The social occasions which I had hated now became opportunities, until at a dance on New Year's Eve and the eve of my departure, I proposed to her. Claudine did not reject me.

Meanwhile, I spent my working hours at the station in a small bare office, unhappily hunched over a typewriter, to set down an account of the Kuba initiation I had attended barely a month earlier. On arrival I had told Jean-Jacques Maquet the story, whereupon he suggested that I write it up and send it to the journal *Africa*. Because he was the director and a veteran researcher, I treated his suggestion as an order, even though it looked an impossible task ever to condense such a rich and complex experience into a mere article. Yet somehow after a long week's work, the whole event had been boiled down into an introductory account.[29]

The seminar opened on December 21, and it was memorable.[30] Looking at the agenda even now, it is striking to see how novel the topics discussed were in the context of the times. These issues were to remain at the center of attention for a generation to come. Urban studies, nutrition, the structuralist views of Lévi-Strauss, lexicostatistics, and the historical value of oral traditions were exciting stuff then. It also was instructive to learn about the research designs, methods, procedures, and assumptions of other social scientists. I learned a great deal about techniques such as sampling and building valid quantitative databases, and about practices in other disciplines, at this and subsequent seminars. On this occasion the differences between the approaches of the anthropologists struck me most. Maquet summoned informants to his office, and de Heusch traveled a lot around his "field," asking questions, getting answers, and moving on. Later I would observe that Daniel Biebuyck, then on leave in Belgium and based in Lwiro, was an even greater traveler. Yet unlike de Heusch, he returned again and again to the same places to talk to the same people. Their practices were all very different from mine.

But despite their brilliance, the researchers at IRSAC, taken collectively, still disconcerted me. The Europeans in town had dismissed them as snobbish bohemians, but to me they were not bohemian at all. Some among them were aping the fashionable young intellectuals in Brussels. They aimed to shock the good burghers by affecting liberal attitudes, shot through with affectation and elitism. It was no accident that de Heusch once gave a lecture about the virtues of royal incest to the townspeople. Other researchers were simply Belgian professionals. They thought of the significance of their experience as it related to the expected reception of their work by an international academic community rather than as the personal opportunity to be involved with another culture, which for me was the obvious attraction of research. Thus they carefully kept a great distance between themselves and the "objects" of their study, an attitude which for my taste slid all too easily into the kind of elitism I had suffered in high school. To me there were no monolithic "Kuba," specimens of study, but rather different people who were teachers, friends, assistants, or acquaintances of a day (informants!). These people were what one talked about to academics, yes, but they were not objects.

It is hard to evaluate to what degree the research I carried out in Kuba country after my return from Astrida was affected by what I had learned at the seminar. While the study of Kuba history and the Bushong language continued as before, my approach to Kuba society and culture took a new turn. From the seminar I picked up technical suggestions, such as how to attempt a photo essay, how to have children play "kinship," and how to organize simple quantitative surveys. Yet on the whole the change in research design was bound to happen anyway. I now knew what the overall social and cultural landscape was like, so I needed to acquire quantitative data on almost every aspect of social, political, and economic life to compare practice with norms. Therefore I hired more assistants to carry out this program. This progression in fieldwork was not very original. It was then standard procedure for social anthropologists. Less usual was my interest in "culture." I started to collect data relating to Kuba culture as it was expressed in accounts about worldview, symbols, religious practice, dreams, gossip, oral literature, art, and language.

Thus I conducted research across a broad spectrum of topics rather than concentrating on political institutions or art, which were the most distinctive characteristics of Kuba society. This recalled the approaches of ethnologists a generation earlier, against which especially E. E. Evans Pritchard had inveighed. Yet even in the fifties anthropologists were supposed to gather every kind of data that could be useful to anyone at all. I once heard Audrey Richards at a seminar in Lwiro declare that anthropology was still the handmaiden of all the other disciplines. Anthropologists were expected to come up with the data needed by nutritionists, doctors, and economists. Yet there were several drawbacks to this broad-spectrum approach. First, it gave me a false sense of security. I thought that I was recording everything of note, from making pottery to making charms, and that if only enough "evidence" was gathered, it would automatically pattern itself and lead to theoretical insights. This was false. I now see, for instance, that my notes on metallurgy and smithing are totally inadequate. Second, as a consequence of this stance I avoided the kind of concentrated thinking and checking against data that would have led to a breakthrough in the understanding the phenomena of symbolism and religion that interested me most.[31] Third, a large mass of the data gathered has never fully been exploited, for lack of both ability and a sustained interest in acquiring the necessary expertise in specialties ranging from technology to demography. Finally, the very breadth of research activities, paradoxically allied to the intensity of interaction with the Kuba, created a sharp boundary between "Kuba" and others. What the Kuba did, felt, and thought was fascinating. What others did, felt, and thought was irrelevant. I was far too much of a Kuba nationalist and reacted to the local situation as a Flemish nationalist would at home.

In the first weeks of my stay in the country, for example, I had seen the atelier of Djilatendo (Tshyela Ntendu), one of the earliest modern painters in the Belgian Congo, and I had even listened to stories about how, long before the war, he had been encouraged to paint by a territorial agent and had settled in Ibaanc (Ibanshe), a Luba/Lulua enclave in Kuba country. Yet I did not even record this. He was not a Kuba, and I saw in his canvases on view merely poor attempts to imitate Kuba decorative patterns. Thus I missed a unique opportunity of recording evidence about the early days of modern painting in the Belgian Congo.[32]

Despite the continuity in research design, my work in 1954 became qualitatively different: I became more of a team leader and less of a lone researcher discovering only through personal experience. I began to feel trapped in a routine as the novelty of "discovery" wore off, despite a few spectacular happenings, such as when a diviner made a corpse confess to witchcraft or when a performance of the great *itul* masquerade occurred on the great town square. The real cause of this lack of absorption was simple. My undivided attention no longer went to the Kuba: I was longing to be near the girl I loved.

In May 1954 I took the opportunity to return to Astrida at the conclusion of a second IRSAC seminar in Luluaburg. I only returned to Kuba country in early July, when an irate Maquet ordered me out of Astrida. By then Claudine and I were engaged, I had received a call-up notice from the military for October 1, I had made up my mind to write a doctorate in history, and we had decided to marry in early September. Back in Mweka, I wound up the existing research program. I took Evariste with me to continue working on a grammatical sketch of Bushong and was again in Astrida a mere month after my departure, all to the ever-growing displeasure of Maquet. Claudine and I were married in Astrida on September 3 with a mollified Maquet as my best man. Still the Kuba struck back: the honeymoon was cut short after four days, so I could complete the Bushong grammar in time.[33] Then I joined the Belgian army at the base of Kamina in Katanga province, where I would be stationed for the next eighteen months, while Evariste made a long, roundabout journey by boat and train back to Nsheng.[34]

One could say that military service was the equivalent of Kuba initiation in the Belgian world and that it socialized me back into Belgian mores, but that is a specious comparison. Certainly I learned a lot about colonial and military attitudes, which I hated, and I learned to hide that passion. But I also learned to use every single avenue open to me to turn situations to my advantage. Eventually I held a job that gave me much time to write the first draft of what was to be a doctoral dissertation on oral tradition and Kuba history. During this whole period Evariste kept working for me, and other Bushong in Mweka also wrote to me, so that I still vicariously participated at least a little in a Kuba way of life. I was now serious about the need for a Ph.D. After years of silence, in 1955 I finally wrote about this to Jozef Desmet, who had supervised me when I was a student in history and who had succeeded to the chair of Albert De Meyer at Leuven. Early in 1956 Desmet tentatively agreed to direct such a project, provided that Vaast (alias Gaston) Van Bulck, an ethnologist, would be a codirector.

Contacts with other Africanists did not completely lapse in Kamina. To begin with, Daniel Biebuyck, a veteran colleague from IRSAC, had also been drafted, and we saw quite a bit of each other. Biebuyck was a large man, a force of nature bubbling with an eloquent vitality, who admired and condemned with equal passion. He was fascinated by the artistic and oral expressions of the intricacies of collective thought in the communities he had studied. He had studied classics at Ghent, then art history with Frans Olbrechts, and later had been a companion of Jean-Jacques Maquet's at University College, London. Ever since he had studied various populations in Kivu. He was an enthusiastic ethnographer, absorbed by concreteness and nuances. But he was also suspicious, and self-centered to the point that he did not easily share information.[35]

At Christmas I returned on leave to Astrida and attended another seminar there. The station now had three new economists, interested in demography, rural marketing, and urban migration, whose communications once again broadened my views.[36] In August 1955 Biebuyck and I were allowed a special leave of absence to attend an Interafrican Conference in the Social Sciences and Humanities at Bukavu.[37] The presence of Biebuyck was crucial to its success, because he had arranged for the participants to attend the performance of an epic by the people in northern Kivu, where he had worked. I was allowed to tag along only for a few days, to serve as rapporteur for one of the sessions. It was a treat. I met J. Desmond Clark, who was to become the undisputed leader in African archaeology. He talked about the potential, achievements, and needs of archaeology. I savored the rhetorical flourishes of Marcel Griaule, even then a legendary figure among French Africanists, whose fame is intertwined with that of Dogon (Mali) cosmology, and admired how Daryll Forde gently brought the discussions back from the heights of potential metaphysics to the pedestrian links between cosmology and social structures. The well-known anthropologists Audrey Richards and Melville Herskovits attended, as did Meeussen. Typically for him, Meeussen took me aside for an hour or two to teach me the rudiments of the new technique of componential analysis in kinship terminology, to discuss points of Bushong grammar, and to share the latest news about comparative Bantu studies. A certain John Fage of the University of the Gold Coast, one of the founders of African history as an academic specialty, also attended. Yet I was still so enmeshed in the networks of anthropologists that his presence escaped my attention. I did not catch the significance of his work, even though it would also be mine.[38]

Then in January 1956 an ancient archaeological site unexpectedly turned up in a sand pit on the base.[39] Biebuyck flatly refused to become involved in the necessary salvage excavation. Two graves containing well over one hundred pots and metal objects had been found. They had to be dug up and secured while the sand pit lay idle for a few days. But I only had time in the early evening after my working day was over. So I dug them up with one of the laborers at the sand pit as best I could, which was not very well. I could not keep the objects all piled up in a corner of the barracks, so I packed them as best I could with the makeshift means available and sent the contents to Astrida. The pots arrived shattered to pieces, and the acting director, an economist, threw the whole lot out. Thus the salvage excavation was a total failure. All that now remains of the site are a few photographs.

Barely a month before I was due for discharge, back in Astrida Claudine bore a son, Bruno. Somehow I managed to obtain forty-eight hours' leave and to catch rides on military and civilian planes for a short visit. Then I returned to Kamina, but not for long. My unit was discharged on March 22, 1956, and we boarded a rickety military plane for home. Even though the plane crashed and broke up on landing at Usumbura, no one was seriously hurt. Soon I was again in Astrida with Claudine and Bruno. But not for long. Two weeks later I had secured a sturdy van and a driver. Bruno was too young for the grueling three-day drive. So back I went to Kuba country alone.

At Nsheng I was warmly welcomed, and soon it seemed as if I had never left. There had been changes there since 1954. A new state school and a hospital were being built on the ruined campsite at the Tail of the Parrot. The Catholic mission was planning to open an art school, in Mweka a genuine gas station had sprung up, and everyone everywhere, Congolese or European, was full of talk about a rosy economic future. My own plans were clear now that the first draft of my dissertation was ready. I first lived in a remote Bushong village to compensate for the biased view I had acquired by living so long at the capital. Then I traveled incessantly, living like a gypsy on the road and having a marvelous time. I went as far as I could with the car, and then I walked to the really remote spots, in one instance over eighty kilometers in a single day. I thus visited the whole country, gathering additional data on the early history of the various chiefdoms and checking earlier information. I also photographed or drew all the art objects people would show me and gathered a sizable collection of Kuba artworks which people wanted to sell. These were not intended for the museum in Tervuren but went to a museum then being established at Lwiro. Everything happened as planned, except that I came down with typhus in a remote village and arrived at a Presbyterian mission hospital

only to collapse on the threshold of the doctor's office. I regained consciousness more than a week later. Then I returned to Nsheng for further
convalescence and a bit of quiet research, before the grand tour resumed
again.

In less than three months I gathered an enormous amount of new data.
That was possible only because I was now a familiar figure all over Kuba
lands. The interruption caused by my military service had not prevented
correspondence and even contacts with Kuba visitors. But three months
was still a short time. Soon I had to go. The day before my departure some
of the most respected elders visited me to say that I was now educated
enough to be taught the more complex features of Kuba thought and to
urge me to return soon. Alas, it was too late for that! On the morning of
the first of July a crowd of well-wishers helped me pack the van. Then I
said a formal good-bye to the king, and off we went. As the van pulled out,
I looked behind me for a last regretful glance at the piece of my life I was
leaving behind forever, yet I was happy at the thought of rejoining my
family and of the life to come. I left sadly convinced that I would not see or
hear anymore from any of the Bushong I had known for so long, for no
other researcher seemed to have kept up with "informants" after leaving
the field. Little did I realize how long-lasting the links forged between the
community in Nsheng and myself would prove to be. Although I was
never able to return to the area, some correspondence was kept up for over
twenty years, and later in Kinshasa I would meet some of the Bushong I
had known in Nsheng. Nor was I forgotten there.[40]

The family traveled to Belgium on leave for six months. I had two precise
professional goals in mind: to acquire a *licence* in historical linguistics and
to defend my dissertation. There now existed an Institute of African
Studies in Leuven, where Meeussen taught courses in linguistics. Desmet,
who clearly wanted to help me but who obstinately continued to label me
as an "ethnologist," now made clear that I should defend a dissertation,
not in history but in "African studies," at that institute. Hence he wanted
Gaston or Vaast Van Bulck to be a major professor also.[41] Van Bulck, a
Jesuit, had studied in Vienna and was a member of the Viennese school of
cultural history. He had traveled extensively in Central Africa and had
accumulated mountains of ethnographic data. Unfortunately he was noto-
rious both for the disorder in his notes and in his mind. I found him totally
unacceptable as a dissertation director because of his theoretical orienta-
tion, which I thought utterly fallacious. When I told Desmet this, he urged
me to defend this Ph.D. with Forde in London. Again I refused on the

grounds that it was a doctorate in history, an application of general historical methodology. I challenged him to show why precolonial history was
not history but something else. He retorted that he and his colleagues were
not competent to evaluate this subject. I came back arguing that if historical critique—also known as "the rules of evidence"—was valid anywhere,
it should be valid everywhere. Hence my topic touched on the core of the
discipline, and historians not only had the competence to evaluate this
dissertation, but they were the only scholars who had. Still he held out.
But two can be stubborn, and in the end he half relented: he would seek
the agreement of his colleagues in the department for this project. Stub-
bornness is a thief of time, however, and it was now clearly too late for me
to defend the dissertation before the summer. I asked and received a
further leave of absence from IRSAC, and the family prepared to live on
our meagre savings.

Fall came, and I had rewritten much of the dissertation. Desmet began
to read and comment, especially on the long introductory chapter, which
later formed the framework of *De la tradition orale*. Claudine, Bruno, and I
were crammed into a tiny apartment on the outskirts of Brussels, an
unfriendly city to outsiders. It was a very difficult year for Claudine and
myself. But the place was within easy reach by public transport of Tervuren, its library, Maesen, and Meeussen. From Tervuren I accompanied
Meeussen when he lectured in Leuven, and I sat in on his lectures and also
did additional exercises for him at Tervuren. In this fashion I had taken the
equivalent of a full M.A. program in African languages by the end of the
academic year, including writing a thesis. With Maesen, who was a reader
of my doctoral dissertation, I discussed anthropology, and I passed chapters to him for comment. But he always promised his observations later. In
the end he had the whole draft, and still there was no reaction. One cold
day in February I finally squatted on the steps to his house until he gave
me the comments he had already made.

This show of determination, though, did not speed up the defense.
Desmet had brought the proposal to the department, which in its collective
wisdom found that it could not decide. The department sent the file on to
the dean of the faculty, who submitted it to his council. In due course they
were baffled, so they sent it up to the *rector magnificus*. Rumor has it that
when the rector saw the file, he brusquely exclaimed that it was not his job
to evaluate the suitability of Ph.D. topics. Back it cascaded down, first to
the faculty council, which promptly followed the rector's lead, and then
back to the history department. I remained obdurate, and Desmet persuasive, so his colleagues finally yielded. The topic was accepted, provided

that the jury would include three readers with specialties in historical critique, from three different universities, as well as an anthropologist (Maesen) and a linguist (Meeussen), and provided that the results of inquiries to be made in the Congo about the research were favorable. That decision came late in the spring, too late for me to defend that year, even though the whole dissertation had by then been approved by Desmet and Maesen. The family was completely broke. Claudine returned with Bruno to her parents in Astrida, while I moved back to Gooreind.

Apparently the inquiries in the Congo established that I really had been there, really had done research, and really spoke the language, so the defense finally took place on October 16, 1957, in the familiar seminar room now packed with curious people. All went well until the ritual query came, asking whether a member of the public wanted to ask a question. Van Bulck, who had been rejected as a member of the jury, rose. He began to ask questions and offer obiter dicta which opened the floodgates. Other people chimed in. Friendly or hostile questions came from everywhere, including a belligerent one to the effect that "all this oral tradition is just tomfoolery." What could I retort except that it was up to the jury to rule on the matter?

The jury deliberated, returned, and announced:

We, president, secretary and members of the committee, charged by order of the Rector Magnificus with the examination of doctor in Philosophy and Letters . . . considering that he has, with the greatest distinction, submitted a thesis, "The Historical Value of Oral Tradition: Application to Kuba History," and a further proposition, "Latin Dirges for Contemporaries Find Their Origin in Germanic Dirges with the Later Addition of Elements Derived from the Classical and Early Christian Literature," have conferred and confer upon Mr Vansina, Jan, the degree of doctor in Philosophy and Letters. Enacted at Leuven, October 16, 1957.

At long last, there it was. My research was now officially sanctioned as history, even though the prevalent stereotypes were still so powerful that nearly everyone in Belgium, including most of the members of the jury, would continue to think of me as an "ethnologist." Yet the struggle to obtain that doctorate left me more determined than ever to be a historian of Africa, if only to show that one could not deny a history to Africans by burying it as "ethnology" or "ethnohistory."

3

Old Africa Rediscovered

AT THE moment of my dissertation defense, the academic practice
of African history was then almost a decade old. I had twice
failed to notice its existençe, once when Daryll Forde spoke to
me about it and once when John Fage attended the conference at Bukavu.
But six months before the defense, the cartographer at Tervuren had
drawn my attention to a conference entitled African History and Archaeology which was to be held at SOAS in July. I decided to attend. It was
sheer delight. Finally I had found like-minded scholars of that still-rare
species "historian of Africa," who were as determined as I was to rediscover the early history of tropical Africa. I learned there what and how
much they had already achieved. That is the story related in this chapter.
Only let us not end it in 1957, just because that was the year I entered this
network of scholars, but pursue the tale to 1960, the year in which nearly
all the countries of tropical West and Central Africa became independent.

"Old Africa rediscovered" was still a triumphant hope rather than a
solid achievement when Basil Davidson, a well-informed journalist, chose
this for the title of his book about the history of precolonial Africa for a
British public.[1] In Europe generally and in Britain in particular, the gospel
had been for well over a century that tropical Africa had no history.[2] As
late as July 1951, the august and informed personage Dame Margery Perham had declared in the influential periodical *Foreign Affairs:* "The deal-
ings between tropical Africa and the West must be different. Here in place
of the larger unities of Asia was the multi-cellular tissue of tribalism:
instead of an ancient civilization, the largest area of *primitive poverty*
enduring into the modern age. Until the very recent penetration by Europe
the greater part of the continent was without the wheel, the plough, or *the
transport animal; almost without stone houses or clothes, except for skins; without
writing and so without history.*"[3] That was the position of the enemy. David-

son, addressing the same public, now assured them that there was a history. He told them "the story of Africa's forgotten past."

His book created a sensation in Britain. A British diplomat passing through Astrida asked me a few months after its publication whether the story of states and trade and great art was really true. Why were such people interested in this issue at that time? Because most of tropical Africa was then on the eve of independence, and Davidson argued that, given a brilliant past, a brilliant future rather than a descent into chaos was to follow. He concluded his account with three pages entitled "History Begins Anew," which contained phrases such as "They [Africans] reappear today in the sad evening of the world of nation-states" and "African peoples followed their own road in the past; there is nothing to say that they will not follow it, constructively, creatively, again."[4]

Academic historians of Africa hailed the book as a first public vindication of their views and a first overview of their achievements since 1948, the birth date, not of African history, but of African history in academia. It was in that year that Roland R. Oliver was appointed as historian of Africa in the history department of the School of Oriental and African Studies at the University of London. Moreover, 1948 is also a special date because in that year Kenneth O. Dike, a Nigerian, began to gather oral traditions at home as part of the evidence to be used for his doctorate.[5] By collecting such data, he was using information which everyone in his homeland accepted as historical evidence to prove to Europeans that there could be history without writing. At the same time his work continued the practices of oral historians from whom he had learned so much in his own youth. The award of a doctorate by London's King's College on October 18, 1950, confirmed his success and constituted an academic recognition as important as the appointment of Oliver had been. In collecting oral traditions and seeing them recognized as valid evidence by his jury, Dike forged the link connecting a flourishing oral and written African historiography and also established a new academic practice. Lest the reader should imagine, however, that 1948 saw an immediate and general change of attitudes about Africa, it may be well to recall that the same year also saw the victory of the nationalists in South Africa and the advent of apartheid.

Historical consciousness and a historical narrative had existed in the various parts of the continent as far back as one could remember and beyond. Everywhere in tropical Africa older people taught their descendants about the past in word and practice, while in many societies some persons became particularly attached to this topic, queried others about it, and acquired prestige as community historians, such as Mbop Louis and other *bulaam* among the Bushong. Some centralized societies even had official historians, entrusted with certain public or esoteric traditions about the past and with the transmission of knowledge to their successors.

A written historiography also existed in tropical Africa. As local historians became literate, some oral materials were committed to writing, annalists and chroniclers appeared, and soon historians followed, to assemble all sorts of evidence to propose a reconstruction of past events and situations. Thus by 1500 there existed a chronicle, written in Arabic, of Kilwa, a city-state on the East African coast. Arabic chronicles from the succeeding centuries have survived from inland towns in West Africa.[6] But in most parts of tropical Africa, writing was adopted only during the nineteenth century; committing historical records to paper soon followed in West Africa, Madagascar, and South Africa. The earliest history of this sort published about West Africa was Samuel Crowther's history of Oyo, an introduction to his *Vocabulary of the Yoruba Language,* and from midcentury onward other books were published that treated other parts of West Africa.[7] In Madagascar, Raombana wrote his voluminous history and annals between 1853 and 1856. At least another fourteen histories in manuscript have survived from the nineteenth century.[8] Elsewhere in South Africa and on the East African coast, some Africans also wrote histories, although there were far fewer than in West Africa.[9] This trend never died out. As they became literate, local historians all over tropical Africa began to write histories in vernacular languages for the benefit of their communities. This process continues.

Some foreigners also had been writing African history for centuries. Before 1500 Arab authors dealing with the history of North Africa included information about West Africa as well.[10] Ibn Khaldun and Leo Africanus are but the best known among them.[11] A few Europeans also wrote histories of particular African societies long before the colonial conquest. For instance, the second book of the description of the kingdom of Kongo by Duarte Lopes and Filipo Pigafetta, published in 1591, was a history.[12] In 1624 a local priest wrote a whole history of the kingdom of Kongo.[13] During the same century several other authors followed suit in Kongo and Angola. Similar examples could be cited for West Africa and other coastal areas.[14]

Africans and Europeans continued to write histories during the colonial period. Among the latter, administrators and missionaries were most active. Administrators especially needed to record political histories as part of their "intelligence reports," while missionaries were more concerned with "general" history and with the production of texts for schools. Very few of these authors had been trained as professional historians.

Only Hubert Deschamps used his research to obtain a doctorate in human geography (1938). At the conclusion of his administrative career in 1943, he became a professional historian. Deschamps would be the first to teach African history at the Sorbonne.[15] The first African academic historians, the Nigerians Kenneth O. Dike and Saburi O. Biobaku, had learned the history of their people as children, both from oral tradition and from Yoruba authors writing in Yoruba or in English.[16] Their merit was to translate this activity into a disciplined "scientific" setting, just as Nigerian lawyers at the time were translating local oral law into written law. The cases of Dike, Biobaku, and Deschamps illustrate the continuity of academic African historiography. From this angle, the academic recognition of African history in 1948 was merely the culmination of a trend and its appropriation by professionals. There is no doubt that colonial attitudes explain why the recognition of a genuine African history was so late in coming and why even Dame Perham, reared in imperial history, could be so ill informed as late as 1951.[17]

After all, the colonial period was the heyday of imperial history. What happened to Africans was only considered at European or at almost all American universities as part of imperial history, or the history of "European expansion," a euphemism much in favor after World War II, with each country having its own imperial history. The gaze of imperial history was firmly focused on the deeds of Europeans overseas, not on any of the benighted natives. Imperial history had a pedigree as long as that of European colonization. It was in full bloom during the early twentieth century, when it was used to justify colonies and to recruit colonials by providing to them shining examples of colonial heroes. Thus at the University of Leuven in the 1940s one spoke only of the greatness of King Leopold II and Henry M. Stanley and the fight against the Arab slave traders. But our professor was sceptical about heroes, and so the "history of the Belgian Congo" merely came as two lectures appended to the history of Belgium.[18] The exemplar of more serious African imperial history in the English-speaking world undoubtedly was South African historiography. Moreover, all historians then were positivists, and imperial historians believed even more than others that there was one historical truth and that it could be known by studying written documents. The fixation on writing was as great as it had ever been. Dame Perham certainly subscribed to Leopold von Ranke's intemperate remark: "Was nicht in den Akten hat nicht gelebt!" (What is not in the documents has not lived!)

African history as such was a subject of some interest to African American academics in the United States, inspired by W. E. B. Du Bois.[19] Carter

G. Woodson founded the *Journal of Negro History* in 1916. The journal drew some attention to African history and occasionally published articles about the topic. Yet in this milieu the focus of interest lay on African American history, and African historical issues remained marginal.

Consequently, most of what is now recognized as African history was left to anthropology, the discipline which coped with the nonliterate (noncivilized) and the exotic. From the 1910s to the 1930s "cultural history" had been a central endeavor of anthropologists both in the United States and in Central Europe.[20] Some anthropologists were interested in the past of African peoples. Yet they were every bit as positivist as historians, so most of them denied any value to oral traditions. In addition, their leaders in Central Europe were not even prepared to make much of archaeology, which was considered there to be a separate discipline. To ethnographers, tropical Africa was a quilt of thousands of tribal territories, or Perham's "multi-cellular tissue of tribalism," yet another justification for colonial rule.[21] At the same time Dietrich Westermann had also written a work on the formation of States south of the Sahara.[22] It showed little clusters of African "states," each evolving its own destiny in splendid isolation like a colony of bacteria in a petri dish.

By the time academic African history arrived on the scene, the search for the history of tropical Africa involved small heterogenous groups here and there, often working in isolation. Academic historians encompassed a general imperial group, a South African group, and a few lonely scholars, such as John W. Blake, who were focusing on early European-African contacts.[23] With the exception of Melville Herskovits and some of his students at Northwestern University, anthropologists were now no longer involved with this topic, and archaeologists were focusing on the earliest ages of humanity. Outside of the university, a number of clerics were producing substantial text editions.[24] They followed in a tradition that had flourished in Portugal ever since that country became concerned about its "historic rights" over the colonies in the nineteenth century. Amateur historians were also flourishing among administrators, whose bastions were the various colonial schools, and among missionaries sometimes inspired by their flock. But African history as a coherent history of the peoples living on the African continent was unknown.

At that time a network of institutions and journals concerned with Africa and directed by academics also existed. "Colonial universities," designed to train administrators, were not necessarily oriented toward Africa, although in France, Belgium, and Germany they focused heavily on African territories. The former geographical societies spawned some institutes which dealt specifically with "Africa," meaning tropical Africa, of which the oldest was the Royal African Society in London. That association was founded in 1901 and remained a bulwark of colonial attitudes. Its counterpart, the Société des Africanistes in Paris, dates only from 1930. Almost all its members were ethnographers. The first institute that was more directly controlled by academics and supposedly embraced all of tropical Africa was the International African Institute in London, founded in 1926 with funding from the Rockefeller Foundation. Its journal, *Africa,* soon became the focal point for what would later be called African studies. Then followed institutions in tropical Africa itself, once again limited to specific territories. The earliest was the Académie Malgache, begun in 1902, which was inspired by institutions in Algeria, Indochina, and France. Britain started the Rhodes Livingstone Institute in Northern Rhodesia in 1938 for the study of the social sciences, and France founded a truly multidisciplinary institute, Institut Français de l'Afrique Noire (IFAN), in Dakar under the polymath Théodore Monod in 1938.[25] A few others followed after the war, including IRSAC. IRSAC was influenced more by French colonial institutions than by the British ones, which were more specialized. None of these institutions recognized any African historians as such, although IFAN knew of "prehistory" and Raymond Mauny was in fact pursuing historical research at the institute after the war.[26] Yet the network of all these institutions and the journals they published formed a ready-made structure which was of considerable assistance to the development of academic African history when it came.

The Second World War was a watershed in European colonial history as in so much else. The two main victors were the United States and the Soviet Union, two powers which dominated the newly founded United Nations and which made a show of being anticolonial. The war itself had also started the process of decolonization in Asia. The heyday of colonial rule in Africa was clearly over. The Western European powers picked up the thread of rule as they had left it in 1939, but business as usual could not go on for long. The British government had long realized that something ought to be done about higher education in tropical Africa. The matter was felt to be urgent enough that the Asquith and Elliot commissions were set up in the middle of the war, on July 13, 1943. At that time only one university college existed in all of the British territories, namely Fourah Bay in Sierra Leone. It had been upgraded from a lower rank by missionaries in 1876, as the result of African pressure in the territory. Its degree program was supervised by Durham University.[27]

The commissions worked in close collaboration with the University of London, and they created a machinery for setting up external degrees to ensure that the degree standards in Africa would be at a level equivalent to those in London. After agreement was reached, the Asquith Commission handed in its report, which was published in July 1945. The Elliot report, dealing specifically with West Africa, appeared at the same time. At least the Elliot Commission had three African members. The commissions designated four institutions, existing and new, as university colleges in tropical Africa: Achimota in the Gold Coast, Ibadan in Nigeria, Khartoum in Sudan, and Makerere in Uganda.[28] The government accepted the recommendations and set up an interuniversity council in 1946. Khartoum was in operation by 1946, the West African colleges in 1948, and Makerere in 1949. In 1955 a College of Rhodesia and Nyasaland at Salisbury followed. Independent of this, the University of Addis Ababa began to function in 1950.[29]

Both reports stressed that each college should institute a post wholly or mainly devoted to history.[30] As the Elliot Commission put it, "Research into the past will not only stimulate local interest in the ancient traditions of the peoples, but will help to maintain a sense of continuity in the rapid changes now coming upon them." The creation of these posts and departments of history was entrusted to the head of London's School of Oriental and African Studies, who was then Cyril Philips, a historian of India. He felt that the supervisory role which his school was to assume over African colleges would require the appointment in London of a specialist in the history of Africa. To fund this post, he sought and was granted financial assistance from the Rockefeller Foundation. Meanwhile, in 1947, on a journey to India, he visited East Africa and "was startled to discover how little was being done there to collect and preserve material on the history of the African peoples."[31] In contrast to India, the museums and record offices here were inadequate, and Philips found no organized attempts to collect tribal traditions. In the mother countries, he concluded, imperial history was studied, but not the history of the African peoples themselves. For him, developments in India provided a model that could be followed in Africa. He proposed to remedy the situation in Africa by making two key appointments, a "homeman" at SOAS and a "fieldman" in Africa.[32] Thus was African history born.

The time was ripe for a history of Africa, and half a dozen or more possible candidates were available to Philips. Their number was a consequence of the war, which had been an intellectual watershed. Many later well-known African historians had seen service in the armed forces, some in extraordinary or glamorous positions as intelligence officers or RAF pilots. Basil Davidson had parachuted in Bosnia and fought also in Vojvodina. Unlike their prewar seniors, the new doctoral candidates had experienced life outside the ivy walls and had lived in trying and diverse circumstances. Their mindsets were simply different from those of their elders before the war. Because they had fought to stamp out fascism and alien rule, such men could not easily accept the role of an uncritical colonial historian. Thus, after the war fledgling scholars interested in Africa, such as Thomas Hodgkin, George Shepperson, Christopher Fyfe, John Hargreaves, John Fage, and Roland Oliver, to name but a handful, all broke in one way or another with the canons of imperial history, even when they were actually engaged in teaching it. This was the case for Vincent Harlow and Graham Irwin, the teachers of Kenneth Dike and Saburi Biobaku. Many among them were attracted to the ideas of the Labour party. Yet even so, these men were not radical anticolonialists, with the exception of a very few, such as Davidson and Hodgkin. They agreed that Africans should direct their own destinies, but they refused to condemn colonial rule totally. Many of them still felt that colonial rule had brought literacy and education, world religions and modernization, and that these contributions were precious. In consequence, their assessment of the colonial period was ambivalent, and it remained so.

Philips chose Roland Oliver, who was appointed a lecturer in African history at SOAS in 1948, and John Fage, who went to University College of the Gold Coast in 1949.[33] We do not know what prompted Philips to appoint Oliver and Fage rather than others, nor why Oliver was to be "homeman" and Fage "fieldman," but clearly Philips' choice was felicitous. Together Oliver and Fage created a new academic field. Oliver spent his first year taking his bearings. He traveled to Ghana and in 1949 met Fage, who had actually begun to teach African history there. Jointly they provided the impetus for other British historians of Africa at that time. From Ghana Oliver then drove across the continent to East Africa, collecting views along the way, from Nigeria to Uganda and Kenya, about what African history should and could be. In western Uganda he briefly visited royal sites, exhorted the anthropologists he met to collect oral traditions, and gathered a few of these himself.[34] Back in London in 1950, he set up the seminar in African history at SOAS and began to train his first graduate students.

Oliver's position was extraordinary, even in those exceptional years after the war. He was only in his mid-twenties when he was entrusted not just with the development of a new specialty at SOAS, but also with the responsibility to maintain degree standards and supervise the creation of a curriculum for the specialty in four and soon five university colleges in Africa. At that time he still had not even completed his Ph.D.[35] In contrast, Fage had already had extensive experience of southern and eastern Africa before 1949, when he defended his dissertation.[36] Together they fully succeeded from the outset. Certainly the circumstances were favorable, and the combination of a "homeman" and a "fieldman" was an inspired move, but the scheme could only work if both men worked harmoniously together. It was lucky for African history that their personalities meshed so well and that together they had the necessary gifts to convince the London establishment of the subject's value, to develop a program of teaching and publication, and to articulate a doctrine for the new field.[37]

This doctrine reflected the fundamental aspiration of African scholars such as Kenneth Dike and Saburi Biobaku that African history should be a history of Africans. It also addressed the objections of imperial historians and anthropologists.[38] Its major points were the following: First, "Africa" should include the whole continent from tip to toe. Oliver and Fage repudiated the then-common division between "Black Africa" and northern (presumably "white") Africa, because they felt that this division was historically unwarranted—much of West African history made no sense without that of northern Africa and vice versa—and was at least somewhat tainted by residual racism. They also rejected the ethnographic vision of Africa as a quilt of isolated "tribes," as an exotic warehouse for anthropologists. They pointed to the basis for a shared history which flowed from the common experiences that had tied many of these supposedly isolated peoples together in the past. Second, African history should focus on the experience of Africans, not of their overlords. Their past had to be studied from "the African point of view," not from the viewpoints of outsiders, contrary to the practice of imperial historians. Third, they rejected the equation history equals written sources. There were many more written sources available that addressed a much wider part of the continent than had been previously thought. Indeed, the earliest continuous written record anywhere began in Egypt. Moreover, African history could be studied, despite the shortage of written sources. Oral and material evidence would allow the historian to reconstruct the African past more fully. Fourth, African history could be studied through terms familiar from European history. States, trade, and the arts had all flourished there. Finally, the study of African history, especially of precolonial African history, showed that Africans had long been familiar with complex technological, economic, political, and religious situations. This was a point of major interest at the time, because it undermined the argument that Africans were not able to cope with the complex requirements of independent rule.

These newfangled doctrines did not just diverge from the prevalent colonialist image of Africa. They also clashed head-on with the convictions of various groups of academics. To them all this was heresy or poppycock. Imperial historians held that before the partition of Africa, its inhabitants had been savages, pure and simple, with only the most rudimentary technology and morals. What history existed there besides mindless violence and endless migrations? There was no substance to African history: nothing ever happened there. And there were no sources. Africans were not literate, and hence their past belonged to "prehistory" anyway. Even historians as well intentioned as Margery Perham, who had been a member of the Asquith Commission, still subscribed to such views.[39] All this "traditional" stuff was for anthropologists. But most British anthropologists abhorred "speculative history." They shared the fetishism of the written document and the view that African history began with the colonial conquest. This belief is evident from the "History and Traditions of Origin" section in the volumes of the *Ethnographic Survey of Africa* commissioned by the International African Institute during the fifties. They also clung tenaciously to a view of tropical Africa as a collection of timeless tribes. Orientalists, including those at SOAS, also opposed a vision of "Africa" that encompassed the whole continent. They were not ready to abandon almost half of their turf! Egyptologists and classical historians involved with northern Africa simply ignored the issue.

Given such a diverse and formidable opposition, what then made the Young Turks succeed? In two words, it was government backing. Their talents were needed as part of the creation of the new institutions of higher learning, which African elites had demanded for so long. The decisive importance of the role of the new colleges in fostering the birth of African history is shown *a contrario* by the lack of developments in francophone Africa during the same period. In 1945 a futurologist would have forecast that the new field would first develop in French-speaking Africa. Had not Maurice Delafosse published the three volumes of his history of West Africa in 1912, and had his example not been followed by several other talented administrators?[40] After the Second World War Charles-André Julien was already arguing for a history of the Maghrib "from the bottom up." Raymond Mauny was quite active as a recognized historian and as an archaeologist in West Africa, and Hubert Deschamps, then in temporary disgrace, had actually earned a doctorate by dealing with the internal history of a portion of Madagascar in 1938. In 1947 Alioune Diop launched the militant journal *Présence Africaine* in Paris as a focus for the aspirations of French-speaking African and Caribbean intellectuals and soon complained about the teaching of European-oriented history in West Africa. At that time Africans enjoyed more political influence in France than they ever would have in Great Britain. But the futurologist would have been wrong.

African history as an academic subject did not develop in France or in the French colonies, despite the favorable circumstances, primarily because it was not a major concern of African intellectuals there. They were so thoroughly assimilated to French culture that their protests were molded by the very same assumptions that underpinned general French attitudes toward history. These were not conducive to a detailed reconstruction of political history. Thus the young African scholar Cheikh Anta Diop promoted a vision of the African past that challenged prevailing European views on African history, but he focused on the origins of "civilization."[41] He accepted that "the" cradle of civilization lay in Greece, held that Greece derived the precious civilizing substance from Egypt, that Egypt was black, and hence that black people had created the civilization Europeans now enjoyed. Nevertheless, he still accepted that Greece was the cradle of a one and only civilization and that this was what mattered. In contrast, his counterparts writing in English and influenced by British empiricism left such grand thoughts aside to get on with the practical task of reconstructing a detailed history of Africa.[42] Unfortunately, as a result of such lofty attitudes, the French speakers lost time. *Présence Africaine* published its first article on the topic only in 1956 and aired the issue fully only at its congress of 1959.[43]

Moreover, African intellectuals from French colonies continued to see the Sorbonne in Paris as the ultimate arbiter of things academic. They did not clamor for universities in Africa. Far from approving the creation of an institute for higher studies at Dakar in 1950, for instance, they were concerned, lest it be an institution that would not be totally equivalent to French universities. So they did not pressure for a history of Africa to be taught there.[44] Thus it came about that I taught the first course about African history in French in 1958, in the Belgian Congo at Lovanium. Around that time Léopold Sedar Senghor is said to have finally begun to agitate for the recognition of the field, albeit at the Sorbonne only. Two positions were created there in 1960, more than a decade late compared with Britain and British territories.

The fledgling subject of African history needed to achieve three crucial goals. A sufficient number of historians of Africa had to be recruited, an African history curriculum had to be set up, and it had to be shown that valid and usable sources were available for practitioners to write "indigenous history." These goals were all met by 1957, the date of Ghana's independence. In addition, it was urgent to convince a wider public, especially among the political elites in Europe, that Africa's past history justified confidence in the future of independent states. Basil Davidson's book attempted to achieve that objective in 1959.

In general, the state of the specialty during the fifties can be assessed by the reports of two successive conferences about history and archaeology in Africa held at SOAS in 1953 and 1957.[45] One aim of both was to bring specialists from the African colleges together with those from SOAS for a joint general overview. The 1953 conference was also intended as a sort of "coming out" ceremony, intended to flaunt the support the new specialty had already been able to accumulate in order to marshal further support. The second one succeeded in attracting "international" attendance, that is, from France, Belgium, and even Portugal. Looking over the names of the participants, one sees eighteen bona fide African historians participating in 1953. Adding the names of those who are known to have been active but who were absent, such as Dike and Biobaku, the number of scholars climbs to twenty-eight. This figure excludes historians of South Africa or of northern Africa. In 1957 fifty-five historians participated, including Dike, Biobaku, and five other West Africans (four of those presented papers in absentia). The number of others active in the field cannot be exactly estimated for that date, but there were more than in 1953. Hence, in four years the total number of historians of tropical Africa seems roughly to have doubled. Later the numbers continued to rise. By 1959 there were enough historians in the eyes of the Rockefeller Foundation to justify a subsidy toward the launching of the *Journal of African History*.[46]

The first conference has been described as a modest weekend school.[47] It presented information derived from archaeology and oral traditions. One of its most striking features is that the conference report reprints the bibliographies used for the papers in an appendix, a practice that betrays the still-recent origin of the field. These bibliographies were intended to help participants justify the introduction of courses on the subject and innovations in the history curriculum. Moreover, the report dealt only

51

with precolonial history, thus sidestepping any direct clash with imperial historians or university authorities.

The 1957 conference was a much more impressive affair. When I entered the conference room, I was taken aback by the size of the crowd. Not only the size was astounding. For the first time a sizable number of social anthropologists, including Daryll Forde, attended the proceedings. It was evident that, in London at least, African history was now a respected field. As its report shows, this conference again dwelled mostly on precolonial history, but the subject was now broken into two parts—pre–nineteenth century and nineteenth century—simply because exactly half of the seventy papers submitted dealt with the period after 1800. The general outline of the precolonial history of Africa presented in the report strikes me today as amazingly familiar. Here was a picture that was soon to be standardized for at least a generation—but only for tropical Africa, for no papers dealt with northern Africa or South Africa. Despite the definition of "Africa" in the doctrine of the school, the historiographies of these areas were not yet affiliated with "African history."

The atmosphere at the meetings alternated between the electric and the dishwater dull. At times participants were enthralled by a speaker whose exposé was revolutionary in its novelty, while at times they were bored by details, say about coins in East Africa, which only the speaker and one or two others understood. The most heated discussions I remember during the sessions dealt with methodology and with a conflicting assessment of the virtues of King Leopold II of Belgium.[48] As a review by Jean Stengers shows, the conference especially impressed the foreign historians in attendance, although they too were mostly imperial historians.[49] The main features that struck Stengers were that African historians were there and that no visible opposition existed between a "black history" and a "white history." Observations such as these betray the prevailing climate of opinion among European academics at the time: they were happily surprised that Africans could be rigorous academic historians but still unaware of the constraints of a colonial situation which made it impractical for Dike or others to express their intellectual disagreements with SOAS in such a forum.

By 1957, also, the battle for the curriculum was being won. The Asquith and Elliot commissions had correctly foreseen that adaptations to the model London curriculum were necessary, but they unfortunately advocated only minor changes, in order to put a greater emphasis on the history of the country where the college was located.[50] This was totally inadequate, however, and the relevant passages in the reports of the commissions soon became a stumbling block, as the texts themselves were authoritative. A struggle for a meaningful curriculum ensued within each college. The first teachers, John Fage, Kenneth Dike, and Kenneth Ingham, were in the front line of that battle. The credit for the first breakthrough belongs to John Fage, Philips' "fieldman." He was the first to face the issue, and in British officials' eyes he appeared to have the right credentials to make acceptable proposals in the matter of adapting the London history degree syllabus to the needs of tropical Africa.[51] It took Fage four or five years of hard work before he could even forward proposals for courses at Achimota to London in 1954. Even then the London board raised questions about the amount and the quality of the teaching materials available. Fage was ready for this. In 1952–53 he had compiled lists of books and documents about West African history, and now he submitted them. Moreover, he had completed a textbook, *An Introduction to the History of West Africa*, in 1953, which was published in 1955. He followed this up with a school atlas.[52] With all the objections met, the syllabus was reformed. Still, the part of African history in the general curriculum remained small.

Meanwhile in Ibadan, Dike, who had been appointed in 1950, made no headway at all. He left the university in 1952 to concentrate on the organization of an archival service in Nigeria. He returned in 1954, but little progress was made until he was appointed as head of the department in 1956.[53] The curriculum was then somewhat Africanized. But a truly new syllabus was prepared only between 1959 and 1961, and it could be adopted only after Ibadan had become an independent university. Only then could Nigerian historians such as Jacob Ajayi or Joseph Anene turn to the question of reforming the curriculum of secondary schools. Still, the new Ibadan curriculum rapidly became an inspiring model for the other universities in Nigeria and in Ghana.[54] Meanwhile in Makerere, Kenneth Ingham, who had arrived there in 1950, seems to have met some resistance from European settlers. Like Fage, though, he finally did obtain some measure of reform, and also like Fage, he published a textbook.[55] Still, by 1959 only two certificates out of ten in the honors program in history dealt with African history, while one out of three was in the general B.A. program. But A. J. Hanna, Ingham's successor, a dyed-in-the-wool imperial historian, abolished the single African history course requirement for the B.A. in 1963.[56]

The second most pressing question for African history in its early years was the issue of sources. If African history was to be the history of Africans, written sources alone would not do. Intellectually, the challenge was to develop an adequate methodology for the use of sources other than written ones. Throughout the fifties this issue dominated all discussions about the field. There was no need to prove the validity of archaeology, a recognized discipline. The main task there was to lobby hard for the appointment of archaeologists. The central methodological problem facing historians was the question of oral tradition, because the evaluation of traditions seemed to be their responsibility and could not be delegated to any other discipline. Nor did most anthropologists at that time agree to collect such traditions for historians. Moreover, the availability of oral traditions was the feature which made the case of tropical Africa different from other "prehistory" situations. Traditions were crucial, but how reliable were they? This question dominated Oliver's introduction to the report on the 1953 SOAS conference (probably written in 1955). He assessed the likely contribution of evidence from this field in light of his experience in Uganda in 1950 and 1953.[57] Of course traditions were much more familiar to Dike and Biobaku. They had used many of them in their research since 1948. But like Oliver, they did not make a systematic effort to resolve the issue of the status of the traditions as sources for the historian. Thus in 1953 Dike concluded: "There is no reason to discard oral tradition provided it is used in conjunction with evidence from other sources and the possibility of inaccuracy is always borne in mind."[58]

In the preceding chapter I told how I came to perceive the issue independently in 1953 and how I tackled it by examining such sources by the rules of evidence. By 1957, at the second conference on African history at SOAS, the validity of oral tradition still dominated the general debate on techniques.[59] At that meeting I reported my results. This exposé convinced most of the participants, although they did not necessarily accept the necessity for historians to engage in fieldwork yet. Henceforth the argument that oral tradition could be handled like written sources was the main argument historians of Africa used to convince outsiders that the oral sources of "indigenous African history" were respectable.[60] For many years to come historians would no longer agonize about the overall respectability of oral tradition as a source but would try to locate and use traditions in different types of societies. In this context the research carried out by Bethwell A. Ogot represented another breakthrough.[61] My research had mostly dealt with kingdoms, and his concerned decentralized societies based on "clans" and age-sets. Despite this, he was able to find and use traditions for a historical reconstruction.[62]

Oral traditions, however, were not the only sources to be used. There were many others, such as archaeological remains, monuments, and objects, as well as linguistic and biological data. Relevant written materials were of course also crucial. From the outset this situation posed a practical problem: how to recover these sources, how to make them accessible to historians, and how to study them competently. First, there was an urgent need to develop archives, museums, and archaeological research. The colonial governments welcomed the creation of archives but were less enthusiastic about museums and archaeological institutes. The resolutions passed at the first conference of African historians at SOAS in 1953 stressed these issues, which were resolved in 1954, when the Colonial Office set up record offices and appointed archaeological officers everywhere. Meanwhile, practical steps had been taken in various territories to create record offices. In Nigeria, Dike, Ajayi, and Ebiegberi J. Alagoa worked for a decade from 1951 to organize archives there. Christopher Fyfe in Sierra Leone was engaged in a similar task.

But given the diversity of sources, the historians of Africa were asking for the creation of specialized interdisciplinary research teams, the so-called schemes, and for specialized, permanent research-oriented institutions. Here the Colonial Office dragged its feet. Early on, Roland Oliver proposed to create a School of History and Archaeology in East Africa, but despite further lobbying, the institute was set up only in 1961.[63]

By 1953 Dike was proposing a different solution to this problem: the creation of interdisciplinary research schemes and African studies institutes attached to the new universities. He claimed that African universities could make outstanding contributions in this area and observed that "the individual can make little impression on fields so vast." He called for institutes of African studies to coordinate research in many disciplines, but this idea would not be tested until the sixties.[64]

Meanwhile, Dike, Biobaku, and Fage all agreed that research by interdisciplinary teams was the best solution. Dike convinced the Carnegie Corporation to fund a "Benin scheme," and he launched it in 1956. The specialists participating were archaeologists, social anthropologists, and historians. It is worthwhile to note that the person responsible for gathering oral traditions for the Benin scheme was a social anthropologist, not a historian. In this Dike adopted the practice of Fage in the Gold Coast. Fage worked closely with David Tait, an anthropologist, who was actually gathering the relevant traditions. Moreover, Fage was convinced that there existed no hard-and-fast dividing line between these disciplines, so that a joint approach could produce an integrated reconstruction of the "indigenous past." Following Dike, Biobaku set up a Yoruba scheme and found funding for it. Meanwhile, Oliver conceived of a cooperative interdisciplinary history of East Africa and successfully lobbied for its implementation.[65]

Yet despite the obsession with methodology, a serious gap soon developed between precept and practice. Even in the late fifties, most historians did not actively work with any sources but written ones. Thus only nine papers, out of seventy, at the 1957 conference dealt with oral tradition. Three of these were by social anthropologists, and six by historians. In addition, no historian had then been involved in any practical archaeological research. Moreover, even the ordinary application of the well-worn rules of evidence for written materials was all too often perfunctory or worse. The rush to construct textbooks and syntheses prevented practitioners from paying much attention to the quality of the texts they used. They often relied on faulty translations and did not worry about the authenticity and sources of the texts.[66]

Most academic historians also despised the vital but pedestrian and onerous task of providing reliable and annotated text editions. Another facet of this ambiguous attitude was the issue of fieldwork. The irresolution of the historians is palpable in the resolution of the conference of 1957 which spoke of "the urgent need for training historians for field-work in Africa, in concert with archaeologists and anthropologists."[67] SOAS never would *require* fieldwork for a doctorate. Moreover, it became clear by 1960 that none of the various interdisciplinary "schemes" were actually succeeding in integrating the work of the specialist participants into a single overall reconstruction of the past, although precisely that was the avowed goal of each scheme. Still, the schemes were young, and historians seem to have hoped that this deficiency would eventually correct itself. The whole situation becomes more understandable when one considers the pressures under which historians were then laboring. For apart from the imperial historians, there were other adversaries.

History and politics were closely allied in the early years of African history. Dike did not choose these words as the title of his first article in 1953 without reason. The prospect of self-rule and then independence in West Africa, especially in the Gold Coast–Ghana, was accompanied by the writing of uncritical histories, which either celebrated "African glory" or emphasized the pivotal role of Kwame Nkrumah and his party.[68] After the independence of Ghana came in 1957, the pace of decolonization unexpectedly accelerated, especially in the French territories. Most of these, as well as Nigeria and the Congo (now Zaire), became independent in 1960. As apologists wrote more and more fanciful but glamorous accounts of past glories, historiography became enmeshed in the nationalist drive toward independence. Indeed, the assumption of the name Ghana by the former Gold Coast, or of Mali by an ephemeral federation of Sénégal and Soudan, illustrates the pivotal role history played at that time as an instrument of political legitimacy.

As both Fage and Dike pointed out at the second conference at SOAS, the task of academic historians of Africa was to combat such uncritical distortions by quickly publishing themselves, not just to provide textbooks for the colleges but even more to inform a wider public in Africa and in the metropoles.[69] Davidson's *Old Africa Rediscovered* was an answer to this demand, hence its glorification of the African past. But it also was a reply to the stubborn opposition which continued in many academic circles. After all, in 1960 A. J. Hanna, a scholar inspired by the conservative historiography current in South Africa, could still write a disquisition about Africa's lack of history, because Africans were "'impulsive children of nature' lacking rationality and condemned by their environment to an attitude of apathy, improvidence, and fatalism."[70] A climate of urgency thus permeated African historiography in the 1950s and grew to a fever pitch by 1960.

At the same time the approach of independence on such a scale in tropical Africa attracted a growing number of historians to African history. Most of the British historians who joined had done research in imperial history for their doctorates. Unwittingly they carried fundamental concepts and attitudes from imperial history into the new field. Indeed, even Kenneth Dike himself, like Diop before him, accepted Perham's and Julian Huxley's definition of civilization in his refutation of Perham.[71] He countered their arguments on the very terrain they had chosen. He stressed political organization, art, and written records, topics which Basil Davidson also highlighted in his work.[72] Thus Dike's proposed vision of African history became an inverted mirror image of imperial history. Moreover, some imperial historians, such as Hanna, and some Belgian critics of King Leopold II thought that to write about tropical Africa, even while focusing on the actions of Europeans, was practicing "African history." Indeed, colonial stereotypes still remained quite strong, even among the most ardent proponents of African history. Today "the essential virtues of the negro" sounds offensive, patronizing, and quaint. Yet the expression occurs on the first page of the 1957 conference report. Although academic African historiography was marked by a break with imperial history, it nevertheless carried a heavy legacy inherited from its adversary.

Meanwhile, a small number of monographs, syntheses, and textbooks in the new mold began to be published from the mid-1950s onward, supplemented by works of amateurs, mainly administrators and cultural anthropologists sympathetic to the African cause. Dike even succeeded in launching the Ibadan History Series, a series of monographs, in 1956. At the same time historical societies and specialized journals began in the Gold Coast and Nigeria. The *Transactions of the Historical Society of Ghana* dates from 1952, and the *Journal of the Historical Society of Nigeria* from 1956. This trend culminated in 1960 with the appearance of the *Journal of African History* edited by Oliver and Fage, which encompassed the whole continent and addressed itself to academic audiences everywhere. Its appearance signaled that the specialty had come of age.

The issues of that first year give a good cross section of the field. African history appeared almost to be an interdisciplinary endeavor. In its first year, the journal published authors who are now well-known African historians (ten out of eighteen), but also administrators, archaeologists, a linguist, an anthropologist, a missionary, and an imperial historian. Among the authors of the fifty-odd books which were reviewed, professional historians were a minority. The journal also concentrated on early African history: two-thirds of the contributions dealt with Africa before 1800, while among the books reviewed, only one-fifth dealt with the period after 1800. This indicates that the editors deliberately focused on the early period. Yet it was also evident that few historians were actually working on the early history of Africa. Most authors who wrote articles or were reviewed were British or American, but the works of a number of French scholars were also reviewed. Today it strikes us that none of the authors of the articles or of the book reviewers in that first year were African, while only two contributions by Africans (two North Africans and a Zairian) were reviewed. Yet African historians were quite active, especially in Nigeria. The first article by an African would be published by the *Journal of African History* only two years later, in the report on the third conference held at SOAS in 1961. This imbalance was unfortunate. It was to lead too many Nigerian and other African historians to submit their articles to their local journals first, and it has deprived the journal of the chance to become a wholly representative publication in the field.

The development of academic African history before 1960 can be summarized as follows: The demands of mainly West African intellectuals in British territories forced the colonial government to open colleges after the Second World War. The views of these intellectuals about their past, along with the appearance of a new generation of British historians marked by their experience during the war, led to the "invention" of African history as a distinct academic field. Stiff opposition to this approach gradually weakened, while a rapidly growing number of historians flocked to the new movement. Meanwhile, the accelerating process of decolonization made it ever more urgent for African historians to publish syntheses and textbooks. This demand was met, but unfortunately by sacrificing rigor all too often. Moreover, major questions about the handling of unusual sources and the proper training for historians of Africa remained unresolved in 1960. Thus African history entered the sixties as a vigorous and promising but still immature specialty.

4

Toward the Millennium of Independence

A T T H E SOAS conference in July 1957, the task of reconstructing a genuine African history seemed to be well under way. To be part of such a collective endeavor, to contribute oneself and to learn from others, to rediscover the fate of a whole continent, was seductive to many who attended. It certainly reinforced our wish to be part of this enterprise. Yet we seem to have understood this goal differently and to have advanced toward it in different ways. As the narrative of my own research goals and practical activities from 1957 to 1960 shows, my work still diverged significantly from that of most other historians, so much so, indeed, that many among them still perceived me as somewhat marginal to their enterprise.

After completing the doctorate, I planned to conduct research in the areas north of the Lower Kasai, whence the Bushong, I thought, had emigrated. In the fall of 1956 I submitted a proposal to this effect. Jean-Paul Harroy had left IRSAC in 1955 to become governor of Ruanda-Urundi, and the new secretary general did not react to it. But late in the spring of 1957 I was called to headquarters and offered Jean-Jacques Maquet's position as head of the Astrida station and director of the social sciences and humanities. Maquet was resigning to teach at the State University at Elisabethville, founded in 1956. He had recommended me as his successor because all the researchers with more experience were also resigning and because my wife's parents lived in Astrida. Indeed, Jean Hiernaux had already moved to that university, whose rector he was soon to be, while André Coupez was appointed there a few months after Maquet. When Claudine returned to Astrida during the summer, the researchers at the station were talking about nothing but Elisabethville. As for Daniel Biebuyck, he had left IRSAC at the conclusion of our military service to accept a position at Lovanium University, which had been founded by the University of Louvain and had opened its doors in the same month in which we had both been inducted into the military.[1] Obviously the context in which IRSAC operated had changed to its detriment. The upstarts, the two new universities, were raiding and making off with nearly all of its experienced researchers.

The creation of the universities was only one sign of the process of decolonization, which was now beginning to unfold. Elisabethville was an official university, and Lovanium a private one. In the Belgian context this meant that the first was anticlerical and in the colony antimissionary, while the second was Catholic and if not directly under missionary control, then nevertheless run by the church. That in turn meant that Protestants had nowhere to go. They worked to open their own university and eventually began the University of Stanleyville. The creation of official schools, especially high schools, in the Belgian Congo by an anticlerical minister in 1954 had led to large-scale protests in the streets, organized by the Catholic missionaries, while counterdemonstrators agitated for government schools.[2] In this way Africans learned, to their surprise, that demonstrations were "legal" and acquired practical experience in organizing mass action to bring pressure on the authorities. Their urban nationalist leaders would not be slow in turning to this avenue of protest. The following year the possibility of decolonization was first openly raised in Belgium itself, only to be dismissed there as ridiculous. Predictably, nationalist groups in the colonies eagerly picked this up.[3] From then on matters escalated so fast that a mere two years later, in 1957, the colonial rulers were forced to organize elections for local government in the major cities of the country, and civil strife had begun to take shape in Kasai.[4] Meanwhile, nationalist struggles were occurring in all the countries surrounding the Belgian Congo. The most important of these to the colony had been the Mau Mau uprising in Kenya, the creation of the Central African Federation (now Zambia, Malawi, and Zimbabwe) in 1953 with the attendant rise of vocal nationalist movements there, and the independence of Ghana in 1957. Soon Charles de Gaulle's referendum on independence and Nkrumah's Pan-African activities were to have direct repercussions on the Belgian colonies.[5]

On my arrival in Central Africa in 1956, Desmet had proposed that I accept an appointment as librarian at Lovanium, a suggestion which I flatly turned down. By the early fall of 1957 Guy Malengreau, the man behind the creation of Lovanium at Louvain and now its representative there, was putting pressure on me to join Lovanium as an anthropologist.[6] In addition, he also wanted me to teach a course on the history of Africa. I replied that I did not see how I could do this because so little information was accessible about African history. He shrugged his shoulders petulantly and exclaimed: "Just take Urvoy's book on Bornu, and you can organize a whole course around that!"[7] I was not at all interested in a university career. I just wanted to stay in research. So I accepted IRSAC's proposal as the least of the two evils and proposed to pursue research dealing with the oral traditions of Rwanda. Yet I also compromised with Lovanium and agreed to teach a full semester's load, but part time, that would include one course on the history of Africa. When I boarded the plane on October 19, 1957, I was therefore slated to do three different jobs at once: administration, research, and teaching.

Symbolically perhaps, I had taken George Balandier's newly published book *Afrique ambigüe* to read on the long trip first to Stanleyville and then the day after to Rwanda.[8] The seat next to me was occupied by a lady who was returning to Stanleyville. After we had read our books, we started chatting about our destinations. It was all very normal: colonials returning to their posts.

Claudine met my plane in Usumbura and told me that Harroy, now vice governor general, had scheduled an appointment to see me the next day. Harroy still looked vaguely avuncular and reassuring, while he played the part of the important, self-satisfied person who knows exactly what is to be done and presents it as the obvious rational and objective course to take. On this occasion his apparent main objective was to encourage IRSAC and myself to undertake more research in Burundi. He pointed out that, compared with Rwanda and with the exception of Usumbura, very little academic research had as yet taken place there. The next day I arrived at Lwiro headquarters to meet Louis van den Berghe, who was still painting grandiose panoramas of the future of IRSAC in an age when the colonies were about to become autonomous and perhaps independent. And it was true that, despite the competition of the universities, a number of new researchers were being or had been hired to replace the defectors. Soon there were as many in the social sciences and humanities as there ever had been, and finally there was even one more.

It was agreed that I would study the precolonial history of Rwanda and Burundi, with the aim of establishing a history manual based on oral documentation. The research was to establish a precise chronological framework and deal with "all the aspects of history, including settlement, economic, political, and religious issues."[9] This broad mandate hid the continuing uncertainty about my precise plans. Two days later I was in Astrida, where I found Maquet still in residence. Immediately we began to initiate the administrative takeover, and I also started work on my research projects.

These projects were soon clarified. In Rwanda I would make use of the considerable amount of earlier research that had been carried out with regard to society, culture, language, and history. I was to seek out and record all the existing formal historical narratives *(ibiteekerezo)* and all dynastic praise poems, with the aim of publishing them in a series of text editions. In my mind the models to emulate were the monumental series of text editions, such as the *Patrologia Latina* or the *Monumenta Germaniae Historica*, that have been so essential to researchers of the medieval history of Europe. In the French or German manner, this was to be solid basic work, but essential to any later historical research. This activity would complement, not duplicate, the research on early Rwandan history in which Alexis Kagame, a Rwandan abbé, had been involved for many years, provided I took care to coordinate his research with mine.

Meanwhile, I started to learn the language from Thomas Kamanzi, Coupez' main assistant. For the first few months I benefited from the services of other qualified assistants who had worked for years with Maquet or Coupez. Compared with my former Kuba helpers, these assistants had a strikingly high educational level. All had at least high school diplomas, and some, like Kamanzi, had obtained the equivalent of a bachelor's degree in philosophy at a seminary. On the technical side, I now had tape recorders available for use in the bush.[10] Maquet liked the research project for Rwanda but tried to dissuade me from the idea of conducting research in Burundi as well. I disregarded his advice because so little was known about the early history of Burundi and research there certainly would be highly productive. Moreover, I knew that a Dutch anthropologist, Albert Trouwborst, was about to begin fieldwork in Burundi, on January 1, 1958, with some help from us for his transport and logistics. I hoped that we could help each other.[11]

On the first Sunday I was in Astrida, I met Kagame after High Mass. Abbé Kagame was a well-known and controversial personality in Rwanda.[12] His admirers regarded him as the scholar whose labors had advanced Rwandan philosophy, ethnography, and history and whose epic poetry constituted a landmark in Rwandan literature. His detractors thought his efforts amateurish, often clumsy, and merely a cover for political activity. He was rumored to be an éminence grise of *mwami* (king), Mutara Rudahigwa, whom he was steering toward independence as fast as possible. I found Kagame to be a tall, massive person with a face that irresistibly reminded me of the impressive masks carved in the Cameroun grass fields. He invited me to his office, a modest room at the end of a long row of such rooms which made up the residence of the missionaries. It was filled with heavy rustic furniture, all made on the mission station. Even the typewriter looked rustic. Around it, books and papers lay in piles, cascading from his work space all over the room. Later, as we became acquainted, I found him to be an amazing personality endowed with a nimble and subtle mind but also a mass of contradictions: he was a committed Rwandan nationalist, yet one who appreciated the pranks of the Belgian comic book hero Tintin, with their endless allusions to the undercurrents of culture in Belgium; a humanist, and yet a racist who firmly believed in the superior talents of Hamites and the lesser ones of Negroes, although everyone was equal in the eyes of God; a detached scholar, yet one who was highly subjective in his interests; a person near the hub of politics in his country, yet also a modest man withdrawn in his humble cell. From the first meeting, we reached a kind of understanding to be both trusting and distrustful of each other, and on this basis we also agreed that each of us would go his own way. We were to remain on such cautiously friendly terms for more than two decades.

Setting up the mechanics for the Rwandan research project posed only one obvious problem. The task at hand was sharply delineated, and experienced personnel were available to carry it out. But how was I to find all the informants in a population of over two million people? Would I follow Maquet's example and ask a number of Rwandan notables and Belgian officials to establish a list of local historians?[13] That was obviously biased. At that time the Rwandans were divided into three recognized, self-conscious, and ranked social categories, an elite of ruling Tuutsi, the mass of the population, the Hutu, and a small group of people who did not farm, the Twa.[14] Maquet's bias was obvious because it favored those Tuutsi on whom the Belgian officials had relied to assist in the administration of the country. Political parties were becoming active in Rwanda in 1957, and local elections had been held in 1956. The ruling Tuutsi, defending their status, clamored for an early independence before their dominant position could erode, while their challengers, the Hutu party, held that Rwanda was in a state of "double colonialism." Independence should be delayed until they had gained full access to the levers of power on equal terms with the Tuutsi, a power they hoped to attain via the ballot box.[15] But unbeknownst to me, there was another problem. IRSAC had the reputation in the country of being "150% Tuutsi," as Anastase Makuza recalled in a reminiscence valid for 1955. He added that the royal court was believed to select carefully even the "few Hutu informants employed by the European staff."[16] Certainly the assistants I inherited were all Tuutsi.

The answer to my problem began with a pilot scheme. First one should track down all the experts on a "hill," the population unit here, and ascertain which historical traditions they knew. Then one would talk to all the adults on the hill and ask them the same questions. I did this at Gisagara, some twenty kilometers away from Astrida, assisted by Alexis Mumvaneeza, a Tuutsi, whose home it was. That yielded both lists of people and lists of the stories they knew and allowed the establishment of the ratio of potential informants to well-known ones, as well as the proportion of commonly known topics and "rare stories." This was in hand by early 1958. Now I began systematically to send assistants to draw up a list of all potential informants from subchiefdom to subchiefdom throughout the country. Later I and one or two more highly trained assistants followed up, to record all the traditions known to the most knowledgeable people and all "rare" traditions. At the same time samples of all other literary genres were gathered, so we could contrast them with the genres of *ibiteekerezo* and dynastic poetry. The pilot scheme had turned up Hutu as well as Tuutsi voices, and so did its application elsewhere. By the end of the project, almost four years later, the views from the Rwandan past were no longer outrageously one-sided.

Still, the planned program had to be improved. In May 1958 a manifesto appeared, issued by the most conservative wing of Tuutsi, the *abagaragu w'abwami*. They justified Tuutsi rule by recalling a story of origin according to which the Tuutsi had "fallen from heaven" and since had lorded it over the Hutu. This was to refute Hutu intellectuals who claimed that the ancestors of the three social categories had been brothers. The argument vividly showed the present use of traditions by the various parties and the need therefore to make certain that all segments of the population were heard.[17] That Tuutsi claim began to make me quite wary about the received reconstructions of the past in Rwanda.

Then around the first of October 1958 I acquired a copy of a little book, *Historique et chronologie du Ruanda*, a collection of condensed accounts of local traditions which had been gathered for administrative purposes all over the country since the twenties.[18] The implicit image of the past given by this book violently clashed with the received wisdom about Rwanda's past. True, almost since the moment of my arrival, I had known that the abundant ethnographic literature about Rwanda really dealt only with the central districts of the country and that little was known about the outlying areas. I had therefore earlier in 1958 sent Marcel d'Hertefelt, an anthropologist and political scientist residing at the center, to Bureera, on the northern fringe of the country.[19] By year's end he was able to prove that the area's social organization differed significantly from that of central Rwanda.[20] Still, *Historique et chronologie* shook me up. Only then did I realize how thoroughly distorted the accepted reconstructions of Rwandan history were: all accounts of local traditions had simply been suppressed, and the scholarly consensus merely reflected the ideological views of the court. To correct this, it was necessary to recover a whole class of data, local political traditions, which had never been seriously gathered outside the heartland of the country. The research design was therefore altered, and a major effort was organized to track down and record these traditions.

Setting up research in Burundi was much more difficult. First, there was only one Rundi research assistant in Astrida, Jean Bapfutwabo, who was trained in transcribing the language. Another one had to be found. It took some time before Lazare Ngendanduwumwe from Kayanza, just over the border from Rwanda, could be hired. After an unsuccessful visit to see the *mwami* of Burundi at Gitega, the capital, research began in earnest in late December, when Lazare and I spent a few days with local leaders (*abashingantaahe*) at Kayanza. To my delight, I learned that the known tombs of the kings of Burundi were not far away and that Kayanza was also quite close to the residences of Pierre Baraanyanka and Nduwumwe, two almost legendary figures in the country. Baraanyanka had collaborated with the German colonizers and then played a major role as leader of the Abatare faction of the Rundi aristocracy during the Belgian occupation, a faction generally allied with the Belgian administration. Indeed, he was still playing this role and was about to launch one of the two main political parties in Burundi. Nduwumwe, a son of King Mwezi (d. 1908), was involved in the death of King Mutaga (d. November 1915). He had assumed the regency of Burundi during the minority of the Mwambutsa, who was ruling at the time of my fieldwork. Nduwumwe had led the faction of the descendants of Mwezi, the Abeezi, who had been and still were competing with the Abatare. By January 1958, however, he was very old, and indeed he died soon after I interviewed him.

The first visit to Kayanza was followed by others, during which I interviewed the keepers of the royal tombs high up in the mountains, where it was bitterly cold but beautiful. Life there seemed freer from the

66

constraints of chiefs. I can still see the big bottle flies familiar from Europe and the Twa of the region, who told stories while sucking beer through straws from a huge communal pot that held enough beer for twenty people to get drunk on! What a contrast this was with Baraanyanka's villa, which was barely visible in the valley below. There I had taped while sitting on a terrace sipping tea, looking out on an impeccable coffee plantation maintained by more or less forced labor, and I had watched the smooth performance of a person radiating power. One other main source of Baraanyanka's income remained invisible from his patio. That was his portion of the gold confiscated from illicit gold panners in the mountains, who smuggled the metal past his residence to the market of Kayanza, where they sold it to South Asians. Nduwumwe, by contrast, lived in a tired, damp, thatched old dwelling hidden in a hollow amid fig trees. Here in the half-light the old man, once massive but now shriveled, sat while he quietly thought about and answered queries by musing about episodes of his past, which he recalled as follies or worse. He only became truly animated when discoursing about the rains and the forthcoming crop of beans.

I also learned that, unlike Rwanda, Burundi had no specialists of history and that the nobles of the land did not care to remember too much of the past for fear of exposing the flimsiness of their titles to land and office. It was going to be very difficult to recover the history of the country. One found only a few anecdotes or short tales.[21] The problem of constructing a valid sample of the existing traditions was going to be much more difficult to resolve here than it had been in Rwanda. The first thing to do was to establish a reliable relative chronology. That could be achieved by finding evidence about the kings and their succession. This led me to visit the tombs of deceased kings and to record the testimony of those who guarded them. This information was then cross-checked by tracing the places of the tombs of the queen mothers and interviewing their guardians. By the time this was done, Albert Trouwborst had finished his research in the center of the country and had just moved to the source of the Nile in the far south. I visited him there several times and through him got to know the wise Masasu, who had been so helpful to him and who now told me what he knew about the country's history. In this fashion a coherent image of what Burundi had been in the 1880s and the 1890s slowly took shape. Only then, in August 1958, could I begin to construct a valid sample. The variability of traditions about the past seemed to be linked to three main factors: proximity to historical sites, distance between communities, and the absence or prevalence of major geographic barriers in the mountainous country. The research design was built around these factors, and we began to carry out the research in the fall of 1958.[22]

The design also took the geography of *umuganuro* into account. By 1958 the political spotlight of the newly founded nationalist (Abeezi) party was agitating for the restoration of *umuganuro*, an annual royal ritual of renewal of the country and allegiance to its king, which had been outlawed after 1929. This ritual tied a score or more of local ritual and political centers in the south and the center of Burundi together. In the past it had formed the backbone of central government. By interviewing the guardians at the sites involved, one could obtain a sense of the overall functioning of the kingdom in earlier centuries.[23]

A totally unplanned aspect of historical research and of the administration of the station was the discovery of archaeological sites, especially in Rwanda. Traipsing about the countryside to meet storytellers, I soon noticed the Stone Age tools and Early Iron Age shards of pottery which lay scattered at or near the surface here and there. Usually I brought some back and recorded the finding place. Then one day in the spring of 1958, Alexis Mumvaneeza told me that people at Dahwe, near his home, had found "bricks from German times." Following up, I found some Stone Age tools as well as the remains of an Early Iron Age smelting furnace there. Having learned from my inglorious experience in Katanga, I did not attempt to dig there but kept recording occurrences of similar sites in the area and notified Jean Hiernaux, who excavated the site. It was to become famous, and archaeologists would dig there for many years.[24]

A few months later workmen at a chalk and gravel pit at Masangano in the north of Rwanda turned up bones and traces of human activity of a much earlier age. I brought back a sample of these and again told Hiernaux, who dug there as well. Then, in December 1958, I was told about yet another type of site east of Astrida (Sakara, Buhanga) consisting of a set of two-meter-deep bottle-shaped underground storage pits filled with debris. The associated ceramics of Later Iron Age vintage dated it to the seventeenth or eighteenth century.[25] I tried to entice Hiernaux or other archaeologists to dig there, but to no avail. Having watched how Hiernaux went about it, I dug up one of these pits myself, but the site still awaits a competent archaeologist, as it is a low priority for them. Archaeologists like older sites better and are not impressed by the interest historians have in a younger site which overlaps a period remembered in oral traditions. As bits and pieces of the past kept turning up in Rwanda as well as in central and northern Burundi, I felt that IRSAC urgently needed the services of a professional archaeologist. I failed to convince van den Berghe to build a complete laboratory for such a person, but finally, in 1960, IRSAC did organize a successful six-month mission by Jacques Nenquin.[26] From that time archaeological research organized by Tervuren and later the Free University at Brussels has continued in both Rwanda and Burundi.

Charting archaeological sites was only a small by-product of administering a station. I was in charge of the buildings, grounds, rolling stock, supplies, capital equipment, and payroll. For the first two years I was aided by a European administrative assistant and a Rwandan staff, so my job in these matters was limited to supervision, decision making, arbitration, and follow-up. I supervised the activities of European researchers, ensured that they had the equipment and the means they needed for their tasks, discussed their results with them, handled relations with the headquarters at Lwiro and with the central and local authorities in Ruanda-Urundi, took care of the many passing visitors and the few foreign visiting researchers, organized seminars, traveled to Lwiro when necessary, and did all the paperwork. The administrator's job was no sinecure, and these tasks gradually absorbed more and more of my time.

Daily life at the station was supposed to be a set of well-honed routines. But I remember them only as a blur, probably because the typical day was so hectic, and the variety of activities so bewildering, that there almost never was a "typical day." Of a morning I might be recording a tale by a Rwandan informant at the station or in the countryside around Astrida, to be confronted in the afternoon by an unexpected visitor who would need to be entertained, housed, and provided with a dinner at home. I might be dictating letters, or checking accounts, and be interrupted with a plumbing problem, a demand for car repair, or exciting news concerning a former royal residence, an informant, or even strange objects found somewhere. Every third week, I disappeared into Burundi, and on my return I feverishly caught up with all the work that had piled up. And let us not forget that in early 1958 I spent three months at Lovanium, followed by another ten weeks there in early 1959. All of this would have been impossible without Claudine, who not only took care of Bruno and the household but also valiantly coped with unexpected visitors. Moreover, she visited some sites with me and in general followed my research so closely that when I was at Lovanium in 1958, she could supervise the research operation in Rwanda. Occasionally she went on taping expeditions herself.

In spite of the pressures, running the station was intellectually quite stimulating, because I came in contact with so many different scholars and learned so much from them. Some belonged to disciplines far removed from the social sciences. I fondly recall a day's excursion to the savannas of Bugesera with an entomologist who caught exactly the right kinds of bugs there to prove that the area had not been recently deforested (in the last four or five hundred years!): the former kingdom of Bugesera had always been mostly pastureland. I learned about volcanoes, the evolution of small fish (cichlids) in sheltered bays of Lake Tanganyika, population genetics, the signs of malnutrition, gorillas, and trypanosomes. Practically every discipline of the social sciences was represented, with one conspicuous exception: history. IRSAC still classified me as an anthropologist, and only gradually and grudgingly was "and historian" appended to the description. The only discussion of history at any of the seminars—three of four every year—occurred at Lwiro in February 1958 and consisted of presentations by the librarian at Lwiro, a historian, called "Historical Method"; by a high school teacher from Bukavu titled "Diplomatic History of the Border of the Province Orientale with Uganda"; and one by me called "The Value of Oral Traditions."[27] With the honorable exception of Louis van den Berghe himself, everyone at IRSAC still shared a narrow colonial view of which stuff was history and what was mere "ethnology."

Among the many visitors who passed through Astrida, only two were historians. First, Roland Oliver and his family arrived in July 1958, full of news and plans. Oliver's biography of Sir Harry Johnston, one of the great proconsuls of British imperialism in Africa, had just been published, and he was now free to turn to other interests.[28] He was eager to compare his findings about the precolonial history of the Great Lakes in Uganda with information known from Rwanda and Burundi. We went with Kagame to visit the burial sites of the early Rwandan kings near Kigali, and during this trip the abbé discoursed on the perfections of precolonial Rwanda. Then I took Oliver to Munanira, a former capital in Burundi, to look at the faint traces of houses and at the fig and *Dracaena* trees which had formed the enclosures. We even found pieces of "subactual" pottery. In the evenings we talked and talked about genealogies, finally agreeing on an absolute chronology for the whole region of the western Great Lakes. It was a memorable visit. From Astrida Oliver drove through the Congo to Northern Rhodesia. Later I learned that his transmission conked out in the first mountainous stretch along Lake Tanganyika and that he drove for hundreds of kilometers in first or reverse gear on the most narrow and twisting roads imaginable. He was not one to give up easily.

The week after Easter 1959 had been set aside six months ahead of time by Claudine, who wished to take me on a holiday to visit the Albert

National Park. I was settling the last details about this with Robert de Wilde, the European administrative assistant, when a messenger came in to tell us that visitors had arrived. We were deploring this in no uncertain terms when the people in question burst in. It was Philip Curtin from the University of Wisconsin and his wife, Anne. The vacation was buried, and I never saw the national park. Curtin told me that in 1957 he had done doctoral research in Jamaica. He then became interested in Africa, and now the Curtins were touring large portions of tropical Africa on a grant to make a preliminary survey of archival holdings in various colonies. Obviously they were also having a grand holiday. He wanted to see the whole operation of recording, transcribing, storing, translating, and indexing the *ibiteekerezo*, to see how oral traditions became "texts." We also went for a climb to the summit of the hill of Sakara.

The stream of visitors from various disciplines of African studies, mostly anthropologists, kept us all up to date on the evolution of theories in academic circles in Europe and the United States. Indeed, the contacts were so effective that Helen Codère succeeded on her arrival in July 1959 in enrolling me as a member of the infant African Studies Association in the United States, although I had never been there and had no intention of going! On the other hand, being on the ground in Astrida gave us a much clearer view of which research was needed urgently and which projects from abroad looked like pure frills, and hence were a waste. The core of the team of the Astrida station consisted of three economists (two in Zaire, studying urban problems and labor migrations, and one in Ruanda-Urundi studying demography) and three anthropologists (two doing general research in lower Congo and Katanga, while Marcel d'Hertefelt in Rwanda investigated contemporary developments and modern social dynamics). This mix of researchers made IRSAC similar to the Rhodes Livingstone Institute in Northern Rhodesia or the East African Research Institute in Kampala. But in addition, we had Coupez' linguistic project, whose researchers were working to produce a large dictionary of Kinyarwanda for use in the country itself. We had also acquired a botanist, who was involved in research on peat bogs, including an assessment of their economic value. His presence was a reminder that the social sciences were only one unit within the whole of IRSAC and that these units often interacted.[29]

Imagine a high, long oval hill overlooking Léopoldville from afar, a hill whose noble brow had been sliced off, so that it looked like an aircraft carrier on whose flight deck superstructures had been and were being built. That was the look in 1958 of Lovanium, the famous university then just four years old.[30] The main access to the university from the city was barred by a gate, where campus police checked credentials. From within, the site irresistibly recalled an oval *laager* surrounded by a fence. Beyond the gate lay what had become a sandy plain, dotted here and there with large buildings, rumored to be in modern prison style because that was the least expensive. A ring road led from the public part of the university, the classrooms, dormitories, church, and swimming pool in the making, to a more secluded portion further away. There the bulldozers had spared at least some of the original soil and vegetation, and houses nestled under copses of trees in segregated splendor. That, of course, was the abode of professors and administrators.

Lovanium was a magic word in the bars of Kinshasa at that time. The whole complex was a focal point for Congolese everywhere in the country. It was a symbol of future salvation. The time was near when the Congo would control its own destiny, and that future was to be entrusted to the capable hands of those who were still students then. Nationalism was nearing fever pitch in the capital. The rival parties of Patrice Lumumba and Joseph Kasavubu were outdoing one another in promises and demands for autonomy and independence. They held their evening rallies on the huge terraces of major bars, sponsored by two rival breweries. There the political allocutions were interspersed with cha-cha-cha dancing and the poetic songs of the new Congolese music.

I arrived in Léopoldville on April 18, 1958, and was picked up by Daniel Biebuyck, now the head of the department of anthropology, to which I belonged.[31] I was whisked away to campus, to a room tucked into the side of the rector's residence, at the entrance of the residential section of Lovanium. The next day, at the ungodly hour of 6:30 A.M., a little shuttle bus brought me to a big auditorium and to my first class, where I faced the task of teaching Introduction to African Civilizations. I would also teach History of Africa and an "in-depth course about an African society." I will never forget my first class. More than one hundred students were ready for me, all very much awake—there were so many because this course was one of the few which every single student had to attend. In 1958 and 1959 practically the whole later elite of the country sat in that auditorium, the largest then available. I entered, and no sooner was I on the podium than a wall of sound greeted me. A cacophony of accusations was showered upon me from all sides. Was I here to teach once more how primitive Africans were and how despicable? Was I here to vaunt, once more, the benefits European civilization had brought to this benighted land? Was I? What-

72

ever I said was lost in the general jeering, banging, shouting, and rolling in the aisles. So I gave up any attempt to speak, picked up a piece of chalk, and began to write slogans in huge letters: "African civilizations are not less glorious than any other." "They are your heritage." "Future leaders of the country need to know and respect the culture of their ancestors." The din lasted for the full hour, although it weakened somewhat toward the end. The next time the class met, it began again, but now at least one faction was shushing the others and yelling at them to let me speak. Once I could speak in comparative silence, the class was saved.

The history course got off to a more quiet start. Here the students were really curious. Ever since my return from Belgium in 1957, I had used whenever time could be found in the evenings to write the notes for this thirty-hour-long course. There was no textbook available to me and only a few relevant books and articles.[32] I had produced a three-part outline. A seven-lecture introduction about sources was followed by a sixteen-hour-long section on precolonial Africa minus North Africa, and the course was to conclude with seven hours on "European Discoveries to the Partition of Africa"—mostly about nineteenth-century explorers and the Conference of Berlin. In practice, that last part was reduced to two or three hours. Precolonial history fascinated the students. As Monseigneur Tharcisse Tshibangu, later rector of the university, told me some years ago, the students were amazed by the feats of their African ancestors. They had never heard before about Ghana or Mali or any other ancient kingdom. I must confess that I went in for word descriptions as graphic as any in the *National Geographic* and was rarely found out. Still, I recall the stubborn queries of a student who interrupted my evocation of melodious muezzins chanting at dusk from an orchard of minarets. "Exactly how many mosques were there in the capital of Ghana?" A "We don't know" would not do for an answer. I was compelled to say, "One hundred three, and keep quiet!" As to the "in-depth" course, there was nothing extraordinary about its reception. It merely earned me the nickname Kuba because that was all I was talking about.

The indignation of the students was easy to understand. In some ways Lovanium was a surrealist joke. Most of its professors were fresh out of Belgium, totally ignorant about the Belgian Congo and uninterested in it. Most of them seldom left the *laager*. They were there to bide time profitably—salaries were high—in the hope of eventually sliding into university positions at Louvain. Most of them were also devoid of any creative imagination, but blessed with many pretensions. The results were sometimes ludicrous. The historians on campus were three medievalists, including an older gentleman, Pierre-Herman Dopp, whose treatise on Emmanuel Piloti's trip to the Holy Land in 1420 had just been published by Lovanium University Press on beautiful paper in elegant covers. This worthy book had been preceded in that press's collection by a philosopher's disquisitions about Plato's ontological methods and by a political scientist's discourses on the ideal international order—that at a time when such a momentous struggle was going on in the Congo itself! Among the first four volumes published by this press, only one, a study by the economist Fernand Bezy, had anything to do with the country. It discussed the structural problems of the Congolese economy and urged, in the name of economic rationality, the development of only the two "poles of economic growth," lower Congo and Katanga, and abandoning most of the country to neglect.

Alone among the universities founded in Africa during the fifties, Lovanium had not set up a history department as such. The historians were there to teach the history courses required in the official Belgian curriculum for students of other specialties, such as law and social sciences. These were all courses in European history; hence, to the historians of Lovanium, my course was rather an excrescence. They were also totally uninterested in the archaeological collection which Hendrik Van Moorsel was setting up with the finds he had made in the area. Among other items, his museum contained wonderful ceramics from a major seventeenth-century trading site near the Pool and an eighteenth-century cannon found buried in a yard near the river.[33] This collection, rather than Luc Gillon's baby nuclear reactor, was in my eyes the most exciting thing one could see at Lovanium, and I could not understand the snobbish disdain both for the objects and for the collector, who became my close friend. No wonder I felt rather lonely in such an ambience.

On January 4, 1959, violent riots erupted in Léopoldville.[34] The crowds attacked schools, dispensaries, and most mission compounds, in fact, all the instruments of European intrusion in the African townships. The riots were so fierce that it took until January 6 for the army to reassert control everywhere. My family and I arrived from Rwanda six days later. The ruins had just stopped smoldering, and an eerie calm lay like a haze over the city, even over the student homes at Lovanium. Lined faces showed both the drain on people's emotions and the continuing tension, as everyone awaited the long-expected declaration by the government about the future of the colony. On January 13 it came, accompanied by a dramatic gesture: a royal message which promised independence and set a calendar for elections for local and provincial councils. No fixed date, however, was set for independence.[35] The reaction of the main competing parties was, of course, to clamor for immediate independence. Yet the declaration had succeeded in lessening the tensions in the urban population at least, while the intricate path of decolonization provided the students with substance for endless animated discussions.

That year we stayed at Lovanium until the first days of April. I recall an immense optimism among the students, untempered with caution. They were dazzled by the vision of a grand future, tinged with millenarian fervor: they saw before them a new Jerusalem in which they were to be the new priesthood, idealistically offering all their talents to raise the splendor of the future nation, while also basking in the kind of prestige accorded Catholic saints: confessors or martyrs. I do not remember many details because I was kept very busy teaching three major courses in just ten weeks.[36] Still, the mood of the students was not nearly as militant as it had been the year before.

This year I was forced to offer a new course, Introduction to Bantu Languages—at first blush yet another example of Lovanium's capacity for the absurd. Here was a large auditorium brimming over with nationalist students—brimming because once more all the students had to take this course. Almost all of them spoke Bantu languages at home. Yet now they supposedly needed to be taught these languages by some foreigner who did not fully master even one of these. Of course, the first observation I heard when I entered the room was that *they* all knew, so why did they need an "introduction"? So I wrote a sentence on the blackboard and asked someone to translate it in his language. The result went on the blackboard. Then someone else translated it in his or her—there were a very few "hers"—language. Soon peals of derision rang out at the ridiculous way such and such a language expressed that sentence. In a similar fashion we soon disposed of two other generally held beliefs: that only some "noble" Bantu languages could be written, languages such as Kikongo or Lingala, for instance, and that Bantu languages had no grammars. When a demonstration showed that I would teach the hidden grammar of their own native languages, the students were intrigued, and I was saved.

My only other vivid memory of those days has to do with another aspect of university development. I still see as a snapshot in my mind the rector, Monseigneur Luc Gillon, touring the campus with two dark-suited gentlemen looking rather like a pair of Mormon missionaries. The three were lone figures on the sandy expanse of the hill, for faculty and staff discreetly hid themselves when they saw them coming. It reminded me of the scene in Kuba villages visited by an unknown colonial agent. These people were officers of the Rockefeller Foundation, and Gillon, a civil engineer who was building his campus himself, was showing them the spot where he wanted to build the university hospital. The gossips at the university had endowed the foundation with almost mythical wealth but also with a capricious generosity which had to be gingerly coaxed into giving by experts. The slightest faux pas could drive away the grants, and the culprit would be branded for life![37]

As the year wore on, the territorial administration began to lose control in other parts of the country, especially in the Province Orientale and in lower Zaire, while by the summer civil war broke out in Kasai between the Lulua and the Luba ethnic groups led by their political parties.[38] The insecurity became so intolerable that an epidemic of poison ordeals broke out among the Bushong. These ordeals had effectively been banned in the twenties, and by the fifties the Bushong had felt that the colonial administration was protecting witches. Feeling insecure and threatened by the civil war while sensing that the administration could no longer prevent it, they subjected some five hundred people to the deadly ordeal, in a great surge of millenarian cleansing, before the administration succeeded in putting a stop to it.[39] Among the victims was an old woman, Mbulapey, who had long been suspected of witchcraft. One day in 1954 she told one of my assistants about a remarkable dream, according to which she had abjured witchcraft altogether. But tragic suspicions lingered on during the next five years and eventually caused her demise. Her case shows how pent-up passions found violent expressions in the rising climate of insecurity.

In the month of June, Guy Malengreau wrote me to urge me to abandon IRSAC and join the University of Lovanium full time, arguing that now was the time to provide the new elite with whatever I could contribute. It was a powerful appeal, and I was quite tempted by it, even though it would mean the end of a research career. Meanwhile, late in May, van den Berghe kept pressing me to drop Lovanium altogether. He underlined the need of the new country for scientific research, both fundamental and applied. He foresaw a great expansion of IRSAC and offered me his position as its director. That possible future was also quite attractive. But I turned it down. I wanted to remain involved with actual research rather than administration. I proposed to continue as an active researcher, while also taking care of the unit for social sciences as before. Then in July, when the river of Congolese nationalism was about to burst its banks everywhere, the historians at Lovanium succeeded in abolishing the course in

African history, replacing it with an Antiquity–Middle Ages–Modern Times course, which was standard in Belgium. At this point I wrote to Malengreau, ending my association with the university, and I received the warning in reply that I was "letting the prey [Lovanium] go for its shadow [IRSAC]." I thought not. All along I had felt that a teacher or an administrator sedately brings up the rear, while the researcher probes the very frontier of knowledge.

In the first days of January 1960 I returned to Lovanium for ten days to attend a seminar on land tenure organized for Daryll Forde by Daniel Biebuyck. Everyone else was waiting for the opening of the round table of Congolese and Belgian leaders in Brussels, where the date of independence was to be set.[40] This time I arrived at the brand-new airport at Ndjili. By the standards of 1960, it had a huge runway, and its terminal was bigger than the one in Brussels, dominated by the majestic cupola of a grand central concourse. None of the passengers had seen this before. My neighbor, a high territorial official, exclaimed, "What megalomania! Yet another example of pandering to the rabble!" thus betraying how blind to the winds of change he still was. In the electric atmosphere of the day, Léopoldville was awash in rumor, the popular sidewalk radio (*radio trottoir*). We traveled up to Lovanium in a car whose license plate started with a *D,* and all along the way we were applauded like royalty. For rumor had it that *D* stood for *dipanda* (independence) and hence identified liberators! Political parties were fiercely competing with each other, and everyone was obsessed with the coming independence, its date, its shape, its promises, and its uncertainties.

On January 27 the date was set at June 30, and the mad rush of institution building and elections began. The fever of independence ran high even back in Astrida. The mood of the Congolese working there oscillated between wild hope and grim apprehension. One day rumor told of miraculous portents: even the "pygmies" were clearing roads in the forest to receive the millennial gifts of independence. On another day it was prophesied that the politicians competing for elected office in Bukavu, the capital of Kivu, would kill each other as soon as independence came. The apprehensive mood was such that one of my cautious acquaintances even tried to have his appendix removed at the hospital in Bukavu before the fatal date, because he believed that all Europeans would leave after June. Who would be left to operate, if ever one caught appendicitis? Independence was the unknown, with the terrors and the promises of all unknowns. Indeed, Europeans, residents and visitors, were equally infected by this climate. Government officials worried about their future, settlers had to decide whether to leave or to stay, and I began to see a stream of strange visitors, some of very high rank and some undercover agents, flowing through the station, supposedly concerned with Rwanda but in practice keen only on information about the Belgian Congo, as they tried to divine the future and report it to their various governments or services.

Meanwhile, political activity also reached a crisis level in Rwanda. Ever since 1953, the year of the first local elections, Hutu intellectuals had been attempting to wrest at least some power away from the ruling Tuutsi.[41] In 1956 they had made some gains at the local level but were even more powerless in the important decision-making councils than before. In 1957 two separate Hutu parties were created, and they steadily gained adherents. Some Tuutsi reacted in May 1958 by issuing their own manifesto and by clamoring for immediate independence, whereupon the Hutu parties retorted that in a state of "double colonialism" Tuutsi domination should end before Rwanda truly could become independent. A United Nations attempt (Ruanda-Urundi was a mandated territory) to prevent the breakup of the territory into its constituent kingdoms was unanimously and derisively rejected by both Rwanda and Burundi. By December 1958 the political situation was becoming volatile.

The political temperature rose further when a Belgian parliamentary committee under the leadership of Auguste de Schrijver, a heavyweight in Belgian politics, held hearings in April 1959. Everyone knew that the conclusions of the committee would affect the existing power relationships. In Astrida the commission heard much testimony about Tuutsi-Hutu relations, including a deposition from one of my Tuutsi assistants, who, like many others, came out in favor of negotiations and sharing power with the Hutu. Meanwhile, the ruling Tuutsi correctly concluded from the hearings that the official mind in Belgium no longer firmly supported them and was turning against them. In that climate of suspicion, King Mutara Rudahigwa suddenly died during a visit to Usumbura on July 25. The news traveled like a shock wave through the country. Most Rwandans were convinced that he had been assassinated and that the Belgians were about to topple Tuutsi rule. In addition, there was a succession problem, as he was childless.

Late the next day I learned that the funeral was to take place at the church of Nyanza, his capital, on July 28. As head of IRSAC, I was to be present with Claudine and those researchers who wanted to come. But on the twenty-seventh I also noticed something very unusual and suspicious having to do with the court, while Marcel d'Hertefelt picked up Hutu

78

rumors about potential danger. So I asked Claudine to stay home and refused to take Helen Codère, an American anthropologist who had just arrived on the station.[42] On the morning of July 28, as I was stepping into the car to leave for Nyanza, an unknown Rwandan sidled up to me and whispered in my ear not to go: there would be a coup at the burial site. I mulled this over all the way to Nyanza. In the church I was placed in one of the pews at the rear, and by the time I had made up my mind at least to warn Harroy, I could not reach him without attracting notice, with God knows what consequences. So I went on to the burial site. This proved to be a hollow in the ridge of a hill. It was clear that something was amiss, because only a small party of Rwandans were present, instead of the huge crowd one might have expected. The casket was placed in the center of the hollow. At its head stood a handful of chiefs, Governor Harroy in ceremonial plumes, and the officiating clergy. I found myself in a small cluster of Europeans and Rwandans on the left side of the coffin behind an honor guard of soldiers. The prayers were read, and the moment came for the graveside allocution. While Harroy spoke, the crowd grew restless.

And then the coup happened. Suddenly the senior Rwandan, Chief Michel Kayihura, was pushed forward by his neighbors to speak. Instead of eulogizing the deceased, however, Kayihura declared that, according to custom, the king could not be buried before the next king had been designated. The *abiiru*, or ritual councilors, had done so. He then faltered and was pushed aside by François Rukeba, then an unknown man, who began to harangue the public. As he leaned forward, I could see the inner pocket of his jacket, stuffed with bills. While he spoke, and while the soldiers linked up to prevent a surge forward into the empty space, many men armed with spears suddenly rose above us all around the rim of the hollow. The trap was sprung. Even the soldiers did not count for much, because as an honor guard, they carried no ammunition. Rukeba insisted that the name of the successor should be divulged immediately, whereupon the head of the *abiiru* stepped forward. He proclaimed that the successor was to be a certain Ndahindurwa, a gangling youth and a brother of Mutara's, who stood perplexed when the chiefs shoved him forward. He was to be King Kigeri V. While the men with spears and the Rwandans in the hollow cheered, Harroy was completely taken aback. He had to respond on the spot, and he could only ratify the new king, although he refused to do so unconditionally. Thereupon almost everyone left the burial site in such haste that they upset the casket and forgot the burial altogether. Suddenly it was very quiet and lonely, and before I really had taken it all in, I found myself helping the grave diggers and the priest to set the casket straight and to reassemble the scattered floral tributes around it.[43]

Back at Nyanza, I found a number of despondent Hutu priests and seminarians congregated in a building near the church. Clearly the coup had succeeded. Yet it did not prove to be a success for the Tuutsi oligarchy. It only seemed to be a decisive victory. For in the following months it became clear that Kigeri V was unable to unite the country behind him. Before the coup only a tiny handful of eccentric Hutu had attacked the monarchy, but now the main Hutu party became republican. Manifestations for or against the monarchy began to occur everywhere. The coup had resolved nothing. It merely raised the issues at stake and heightened tensions. Still, life also continued as before, and my own research, for instance, was not affected. I had known about the *abiiru* before and indeed had tried to reach some of them. As early as 1945 Kagame had been co-opted among the *abiiru* and had written down the text of their esoteric sacred liturgies. He had published an article about their role in 1947.[44] Since their role was now out in the open, I tried to obtain permission from the regent, Michel Kayihura, for the king was not yet ruling, to interview the *abiiru* about Rwanda's history in general. To no one's surprise, that attempt failed.

Nineteen years later, in 1978, on my arrival in Nairobi, as I entered a hotel I saw Kagame, Kayihura, and the widow of King Mutara in the lobby and was discreetly but warmly greeted by them. Only a few days after this meeting did Kagame ask me how I had known about the coup ahead of time. I replied, "Somebody's mother's brother was not where he was supposed to be the day before." After a minute's reflection, he retorted, "Ah yes, I see." This baffling exchange referred to Kagame's 1947 article and to his absence from the mission the day before the funeral. Kagame had been one of the coup plotters, and I had learned from his nephew that he had absconded. I cite the anecdote here mainly as an illustration of the very indirect and discreet ways in which information is conveyed in Rwandan culture, and as an example of the quality of Kagame's and my relationship.

In the fall of 1959 the political climate began to cause anxiety in even the most remote corners of the country, and my research assistants spent more time than before explaining their presence and their purpose. More parties were created, the old ones reorganized, and the oratory at various meetings became menacing. On October 31 a group of Tuutsi youths attacked one of the few Hutu subchiefs in the heartland of the main Hutu party. The next day unrest broke out, and groups of Hutu and Tuutsi youths began to roam the countryside. Two days later violence erupted.

Within a few days the whole country was engulfed by it. At first the Hutu jacquerie seemed to be ascendant, but by November 7 the Tuutsi, who reactivated the almost forgotten system of army regiments, began to gain the upper hand, at least in the central parts of the country. The available police force in the territory was totally inadequate to cope with an insurrection on this scale. A military emergency was therefore decreed, a colonel was put in charge, and Congolese troops were brought in from Kivu. Even so, the police force went into action only on November 10, when the small force available in Astrida sallied forth to assist an embattled Hutu leader nearby and drove off his assailants. Large-scale operations ended by November 14. An uneasy truce followed, punctuated from time to time with surprise attacks at night on one hill or another.

At IRSAC I was faced with a power vacuum. On the first or the second evening of the jacquerie, Harroy suddenly arrived at my house at night with a military adviser. He looked harassed and somewhat bewildered. They wanted to know which role the Twa played in the military organization of old Rwanda and where the nearest Twa groups resided. The Twa were the lowest-ranked social category in Rwanda. They were hunter-gatherers and potters, and in time of war they formed feared commando units for the Tuutsi lords, who were their patrons. In this fighting some Twa had answered the call of their Tuutsi patrons. I could not say much, but Harroy's visit by itself told me that chaos reigned: I had to fend for myself. The next day the panicky Europeans of Astrida set up a vigilante group in town, itself a potentially disastrous move. I decided to confine the Europeans of the station to a single building. I made sure they had no weapons and conveyed the large stock of spears kept in our museum myself to the police post in town. During the day we continued the pretense of normalcy by going to the offices and sheltering a number of workers and relatives of workers at IRSAC, pretending that they were not refugees. In the evening we remained in the refuge building, except for Marcel d'Hertefelt, who thought that all this was ridiculous. From time to time we would catch glimpses of troops on the heights beyond our hill. D'Hertefelt, meanwhile, was glued to the police frequency on a shortwave radio. Ever since he had gone to Bureera, he had become an ardent Hutu supporter, and he was now, to my dismay, rejoicing at their successes. I was merely stunned by the extent of the devastation and the attendant loss of life. So much for scholarly distance from "the objects of study."

Finally, one morning we sighted clouds of dust along the hillside where the road to Usumbura followed the contours of a nearby valley. It was the harbinger of an army column that brought relief. A day or two later I was called to the local jail, where I found the assistant who in April had talked in favor of the Hutu. He had now been captured red-handed during a Tuutsi attack on a Hutu stronghold. He told me that the emotional pressure of his Tuutsi peers, and the call of the war drum of his regiment, had been too much, and he had been swept up in a collective frenzy. Unfortunately there was not much I could do about this situation beyond leaving a statement testifying about his previous good intentions.[45] A few weeks later Thomas Kamanzi, by now a full-fledged researcher at the station, came in the evening to the house and asked me to rescue his father and family, who had fled their home and were hiding in a papyrus swamp. We took a small Volkswagen Beetle and drove off without headlights. The hill was easy to find, for it was illuminated by flames shooting up from houses being torched and we could see shadows running around between them. We cut the engine and coasted down to the marsh at the bottom of the hill. Kamanzi got out and some time later returned with five or six people, three of whom were adults. We managed to squeeze everyone into the tiny car and to drive away undetected.

The jacquerie of November 1959 was only the first in a seemingly unending violent and tragic cycle of Hutu and Tuutsi struggles for power, first in Rwanda and later in Burundi as well. In Rwanda the elections in July 1960 were accompanied by further violence. Then followed the overthrow of the monarchy in January 1961 and independence in 1962 under the rule of a single Hutu party. Each of these events produced renewed fighting and ended in massacres of Tuutsi. Large numbers of Tuutsi fled abroad, whence some organized raids into Rwanda to overthrow the government. This only provoked more repression, more massacres, and more refugees until a major bloodbath occurred in December 1963, whereupon the attacks stopped. The problem faded away but was not really gone. Late in 1990 well-armed Tuutsi from Uganda invaded Rwanda, and they have waged a low-level war in the north of the country ever since.

Meanwhile, in Burundi the struggle between the two parties which had taken shape around the rift between Abatare and Abeezi gave way after independence to a tragic polarization between Hutu and Tuutsi. There followed an attempted Hutu coup in 1965, a Tuutsi reaction, the proclamation of a republic under a ruthless military ruler in 1966, and, in 1972, a mixed Hutu and Congolese rebel incursion, which sparked a major Hutu massacre, leaving between one hundred thousand and two hundred thousand dead and countless refugees. A period of ominous calm followed these *évènements*, as the Rundi call them, but in recent years the infernal cycle of sporadic Hutu raids and substantial retaliatory killings has begun again.[46]

The research activities of our center were greatly affected by the events of November 1959. Research was resumed to some degree in December. The Hutu, actively bolstered by the Belgian colonel in charge, were now ascendant. They still saw IRSAC as a nest of Tuutsi, despite the fact that d'Hertefelt was well known as a champion of the Hutu. It became more difficult to convince local historians to tell us stories, and travel became less secure, but those were not the biggest impacts. This could be seen on the station itself. There large numbers of people began to flock to the residence of Helen Codère, who had arrived to carry out a study in "acculturation" just before the coup of July.[47] Suddenly she was perceived as a safe confessor, and Rwandans of all ranked groups, who had hitherto been so secretive and reticent to talk about their own intimate affairs, began to confide their deepest shocks, doubts, bewilderment, and fears to her.[48] The jacquerie had traumatized the whole population. People felt as if a familiar way of life, whatever its injustices, had abruptly ended. They had been thrown into the unknown, they did not know what to expect, and hence they could not foresee how to cope or to plan for tomorrow. The events had also raised strong emotions in the hearts of the three social scientists at the station, and it is easy to see from our writings how they affected Codère's, d'Hertefelt's, and my interpretations of Rwandan society and culture. The events also vindicated the need for local research in the outlying parts of the country. So when Pierre Gravel, a Canadian anthropologist, arrived shortly thereafter for a stint of fieldwork in Rwanda, he chose to work in the far southeast of the country.

Meanwhile, my research trips in Burundi had come to an end in October 1959. One more trip had been scheduled but was canceled because of the events in Rwanda. The research design had been fulfilled, except for two marginal areas, the Ruzizi Valley in the west and low-lying Mosso in the south. I now decided to abandon these and to close down the project. The collection of data in Rwanda was to be halted, but the transcriptions of tapes and translations would continue. So in July 1960 I was ready, albeit somewhat reluctantly, to go on a scheduled six-month leave to Europe. Claudine and Bruno had preceded me. I recorded a last interview high in the mountains on July 2. Four days later, just before scheduled elections in Rwanda, a melancholy good-bye ceremony was organized by my Rwandan collaborators, who urged me to return soon. Then I was off to Usumbura, with tickets for Léopoldville-Kinshasa and Europe. I had no inkling then that I would not reach Kinshasa nor ever return to Rwanda.

"Fieldwork" in Rwanda and Burundi had been very different from previous experience in Kasai. It had not included any significant measure of "participant observation." In the Rwandan project I had acted very much as a manager, receiving, checking, and assessing information in preparation for its publication. I had been so much aware of my role that I proposed to have these text editions authored by the IRSAC team as a whole and to confine publications under my own name to conclusions derived from the data. The Burundi project, however, had been very much my own work. Nevertheless, it had been a strange form of fieldwork, as it consisted of "raids" of a few days each (never more than ten days or so) into the country. Many of the informants had been spotted beforehand by Lazare Ngendanduwumwe, although I searched for and found others on my own. This project could never have succeeded if not for the parallel research project that Albert Trouwborst had carried out in 1958 and from which I had learned so much about Rundi society and culture. It is telling that, in contrast to the Kuba situation, I had lost contact with Rwandans and Burundians by 1962. It is also telling that the contacts that were maintained for a year or two after my departure were not with ordinary people but with the assistants at the station with whom I had rubbed shoulders for nearly three years.

The lack of fieldwork left me somewhat unfulfilled, but the amount of data gathered, especially in Rwanda, was enormous and a source of a good deal of satisfaction, especially as I expected to return within six months for another two-year stint, which would lead to the publication of all of these data. This never happened. Even though the texts are now available on microfilm, at Tervuren and at the station in Butare (formerly Astrida), most of the information they contain, especially for local history, has still not been studied.[49] In contrast, the results of the much smaller Burundi project were eventually published and have been used as a starting point for research from the 1970s onward, despite their weaknesses. The most important of these was that I did not systematically search for written accounts of oral traditions in unpublished records or in newspapers or magazines published in Burundi. I thus missed much about the context of these tales as an expression of the historical consciousness of various contemporary groups.[50] With hindsight, one now sees that the research design of the Burundi project especially was a precursor of the later research practices of many historians of Africa. While such later "historical fieldwork" has often shared the strengths of the research in Burundi, it unfortunately has exhibited an often less than careful attitude toward sampling and has also partaken from the Burundi project's major weakness, an underestimation of the meaning of traditions for their present-day carriers.

On arriving in Usumbura, I was met with the news that an isolated upheaval in the Congolese army had turned into a general mutiny and that plane service to Léopoldville, soon to become Kinshasa, had been canceled. I had no choice but to stay in Usumbura. Two days later, while the mutiny was spreading to major cities all around the country, the Europeans of Léopoldville, in panic, attempted to flee the city, but soldiers had closed off both the airport and the wharf. By then I had been asked in Usumbura to volunteer in a relief effort for refugees as a monitor at the radio station. From then on I stayed there, listening to messages from incoming aircraft stating how many refugees they carried and planes from Belgium announcing their arrival and their carrying capacity. That information was then relayed to the refugee center in town. Meanwhile, the person seated next to me checked the shortwave radio bands for messages from Europeans trapped in various towns of Kivu, Province Orientale, and Kasai and relayed that to the airport. So it went on night after night and most of the days as well. I only got out of the building to sleep for a few hours in the house of Etienne van de Walle, in the foothills above the town.[51]

I remember one day, at van de Walle's house, especially intently watching the military camp in town, over which a helicopter was hovering. I knew from radio signals that an attempt was being made to disarm the Congolese garrison there, because a mutiny could break out at any moment. But I could not say a word to anyone, including the van de Walles, for fear of creating panic. I knew that as long as the helicopter behaved normally, all was well. It circled peacefully for hours and finally flew away. Usumbura had been lucky: the soldiers had surrendered their arms without a murmur. Another day a message called me to a refugee shelter at the request of a person whose name I did not recognize. On arrival there, I found tiers of beds and cots filled with exhausted women and children occupying every inch of a set of rooms. When I found the bed of the person who had called me, it turned out, to my surprise, to be the lady with whom I had traveled from Brussels to Stanleyville on my return from Belgium! She was recovering from the shock of finding herself here just with the clothes on her back, and she was seeking shelter with a family in town. Day after day a flood of refugees reached Usumbura, to be flown out to Belgium as fast as the planes could turn around. During the first weeks the arrivals were outstripping the departures, but then the tide turned, and the shelters gradually began to empty.

As a reward, I was put on the last refugee flight, very late in July or in the first days of August. The heavily loaded plane took off slowly, and I watched as the morning sun slowly crept over the foothills of the Congo-Nile divide, not realizing that I would not see these hills again for twenty-three years. We arrived just before dawn in Brussels, quite hungry and thirsty, for we had been given little food and not much water. The plane was parked on the apron, and as we descended the steps we were met by gendarmes. I was questioned. Where did I come from? Had I been sub-jected to ill treatment? They refused to accept my statement that I was not a refugee: it was a refugee plane. And they kept insisting: "Not even a little ill treatment?" When they let me go, I was waved through immigra-tion. Then I arrived at a work station where a row of clerks, armed with pens and huge sheets of paper, were seated on stools at high nineteenth-century writing desks: it was a scene out of Dickens! One of them beck-oned to me from his perch. His job was to give refugees some money to help out with their immediate needs. I refused, but once again I was firmly told that I was a refugee and could not leave without money. Yet Belgium being Belgium, this money was a loan, and numerous signatures were required in return for a few banknotes. On leaving the airport, I was stopped again at the exit, this time by a bunch of civilians who wanted to know where I was going. They were volunteers ready to drive refugees to their homes, wherever these were. At that point I caved in and just let one of them drive me a few miles to the house of one of my sisters.

This welcome expressed the cataclysmic shock which pervaded the country at the time and which carried an undercurrent of ambivalence toward colonials. Even while it commiserated, public opinion could not help but blame the catastrophe on bad colonial management. When I left the country in the last days of August, bound for Salisbury in Southern Rhodesia, the shock had still not worn off.

I went there to attend a conference on African history organized at Roland Oliver's initiative by the University College of the Rhodesias and Nyasaland. In Salisbury I found "normalcy." I was welcomed at the air-port by Richard Brown, a university lecturer, who happily chatted away about his research on Ndebele history. Then I mingled with the other assembled historians, all equally insouciant and comfortable in their infor-mal clothes. By the deference accorded to him, one sensed immediately that Oliver was the leader and the fulcrum of authority here. But I was also struck by a pensive person of good dark looks, dressed in a formal suit, who was usually listening to the others. It was Terence O. Ranger.[52] He was teaching African history at the college, but he still pursued his earlier research on Stuart England. In the general conversation later on, he talked mostly about actions to protest the color bar and the tense race relations in the country. At the conference itself, we heard some remarkable papers, but I enjoyed none more than an elegant presentation by Leonard M. Thompson on South African historiography.[53] He interrupted his talk once to exhort two gentlemen of the South African security in the front row to be diligent recorders.

At the conclusion of the conference the participants toured the country for a few days. We began by visiting the site of Great Zimbabwe. As we drove on the main road south, we met a wide-open, empty, and seemingly endless vista, interrupted only by a fence some distance away. As we traveled from hill brow to hill brow, it accompanied us, tirelessly running along all day long. This was a boundary between white and black lands. As I saw this instrument of racial segregation continuing mile after mile, the ruthlessness, the monumental stupidity, and the scale of segregation sank in. Not even the sight of Great Zimbabwe was as impressive as this. During the following days, such instances of the color bar, as well as the kind of comments I was hearing from Rhodesians and even from some historians about the ongoing tragedy in the Congo, began to enrage me more and more. I left the country none too soon and vowed never to return there or to go to South Africa as long as this outrage endured.

On returning to Belgium I found that the gloom had deepened. The public was turning against colonials: if they had done a good job, none of this would have happened, and Belgium would not have been put to shame. In addition, who was to pay for the integration of ten thousand colonial administrators into the civil service, and how would that affect the normal career patterns of Belgian civil servants? No wonder that former colonials and the staff of colonial institutions felt betrayed and disheartened. The result was a rout: within the next two years most of the institutions, including the academic institutes, which had been concerned with the colony disappeared.

5

On Wisconsin!

JAN, telephone!" I heard one of my sisters calling through a window. I
ran in and up the stairs and picked up the phone. It was a transatlantic
call, and it certainly sounded as if it came from the depths of the
ocean. The caller was Philip Curtin. He offered me a short-term appointment for up to three years at the University of Wisconsin in Madison and
wanted me to come "right away." When I retorted that I had a job, he
answered that what with civil war in Rwanda, chaos in the Congo, and
unrest in Burundi, I would be unable to do research there. "So why not
take a year or two off?" He wanted an instant yes or no. "This is so
sudden. I need time to think this over," I answered in the best novelette
tradition, to which he replied that transatlantic calls were very expensive
and I had a minute! So I ran away to consult Claudine. We had never given
even a passing thought to the United States. But the proposal sounded as
though it would offer an adventurous interlude, and the situation in
Africa was bad. The appointment would be half-time teaching and half-
time research, and I could use the time to write up the results of my earlier
research. So I told Curtin we would come "immediately" but half the
appointment had to be in the department of anthropology. We did not
even know where Madison was. Looking it up in an atlas, we discovered
that the climate of the place was indicated by a sickly purple, which also
occurred in Siberian Omsk and Tomsk. That, we decided, had to be a
mistake. It was not.

The next day we went to the consulate and met its endless forms, then
we obtained doctors' certificates, x-rays, and so on. The file was ready
within a week, and I innocently insisted on getting a green immigration
card right then. A delay followed, and then I was summoned to swear a
litany of oaths at top speed. Some of these sounded surreal. The question
whether we intended to assassinate the president followed one about our

plans for opening a house of prostitution. In retrospect, the amazing thing was that the green card did come within weeks. I still do not understand how or why that happened. Meanwhile, the Congolese establishment in Belgium was in total disarray. Institutions like the "colonial university" in Antwerp and the African Studies Institute at the University of Louvain were summarily abolished. When I went to consult the new president of IRSAC, I found him so disoriented and demoralized that I resigned on the spot rather than asking for a leave. At the same time a call came from Brussels to meet a colleague of Curtin's there. He wanted to rent his house in Madison, and continent unseen, we signed a lease. We did not understand an iota of his long disclosures about domestic appliances (What was soft water?), but never mind. The house turned out to be wonderful: it is the one we live in now. In a whirlwind of activity, myriad details were taken care of somehow. On November 24, 1960, we arrived in New York, in time for a holiday unknown to us: Thanksgiving. Two days later, bewildered, disoriented, and thoroughly exhausted, we were in Madison.

The offer of a position by telephone itself was the result of sheer serendipity. I had met Curtin in Astrida on Easter Eve of 1959, but he had been one visitor among many. Late in August or September 1960 he accidentally met Allan Merriam on a plane returning to the United States from Europe. Merriam was an anthropologist and musicologist from Northwestern University who was on his way back from the chaos in the Congo, where he had just completed a spell of fieldwork in collaboration with IRSAC. Gossiping on the plane, Merriam told him erroneously that I was out of a job. Curtin seized on this with alacrity. He went straight to Fred H. Harrington, the vice president of the University of Wisconsin, who was mowing his lawn, and asked for a "short-term" appointment. He was told to go ahead, and the vice president went back to tending his lawn. Later Harrington convinced the Rockefeller Foundation to provide the funding. Meanwhile, the history department took only a quarter of an hour to agree to hire me on "soft money." Curtin then somehow found the correct unlisted telephone number and called right away. But I was in Salisbury, and he had to wait until I was back to try again. Hiring in those days certainly was more informal than it is now.

In those early days nothing seemed unusual to me because everything was novel and totally unreal. We had to adjust to jet lag, a new country and its customs, a real winter, and a new university system all at the same time, and only I spoke or understood English. In the first weeks the merest trifles baffled us. We were barely in the house, for instance, and exploring its exotic gadgets when we heard soft chimes. We wondered what it was but shrugged it off: probably some strange cuckoo clock somewhere. There were more urgent things to do. Over the next two days this chiming occurred a few times at irregular intervals. Finally one of us happened to be near the outer door when the sound rang out and in a flash of insight understood that this was the doorbell! Some of our neighbors had been calling to help us out and could not understand why we did not answer the bell.

The house was like a dream world. The reliability of the electricity, gadgets such as television and a washing machine, and the complexities of soft water and the heating system perplexed us and challenged all our ingenuity. Neither we nor our hosts realized how much we were attuned to conditions of life in Central Africa, rather than those of Belgian cities.[1] Hence no one in Madison realized how profound the transition really was. Bruno, then four years old, captured the atmosphere of the first day best when he saw an abstract painting over the mantel in the living room, ran to his mother, and declared: "Look, a painting in English!"

The university was a mixture of the known and the unknown. On the whole, Curtin's lecture courses were familiar, despite the existence of "readings" and "discussion sections" unknown in Europe. The working of his seminar was also familiar to me, despite the relaxed setting at his home during the evening. The informal code of behavior between students and faculty delighted me. In Belgium professors tended to be unapproachable and used their magisterial authority as a weapon to back up the infallibility of their pronouncements. Of course I realized that the relationship was unequal, but it looked like a relative inequality, as in the relationship between older and younger siblings, not an absolute caste system, as in European universities at that time, where professors were inaccessible oracles.

It took more time to adapt to the differences between the behavioral codes that were then current in the history and the anthropology departments. The historians were conservative and even dreary of dress, urbane in conversation, and often pedantic, even pompous, in demeanor. Rank and age among them were unmistakable, and their meetings were structured by clear rules of debate, although they often more than verged on the boring. Yet the historians had a sense of humor: soon they nicknamed me the Louvain Leprechaun. Anthropologists were different. Their welcoming party for us set the tone. It was chaotic. Drinks flowed too abundantly, here and there small clusters of people, faculty and advanced graduate students alike, sat on the floor, absorbed in ardent recrimination, a few feet away more decorous faculty discussed the issues of the day, and

90

others in another corner swapped tall stories "from the field." No one paid much attention to Claudine and me when we came in. Anthropology was a small and young department then, deeply split into its components: biological anthropology, archaeology, and cultural anthropology. Its internal dynamics were those of a very small community, and intense personal relationships overrode any formal structure. That and the absence of clearly delineated and impersonal roles made it much more difficult for me to adapt to their community than to that of the well-regulated historians.

The third specific community we had to fit in with was that of the dozen or so graduate students interested in African history and one or two anthropologists. Those students were about my age, some even a little older. Despite the sometimes unfamiliar accents in which I spoke and my unfamiliarity with local conventions, which intrigued them, the facts that Claudine and I were their coevals and that we obviously needed pointers about practical life reassured them. Soon they accepted us warmly. They spontaneously enlightened us about a wide variety of social usages and relationships. In the first two years they, more than the faculty, which took knowledge about such things for granted, taught me how to behave in American middle-class society. On my side, I was struck by their overall maturity and their motivation. Some of them had waited for years until they could study African history somewhere, and now they wholly committed themselves to it with youthful enthusiasm. This was very different from Belgium or the Congo, where the goal of most students was simply to obtain a diploma as a gateway to a good practical future.

The students were in their late twenties or even over thirty, and their age came as a shock to me. At that time in Belgium, formal instruction ended with the acquisition of the *licence* diploma (an M.A. equivalent), usually at age twenty-two. Thereafter a few pursued doctoral research on their own. One then taught oneself whatever further skills were needed. Here, in contrast, students seemed too insecure to learn on their own. Whenever they needed an additional skill, they sought further formal training. While this attitude was certainly sensible, it also delayed the onset of original research until the student scholars were in their late twenties. I believed then that the peak of a person's originality and dynamism had already passed at that age and that therefore these graduate students were squandering the most fruitful years of their lives in classrooms. Of course I was young and naive myself, and I had hated being the passive recipient of formal lecture courses. Still, it is true that the most original insights often come when a field is still a novelty, when one still enjoys the exuberant energy of youth, and when one is not yet set in one's personal ways. Hence the younger one undergoes the learning experience of fieldwork, the more one can benefit from it.

Adapting to the general middle-class culture of the United States was all the more difficult because we had been totally unaware that there were any differences with Europe. In a sense Madison was a company town. The distinction between a professional and a personal life was much less rigid than in Europe. People seemed to thrive on acquaintances but often missed the support of either a wider family group or long-standing friendships. Somehow parties were crucial in establishing and maintaining social relationships here, but at first we could not make head or tail of them. Why did they exist? How was one to behave at them? They might be crucial to social life, but no one could enlighten us as to their meaning or functions because the participants were themselves unaware of them. It would take us more than a decade to fully realize how parties fit into the overall configuration of middle-class American society.

Other small pointers also vividly underlined big cultural differences. They ranged from the proper use of first names, to the occasions when it is proper to smile, to the question we were soon asked over and over again, "How do you like Madison?" and even to Curtin's anxious question about whether we were growing roots. Meanwhile, there was no time to get used to our new environment. We were expected to function amid all these novelties within days. Luckily for us, this community was also accustomed to immigrants. Thus a number of ladies soon volunteered to help Claudine, from tutoring her in English to taking her bird watching. One family in particular took us under their wing and informally helped us a great deal.[2] As for us, we were used to fieldwork situations, and we treated our circumstances as a stay in the field. This culture, like any other, was a stage, and we began to play our bit parts, using whatever cues we could discern.

We had to learn to play our parts very quickly indeed. Barely two weeks after our arrival I accompanied Curtin on a day trip to New York to assist him in his successful attempt to secure a large grant for his brainchild, the Comparative Tropical History Program, from the Carnegie Foundation. Three weeks after that Claudine and I drove over frozen roads to Northwestern University, where I gave a lecture. After its conclusion Melville Herskovits ushered us to his car, sat beside me, assumed a conspiratorial mien, and started a conversation. The scenery was fit for a Chicago gangster movie: a dark, badly lighted and deserted street in the shadow of the elevated train tracks that loomed overhead. He offered me a position at his university and urged me to abandon Madison. I was taken aback—after all, I had a three-year commitment to Wisconsin—and the setting suggested an improper offer. So I summarily rejected it, as I would several other offers in the following years.

In hindsight, it is evident that the early 1960s was a time of unusually tumultuous university growth and of exceptional mobility among faculty. New programs of African studies, for instance, appeared every year. But at the time I saw nothing unusual in all of this. Such incidents simply fed my impression that universities in the United States were very loosely organized and almost instantly adapted to new fields of research and study. The faculty was seminomadic and flitted from post to post according to the changing configuration of new research. Such a dynamic dispensation was greatly to be admired. Unburdened by centuries of tradition, the American university was more open to new imaginative ideas and more attuned to the present than its European counterparts. What could be better for the development of a new field such as African studies? In short, I thoroughly misunderstood the institutions I encountered. Even almost two years later I was still so ignorant about the structural aspects of universities that when some colleagues began to congratulate me one day in 1962 about something called tenure, I had no idea what was up. I had done nothing, so why these sudden congratulations? That tenure meant permanent employment did not even cross my mind. After all, I was on a short-term appointment in Madison, and no one had asked me if I wanted to stay beyond the agreed-upon three years.

My family's lifestyle and outlook certainly were geared to a short-term stay. Every year we moved houses, we evaluated Bruno's performance in school by comparing his grades with equivalent grades in Belgium, and I kept in close contact with the research institute in Rwanda and with various scholars in Belgium and in Britain. A number of visitors from the Congo and some IRSAC colleagues made it to Madison, almost all my writing was in French or Dutch, and I constantly corresponded about publications with the academy in Brussels or the museum in Tervuren. Like so many short-term visitors, I attended many professional meetings and agreed to deliver lectures at various universities mainly to do some tourism, visit the major cities of the country, and become acquainted with what were becoming major centers of African studies. I did not fully realize that in many cases those who extended these invitations had ulterior motives and that job offers from Northwestern, Berkeley, Chicago, and the University of California, Los Angeles came as a consequence of them. Nor did I understand the relationship between this and the offer of tenure.

By 1962 it was time to look for future employment. Several new possibilities were beginning to shape up. The obvious one was a position at Leuven, my alma mater, urged on me by my cousin who was in the faculty of medicine there. Although they never talked about it, I suspect that my parents would have liked me to take this route. Indeed, I finally did receive a letter from the *rector magnificus,* but I turned the offer down. I explained my reasons in a letter to my parents: "For years and years I told and let it be known to everyone that I want to do *research* and not to teach. That was the reason, e.g., to reject Lovanium. And it was THE reason. Madison we accepted because it appeared to be the only place where I could at least do research half time. But now the problem is to arrange for [the return to] Belgium."³

The possibility I was most keen about was to be appointed at Tervuren to do research, with the prospect of being sent on year-long stints in Africa. Later—maybe after eight or nine years—I wanted an appointment in Leuven, and then I would turn from a research career to teaching. The Leuven offer was premature. To refuse it would mean to close that avenue for a later career, because no one would believe that anyone would really prefer to do research. So I refused Leuven and pursued the Tervuren option, little knowing that I had in effect breached custom by doing so.

I was made a full professor at Madison in the spring of 1963, still not aware of the relationship between outside offers and this astonishingly rapid promotion. Indeed, Northwestern was so persistent that I undertook to teach a seminar there in addition to my duties at Madison. Contrary to all precedent, the dean in Madison agreed to let me do it. So once a week I commuted by train and taught a seminar with twenty students. That was not the only strange development. In May 1962 the Social Science Research Council wrote to me out of the blue, telling me that they had money left over after having funded all the requested research propositions. They offered me four thousand dollars to do fieldwork in Africa, wherever and for whatever project I wanted. They even agreed to carry it over to 1963–64. In the spring of 1963 I was also approached by Roland Oliver about an appointment at SOAS in London. So when our family left for Europe with all our belongings in June, it was with the prospect of doing a year of fieldwork and the strong possibility of a position either at Tervuren or in London. Still, as a precaution for the future, I had not formally resigned from the University of Wisconsin (possibly on the urging of Philip Curtin) but instead took a year of unpaid leave.

I had gone to Madison mostly because I was offered a half-time research position in a newly created humanities institute.⁴ Housed in an old observatory on a small hill with a spectacular view, the institute was not yet well known on campus, which meant that one could hide there to work uninterruptedly. A handful of other researchers there were also devoted to their studies, so the atmosphere was truly scholarly. One could and did get much work done there. I was also assigned a graduate student in anthropology as a research assistant, mainly to fetch books from Madison's fine university library and to write summaries of articles I asked her to read. The library was extremely well stocked with works on Africa, and its open stacks allowed accessibility to its resources. What a difference this was from European libraries, with the dreary waiting for books that trickled in one at a time from the closed stacks. So it was paradise to me actually to have materials delivered to my desk at the institute when I needed them.

The research agenda was full. After so many years of fieldwork, I urgently needed to write up the results. Indeed, I had been taught by word and by awful contrary example that a research project is not finished until the results are published. Publication, I had been told, was the essential obligation to the scientific community of anyone fortunate enough to have been entrusted with research. My stand on that score was not brilliant. Yes, the manuscript of my book *De la tradition orale* had been delivered at Tervuren for publication on my return from Rwanda, but that was all. Meanwhile, a few IRSAC assistants were still copying and translating Rwandan *ibiteekerezo* in Astrida, and I was directing their work from afar. As I still planned somehow to return there after my stay in Madison and still intended to edit several volumes of oral documents, that material did not demand my most urgent attention. I should now be writing a monograph about Kuba society, especially about its political organization. But I felt that I should first write at least a short study of the major distortions which were then current in the historiography of Rwanda, if only because the topic was so relevant to the political convulsions shaking the country.

Past historians had been inspired for their conception of the history of Rwanda, by French history. In their view the Rwandan state had expanded by conquest from a small cradle, just as France had grown out of the Ile-de-France.[5] The country was the creation of an enlightened Tuutsi aristocracy, who had set up a benevolent feudal system by which they both protected and exploited the less intelligent rustic farmers. Works espousing these views, such as Maquet's *Le système*, legitimated Tuutsi rule, and it was urgent for me to counter such myths. So while it was all still fresh in my mind, I wrote a short, condensed volume about this topic. It consisted of a critical discussion of the historiography of Rwanda, an overview of the available sources, a discussion of chronology, a concise exposition of the history of Rwanda's major institutions, and a systematic examination of the role of conquest in Rwanda's expansion. By mid-February 1961 the manuscript was completed, and I turned to the Kuba project. In reality the study on Rwanda was more an essay than a monograph. It was directed toward historians, both Rwandan and foreign, and with the exception of its next-to-last chapter, it reached its goal. Its positions came to be accepted by all. But the course of the Rwandan revolution ensured that for a generation no one pursued research in the history of a proscribed dynasty.[6]

Toward the end of the spring I learned that as an inmate of the institute I was expected to give a public lecture in September. Curtin asked me to deliver the Knaplund Lectures, a series about the history of the British Commonwealth, sponsored by the history department.[7] I proposed a set of three lectures about the overall political history of precolonial Central Africa. The goal was to show to a general university audience that Central Africa had experienced a complex precolonial history. The slight difficulty in my proposal was that so far no one had even begun to find the major outlines of this past. Hence I had to drop the Kuba project and hurriedly start on this new topic. I began to read the available literature at top speed, and by summer I was deeply immersed in text editions of the sixteenth and seventeenth centuries.

During the early 1960s Africa and especially the Congo were very much in the news, so a sizable audience thronged to hear the first of my lectures. The material was so novel to them that it piqued the curiosity of many of their friends as well. The second and third time around, the large auditorium was overflowing. A few weeks later during a lunch at the university (Curtin always set up such propositions during a lunch!), Curtin proposed that I publish the lectures. At first I refused because the work was not based on original research. It was merely something for an uninformed general audience—useful, no doubt, but just then not a priority. My views of what was important were still shaped by the opinions of Jozef Desmet, my former teacher, for whom well-done research monographs and text editions were gold for the ages, while surveys were dross for the decade. But after a heated discussion, Phil convinced me that a synthesis, even if I felt it to be provisional, would be of great assistance to students, researchers in the field, and an imaginary public at large. So I agreed, even though it meant adding yet another book to an already overloaded schedule.

Apart from historical traditions, the largest block in the mass of the materials I had gathered about Kuba society dealt with their social and political life. Even though to my mind the political institutions of the kingdom were by far the most interesting, in writing my study I did not privilege them. Influenced by the stress on kinship and small social groups then prevalent in British functional anthropology, I decided to give a full account of these topics as well. But watching the way linguists like Meeussen worked had convinced me that conciseness was a cardinal virtue: one should not pile case on case when one example would support a general statement. So I ruthlessly reduced the wealth of data to ten chapters, half of which described kinship and the local community and half the wider political institutions. This worked out quite well for the first half, in part because the phenomena to be discussed were relatively simple and in part because I could quantify many data. But it did not work nearly as well for the political system.

In retrospect, I can see how this tyranny of conciseness and imposed chapter length led me astray. I made short shrift of the discussion of kingship, the aristocracy, and political dynamics. Yes, it was all there, but the treatment was far too condensed, and too many of the concrete data at hand were omitted. The purported original contribution to anthropological theory was the provision of a process model which sought to establish generalized rules to account for recurrent political change, valid over three centuries. That was so condensed that no anthropologist ever picked it up. It also suffered from the flaw, obvious in hindsight, that I did not seriously tackle the impact of the colonial situation. The whole book was thus lifeless and static, even though it had been abstracted from a myriad of detailed concrete sources, ranging from participant observation to proverbs and even dialogues jotted down by Bushong in Bushong on the topics at hand. The result certainly was thorough but badly flawed.[8] No wonder that its publication passed by without much comment and that its impact has been practically invisible. Moreover, the Kuba themselves had no access to copies, although later some books apparently reached the country, where they are still in use.

The bulk of my dissertation had dealt with the precolonial history of the Kuba, and that too needed to be published. The text was a blow-by-blow account of the traditions which I had collected about the origins and migrations of various Kuba groups, and it chronicled events in each of the succeeding reigns. The interpretation remained quite timid. In short, this was a typical Ph.D. effort written for a positivist jury. Tervuren agreed, however, to publish it as it stood, in the original Dutch. That suited me for several reasons. This solution required no new efforts, the result would contribute to the increase of scientific literature in Dutch rather than in French—something I applauded in a context in which the hegemony of French in Belgian scholarly life was still nearly absolute—and Dutch seemed to be perfect to avoid feedback from this book into Bushong traditions. For I had not forgotten the tales of Frans Olbrechts about his research among the Cherokee. When he asked them about magic, they surreptiously consulted a book written by a previous ethnographer who had worked there on this topic and repeated it all back to him.

My book, therefore, merely reflected the views of the Kuba (mostly the aristocracy) about their own past.[9] It was thus quite similar to the local works of African historians, only on a larger scale.[10] Years later I saw the need to rework the data and interpret them more. Yet it was only in the late 1960s that I grasped why the book should have been written for its "natural" audience, the Kuba, and in a language accessible to at least some of them. Meanwhile, the combination of the topic and the language in which it was written ensured the book's almost totally obscurity.

It was late in 1961 before I turned again to the kingdoms of the savanna. With the help of Lois Marmor, I worked through the whole bibliography, summarized it, and was able to present a reasonably well-founded overall reconstruction of this large area a year later. The writing up which followed, however, was hectic, too hectic.[11] Still, the speed of composition influenced the unity of conception which marks the book. It was destined to be an "exploratory work . . . to arouse interest" or a "workbook."[12] The trouble has been that a whole generation of historians took it as a definitive synthesis. It has had too much success.[13]

Whatever their defects, these books still achieved one goal: to make the results of my research available to my academic peers. It still astonishes me now that I managed to write all of them within two and a half years, working half time. But with the exception of the last one, they were the fruits of the years of research at IRSAC, and none contained any startling breakthroughs of more general interest. Moreover, the research about the kingdoms of the savanna was widening my own horizons.[14] In those years most historians of Africa were still fascinated by questions of method, and I was no exception. Oral traditions no longer weighed so much on my mind, even though I was much solicited to restate the conclusions of my earlier work with the addition of further curlicues.

What fascinated me now was to find a sound methodology to tap the huge mountains of existing ethnographic sources about Africa. I had read most of the works of the American and Central European schools which had attempted to use ethnographic data directly as sources for history. All of these had failed. More recently, George P. Murdock's *Africa: Its Peoples and Their Culture History* had provided a grand sweep of issues and adduced a set of fascinating questions, but it had solved no problems of method and had actually added little to the historical record.[15] David Baerreis, an archaeologist and colleague at Madison for whom I had great respect, espoused the new evolutionary theory proposed by Julian Steward.[16] Yet the problems with this approach were obvious: basically there was too much *a priori*, which led to circular reasoning, while the theory actually fitted only a tiny minority of historical cases. For a while I played around with the notion that historical reconstructions could be cast into strict process models. That would boldy reveal the subjective features of the historian's interpretation, since they would have to be stated in the open rather than merely being assumed. Moreover, I felt that process models allowed one to bring dynamic perspectives to a hitherto static functionalist comparative anthropology. Michael G. Smith, who had published a book titled *Government in Zazzau (1800–1950)*, seemed to have achieved just that.[17] As a result I went to Dakar in December 1961 to attend a conference on African history with a paper about process models. By chance, I met Michael at the airport in New York. We spent the whole long flight from New York to Dakar discussing the then-unusual notion of the process model.[18]

The Dakar conference had been organized by my old mentor Daryll Forde, director of the International African Institute. It was attended by thirty-nine scholars, anthropologists and historians, most of them francophone historians and members of the SOAS network, including a number of African scholars such as Jacob Ajayi and Bethwell A. Ogot.[19] But the older leading African historians, Kenneth Dike and Saburi Biobaku, were absent.[20] In addition, there were a few others: three Americans, one Belgian, one Italian, and a representative of UNESCO.[21] This occasion brought the SOAS network face to face with its francophone counterpart for the first time. Once the conference was under way, it turned out that there was no translator. Hence I was drafted as a near simultaneous translator for French and English, while the host, Raymond Mauny, recompensed me by feeding me white wine, which seemed to stimulate wonderfully fluent translations and summaries. By its nature, this activity forced me to take copious notes. Hence, near the end of the meeting Forde prevailed on me to undertake the general editing of the conference papers then and there. I was to stay in Dakar, review the papers, and write the general introduction. It was a lot to ask, because I had planned to visit my parents in Belgium before Christmas and to be back to celebrate Christmas with Claudine and Bruno in Madison. But I did it, and during the next three weeks I stayed in a room at the IFAN compound and wrote all day and much of the night, notwithstanding a bout of malaria. Each afternoon

I would deliver the product of the day to Mauny. It felt a little bit as if I were being held as a hostage, although I do remember one afternoon off. In this fashion the introduction in both languages and all summary translations of the papers had been typed, approved by Mauny, and made ready for the publisher before New Year's Day.

Although most papers were devoted to techniques or specific reconstructions on topics of "state and trade," they were not the most remarkable feature of this conference. That was the discussion of the meaning of African history to contemporary Africans and the legitimate role of "historical imagination" in what now would be called "the production of history." It buried all forms of historical positivism and underlined some positive uses for contemporary subjectivity. In 1993 the section of the conference report that addresses these issues seems very modern indeed. It resonates with questions much debated today and shows that historians even then were not as naive as contemporary polemics sometimes make them out to be![22] At that time the discussion was triggered by the concerns of Jacob Ajayi and other African scholars about the impending reforms of curricula for West African schools and textbooks, and by the reflections of African historians and European anthropologists on the uses of history in Africa for contemporary political purposes. It seems paradoxical that most of the work of the conference dealt with source criticism and methodological practices to increase objectivity, while recognizing the essential role of subjectivity. Yet there is no paradox: good history finds its shape in the spark between these two extremes.

In the context of the historiography of African history, the most significant process I participated in during the early 1960s was the creation of programs in African history and in African studies at Madison, because so many of their features were later adopted by almost all colleges in the United States. That development was as much intertwined with the views and experience of Philip Curtin as it was with mine. After service in the merchant marine during the Second World War, from which he returned with a global view of the world and a passion for history, Curtin had studied the history of the British Commonwealth. Although he himself came from a well-off family, he disliked elitist views. He wanted to study commonwealth history from the "grass roots" up. Hence, for his dissertation he disdained the archives of the Public Record Office but focused on local archives, a step which was then considered nothing short of revolutionary.[23] He first taught in the genteel surroundings of Swarthmore but in 1956 accepted a position in Madison, where he was hired as a replacement for a historian of the British Empire but was asked to combine this subject with Latin American history. By 1957, the year of the independence of Ghana, he began to develop a special interest in the history of Africa, which would henceforth become his area of specialization. Moreover, he was widening and transforming the notion of commonwealth history into something he labeled comparative world history, of which African history was to be a subfield. And in 1960 he had approached the Carnegie Foundation to fund the whole Comparative Tropical History Program.

Within a week of my arrival in Madison, Curtin, decisive and impatient as always, involved me in developing a program in history and an African Studies Program. I naturally viewed this as part of the job I was hired to do. His views on comparative tropical history as a history of European empires seen from below did not carry universal approval in the department, however, which led to many a spirited and sometimes quite vocal argument there. His main ally was Fred H. Harrington, a historian of U.S. international relations who was then vice president of the university. Harrington was convinced that decolonization inevitably led to greater U.S. involvement with the former imperial dependencies of other countries across the world and that this in turn would create a demand for area programs. The University of Wisconsin should steal a march on all others by creating area programs for all the major parts of the world and make this a specialty now.

Part of my job, as I understood it then, was to help Curtin set up such a program for Africa. We first had to decide whether the program should become a department of its own, as it was at SOAS and soon would be at UCLA, or whether the teaching of area courses should be done in existing departments.[24] We decided for the second alternative because the goal was to spread awareness of African studies throughout the university, rather than to create a ghetto for it, and also because we believed that professional training in a discipline should come first, the geographic area second. The African Studies Program was then merely to be a coordinating agency whose goal would be to place African specialists in the main departments of social sciences and the humanities. The second question dealt with the curriculum within history. Once again, unlike the authorities at SOAS, we took the stand that both intensive language training and experience in Africa (fieldwork) were to be essential parts of the curriculum. There would be a major in African history and a minor in African studies outside of history. A stiff language requirement would include a reading knowledge of French within the first year of graduate studies, a two-year language study of an African language, and reading knowledge of a third language, African or European as indicated by the research topic. Doing fieldwork was also required. The requirements were unusually severe. They were to have the side effect of instilling a special esprit de corps in our African history graduate students, who interpreted such uncompromising demands as a reflection of the depth of their commitment to the field, a vocation that set them apart from the run-of-the-mill graduate students in the department.

A program of courses in the major could be set up without further ado. The goal in 1961 was to train historians of Africa who were also well grounded in comparative history. Therefore we created advanced graduate courses covering the various areas within Africa and methodology, as well as a seminar in African history. Moreover, we both agreed on the necessity of a broad outlook. But the specific form the requirement took reflected Curtin's views rather than mine, which would have steered students more to courses in anthropology. Curtin's preferences had the advantage of keeping the requirements for the major within the department of history, and he cleverly legitimated them by referring to the better prospects of future employment for doctoral graduates. At that time African history was still considered to be too narrow a specialty, and colleges wanted "Third World" historians or those who had studied a combination of African and European history. As a result of this, the students in the major were then also required to take a seminar in comparative tropical history (popularly called Compswamp) and had to attend at least one course dealing with another part of the Third World. Their final examinations tested them both on African history and on one other "world area."

The other parts of the projected program, however, required further inputs from the outside. We needed financial support for the students and for hiring new faculty, we needed to set up an infrastructure for African studies, and we needed an institutional framework for the teaching of languages. Funding for graduate student support was essential to attract the best possible candidates, to allow us to require them to follow a rigid timetable, a "track," and to require fieldwork. Curtin received the grant from the Carnegie Foundation, which allowed him to fund graduate students and begin "headhunting" for faculty. The creation of a program in African studies with core appointments in anthropology, political science, geography, and languages was in line with the general policy of the university. In the fall of 1962 Bertram Hill, a specialist in French history, was appointed as dean of international studies and programs. He worked out the overall structure of such area programs and prepared to create them. That year Curtin was on leave, so I was involved with the program for

Africa. Apart from identifying potential faculty recruits, my major responsibility consisted of proposing a budget, which I completely forgot to do. When the deadline came, Hill and I quickly had to concoct one over the telephone!

The program really began in the fall of 1963, with Curtin as its first chair. At that time an anthropologist, a political scientist, and a specialist in South African languages were on board.[25] The question of a permanent academic home for faculty in African languages was not easily solved, however, because there existed no suitable department in which they could be recruited. It took time to sort out the various possibilities, but eventually Curtin and I won the day. The university authorities eventually concurred in the creation of a special department of African languages and literature, the first and still the only one in the United States. A. C. ("Joe") Jordan was its first incumbent.

When I left Madison in June 1963, the whole program had been worked out in theory, even if it was not yet fully in place. The formula we developed for African studies (interdepartmental programs) was quickly imitated by most universities elsewhere in North America, despite the fact that it was so different from the solutions worked out at the SOAS and followed at UCLA. In history, the African language requirement became a standard expectation, while fieldwork experience was strongly encouraged in all departments. But other programs did not adopt the whole Wisconsin model. They ignored the comparative aspect in history (a market for African history specialists was only then developing), and they balked at the cost of setting up departments of African languages and literature.

Finally June 1963 came. Loaded down with belongings and dreams of a bright but uncertain future, we were off to New York, onto the freighter *Lulua,* and then straight to downtown Antwerp and to a warm welcome from the family waiting there. To be in the Old Country, as Bruno called it, was soothing and deeply satisfying, even to Bruno, who was a little Americanized. Indeed, the first time he went upstairs at my parents' house, we heard him excitedly running down the stairs again, shouting, "George Washington!" He had misinterpreted the oval-framed portrait of a family patriarch in ancient costume.

This peaceful pause was short. A week or two later I was in London to see Daryll Forde and Roland Oliver, who put me up. I had decided that I would not accept the SOAS position because it involved more teaching than research. I was counting on the position at Tervuren instead. When I arrived in London, the first thing Oliver told me was that I was to be interviewed by the SOAS board the next morning. Then I told him the bad news. He blanched visibly but remained courteous as ever, although he immediately began to take steps to present an alternate candidate to his board. Only then did I begin to have an inkling of the complex maneuvers and calculations that had preceded the creation of this position and Oliver's offer to me to teach at SOAS. Still, I understood that by refusing I was burning a bridge: SOAS would never be an option for the future again. The episode left a haze over the cordiality of my relations with Oliver for many years thereafter.

A week later I was in the office of the director at Tervuren, who congratulated me on having been appointed to the position he had secured. But the terms were a letdown. Only a month or two earlier, when Harroy had visited me in Madison, he had believed that I was to be offered the directorship itself. He was obviously ill informed. Nevertheless, on paper the position seemed quite attractive. Now the director was telling me that the job carried a salary less than that of a beginning high school teacher and recommended that I try to secure a half-time position at a university to complement it. The position basically was that of a bibliographer, with additional ill-specified duties. For the moment it was temporary, but in a year or two it probably would become permanent. No possibilities for any fieldwork existed. On the contrary, he wanted me to hand over the four thousand dollars from the Social Science Research Council, so that someone else at the museum could use it for research in Africa! He then expatiated at length on my luck in landing this position. My linguistic, religious, and educational background, allied to my regional ties, had allowed for this piece of good fortune. These were Belgian realities about which no one had briefed me earlier. If I had been properly informed, I would have accepted Leuven's invitation in 1962 and then sought this post in addition. Now it looked as if I was hooked. But I refused to accept this and resigned a few days later, even though I realized the magnitude of the step. This was a loss of face which the director never forgave. From then on my relations with the directors at Tervuren, an institution which was absolutely crucial to my research interests, would remain strained.

There was nothing unusual about this treatment. It reflected the prevailing practices of official appointments in Belgium, and the creation of the post was an achievement at a time when the public wanted to forget the fiasco of decolonization in the Congo as fast as possible. The "colonial university" and the program in African studies at Leuven had both been summarily abolished. IRSAC was absorbed by the government department responsible for foreign aid. Moreover, a latent resentment of the faculty already ensconced at the universities at the facilities which those who had pursued research careers in Africa had enjoyed there prevented the appointment of most of the former researchers of IRSAC. As a result, Belgium had squandered most of its academic infrastructure related to Africa by 1963, and many of IRSAC's researchers in social science had immigrated to the United States or to France.

In August it was clear that our family would have to return to Madison. Meanwhile, however, we could go ahead with fieldwork. This was to be the first time that a field was not imposed on me. I chose to study the precolonial history of the Tio kingdom in Congo-Brazzaville. That kingdom had been known since 1506, and old sources extolled it as a state as powerful and larger than the celebrated kingdom of Kongo. It was also famous because the treaty of 1880 between its king, Macoco, and Pierre Savorgnan de Brazza became the starting point of the scramble for Central Africa. But the history of this major kingdom had never been studied. Was this not a splendid opportunity to record its traditions and reconstruct its history? Moreover, I then thought that a connection had existed between the early Kuba and Tio kingdoms. In addition, Tio society, culture, and language still remained almost unknown, in spite of the fact that the Tio lived close to Brazzaville.[26] In short, any fieldwork was certain to reap rich results. Correspondence with the geographer Marcel Soret, then at the Office de la Recherche Scientifique et Technique d'Outre-Mer (ORSTOM) had prepared the ground, and I had also studied the two known seventeenth-century reports about Kinshasa, which was then governed by a Tio lord.[27] But plans soon seemed to go awry: in mid-August the government was overthrown during the so-called three glorious days.[28] As it happened, the ensuing confusion actually helped us to secure research visas. On October 11 Claudine and I arrived in Brazzaville with most of our field equipment. Bruno stayed with my parents in Gooreind. Soret was waiting for us and put us up in the guesthouse at ORSTOM.

ORSTOM was a research organization with stations all over the world in former French colonies. Like that at IRSAC, its atmosphere was interdisciplinary because researchers in many different disciplines worked side by side at each station. Thus the staff at Brazzaville then included a geographer, an archaeologist, a linguist, and an anthropologist, just in the social sciences. But unlike IRSAC personnel, most ORSTOM staff were supposed to carry out research projects that had practical uses. The anthropologist at ORSTOM, for instance, was then studying the social organization of labor on cocoa plantations, and Marcel Soret was engaged in establishing a detailed ethnic map of all of French Central Africa. He had just finished a study of the impact of the Congo-Océan Railway on the Congo. Nevertheless, there was some time for basic research, and some specialists, such as linguists and archaeologists, had more time for this than others.

ORSTOM researchers were career civil servants. Most of them aspired to complete a "state doctorate" and to secure an academic post in their fifties. The civil servant status helps to explain why so many researchers in Brazzaville "did fieldwork" in a perfunctory way. Once or twice each month they left the station on a Monday "to do fieldwork," only to return late on Friday. The rest of the time they were in their offices, like other civil servants. Moreover, the ORSTOM compound was isolated and insulated from the townships of Brazzaville. Even the momentous events of August, for instance, had passed by without an impact.

ORSTOM provided just what we needed. We had arrived on a Friday, and we were strictly left to fend for ourselves during the sacred weekend. On Monday, though, Soret introduced us to the Congolese administration, on Tuesday an ORSTOM jeep drove us to Mbe, the center of the Tio kingdom, for a one-day visit to settle matters there, and exactly one week after we stepped off the plane, on October 18, we were in Mbe ready to stay and work. Without ORSTOM, such efficiency would have been imposs- ible. We had also helped ourselves, though, by bringing with us the bare essentials for camping and by deciding not to buy or hire a car.

The trip to Mbe had brought us first out of the depths of the valley of the Congo River and then onto a sandy, endless, treeless, waterless, and practically level steppe. It looked completely uninhabited. Indeed, we pas- sed only one small hamlet in the final hundred kilometers or so. This was not like anything we had seen before in Central Africa. Then at one of the rare turns of the usually straight track was Mbe. No one would have guessed that this was a capital. It was laid out and looked just like an ordinary village. But there was a central plaza at a road junction, and on one side of the plaza stood an unusually large house surrounded by a fence—the royal palace. And one of the three quarters abutted on a wood with large and tangled trees. It took an experienced eye to see that the school building nearby and a dispensary about a kilometer away indicated that this was a central place.

On our one-day reconnaissance, the curious young men about town had gathered to hear "the news" as soon as the ORSTOM car arrived. Even more unusual, by the time we left Bernard Ngaayüo had already volun- teered to be a translator and to teach me the language. That, of course, was no accident. I soon found out that he was a son of the most influential leader in the village. Meanwhile, though, early on the morning after our arrival to work, the first language class was under way, the first notebook opened, and I began to write: "A person: *mbuuru.*" We were off to a flying start. During the first weeks the research went as planned. I took notes on the language, and I met the elders of the village in a series of general introductory sessions, so that they could size me up while I systematically asked questions in the fashion of an ethnographic survey. Then came the time to seriously inquire about the past. To my dismay it soon became painfully evident that nobody remembered anything before King Iloo, the one who had signed the treaty with Pierre Savorgnan de Brazza. What happened before that time had receded into a time before history. I even found out why this was so. It had to do with the watershed, the advent of colonialism, of course, but it was also due to the Tio's system of kinship terminology, which allowed them only to name two generations back. Any person more remote automatically became a parent or a grandparent, and their memories were fused with those of the generation of the speaker's real parents or grandparents. It was a neat find. It also was a disaster. There was no way to recover the history of this ancient kingdom from its oral traditions.

As this finding sank in, I realized that it would be hopeless to search hard for a few scraps which might somehow have survived that barrier of time. One should tear up the whole research design and start again. But what to do? Gather linguistic materials and general ethnography? Then it dawned on me that I actually was collecting historical materials: data about daily life one or two generations ago. Why, then, not describe Tio society and culture as it was on the eve of the colonial occupation? Was it not the implicit assumption of all anthropologists at the time that they recorded a pristine, that is, a precolonial, way of life? Yet their timeless descriptions never systematically referred to that time, because they did not rely much on the concrete reminiscences of people, nor did they attempt to date the reminiscences which they did record. Why not be systematic, date every little bit of description and evidence, double check it by recording the reminiscences or oral traditions of others, and write a monograph, based not so much on participant observation as on the memory of people? The drawback was that it was then universally believed that one could only write a valid study of society and culture through the use of that shibboleth "participant observation." But given the importance of "informants" in all such research, that could not be entirely true.

The project looked sensible, feasible, novel, and tempting. Indeed, part of its appeal was the opportunity to challenge anthropologists and see whether I could be convincing enough so that they would accept the results. I reoriented my plans and focused research toward this goal. It worked like a charm. The data were rich, and I even met two very aged informants. Lipie, a slow-moving, withered giant, was so old that he could reminisce about the years before 1880, and Abili Ndiõ, a gnarled but lively woman, remembered much from her youth only a decade later. The new research design yielded everything expected of it, it was ideally adapted to the local conditions, it allowed me truly to carry out the whole plan, and it even yielded a few bits about early Tio history.

The new goal was a blessing also because it allowed me to work just with Bernard, to stay mostly in one place, Mbe, and to become well acquainted with its three hundred–odd inhabitants. It would only require a week or two at one of the tiny villages and another one in Ngabe, the Tio harbor on the Congo River. Certainly it would have been nice to visit the tombs of the eighteenth-century kings at Mpiina Ntsa, 120 kilometers away, but this was not essential. We had no car, and we did not need one. In the end we even managed to accompany Soret on a visit to Ngwi, the spiritual cradle of kingship, more than 160 kilometers to the north. Nor did this research project require any special tools. I did not have a tape recorder. We had a cheap camera, but it died after the first roll of film had been shot. This inspired Claudine, who in her school days had been taught to draw somewhat, to sketch what she or I thought was interesting, mostly objects. In doing so she really learned to see and to understand what she was sketching. The sight of her seated on a low local basketry tripod in front of a pot, a basket, or a knife became part of the local landscape. The local people, who were allergic to being photographed, loved to watch how the pencil slowly created an image of the object. Soon they arrived with objects of their own and begged her to draw their favorite things, a spearhead, a copper bangle, a jug, or a guitar. Moreover, it turned out later that such drawings were more precise than any photograph could have been, when one needed to compare objects Claudine had drawn with similar objects that had been sketched in the late nineteenth century. Both of us had a happy time, and in the end the research was completed in the short time we had—barely five and a half months in the field. Bernard worked an additional three months.

Success was only possible because the villagers were so helpful that we never lost a moment. They helped because they liked us. They liked us because we only had the barest necessities: no radio, no refrigerator, none of those things that were thought to be essential to Europeans. We lived in a rented small adobe shop on the main square in a row of other houses and in full view of everybody. We lived off rice and local onions, just as they lived off cassava and onions. The rations were meager, for at that time poor weather and bad government policies had left the local people and us short of food. Only the onion harvest had been abundant. When we needed to go to Brazzaville, we had to wait until the local schoolteacher, who owned a small car, was going. Then we had to beg a place. He loved it. To go to another village, we once bought a ride on the back of a truck that was carrying a whole soccer team. The soccer team was tickled.

One day a truck driver from Brazzaville told us that President Kennedy had been killed and that his attacker had in turn been shot. We derided the whole rumor, just as we had denied a rumor from the same source that the Americans were planning to go to the moon to paste it over with a huge Coca Cola sign. But then, alas, the lone radio in the village confirmed this story, and the people were proud that *they* had told *us*. I suspect that they really liked us because we stayed there and were dependent on them, unlike the few earlier researchers, who had been there for a day or so, just like tourists. A few times during our stay a couple of jeeps arrived unannounced from Brazzaville with European explorers curious to see the savages in the bush and the butterflies at the river. They wandered about, took pictures, and tried to enter our houses. We resented it just as much as any Tio did, and we got just as upset as they did about such an invasion. We were just as angry and envious when the stupid tourists spread out their lavish picnics on the main square and gorged themselves. They did not even know enough etiquette to bring bread for the villagers, and they knew nothing about a food shortage. So perhaps the villagers simply liked us in contrast to them.

We were mostly cut off from the outside hectic world—but not entirely. Every night we were treated to the sight of a satellite lazily drawing a figure eight on the horizon, and once or twice another one slowly promenaded along the vault of the night sky. Other signs of modern life intruded from time to time. The isolation of Mbe was half illusory. Socially it was a distant dormitory of Brazzaville and a place where urban Tio retired. Indeed, the old man Lipie, rumored to be the oldest man in the whole country, lived in Brazzaville. I interviewed him when he came to visit a leading elder in Mbe. Politically Mbe was not isolated either. The previous president, Abbé Youlou, had been given magic charms for office there; Mr. Nonault, our friendly schoolmaster, kept in constant touch with political friends at the capital. Indeed, a few months after our departure, he emerged as a senior ambassador and was later minister of foreign affairs.

109

Late in March 1964 we were treated to the spectacle of a bunch of "gorillas" (the Franco-Congolese term) coming to intimidate the Tio king, who was too close to the deposed Youlou. Just after we left, in April, the king was deposed by middle-aged city slickers, called "the revolutionary youth." Mr. Nonault taught us much about the practical workings of politics, while we learned from the Tio around us just how dismissive they were of the professed ideologies of government. Three years after independence, the main legitimacy of the government was its peacefulness in comparison with the volatile Kinshasa next door. Thus living in Mbe taught us much about the postcolonial state and about the irrelevance of many of the political science theories of the day.[29]

We could go to Brazzaville and stock up there when Mr. Nonault went for new provisions and mail, and we received supplies when someone from ORSTOM came to Mbe, such as the archaeologist who came to look at some of the sites I had reported or Marcel Soret, who took us north in search of the cradle of the Tio kingdom. But we were largely shielded from pressures until we returned to Brazzaville in early April. Covered with the red mud of the journey, I went straight to the posh hotel there to meet the eminent professor Jim Coleman from UCLA.[30] Eyebrows were raised when this red bushman in shorts arrived in the elegant lobby, and Coleman was a little startled too. But he hid it well and proceeded to cajole me to sign on at his university. Once again I refused. A few days later Professor Benoît Verhaegen, the most dynamic of Lovanium's faculty members, came over from Kinshasa. I caught up with the news about the university, while he urged me to translate *Kingdoms of the Savanna* into French for the benefit of the Zairian students, as well as to write a book-length *Ethnographie du Congo* for them as well, both to be published in Kinshasa itself.

He convinced me easily, because the people at Mbe already had. They told a story in Mbe that researchers came there for a few days to write up papers. Then they returned to Brazzaville and took the plane for "France," and once on the plane they tore up their notes and threw them through the window. I had promised I would not do that. I would really write a book about them which they could read. The book would be in French so that it would be accessible to them. Worse luck, though—Soret's closest friend at ORSTOM warned me that he and his colleagues would resist such a move, because a publication in French could interfere with Soret's projected doctoral dissertation on the general topic of the "Bateke." So we left Brazzaville in the glow of a spell of fruitful fieldwork, marred slightly by that one sour note.

6

The Roaring Sixties

THE STORY of my own experience is now approaching the middle of the 1960s. It is appropriate to interrupt it for a moment to sketch what was happening to the specialty of African history. For that specialty was spreading like wildfire in the bush during the dry season: the number of historians of Africa was increasing by leaps and bounds, new universities, departments of history, and African studies programs appeared almost every year in Africa itself and almost as quickly in the United States, and public recognition for the field was finally spreading also to France and its African colonies. "Unbound optimism" is the expression which best captures the mood of those who flocked to the standards of African history. As Martin Klein put it: "In retrospect the appeal of Africa for myself and many of my generation of Africanists was very much the excitement of watching the destruction of an oppressive colonial order and being involved in the creation of a new one." He links this attitude to the quest in the United States for equality and justice at home, the main goal of the contemporary civil rights movement.[1] Such optimists could not really accommodate the jaundiced stance of classical Marxist doctrines and its class struggles. Instead they focused romantically on the heroism of those who had led the resistance to colonialism and were now the founders of new countries. Martin Klein certainly was one of these historians. He had attended my African history seminar in Madison during the spring of 1963, and I remember him as one of the students whose intense preoccupation with the present shaped his interests in the past.

For some other students, as for me, the appeal of the history of Africa lay more in the sheer novelty of the field than in any contemporary effects, however gratifying. To be a historian of Africa in the sixties was an exciting intellectual adventure. New "discoveries" occurred all the time. For instance, I vividly recall the intense satisfaction with which I read a typed French translation of a hitherto "unknown" text by al-Djakhiz about the East African coast in the ninth century, which Raymond Mauny had sent to me.[2] I also remember the thrilled attention of a small international group of scholars at an informal evening and their subsequent happy speculations when they heard news about the extent and the potential of recent archaeological investigation in a necropolis in Shaba. Sheer intellectual curiosity was intoxicating to many who felt that in this field they could hope to contribute more to the advancement of knowledge than they could ever aspire to achieve in older, more established fields. Hence this group of scholars felt just as optimistic about the field as those who were inspired by the present. They too had no room for any heavy-hearted historical materialism. Actually the difference between the two groups I have sketched was so small that a single person often combined the inspiration stemming from the grand spectacle of the coming of independence to so many countries with the excitement of sharing new discoveries about the distant past.

The single overarching feature of the academic field of African history in the sixties was its phenomenal growth, estimated to be fivefold or a little more. The number of historians and archaeologists concerned with African history rose from about one hundred in 1961 to well over five hundred in 1970.[3] The number of departments in which African history was taught grew about fivefold in Africa, perhaps tenfold in the United States, but only tripled in Britain. In France three departments, all in Paris, began teaching the subject. Publishing research about African history outside of Africa increased almost fourfold.[4] In Africa the number of journals and pamphlet series mushroomed in proportion to the increase in the number of departments.

The overall increase in a decade left a lasting mark on the field. In hindsight it is not surprising that this phenomenal growth spawned various new "schools" or styles of interpretation, but it is surprising that they all continued to share the basic "paradigm" that had been proposed by Oliver and Fage in the early fifties, with the exception of scholars in Eastern Europe, where Endre Sik had developed a rigid Stalinist view as early as 1961.[5] Yet even this was not so surprising: growth was so fast and the general atmosphere surrounding it so compelling that not enough time had passed for second thoughts to ripen into alternative paradigms.

For most of us at the time, general growth of the field in itself was not enough: the goal was growth in Africa. The concluding statement of the

participants at the third SOAS conference in July 1961 expresses this sentiment: "This third Conference on African History and Archaeology hopes
that the centre of gravity of African historical studies will shift increasingly
to the continent of Africa itself . . . so that the best conditions will prevail
for these studies throughout Africa."[6] A decade later that goal was nearly
achieved in most of tropical Africa. In 1960 African scholars and their
expatriate colleagues at the existing departments in English-speaking West
Africa, especially at Ibadan, freed themselves from the tutelage of the
University of London and SOAS. They first reformed the curricula inherited by the British metropolitan authorities and then more slowly "Africanized" the departments. National scholars began to take over the direction of the departments of history, and later expatriates were replaced
when national scholars became available. The last step was to institute
an autonomous doctoral program of one's own. But rapid growth also
occurred outside of tropical Africa. In 1960 the first appointments in African history were also made in the United States and in France. In Eastern
Europe a few Orientalists, specializing in the "Middle East," had shifted
their focus to North and West African issues even earlier.[7] By the end of
the decade African history occupied center stage in departments of history
at African universities and had become a "normal" specialty at major
universities in Britain and North America.

Ibadan took the lead. Freed of control by London and SOAS in 1960,
Kenneth O. Dike, the leader at Ibadan, assisted by a faculty which included
the Nigerians Jacob Ajayi, Christopher C. Ifemesia, and Joseph Anene, as
well as the expatriates H. F. C. (later Abdullahi) Smith, who succeeded Dike
as head of department in 1960, and John O. Hunwick, was ready to initiate
a total revision of the history curriculum at all levels, especially for high
schools and universities.[8] Funded by the Carnegie Foundation, Ibadan, by
drawing the other West African history departments into the process,
succeeded two years later in establishing a common West African curriculum for schools.[9] It was a considerable achievement, all the more so
because this curriculum laid the foundation for a common new university
curriculum as well. Ibadan also pioneered by establishing a university
press and the first history series in it, while the faculty there took the lead
in publishing textbooks to accompany the new curricula, first for the
schools, later for the universities.[10]

The main difference between SOAS and Ibadan lay in the confident
nationalism of the latter.[11] The "West Africans" rejected any balance sheet
approach toward the colonial period in which one weighed "benefits,"
such as the creation of large and bureaucratic states or the introduction of

Christianity, against "liabilities," such as forced labor. They vehemently rejected the view that West Africa had been "pacified" by Europe, but rather stressed the harsh realities of colonial conquest. They soon tackled topics dealing with the heyday of the colonial period, a period which was still being avoided in Britain at the time. Most spectacularly, they rejected the exceptional importance given in European historiography to the colonial period. Jacob Ajayi, who emerged as the most influential Nigerian historian in the later sixties, entitled the concluding chapter in a volume devoted to colonialism in Africa "Colonialism: An Episode in African History."[12] Yet West African scholars were confident enough to strive for historical reconstructions which avoided undue glorification of the precolonial past, no doubt in reaction to the more uncritical popular writers.[13] They told the story, warts and all, rather than always placing all Africans in a flattering light. On that point their outlook was indeed similar to that of most Western academics of the time.

While these programs were being elaborated, more and more Africans were acquiring doctorates in history at universities abroad. With independence the monopoly situation of the former metropoles in this matter disappeared, and several other foreign countries, from the United States to the Soviet Union, began to offer scholarships, as they competed for influence with the former colonial powers. All these countries believed that students trained at their universities would help them to maintain or increase their influence. Hence many scholarships were made available, and West Africans enthusiastically took advantage of such opportunities. Those from former British colonies mostly went to colleges or universities in English-speaking countries, especially to SOAS, Birmingham, and campuses in the United States, while most of those from former French colonies went to Paris.[14]

This soon made the expansion and the gradual replacement of expatriates by nationals possible. With the exception of Ibadan itself, the departments were still chaired by expatriates in 1960, and most of the faculty were also expatriate. Five years later the history departments were led by nationals, and their faculty members had made African history the centerpiece of their research, sometimes with the enthusiastic help of expatriate but "naturalized" teachers such as Abdullahi Smith, Michael Crowder, or J. Bertin Webster at Ibadan.[15] By the end of the decade expatriate teaching staff had become a minority, at least at the older universities. For at the same time the number of universities and history departments in Nigeria mushroomed.[16] By the end of the decade West African scholars with doctorates in history were no longer a rarity. Despite the fact that the shortage of highly qualified cadres was so pronounced that senior historians were often called to assume high office, most of the history posts were filled, the departments had been Africanized, and Ibadan was producing its own doctoral graduates. The goals were achieved. The universities, and the departments of history within them, were now thoroughly integrated into the general life of their countries, for better and worse. While the underlying strength of this integration led to predictions that West African historians, especially the group at Ibadan, were poised to take the lead in the study of African history as a whole, it also contained the bitter seeds of future convulsions. Perhaps the first sign of these also became apparent at Ibadan: Kenneth O. Dike was forced into exile late in 1966, a victim of the civil war which then broke out in Nigeria.

Considering that independence came later to most of the countries in East Africa, the growth of African history there seems at first glance to have paralleled developments in West Africa. In this region the number of universities and, with them, departments of history tripled.[17] Here too the departments of history were faced with the need to reform the curriculum and to Africanize. They succeeded. By 1970 the departments were in the hands of nationals, the number of expatriates had diminished, and the teaching programs had been restructured. Yet these superficial analogies with West Africa are misleading. The climate was totally different. European settlers remained entrenched in Kenya and in Central Africa. They tenaciously clung to their own version of imperial history and fought every step to introduce the spirit of African history at the local universities. In addition, the direct influence of the University of London and SOAS in the region persisted. The Africanization of programs and faculty thus made only a slow headway. At Makerere the existing modest emphasis on African history was actually rolled back in 1962, to be reversed again only in 1968. At Nairobi, Bethwell A. Ogot could only begin the process of Africanization in 1965 after a power struggle in the department. From then onward Africanization in all its aspects proceeded smoothly under his direction. Among the solid achievements of the department was the publication of textbooks and of a pamphlet series for secondary and university education from 1968 onward, as well as of the proceedings of the annual conferences held by Kenyan historians and the *Kenya Historical Review*, launched in 1973.[18]

The success story in this region, however, was the history department at Dar es Salaam, founded in 1963. Its leadership was entrusted to Terence O. Ranger after he had been expelled from Salisbury for supporting the cause of Zimbabwean nationalism there. His populist leanings and his belief in an activist role for historians perfectly fitted the tenor of political life in Tanzania. A year later he had assembled a team of dynamic and dedicated scholars, including the first professional Tanzanian historians, Isaria N. Kimambo and Arnold Temu.[19] In October 1965 Ranger organized the most influential international congress of African historians ever held in East Africa, at which he proposed a new doctrine for African history.[20] Historians should study the colonial period especially, look at it from the perspective of "African initiative," and thus reconstruct what he later called "a usable past," useful for the new political regimes. Despite some opposition, his views soon exerted a strong impact on the whole field, especially in the United States, and first gave rise to the expression "Dar es Salaam school," a term which Ranger rejected.[21] Meanwhile, the department remained actively involved in research everywhere in the country and published the first basic textbooks required for high school teachers and university students, making use of the East African Publishing House in Nairobi.[22] Yet Ranger's "usable past" was already out of step with the official socialist ideology adopted by the regime in its famous declaration of 1967 at Arusha. Consequently, when Ranger left in 1969, his successors deserted his views in favor of historical materialism and founded a new and even more influential "Dar es Salaam school."

In central and southern Africa, such developments did not occur at all during the sixties. The only history department in the region had been that of Salisbury in Southern Rhodesia, which lost its most dynamic teacher, Terence Ranger, in 1963. In 1965 the settlers there declared a unilateral independence, or UDI. These actions effectively prevented the history department from providing leadership for the region. Hence the first stirrings of the process of implantation of African history began only in 1972, when J. Bertin Webster was appointed at Chancellor College, University of Malawi.[23] A year later Zambia was still looking for a suitable expatriate head for its department of history. History departments led by nationals would only take shape there and in the independent countries of southern Africa from the later seventies onward.[24] Meanwhile, the universities in South Africa were hobbled by the legislation on apartheid. In that hostile climate, even the partial recognition that history from an African point of view was a legitimate field of study developed only in the seventies.

While these developments occurred in tropical Africa, the universities in North America and Europe were going through a period of rapid expansion, as a result of a general economic boom. In addition, the launching of *Sputnik*, the first Soviet satellite, in 1957 provoked strong support for a strengthening and expansion of higher education in the United States.

But the growth of African history specialties in history departments was much stronger in the United States than in Europe. *Sputnik* had nothing to do with that. The history of Africa was especially significant for the public in the United States because it was the heritage of its large African American population, which was then involved in the civil rights movement. This and the increased political role of the country in the affairs of tropical Africa account for a seemingly insatiable demand for African history and the rapid multiplication of teaching positions in that field, as well as for the development of programs of "area studies" at the major universities.

At first, many established historians "retooled" in order to teach the odd course on African history. Then, from 1964 onward, the first doctoral graduates trained in the subject became available. Within the next eight years, so many of them graduated that the demand peaked and declined. By 1972 the "market" had collapsed. The largest block of these graduates (some forty) may have come from Madison, although a few other centers, especially Boston University, the University of California, Los Angeles, and Northwestern University, also had sizable doctoral programs. As a result, whereas two or three specialists were available in 1960, an estimated 350 historians of Africa were in place by 1970. About three hundred doctoral graduates had specifically been trained in African history by 1972. Most of those were North Americans, not Africans on scholarships.[25] Whatever the precise figures, it is evident that historians of Africa became a sizable academic community, large enough to warrant the launching of several journals, among which *African Historical Studies* became the most encompassing.[26]

The intellectual stance of most historians in the United States differed from that prevalent among the SOAS network, in a direction similar to that of Ibadan and Dar es Salaam. These scholars held strong anticolonial convictions, and at home they were repulsed by racial discrimination. Some among them were quick to join political scientists in focusing on resistance to colonial rule and the study of nationalist movements.[27] At least some of the senior historians, including Philip Curtin, John Rowe, Leonard Thompson, and myself, wanted a history of the "majority of Africans at the bottom of the political pyramid."[28] But in other important respects, the North Americans differed from the Dar school. They were more detached and repudiated the activist view that their studies had to be useful to contemporary African regimes to be acceptable. Most among them were driven by a sense of mission to debunk racism, implicitly or explicitly, stress the harm done to Africa during the era of the slave trade, and defend the equality of African cultures to those of the West. Yet they

117

also strove for "objective" scientific detachment, a position which was the accepted hallmark of professionalism at the time, even though it began to be contested.[29]

But many urban African American intellectuals disagreed. For them African history was their history, and they were as stridently nationalist as anyone in East Africa. Cheikh Anta Diop's Afrocentric view of history was beginning to be known in Harlem, and it found ardent supporters there. This current was scarcely noticed by most mainstream historians until the clash between the two views erupted at the Montreal meeting of the African Studies Association in the fall of 1968. A number of African Americans seceded to found the African Heritage Association.[30]

The expansion in Britain was more modest and slower than in tropical Africa or in North America. The department of history at SOAS gradually lost its position of authority over the African colleges after 1960, but it became stronger locally. In 1960 the school submitted proposals for an undergraduate degree in the specialty, which were accepted.[31] SOAS awarded its first doctorates in 1963. In that year John Fage organized the Centre of West African Studies at Birmingham and began to teach history there. Birmingham soon developed a collegial relationship of equals with the West African universities. Contacts between the universities in Africa and in Britain remained close, partly because a sizable number of Africans still went to Britain for their doctoral training, at least until postgraduate programs were set up in their countries. In 1964 ten African students were studying in London, and four other Africans had already obtained their doctorates there and were teaching in Nigeria, Ghana, and Uganda. In the same year Ibadan had eighteen postgraduate students.[32] Nevertheless, throughout the decade significant numbers of students still enrolled at British universities, especially at Birmingham and at SOAS. While these two institutions flourished, African history was introduced only at a few other universities such as Sussex, Edinburgh, and Aberystwyth, but significantly not at Oxford or Cambridge. These institutions remained bastions of opposition to the new specialty for a while longer.

In 1960 African history finally acquired a foothold in France, when Hubert Deschamps was appointed to a newly created chair at the Sorbonne. François Braudel, the foremost historian in France at that time, was so disappointed that Henri Brunschwig had not been chosen for the post that a year later he created a position for him at the Ecole des Hautes Etudes, which was under his control.[33] A year later Raymond Mauny joined Deschamps at the Sorbonne. But no further appointments at other universities in France followed. Moreover, few African historians were appointed at the Centre National de la Recherche Scientifique (CNRS), the famous French research institution which offered very long-term support to researchers.[34] In Paris, even more than in London or Birmingham, most of the postgraduate students were Africans who studied there for the *doctorat d'université* or the *doctorat du troisième cycle* on scholarships from development agencies.[35] But few among them could find the support necessary to continue for the *doctorat d'état*, which required many years of research.

Meanwhile, the development of the field in French-speaking Africa itself was very slow. The former French colonies were slow to establish universities, and as late as 1971 only Dakar conducted vigorous research in the history of Africa.[36] The history programs at these universities did not focus on Africa, no trained national historians were in charge of the departments, and expatriates still dominated them. Yet excellent textbooks in African history for the high school level had been developed in some countries, such as the *Histoire de l'Afrique à l'usage du Sénégal* or Joseph Ki Zerbo's *Le monde africain noir: Histoire et civilisation*, the earliest general text about African history written by a professional African historian.[37] It was typical for the times and the relative isolation of African historians in these circles that "Africa" was practically equated with West Africa. Later Ki Zerbo's own *Histoire de l'Afrique noire* was to redress the balance.[38] The curriculum for high schools remained patterned on the French model, uniform for all former colonies and centralized during most of the decade. Reformed secondary school curricula were introduced in 1963, and new university curricula in 1968.[39] As a result, the secondary school texts on world history in French-speaking Africa were more thoroughly and thoughtfully "Africanized," mostly by African historians, and they were of a higher technical quality than those developed anywhere else.[40]

The slow development of African history in France and its former colonies was due to a series of circumstances, ranging from the highly centralized structure of university education and the place which Paris as a cultural capital held in the hearts of most African intellectuals, to the prevailing conceptions about "Africa" and the proper role of the historian. In intellectual milieux, even for French intellectuals knowledgeable in African affairs, such as Jean-Paul Sartre, "Africa" was equal to "Black Africa," something radically different from "North Africa." Most African intellectuals agreed with the position expressed by Henri Brunschwig in his plea "pour une histoire de l'Afrique noire." For him the proper domain of historians was the study of written texts.[41] He held that a disparate collection of sources such as anthropological, archaeological, sociological, and ethnographic data, including oral traditions, if confirmed by written texts, helped to reconstruct history. But this situation did not justify the creation of a special discipline "ethnohistory," which he dubbed a "history written by ethnographers," because such an approach could not avoid the fatal flaw of anachronism. The task at hand was not to "deplore the lack of sources for a faraway past, but to explore the archival holdings for the precolonial [nineteenth-century] period," and in that endeavor oral traditions could illuminate the written record.[42]

Brunschwig's stance restricted the role of the historian far more than the positions adopted by his English-speaking counterparts, and it had unfortunate practical effects. By defining the craft of the historian in relation to written records, if not written records only, he in fact left the study of much of "Black Africa" to "ethnologists," including sociologists, sociocultural anthropologists, and human geographers. One might be excused in thinking that it would make little difference whether scholars labeled themselves "ethnologists" or "historians," but one would be seriously mistaken. Disciplinary training mattered. Most social scientists lacked a sense both of historical contingency and of the crucial importance of historical time. But social scientists, who feasted on regularities, large generalizations, and laws, or at least norms, and for whom concrete societies or cultures were mere "cases," dominated the impressive academic African establishment which had taken shape in Paris by 1960. As a result, historical research did not flourish, and Brunschwig's position did not help. Moreover, the internal structure of academia in France at that time was such that it was usual for one person, nicknamed the "mandarin" or the "patron," to control a whole discipline, often on a nationwide scale, because the universities were so rigidly centralized. The views of the mandarin mattered very much. For African studies that person was George Balandier, a brilliant sociologist. He launched *Cahiers d'Etudes Africaines* in 1960 as an outlet for studies about tropical Africa.[43] Balandier saw a need for historical context but thought that sociologists rather than historians were best equipped to write history from an African point of view.[44] As a result, his relationships with most historians of Africa were not good.

Given the restricted role ascribed to historians and the overall structure of the university establishment, research in the precolonial history of tropical Africa remained in the hands of "ethnologists" such as the Marxist anthropologist Claude Meillassoux, whose article on the "lineage mode of production" appeared in the first issue of Balandier's journal, and Joseph Tubiana, a human geographer, who published a document about the Sultans of Wadai in the second one. The situation changed only after the student uprising of 1968, which forced a total restructuring of the university system and, at least for a while, doomed the mandarinate. For African history in particular, change came in 1971, when Yves Person succeeded Hubert Deschamps at the Sorbonne (Paris I) and Cathérine Coquery-Vidrovitch was appointed at the new University of Paris VII.

African history failed to gain any foothold at Belgian universities during this decade, after the Congo debacle.[45] Yet at Lovanium a complete turnaround did occur, with the foundation of a proper history department in 1966. Its whole curriculum was designed from the start to focus on African history. By 1971 all its faculty were historians of Africa, and the department was embarking on a doctoral program. But that is a story for the next chapter.

Any description of the institutional buildup of the field must refer to the role of conferences. There were conferences of absorbing interest every year, either large ones, such as the one at Dar es Salaam in 1965, or small gatherings devoted to particular issues, such as the seminar on chronology held at an English manor (Farnham) in 1966. Besides their role as forums for debate and for disseminating the results of scholarship, these conferences had two major effects. They maintained morale, and they created links between scholars who had not known each other before or knew of each other but had never met. This resulted in the forging of a single network that encompassed most of the scholars in the field, wherever they worked, and maintained unity. The atmosphere at many conferences was electric, as everyone listened intently to accounts of new "discoveries" or plans for further research. One met new kindred spirits at almost every gathering, and a general atmosphere of camaraderie pervaded the conferences. Attending such a meeting gave one a sense of belonging to a "movement," of carrying out a "mission." Most scholars were convinced that the new countries of tropical Africa were headed for a glorious future, and this general atmosphere of goodwill and optimism molded the attitude of everyone in the field, even that of those among us who were not so sanguine about current developments on the continent.

The general consensus on what African history was all about, even though it remained somewhat fuzzy, owed much to the spirit of such conferences. There were no bitter debates about the nature of the field, its epistemology, or the social science views implied in its practice. The general optimistic attitudes prevalent among most students of the subject, and the urgency to reconstruct a concrete view of the past, precluded much introspection. In hindsight it is clear that most historians, like their brethren in the social sciences, were functionalists.[46] A few, such as Ivor Wilks, were followers of

Max Weber, but most historians eschewed any direct link between their reconstructions and social science theory.

This feature was strikingly shown by the discussion of "African feudalism." Feudalism in Europe had been characterized both by bonds of fealty and by the fief, a unique set of relations between servile producers and a lord of the manor. In social science theory, Max Weber stressed the bond of fealty as the "essence" of the regime, while Karl Marx emphasized "the mode of production," the fief. Anthropologists studying the kingdoms of the Great Lakes had debated in the fifties whether these kingdoms were feudal or not, mostly according to the views of Weber.[47] Jean-Jacques Maquet had claimed that Rwanda was feudal because the state rested on bonds of fealty between lord and vassal, sealed by feudal contracts.[48] In 1961 Maquet's position shifted cautiously toward an overall Marxist view of evolutionary stages in history in which the feudal regime precedes the capitalist one. He approved of the stress on the fief ("the production of material goods"), yet he still berated the theory because it neglected the bonds of fealty, and he pleaded for a reexamination of the fundamental concepts used in thinking about African "states."[49] No historian reacted to this challenge. It was left to Jack Goody, another anthropologist, to rebut Maquet's view at a SOAS seminar the very next year. His rebuttal was published in the *Journal of African History*. Goody took the opportunity to lecture historians on the study of the state: "Social anthropologists are sometimes surprised at the sort of statements historians make about the social organization of African societies."[50] While he dismissed the concept of feudalism as too Eurocentric for comparative usage, Goody also side-stepped the relevance of either Weber or Marx. It seems incredible that still no historian was goaded to intervene in the debate. After all, the study of precolonial states was often their main concern, the meaning of feudalism was much debated among scholars of European and comparative historiography, and the evolutionary Marxist thesis challenged the fundamental beliefs which they all held, barring a few Eastern Europeans.[51]

The case of feudalism was only the most extreme example of the prevailing attitude. Most historians of Africa were indifferent or hostile to Marxism: it was too pessimistic for the times. Thus the Marxist readings of African history proposed by Jean Suret-Canale or Claude Meillassoux in France, or by Endre Sik in Eastern Europe, were virtually ignored. Most historians of Africa also remained indifferent to particular social science theories. Their general consensus remained merely that there was a history of Africa, and it was to be a history written from "the" African angle, without any differentiation among "Africans."

Most historians in other specialties, especially on the European continent (including France), remained tenaciously but often silently opposed to any views with an African angle. When challenged, they merely retorted that the African angle was a matter for ethnologists, or they strictly limited the job of the historian to a study of written texts. In Britain the last stand of the waning opposition was perhaps H. R. Trevor-Roper's celebrated tirade on television in 1963. His "unrewarding gyrations of barbarous tribes in picturesque but irrelevant corners of the globe" became a favorite quotation destined to rally historians of Africa to the common cause.[52] By then the battle for academic recognition was over. Both Oliver and Fage achieved professorial rank in 1963. Both used their inaugural lectures to chart the progress made and to reassert their earlier views.[53] Oliver stressed the significance of African history for the outside world, and Fage dwelled on the African achievement and its place in the future history of Africa.

For them and for most others, the history of Africa was a story about political structures. It was a progression from ancient and humble communities to complex states by an almost magical process of "enlargement of [social] scale."[54] Thus the lion's share of attention continued to be lavished on the precolonial state as a purely African achievement and a matter of pride. The strength of the feelings involved can be gauged by the universal condemnation of a book that underlined the significant role terror had played in the maintenance of previously celebrated African states.[55] Its main example was Shaka, the "Napoleon" of the Zulu kingdom. That choice in particular grated, for at this time Shaka was universally praised as a great man who single-handedly had "enlarged the scale" of the African state in South Africa.[56] As a corollary to this emphasis, precolonial history remained at first the favorite time period, as it had before the mid-sixties, and for much the same reasons. In practice, though, many historians, perhaps most, worked on the very end of this period, the late nineteenth century, simply because many written sources were available for study. Yet most of them studiously eschewed research about the following decades, those of the colonial conquest and later. In part this reflected the fact that this phenomenon was still recent and therefore was considered to be the preserve of political scientists, in part it was a continuation of the habits of the fifties, and in part the "enlargement of scale" slogan sounded distinctly ironic in that context. Clearly there was an impasse here.

It was broken by Terence Ranger and the "school of Dar es Salaam." When I met Ranger at the Salisbury conference, he was a specialist of the early Stuarts but was beginning to feel his way into Rhodesian history.[57]

At the conference he only lit up to denounce the blatant color bar which then ruled life in Southern Rhodesia. He had begun actively to participate in protests to challenge it. From an early emphasis on the study of state and church in colonial Southern Rhodesia, his academic interest soon aligned itself with his activist convictions. Now African resistance to white rule in the country became his major concern: he began to do archival research on the *chimurenga*, the epic uprising of the inhabitants in 1896–97.[58] Eventually Ranger's prominent involvement in protests against the color bar, including a famous swim-in in a segregated pool, goaded the local government into expelling him from the country in 1963.

This was the man who was now put in charge of the new history department of Dar es Salaam in Tanzania. The tenor of political life in Tanzania at the time was totally in harmony with his populist and activist leanings. By the time he convened an international congress of African historians in East Africa in October 1965, his ideas and objectives had crystallized. The scholars invited came from many different backgrounds— West Indian, French, Eastern European, North African, as well as English-speaking—exhibiting different intellectual orientations, such as North African, Orientalist, and neo-Marxist views. This was an ideal forum in which to challenge the dominant SOAS consensus by asking "whether African History was sufficiently *African*." In his evaluation of the state of the field, Ranger went on to contend that African historians had not yet asked themselves whether the European sets of concepts, including those of time and causation, which they used to write African history were adequate. He doubted Oliver's magisterial assertion that historians of Africa in Europe and America dealt with the same issues, from the same points of view, as African historians did. Ranger felt that African history needed to focus on the lives of ordinary people rather than on those of the elites, and he particularly approved of the contemporary mainland Chinese stand on this question.[59]

The congress focused on "emerging themes," which included well-established issues such as the slave trade and colonialism but also presented some new topics, such as African religion, the history of ideas, and "the roots of nationalism." These were precisely the questions which the SOAS school had avoided, and they gave the new "school of Dar es Salaam" its distinctive "nationalist" style.[60] By 1968 Ranger had summarized his message in the catchphrases "African initiative," for the interpretation of Africa's history, and "a useful history," for an activist role for historians, that is, a role that was directly related to the contemporary concerns of the country.[61]

Three interconnected issues affected Ranger's view. First was the question of resistance. The early resistance against the colonial onslaught was labeled "primary" resistance and was linked to later movements of "secondary resistance," which in turn were to lead to the birth of nationalist political movements. The movements of the middle period were not fully nationalist, but they betrayed the famous "enlargement of scale." Ranger colored the whole sequence in a positive way by focusing on "African initiative" rather than on the colonial initiative. These views made history "usable" indeed. They provided nationalist leaders and parties with an impeccable ancestry for "nation building." At the same time they eliminated the earlier awkwardness of the "enlargement of scale" argument by recognizing the same process in the growth of resistance movements. They also made colonial history meaningful from the African point of view by invoking "African initiative." In practical terms, and especially in the United States, the study of the colonial period, with its rich documentation easily accessible to doctoral candidates, now became just as fashionable as the earlier period had once been. Once known, Ranger's views took academic public opinion by storm and became established as the dominant creed among most English-speaking African historians.[62] Nevertheless, there were reservations. Many British and West African historians felt uneasy about "historicism," the tailoring of historical interpretation to the ideology of the times. They thus objected precisely to Ranger's plea to make history "usable."

The success of Rangerism after 1967 led to a noticeable shift in the time periods and the areas most esteemed in the field. The old preponderance of precolonial history gave way to colonial history. Whereas West African historiography had hitherto been seen as a model to be emulated (no doubt because this area had an early lead), now the spotlight shifted to East and Central Africa as the locale for studies of African resistance, whose ultimate triumph made history "usable."

Still, until the last years of the sixties, "Old Africa" remained the favorite. Yet to reconstruct its history raised a nagging problem: Where was the evidence to come from, given the scarcity of written sources for so many periods and places in Africa? During the fifties, historians of Africa had claimed that a history could be reconstructed. In 1961 Raymond Mauny published the crowning work of his career, the massive *Tableau géographique de l'ouest africain au moyen âge*, which achieved that goal for West Africa. As his subtitle put it, he had done it by using *les sources écrites, la tradition et l'archéologie*. Still, issues of method were not wholly resolved with this proof. They continued to fuel debates and provide food for seminars and conferences throughout the decade.[63]

It was not even evident at first that this whole line of research was in the purview of historians. Up to then cultural anthropologists and archaeologists had been most concerned with it. Indeed, throughout the sixties the very expression "culture history" signaled that this endeavor belonged to the realm of anthropology, just as the term *ethnohistoire* signaled the same in France.[64] After all, George Peter Murdock, a senior anthropologist, had then just published a general culture history of Africa.[65] It was also an anthropologist, Daniel McCall, who in 1964 published the first book-length discussion of the main sources which could contribute evidence to the historian—with the interesting omission of written data. He devoted a chapter each to archaeology, oral tradition, language, ethnography, biological data, and art.[66]

McCall's book was well received. Surprisingly, the historians did not dispute his reduction of "history" to "process," nor were there remarks about his superficial treatment of how historical synthesis proceeds. Rather, objections focused on his proposal to entrust such research to a team effort, a team in which the role of the historian was . . . to study written sources. At the time this view was widespread. Kenneth Dike and Saburi Biobaku had based their Benin and Yoruba schemes on this division of labor. Yet most historians in Africa and in the United States rejected such views. They asserted rather that reconstructing the past was the task of historians, whatever evidence was adduced to do so and whether the evidence had been acquired by a team or not. Moreover, such reconstruction was best worked out by a single mind. Therefore, a historian of Africa would have to become an expert in several disciplines and be competent enough in all of them to use the data they provided for an overall reconstruction. This opinion prevailed among historians in the United States, especially at Northwestern University, and also partly in Zaire and in Eastern Europe, where archaeology was viewed as a special field of history. Historians of Africa were therefore called upon to become polymaths, to run a "decathlon" of disciplines, as an ironic, demurring anthropologist put it.[67]

This debate had practical consequences for both the pursuit of research and the training of historians. Those who favored teamwork set up institutes of African studies entirely separate from other departments. The earliest one was founded at the University of Ghana in 1961 with Thomas Hodgkin as director, and Dike followed suit at Ibadan in the following year.[68] But that soon aroused the ire of academic "teaching" departments, left the issue of the historian's role in reconstructing the past unresolved, and did not bring the study of other disciplines into the formal training of historians. At the other extreme, a handful of intrepid younger North American scholars, especially but not exclusively at Northwestern University, mastered another discipline along with history. This second discipline was usually cultural anthropology, as in the cases of Steven Feierman or David W. Cohen, but it could be archaeology, as in the case of Peter Schmidt, or historical linguistics (Christopher Ehret), or linguistics (Leroy Vail, at Madison). Still, such cases were exceptional, and this practice had no effect on any curriculum in history proper. Most history departments were content to make the evaluation of oral traditions part and parcel of the curriculum, and in many a general course on methodology introduced students to other kinds of evidence. At least one agreement had emerged: oral traditions at least were fully the responsibility of historians.

Thus the validity and usefulness of oral traditions continued to remain at the center of the debate. My own propositions about the application of the canons of evidence to oral tradition were well known by 1960 and 1961.[69] They were well received, although some leading historians viewed them—mistakenly, I thought—as the application of the methods of the social anthropologist to the purposes of the historian.[70] By 1960 Bethwell A. Ogot had shown that traditions from societies other than kingdoms could also be used for historical reconstruction.[71] These positions served as a baseline for further elaboration, both in the techniques of collection and in the canons for evaluation.[72] Meanwhile, oral history in general was becoming fashionable among historians other than African specialties, especially in the United States.[73]

Later work, especially in Tanzania and Uganda, however, apparently produced such discouraging results that by 1968 Ranger became convinced that the treatment of oral traditions I had proposed dealt with situations that were the exception rather than the rule.[74] That was confusing the genre and content of traditions with the method to evaluate them, and anyway he was exaggerating.[75] Nevertheless, the general climate of optimism reigning in the discipline was such that not only did the validity of oral traditions as sources for history remain unchallenged but also obvious instances of shoddy collecting of traditions or arbitrary interpretations of their content were often not criticized either. In 1970, however, Tom Beidelman, an anthropologist, laid down a radical challenge. Since traditions were told in the present, he argued, they were valueless as sources about the past. This was an extreme position, if obviously flawed, and it sounded the gong for a fresh round of debate about the question.[76]

The other major issue pertaining to the reconstruction of early African history was the question of chronology. Without chronology there can be no history. Hence, anxiety grew about the possibility of deriving valid chronologies from other than written sources, especially from oral traditions. Oral traditions recorded in the present raised particularly awkward problems of chronology, and eventually these had to be addressed head-on. Oliver devoted his seminars from 1964 to 1966 to this problem and called a working conference at Farnham in July 1966 to present the results: forty regional papers which systematically set forth the evidence for every part of tropical Africa, using mostly genealogies and king lists.[77] The inescapable conclusion of this effort was that the literature was "sadly deficient both in territorial coverage and academic quality." Still, the situation was not hopeless. One could establish valid figures for the average lengths of a dynastic generation and lengths of reign in each part of Africa. The SOAS team had done this, and its results were published. But the participants at the conference were impressed above all by the limitations of this approach. Such calculations glossed over too many idiosyncratic variables to yield solid results. The reception was sceptical enough that plans for the publication of a handbook of African chronology were shelved. In reporting on the conference, David H. Jones ended his assessment by proposing that no calendar date should ever be introduced if it was not securely related to a contemporary *written* source. A few years later David Henige was to demonstrate, on the basis of huge sets of well-documented genealogies and king lists, that while genealogical averages can be realistic, averaging lengths of reign yields wholly unreliable chronologies.[78]

What really united the practitioners of African history, beyond their adherence to the common goal of looking at history from the African point of view, was their common interest in specific concrete issues or themes. Working on the same problems created a dialogue between them, brought them together at meetings, turned them into friends or rivals. Yet at the same time most scholars were not totally involved with the study of a single topic. Every researcher pursued several interests, and everyone had a unique angle of vision about the topic under study. As a result, every scholar participated in several groups concerned with different issues. Thus historians of Africa formed a single decentralized intellectual community of interlocked groups, despite the lack of a common detailed doctrine.

The issue that was most intertwined both with "the grand picture" and with the methodological debate was certainly the question of Bantu origins. By A.D. 1500 well over a third of the continent had been settled by people who spoke closely related languages which had been labeled "Bantu." Ever since this relationship had been proved in the late nineteenth century, it had been explained by assuming that this situation resulted from a huge migration. The people who spoke the ancestral language common to all the Bantu tongues had spread from a single region to occupy a whole subcontinent, in the largest migration that had ever occurred in Africa. To elucidate the particulars of this migration and its effects was a grand challenge: there were no written sources, and only a combination of evidence from various disciplines could provide a solution. If one could solve this problem satisfactorily, no one would ever again claim that African history could not be written for lack of written sources.[79] The quest for the Bantu expansion was the perfect topic for a common pursuit by historians, archaeologists, and other scholars interested in the methodological issues involved in using such disparate sources for a historical reconstruction. It was a much better approach than any purely a priori discussion could be, precisely because it was a concrete problem requiring a concrete solution. The common pursuit of a solution has kept an interdisciplinary group of scholars in contact with each other ever since the early sixties.

The topic fascinated Roland Oliver from the mid-fifties onward, and it became a staple for discussion at the SOAS seminar. Some anthropologists, archaeologists, and linguists elsewhere were also involved. Unfortunately, though, more or less informed speculations ran rife. How could the Bantu speakers overrun a subcontinent? The answer: they had iron and the autochtones did not, or they had crops and the original inhabitants did not. Why? Was it population pressure in their homeland brought on by the dessication of the Sahara? At what time? What was the archaeological evidence for this vast migration? The response: ceramics of a certain style were. In its first issue, the *Journal of African History* carried an article on the question, and it was followed by others. In 1966 Roland Oliver, using the linguistic data which his senior colleague at SOAS, Malcolm Guthrie, had gathered for many years, published an elegant article in which he described why, how, from where, and when the Bantu migrations had occurred.[80] Initially it utterly convinced most of his fellow historians, and it spawned a series of other articles to approve or modify his hypothesis.

But the core of the evidence was linguistic. It became available for scrutiny only when Malcolm Guthrie began to publish his magnum opus.[81] In 1968, when the first volume was out and proofs of some of the others were available, the Wenner Gren Foundation sponsored a conference at Chicago to assess the state of the question of Bantu origins.[82] There Oliver presented his hypothesis, and David Dalby, a linguist from SOAS, presented Guthrie's materials. Like my colleagues, I had eagerly looked forward to this meeting and was thoroughly prepared for it. It was a cordial and cozy gathering, yet most of the participants refused to endorse Oliver's hypothesis. It turned out that Guthrie's statistical procedures were hopelessly flawed, the linguistics did not support Guthrie's proposed cradle of origin for the languages, and the archaeological evidence did not seem to support Oliver's proposed migrations either.[83] The only linguist speaking at the meeting was Dalby, who was not a specialist in Bantu languages, nor was he well versed in general historical linguistics. Even today I vividly recall the red-faced indignation of Chris Ehret, the historian-linguist, who was then a graduate student and not entitled to speak, while he was urging me to challenge some of Dalby's more outrageous statements. But I merely listened. The attempt to forge a consensus at this meeting failed. Yet Oliver's hypothesis left a crucial legacy: the recognition of the link between the introduction of farming and the expansion itself.

Another major issue was the question of the slave trade. It interested many historians of Africa, especially in the United States, and had been the subject of much writing before "African history" ever appeared. Much of this early work had been apologetic and romantic in a tragic vein and was still so in the early sixties.[84] Then in 1962 or 1963 Philip Curtin observed that the figures of slaves quoted by various authors were spurious. Authors had copied numbers from each other all the way back to some inspired guess made a century or more before. He set out to find what the archival records actually had to say, and he even learned about quantitative demographic techniques so he could handle the figures intelligently. This allowed him to calculate new figures for both exports from Africa and imports in the New World, which he argued were correct, give or take 20 percent either way. His book *The Atlantic Slave Trade: A Census* was an immediate sensation in both African and American history.[85] It provided a focus to all those who were interested in the slave trade, it set an example which turned the standards of quality in that field around, and it provoked a series of further publications, meetings, and debates which are still being pursued today. Moreover, the common pursuit of this issue has ever since united many historians of different theoretical persuasions.

The issue for African history which raised the greatest interest, because it seemed to go to the heart of the matter, remained at first the history of precolonial states. Later the interlocked issues of resistance to colonialism, religious movements, and the rise of nationalism became equally central. Because it often appeared as if the origin of states was linked to the development of long-distance trade, especially in West Africa, the focus on states generated some interest in the study of such trading patterns. This study included the successful neo-Marxist proposal that this sort of trade was a special "African" mode of production.[86] This interest in trade further led to a study of economic history in general, and that then involved historians in a debate which was then raging among anthropologists about economic theory. There were the formalist and the substantivist schools. Both held that economic distribution was crucial, but the formalists held that a single market existed for all commodities, that price was the product of supply and demand, and that economic rationality dictated all behavior. The substantivists argued that most trade in Africa had been managed, that it involved a series of different markets (e.g., goods of subsistence, social payments, exchange of people) which were not linked to each other, that prices were set by political authorities, and that social rationality had priority over economic incentive.[87] Meanwhile, some scholars, such as Polly Hill, Marion Johnson, and Anthony Hopkins, were quietly laying the broad foundations for a specialized subfield in economic history. Its first synthesis would be *An Economic History of West Africa* by Hopkins.[88]

Political scientists had been the first to argue that during the heyday of the colonial period political protest was disguised as a religious movement because its direct expression was forbidden.[89] Soon Robert Rotberg and Terence Ranger also adopted this view of religion as resistance. One of the results of this stance was the appearance of a new subfield, the history of religion.[90] Ranger was one of the first to focus on the history of religion beyond its putative function as resistance. Support from the Rockefeller Foundation allowed him to hold a conference on the topic at Dar es Salaam in 1970 and to publish a volume dealing with East and Central African religious history.[91] Nevertheless, even Ranger wanted to study religion as an expression of social aspirations rather than "for its own sake," and he avoided a discussion of what this "own sake" could be.

Naturally there existed historiographies of Christian missions and of Islam in Africa well before academic African history appeared, both biased by colonial prejudices. The new approaches were slow to affect them, especially the study of Islam.[92] Scholars remained imbued with biases such as those shown by J. Spencer Trimingham, who published a set of volumes about Islam in tropical Africa from 1959 onward. The first one dealt with West Africa. In it he noted that "Islam adapts itself well to animist peoples." It contained sentences such as: "But people are atavistically resistant to change in their psychological attitudes, and their attitudes towards nature-spirits and powers of magic may acquire renewed vitality through association or coalescence with their counterparts in Islam, hence the value of its spiritism and magical practices derived from similar elements in the religion of the pagan Arabs, whose incorporation into a universal religion naturally aids its assimilation by animists." "Negro peoples have given it their own distinctive stamp" was the way he put it, but it was clear that he meant an Islam shot through with superstition.[93] Similar sentiments were common currency at the time and represented the long-standing views of French colonial administrators.[94]

Such a condescending and dismissive attitude naturally outraged Muslims, especially in tropical Africa. The first among the new historians of Africa to react were J. Humphrey Fisher, Jamil Abun-Nasr, and Vincent Monteil.[95] Nevertheless, the stereotypes clung. In his introductory essay to the proceedings of a seminar, Ian M. Lewis demurred somewhat, yet he still used Trimingham's distorted framework in his overview of "Islam and traditional belief and ritual." Less dismissive views than Trimingham's became dominant only after 1968, when Nehemia Levtzion published his *Muslims and Chiefs in West Africa.*[96]

In addition to those topics, elites, education, and urbanization also attracted some interest. In hindsight, though, it is striking that major issues which later became the focus of intense interest attracted so little attention in the 1960s. Thus questions of class, social inequality, exploitation, peasants, gender, health and society, ecology, identity, ideology, and art were largely left unexplored, as were subfields such as biography, technology, and material culture, which would only begin to be seriously explored around 1990.[97] Even at Dar es Salaam in 1967, none of these issues were on the research agenda as yet.[98]

What was it that led historians of Africa in the sixties to choose the issues which they thought were most significant? First there is the obvious. As one commentator of this manuscript, who will remain anonymous, put it, "I don't think that any particular 'paradigm' is at fault. Rather a lot of these people had a very narrow view of history, just as historians of America or Europe did (and often still do): e.g., big political structures, famous people, events, a history of grandiose themes—in which there was no room for the majority of the human race."

Nevertheless, the influence of the general political climate at the time and of the optimistic expectations about the future of tropical Africa which historians entertained certainly also explains in large part why they chose to focus on the political realm and refused to study internal cleavages and tensions within African groups. What they produced was also what was expected of them. The attitude toward biography at the time is particularly revealing in this regard. Nationalists in tropical Africa, like all nationalists everywhere, needed a hagiography, and historians obliged: heroes were forthcoming to a degree. For instance, even in the more detached climate of Ibadan, the first issue of its popular booklets for use in schools was an anthology of the great deeds of such heroes. Despite this, only three historians of West Africa wrote book-length biographies.[99] Among them Yves Person stands out. He erected a literary monument to Samori, an empire builder in West Africa at the time of the European partition, which still is the longest single book (2377 pages, without an index) published in African history.[100] The irony in these publications was that historians of Africa generally rejected a history focused on "great men," which was so common in imperial history. They rather tended to believe in the action of masses driven by social forces. Great men were too elitist anyway. Yves Person, more than anyone else, embodied the paradox. He was both an ardent Breton nationalist and an ardent socialist, indeed a close collaborator of François Mitterand, the leader of the French Socialist party. As a nationalist he was attracted to Samori as a classical hero of resistance to imperialism, while as a socialist he saw this captain of war as the embodiment of a "Dyula revolution," the rise to power of a class of successful traders.

In addition to the influence of contemporary developments, one should not forget that these historians of the sixties were still pioneers. Especially in the earlier part of the decade, they continued to be faced by the unknown and lacked a sufficiently rich academic historiography to guide them in their research. I still can hear the scorn in the voice of one of my colleagues in American history remarking that it was easy for African historians to publish books. They did not have to cope with any earlier work on the subject! Our first task was to reconstruct an overall political framework and its chronologies and to illuminate "trends" affecting large areas of tropical Africa, not just one or another ethnic group. Any other approach remained meaningless until such an overall framework had been erected. At the time the enthusiasm among most of us was fired up more by the search for the unknown than by the wish to vicariously participate in the momentous events of the day.

One who reads the intense discussions about sources and methods in this period can be excused in thinking that a legion of researchers was busy dissecting "exotic" sources using rigorous protocols. That was far from the truth. Most historians continued to rely on archives and on library work, especially in Britain and continental Europe. Fieldwork was common only in North America and in Africa. Usually it entailed the collection of traditions relevant to the topic studied. Often foreign researchers arrived in the field without mastery of the language in which these traditions were told. Like anthropologists, they hired interpreters and "picked up" the language as they went. Most of them taped traditions and had them transcribed and translated. But there was no standard research design at all.[101] In practice, scholars took into account how long their grants would allow them to stay "in the field" and then tailored their research design accordingly. Many researchers fluttered from place to place, sipping narrative traditions here and there. They simply could not be sufficiently aware of the context in which these stories thrived. Some others simply stayed in a comfortable place and read archival materials which contained a record of traditions and questioned a few informants they found there. At the other extreme, however, a few began by residing in a single place until they felt comfortable with the basic cultural and social situation and felt trusted enough, before they even started to gather traditions. Hence the thoroughness of field research varied enormously from researcher to researcher.

Such a pioneering spirit had drawbacks. Graduate students were well aware that the faster they obtained their doctorates, the more rapid their ascent could be: the first to finish occupied the best positions in academia. Until about 1970 that was as true of North America as of tropical Africa. Moreover, in Africa a degree also gave one access to other high-ranking positions. Meanwhile, the urgency to publish for a more general public had not abated. Especially during the first half of the 1960s, the more advanced scholars were still pressured to produce provisional syntheses. The only hitch was that "provisional" often became "permanent," as happened with my own *Kingdoms of the Savanna*. As a result, all too many publications were less than thorough. The shoddiness which David H. Jones denounced in the literature about chronologies was not limited to chronology, and the snide remark of my colleague in American history was not altogether without foundation. Even with written sources, too many shortcuts were being taken. The use of very deficient translations— often from secondary compilations at that—rather than originals was common, and the authenticity of compilers was rarely examined. This had disastrous results, especially for West African history. So-called new text editions were often no more than reprints without editorial notes, graced by a hasty introduction which eschewed any serious discussion of author and original text. In the end too much research was too superficial, and too many books were too carelessly written and too hastily published. The thirst for new information had overcome a concern for high standards. In this regard the indulgent tolerance with which such inferior work was reviewed was particularly worrying, because this lack of criticism ensured the survival of such practices well beyond the sixties.

On the other side of the ledger, however, the high rate of publication produced a huge increase in the amount of knowledge available to scholars over a very short span of time, even if some of that knowledge was unreliable. Year by year vast heaps of knowledge were quarried and made available, usually in English. Year by year more flesh and bones were added to the skeleton of a history of Africa. At the same time serious research in archives and the collection of oral traditions in the field further enriched the body historical. In the end a large amount of valid data was gathered and made accessible to future researchers, in spite of the dubious quality of some information and the superficial character of most interpretations. In 1960 most of the archival data, oral traditions, and archaeological sites were still unknown. By 1970 one had a general overview of the potential of these sources, and one knew better the materials needed to reconstruct the history of the various places and times in tropical Africa.

In 1962 the only available competent overall view was Oliver and Fage's *Short History of Africa*, a book that was still sketchy in many places.[102] By mid-decade the situation had changed so much that the same scholars felt secure enough to embark on the publication of a *Cambridge History of Africa*, planned to be eight volumes long, and UNESCO began to plan its own *General History of Africa*. The *Cambridge History* was intended to be a general reference work for scholars, its models were previous Cambridge histories, and its unifying spirit was provided by its editors.

The UNESCO project was quite different. It represented a unique departure in historiography, because it was the first attempt anywhere to write a history under the direction of a large committee.[103] Its goal was far broader than that of the *Cambridge History*, for it aimed not only to produce a general reference work but also to provide a work to be adapted for use in secondary schools, and later in elementary schools, all across the continent of Africa. Moreover, this work was to be written without partisan chauvinism, so that the schools of all the countries in Africa could indeed adopt the same textbooks. That would forestall the rise of divisive nationalisms between African countries like that which had done so much harm in Europe. There the stereotypes of such texts had contributed much to keeping hatreds alive, and these hatreds had led to two world wars. That error should be avoided in Africa.[104]

135

In 1960 a small group of African and European historians were already concerned with the urgent need for the newly independent countries of Africa to replace a history of European imperial endeavors with a history of Africa and to do this without sacrificing rigorous professional standards. The next year they convinced UNESCO to coordinate the edition of a series of guides to archives.[105] Then they successfully lobbied participants at the first meeting of the International Congress of Africanists in 1962 at Accra and at the first meeting of the Organization of African Unity in 1963 to request UNESCO to undertake the writing of a full-length general history of Africa. UNESCO accepted the charge in 1964. The same scholars also convinced the agency to foresee the organization of symposiums devoted to questions in dispute and to complement its support for archives by setting up institutes to gather oral traditions. By 1967 the agency decided to set up a center for the collection of oral tradition in West Africa and a center of Arabic documentation at Timbuktu. From 1966 onward numerous preliminary conferences and consultations brought African and other historians of Africa from all over the world together and provided them with a forum to exchange views, thus overcoming the barriers imposed by language (Arabic, English, French) and ideology.[106]

The meeting which launched the project was convened in Paris in 1971. It set up a practical organization for directing and editing the work and procedures for recruiting authors and evaluating their texts, it hammered out a general plan for the substance of the eight volumes planned, and it laid down basic rules to resolve ideological differences. No argument was to be rejected, whatever its ideology, provided that it was backed up by all the known evidence and not contradicted by other evidence. The *General History of Africa* would therefore consist of chapters reflecting the most diverse approaches and ideologies. If two different interpretations clashed with each other, this was to be noted in one of several ways, depending on the scope of the issue. In the most extreme cases two parallel chapters would be devoted to conflicting interpretations.[107]

"Perfection is the enemy of the good," as the French adage has it. That also holds true for the hoard of knowledge accumulated during the sixties. The existing practices, hasty as they were, yielded a treasure house of information which became a lasting legacy for the future. But let users of that knowledge beware: not every nugget is sound gold!

7

A Restless Temperament

WHEN Claudine, Bruno, and I returned to Madison in the summer of 1964, the United States had become a different country.[1] The "nation," as the news announcers liked to call the country in times of internal stress, was in the throes of a civil rights movement, while the military buildup in Vietnam was beginning to evoke strong reactions.[2] During our first stay the Kennedy presidency had convinced students that a new, better world was about to dawn. Yet even then Vietnam was already a dark cloud on the horizon. I remember joining my colleague William Appleman Williams on a platform in the spring of 1963 to denounce intervention in Vietnam. But the audience was small and hostile to our warnings. By late 1964 the Kennedy years were already a foreign country for most. A minority, though, especially in California, but also in Madison, turned into alienated "peaceniks" or "flower children." Nearly all of the students who enrolled in African history were involved in the struggle for civil rights, and some participated in the celebrated marches.[3] Yet over the next years this concern gradually was superseded by a slowly rising mix of anger and anxiety over Vietnam. Vietnam poisoned the atmosphere for almost a decade.

Vietnam led to the radicalization of large numbers of students at many universities, especially in departments of history all over the East, Midwest, and California. By the spring of 1968 the Madison campus, like other campuses worldwide, exploded. The uproar reached a peak in 1968–69, subsiding only when the National Guard occupied the campus. Other long-repressed grievances also found expression in this atmosphere, for instance, demands for drastic reform of the curriculum, demands for the creation of "black studies," and demands to redress the gender imbalance in university appointments.[4] In March 1970 a newly formed Teaching Assistants' Association, affiliated with the AFL-CIO, went on an effective

137

strike at Madison, an action originally triggered by a dispute over the amount of tuition the teaching assistants would have to pay but which soon expressed the general hostility of the student body.[5] That successful strike demoralized the faculty of the history department more than any of the preceding events, because it constituted a repudiation by the graduate students. Hitherto most faculty members had thought of the relationship between themselves and graduate students as one of professional and apprentice. The union totally rejected this, and the strike showed that our graduate students accepted those views. Later in the summer of 1970 a building on campus was bombed. This provided a sobering shock to most students, who were avowed pacifists. The turbulence then petered out in the early fall. The creation of a department for African American studies had been authorized in late August 1970.[6]

Radicalization grew apace. The most active students adopted Marxism as an expression of their alienation.[7] But they did not know much about the doctrine, and they were not in a mood to study the works of Marx or Engels. I vividly recall the ironic picture of a small group of conspirators in the library, all students in our department, discussing how they could catch up quickly on Marxist doctrine! Meanwhile, the practical goal of the communards was to take power to shape the curriculum and to govern the department. The professors were to be reduced to "walking reference books." Ironically perhaps for Marxists, the radicals wanted a "consumer" society where the consumers, the students, decided what the intellectual menu should be, rather than have it dictated as a plat du jour by the faculty. Such an agenda met with spirited resistance. Dramatic, nay histrionic confrontations succeeded one another as the faculty of the history department tried to come to terms with the rebellious graduate students. But somehow in all the muddle teaching continued, and students were educated.

We arrived in the middle of this turbulence for an indefinite stay, albeit one, we hoped, that would merely be transitional. Still, we bought a house. I was unhappy, still yearning for "the" position that would allow me the most leeway to do research, but meanwhile I was soon immersed in Madison's programs. During my leave the year before, the African Studies Program at Madison had become operational. People whom Curtin or I had interviewed earlier were now in place. The linguist and novelist A. C. Jordan at the department of African languages and literature was soon joined by others, and I became the department's first acting chair. In the fall of 1965 the first two graduate students arrived, and in the fall of 1968 the department was turned over to one of its members.[8] Appointments had also been made in anthropology and in political science, further faculty appointments were being considered, an African bibliographer had been hired, and there were ample funds for acquisitions. I was especially pleased to find M. Crawford Young in the department of political science, because he was a specialist on the Belgian Congo.[9] Here was someone I could really talk to. Indeed, twice we organized an interdisciplinary seminar on that country.

After 1965 I became less and less involved with the direction of the African Studies Program itself.[10] The program continued to grow without letup. Throughout the sixties faculty appointments continued to be made, and financial support for graduate students was forthcoming. By 1970 the program was large and flourishing, but inevitably its size spawned bureaucracy. It then encompassed over twenty faculty members and had acquired offices, an administrative director, and even an outreach program. All this growth was due to a continued flow of funding which lasted until 1972. Fred H. Harrington had secured a large Ford grant for area studies in 1962, which supplemented the earlier Carnegie grant in comparative tropical history, which was also renewed. In 1965 federal grants under the National Defense Education Act, Title VI, became available. The Ford Foundation renewed its grant in 1967.[11]

To me research remained my proper avocation, however. From that perspective the teaching environment of a large university was somewhat trying, and I perceived it as a barrier to research. The foremost barrier was committee work![12] It comes as no surprise that the only committee work which I really enjoyed was a six-year stint on a graduate school committee for the evaluation of research projects. Yet I also liked teaching. I was fascinated by the task of preparing graduate students to conduct research on their own. And as soon as I returned, my hands were full. There still was no formal doctoral program in African history, only the Comparative Tropical History Program (now Comparative World History) in which Africa was only a special topical field, and Curtin was not keen to create one. This would be a struggle. Moreover, Phil desired to secede and set up his own department of "tropical history," a development to which most of my colleagues in the department and I were totally opposed.

In 1965 I used the occasion of an offer by Northwestern University to air my grievances to the department.[13] I also critiqued the Comparative Tropical History Program and pushed for a full-fledged African History Program.[14] As a result, such a program was created and in operation by the fall of 1965, although it still included the obligation for students to take two courses in a second "comparative area" and the students who chose this specialty were penalized. For while almost all the comparative tropical history students were on Carnegie scholarships, which were in the gift of Curtin, very few students in African history received such largesse. Not until 1968 did another opportunity arise for me to air my dissatisfaction with both the Comparative Tropical History and the African History programs.[15] The African History Program was now reorganized, the "second topical area field" was abolished, and I resigned from the Comparative Tropical History Program.[16] While I did not realize it then, this struggle to free an autonomous African History Program from a wider framework of imperial or "tropical" history in which it was enmeshed was typical, even banal, for the times.[17]

Just as the African History Program was established in the fall of 1965, the first large influx of graduate students came, two-thirds of them being Africanists in comparative tropical history and one-third in the new African History Program. There were now twenty-one graduate students, all in my care, because Phil was on leave that year. Four of my first advisees were back from the field, two were in the field, and there were ten first-year students, compared with only three the year before.[18] Such a graduate student load became the usual condition during two years out of three, because one of us was on leave every third year, while the other took charge of all the students. Hence we both followed the progress and the research work of all the students in practice, although each of us was supposedly responsible only for the students who had chosen us as major professor. The African History Program was my responsibility, while Phil supervised the Comparative Tropical History Program. I also ran the African research seminar, and Phil took the comparative tropical history seminar, at least until 1969.[19]

The division of labor was not just accidental; it reflected a basic difference in our attitudes toward African history. Phil saw Africa in a worldwide context, and I envisaged an African history for its own sake. Yet this divergence did not interfere with teaching. We both made certain that individual students never had to choose between Phil's basic stance or mine. True, I often insisted more on concrete knowledge of contents, on insights derived from social anthropology, and on the indeterminacy of history, while Curtin liked to underscore general trends, economic processes, grand intellectual conclusions, and parallels with historical processes outside of Africa, but these differences enriched the students, rather than disorienting them. Our research experience was also complementary. Phil was familiar with the large archival repositories and microfilming,

140

while I was at home with nonofficial archival collections, oral material, and tape recorders.

Thanks to the climate of the times, the availability of funding, and the scarcity of other programs in African history, many graduate students continued to apply annually. In January each year Curtin and I pored over a stack of files in search of the most promising candidates. That was somewhat of a hit-and-miss affair, because none of the indicators (grades, letters, schools of origin, written samples of work) were fully reliable, except for experience with the Peace Corps in Africa. Then we closely followed the progress of first-year students to see if they would make it. Many of them met our expectations because they were totally committed to succeeding. But then only very committed persons would apply to such a forbidding program, one that required three languages and, in effect, two minor fields. Students who did not perform well, even in the first year of study, were usually marked for a terminal M.A. or in some cases for outright dismissal. Most of the students who gained their M.A.s also made it through the doctorate, although the comprehensive preliminary examinations which ended their formal training were a genuine and feared hurdle. Indeed, the very first time these examinations were given, one of our most promising students failed and had to retake them. In June 1971 four students at once failed. Nor was the final doctoral defense a formality. One doctorate was remanded in 1968, and around the same time one candidate failed. Several times candidates barely scraped through. Our students were well aware of this. Phil's stern stance in his seminars became the stuff of folklore, still recalled when veterans of these battles meet. No wonder that so many of the survivors became dedicated and famous scholars in their own right!

Women students had a harder time of it than men. For me, women students were not unusual. Most of my siblings were women, and several had taken university degrees. Nearly all my classmates in Leuven had been women, and half of my teachers in London were women. So I saw nothing unusual in women studying, and this may be the reason that a majority of the women students wanted to work with me. But most of my colleagues held other views. According to the prevailing and uncontested opinion in the department during the sixties, as I recall it from informal conversation in the halls, women should obtain undergraduate degrees, or even on occasion M.A. degrees, but should not study any further than that. It was a waste of time to accept them in doctoral programs because most of them would abandon their studies either before or after the doctorate to marry and raise a family. Such attitudes played no role in the acceptance of graduate students, but they created discrimination in the allocation of scholarships and in the evaluation of academic potential after the M.A. One female student participated in the first African history seminar in 1961. She persevered, gained her doctorate, and pursued a professional career. Others entered the program from 1965 onward. Half of those enrolled between 1965 and 1972 left after the M.A. The other half gained doctorates, and all but one of them have pursued professional careers in African history.

The large number of students in the seminars meant that my relations with students were less personal than they had been before 1963. They also needed me less, because they now formed a sizable community which developed its own life and because they were now all younger than I was. Many among them also saw me more as a "professor" than a fellow historian. Closer relationships often developed only with those whose master's theses I directed and later with almost all of those who were engaged in doctoral research. Because of my own experiences as a student at Leuven, where professors were magisterial, not to say autocratic, I hated to be a "professor," a role which I equated with pontificating. Rather I saw my role as helping students to develop the talents with which they were already endowed.

That was quite different from Phil's style of leadership, which was both more distant and more decisive than mine. Disagreements between him and one student or another were not uncommon. He certainly disliked the proverbial "late bloomers." I found him not patient enough with those students whose potential was not obvious at once. As a result I was quite often thrown into the role of counsel for the defense. The students did not realize that behind the scenes Phil and I had bitter rows over such issues. Moreover, for my taste Phil did not follow his students closely enough when he was very busy or on leave, and he left their day-to-day supervision too much to me.[20] Given the large number of graduate students we had to supervise and the many other obligations which impinged on Phil's time, that was to be expected. Yet in the end Phil's policy of ruthless elimination, allied to our common uncompromising enforcement of the stiff requirements, joined to the availability of student funding, made the program efficient, at least as measured by the later scholarly successes of the forty who obtained their doctorates in the decade between 1964 and 1974. Most of the leaders of this generation were trained at Madison, a fact that was generally recognized by the end of the decade.[21] The tension between Phil and me was fruitful. As Phil later put it, "It has struck me many times over the years, indeed, that our association here in the training of graduate students in African History was as productive as it was because we *were* different in our attitudes and demands on them." This sentiment was recently confirmed by a reminiscing graduate student: "I received a spectacular education there—from you and Curtin mainly through the 'interaction' between you two."[22]

The program developed rapidly during this period. The three first doctorates (Comparative Tropical History–Africa) were awarded in 1966, and the numbers of students we admitted were swelling each year. In 1967 I began the practice of splitting the research seminar that now numbered up to twenty students into two concurrent seminars. That year there were seven doctoral defenses.[23] The load was becoming too heavy, especially because either Phil or I was usually on leave. By 1968 we were allowed to search for a new person. Meanwhile, the department of history itself had become much larger and more organized. The early days of informal hiring were gone. Standard procedures and interviews were now scheduled, and a prospective candidate was promenaded from office to office to talk to our senior colleagues and give a lecture for the faculty of the whole department. The first person Phil actually brought to the department was Martin Legassick, a scholar of South Africa, then living in California. The instant he arrived, we both realized that our sedate colleagues would not approve of him. From long hair and earring to flowery shirt, tight dungarees, and pointed shoes, his appearance shouted the arrival of the conventional nonconformist rebel. Here was a precursor of the student revolution on the eve of its eruption. His lecture was a fiery, populist, but still pre-Marxist denunciation of South African liberal historiography. Realizing that the department would reject this candidacy, we did not push it.

Phil then brought Steven Feierman to campus. I had known Feierman, a specialist of East African history, as a student in the seminar at Northwestern. Since then he had nearly completed a doctorate there and was planning to write up another one in anthropology for Oxford University. He arrived in an impeccable conservative outfit, accompanied by a sort of nineteenth-century romantic, faintly melancholy demeanor, as if Chopin was in our midst. The department was impressed by his academic record and loved the demeanor. He joined us in the fall of 1969 and soon began to direct the work of several graduate students who were interested in East Africa.[24] At the same time we also attempted to recruit John Ralph Willis, a noted African American specialist on Islam in West Africa. He taught for us in 1968–69 but then accepted a position at Princeton University instead.[25]

From 1972 onward the program began to run into difficulties. Funding became scarcer, and it was clear that an employment crisis loomed on the horizon. This I had foreseen as early as 1968, when Phil proposed to admit "fifteen men" per year to the program.[26] But my fears were disregarded. The result was that in 1972 we granted eight doctorates and as many in 1973. Too many historians of Africa were now chasing a dwindling number of positions. Indeed, I told the new students in the introductory session of the seminar in the fall of 1972 that the boom which had lasted for more than five years was about to end.[27] When I left for Leuven a year later, doctoral candidates were jostling each other in the field, especially in Kenya, and the job market had collapsed. Quite a few promising and trained scholars were forced to find alternative careers. The great American boom in African history was over indeed.[28]

Did our program give rise to a "Wisconsin school," as some maintain? At the time Phil and I both denied it. Our overall outlook was shared by all historians of Africa, and we studiously avoided imposing doctoral subjects on our students. Among the M.A. and Ph.D. topics chosen by our students, precolonial history, political history, and the use of oral traditions were preponderant (nineteen Ph.D.'s), as were studies in economic history and trade (six Ph.D.'s). Yet there were studies of religion (five Ph.D.'s), education (four Ph.D.'s), and urbanization (three Ph.D.'s). One dissertation each was written on cultural history, gender, settlement, methodology, and military history.[29] The most frequent subjects chosen were then favorites in the discipline as a whole, but among the others some were then quite unusual. In general our policy of letting the students choose produced a greater diversity of topics than was typical in the field. How could there then be a "Wisconsin school"? Nor did the subjects of our graduate seminars in African history mold a common school. They were the usual ones: methodology, states, trade, and "resistance." But from time to time there were also unusual ones, such as religion (fall 1965), art (fall 1968), migration (fall 1968), and "the outcome of planned development" (fall 1973).

Was there then a "Wisconsin school" in the sense of a common intellectual style, perhaps linked to the common experience of the students who were enrolled here? While the requirements of our program were different and the exposure of our students to social anthropology, comparative history, and especially language study and fieldwork left a clear imprint on their work, still most of the reminiscences of former students do not focus on this. Rather they celebrate with relish horror stories about the high standards set in the graduate seminars as regards historical methods, from getting sources and analyzing them to writing them up. These challenges seemed to them outrageous, and they recall how they girded their

loins and met them. Perhaps, then, the seminars rather than the requirements created a common attitude?[30] Just as important, however, is the fact
that all the students formed a single coherent body. The deep divergences
of outlook between Curtin and myself did not influence them in choosing
their advisers. Thus Paul Lovejoy, who spent well over twenty years working on northern Nigeria, was advised by Curtin, while David Henige, a
hard-core comparativist, worked with me. Nor did our respective specialties, regions, or periods account for student choices. Not all students
interested in economics, West Africa, or colonial history worked with Curtin, nor did all those interested in oral traditions, East Africa, South Africa,
or precolonial history work with me.

Sometime in the early seventies, the expression "Wisconsin Mafia"
appeared, designating members of that single body of students at a time
when many among them were obtaining most of the first available positions in the field. As we had started to train students earlier than others
and we had trained so many, this was only to be expected. Yet there is, on
reflection, more to the "Mafia" expression. The students of this decade,
starting with the class that entered in 1964, formed a distinctive cohort.[31]
They came motivated to the point that for them choosing African history
was affiliating with a movement rather than choosing just another specialty. To select this field in the turbulence of the sixties constituted
a commitment to the generosity of contemporary liberal values, which,
for some, shaded into greater radicalism. Once at Madison they struggled
together as they undertook an arduous curriculum that set them apart
from most other students in history. They suffered and triumphed together
through the tribulations of the advanced seminars. They looked forward
to fieldwork, rather than archival work, as their mystical ritual of initiation into the profession. They took pride in the onerous demands that were
made on them to set themselves apart from "ordinary" students, as if they
were the Green Berets of history. All of that produced an extraordinary
camaraderie which engulfed nearly all of them. The most obvious sign of
this was their initiative in setting up their own weekly brown-bag lunch to
listen to the experiences of veterans fresh from the field and to discuss
their own projects. They also began to go over every seminar session
among themselves out of our sight, and they supported each other to an
exceptional degree. Indeed, they did create a closely knit community
based on common experience during their formative years. That naturally
led to enduring friendships among them and often with one or both of us,
their teachers.

If indeed there was a common intellectual attitude which can be dubbed to be a Wisconsin school, it stems not just from an approach or a method but also from that esprit de corps. The contrast with the situation in cultural anthropology makes that clear. There the situation was "normal," and no one has claimed that there then was a Wisconsin school in cultural anthropology. Rather than proposing a unified program with clear goals, each faculty member promoted different theoretical views, so that the graduate students felt confused and uncommitted. Their approach to seminars was passive and distant. For them seminars were just another hurdle to clear. As a result of their apathy, I soon found myself tutoring a few individual graduate students rather than working with groups. It is telling that I forged a lasting relationship with only one of these students, but with many history students.

I returned to Madison in 1964 with an agenda for publication almost as full as it had been in 1960. Many of the results of the earlier fieldwork still remained to be published. My plan was to "do" first Burundi, then the Tio, later Rwandan history, and then two or three volumes from the storehouse of Kuba data, beginning with "religion." In addition, there were also "chores" to be done, articles of vulgarization or textbooks such as the *Ethnographie,* which I had promised to Benoît Verhaegen for the students at Lovanium. And then I had new insights for further research on methods.

I began with the *Ethnographie.* This book was to replace three wholly unsatisfactory earlier texts, which were marred by underlying evolutionary assumptions, overly vague generalization, the absence of any social anthropology, and a strong colonial bias.[32] My inspiration for this project derived from Ruth M. Underhill's *Red Man's America,* tempered with the experience I had of the celebrated Ethnographic Survey series set up by Daryll Forde from 1951 onward.[33] This new book would discuss the peoples of Zaire, eschewing the ethnographic present, grouped in ethnographic clusters according to flexible criteria of similarity, while greater weight was to be given to precolonial history than was common in the Ethnographic Survey. The clusters were eventually grouped in four main blocks determined by the dominant natural environments. The data were rapidly gathered by myself and by two graduate assistants.[34] Two of my former colleagues at IRSAC, Albert Doutreloux and Jan B. Cuypers, wrote one chapter each. But the task was not very challenging, and I remember it as the most tedious project I ever undertook. In the end its main revelation was to show the cultural unity of the Congo, a hitherto unrecognized fact, and one which could give considerable hope for contemporary nation builders there.[35] The book scarcely caused a ripple in the specialized literature, but it provoked a plethora of discussion among students in the country. Much later it was learned that President Mobutu used it to balance his ethnic appointments so that none of the sixteen clusters held a disproportionate number of positions. So much for my good intentions. It just goes to show that once a book exists, it takes on a life of its own.

After the completion of this chore came more pleasant work. In 1963 I had written to my parents that I thought there was a way to use ethnographic data as sources for history, a goal that so far had eluded scholars altogether. If this approach worked, it would open new vistas, for then one could write a cultural history of the continent, perhaps covering the last one thousand years or so! Hence after *Ethnographie* I spent the summer of 1965 at Tervuren gathering data about the peoples living in the Lower Kasai between the Tio and the Kuba to test these ideas.[36] The idea was to record carefully the political and commercial vocabulary given in reports about them and to use it as historical evidence. I reasoned as follows: the form of these words was linguistic, and hence their history could be examined by the tried-and-true techniques of historical linguistics. A history of the form, however, also yielded information about its meaning: the ethnographic item which it designated. Thus ethnographic data could be given historical markers. By itself this technique, called Words and Things, was not new, but it had never been systematically applied, and very few scholars at the time were interested in it.[37]

The data were gathered and confirmed the potential of the approach. Later I used these data to write two articles about the history of institutions in the area.[38] I ended the summer, though, by distilling this experience in a paper for the famous general conference on African history organized by Terence Ranger at Dar es Salaam.[39] In subsequent years I kept revising and refining this contribution but never published it again. The article itself did not attract much attention. Nor did a subsequent, even more general article about the historical foundations for comparative cultural anthropology, although this has been cited more.[40]

For some time I had been aware of strange metal bells without a clapper, fashioned out of a sheet of folded and flange-welded metal. These objects were fascinating because the method of the production was so unusual, and their shape, especially when two bells were linked together, was so unique that one could hardly believe that such objects had been invented more than once. Their distribution in Africa ought to reflect an ancient diffusion. Moreover, wherever they were found, they were used as political and military emblems. Such objects were ideally suited for historical research: archaeological finds yielded some dates, the study of style yielded hypotheses about their area of origin, Words and Things could confirm parts of the total pattern of diffusion, and the ethnographic associations were so stable that the spread of this emblem had clear implications for political history. Moreover, later archaeological research could confirm or modify an initial reconstruction. This research led to an article published in 1969 and also provoked an argument.[41] The *Journal of African History* refused to publish its second part, which presented the linguistic material. It was refused on the advice of David Dalby, who claimed that the forms were onomatopoeic and hence of no value in historical linguistics. Later I was able to show exactly how this position was mistaken, but I never published this argument nor what these terms tell us about the diffusion of the bells.

These research interests in method and technique were but minor distractions from the next major task: to write up the materials about Burundi. I worked at this first in Madison and later in Kinshasa, finished the manuscript in Belgium, and gave it to the museum in Tervuren for publication in the late summer of 1967. Writing this book was pure frustration. No one was interested in it, not even in Kinshasa or at Tervuren, not even the Rundi I met at that time in Kinshasa, who were much more preoccupied by the fall of their monarchy, a development then unfolding. Moreover, I constantly felt handicapped by the fact that I was not in Burundi and could not check up on details or verify the correct linguistic notation of texts. Since I had made up my mind that the core of the book would consist of texts and their translations, this was crucial. François M. Rodegem, the only specialist of Burundi oral art, whom I met at Tervuren, refused to check the texts. They did not appeal to him. But the main reason for my frustration was that Rundi oral traditions presented intractable problems. I concluded the work as follows: "The oral sources for the history of Burundi are a scandal, at least for the historian. They are not at all serious, and yet they are indispensable. This constitutes a genuine challenge."[42] I labeled the sources "legends" in the title to underline this situation. The book was not a reconstruction of the early history of Burundi, but merely a presentation of the sources I had gathered. To go further raised knotty questions about the validity of any interpretation of these materials, which I was not in a position to tackle because I had no access to Burundi. Moreover, I was discouraged by the general lack of interest in the questions I raised about these sources ("They were without value, were they not?") and because I was in a rush to start on the Tio book.

Trouble followed. I had met Lucien Cahen, the director of the museum in Kinshasa, in 1966, the same one who had offered me the position there three years earlier. Now he took it amiss that I did not propose to publish the Tio book at Tervuren. For him this work on Burundi was at best a second choice. Nevertheless, when I submitted it, he did accept it. Nearly three years later, early in 1970, I received a letter from him in which he summarily retracted his earlier acceptance, citing uncertainties in the tones of the Rundi transcription, shoddy typing, and the general lack of interest in such an inconclusive work. This cavalier treatment enraged me. Intensive correspondence followed, and finally it was agreed that the book would be published, but without the Rundi texts.[43] It finally appeared in 1972 and was received with indifference.[44] Yves Person, the leading historian of Africa in Paris, berated me for not being bolder and not presenting a historical reconstruction. But one person in Paris, Jean-Pierre Chrétien, then with CNRS, was interested. He was just then becoming involved with the creation of a history department at Bujumbura (as the colonial town of Usumbura was now named) and was himself studying the nineteenth-century history of Burundi as a subject for his *doctorat d'état*. Thanks to him, the book became quite useful during the next decade as a first database about precolonial Burundi, and its presentation of sources also inspired later work.[45]

The story of this book verifies the adage that bad news finds no ears. My first work on oral tradition had been well received when it was finished in 1961, and after the English and Spanish translations appeared it became well known.[46] It became the book that legitimated oral traditions.[47] The book generated mail from all over the world, as far away as Sarawak and Buenos Aires, and I was constantly asked to lecture on oral traditions. Yet I was dissatisfied with the mechanical and the cavalier way in which many gathered traditions.[48] I myself was puzzling about the proper criteria to use for a sound interpretation of "mythical" oral traditions. But I kept quiet. At first I reasoned that historians of Africa were still struggling with their imperial counterparts and that any public pillorying would merely abet the opposition. Later, as the fate of the book on Burundi shows, no one cared to listen to that kind of talk. A more critical stance about oral traditions would only find an audience after Tom Beidelman's challenge in 1970.

Meanwhile, one day in the spring of 1966—I was then in Kinshasa—I received yet another inquiry about a case involving oral tradition. This one came from a certain Alex Haley, an African American. He wrote that he was engaged in writing the history of his family. It seemed that the earliest known ancestor in one of his family lines had been an African slave who had bequeathed a couple of African words to his descendants, which Haley listed. One of these called the River Gambia to my mind. I replied to this effect and forgot about it.[49] When Claudine, Bruno, and I docked in New York on our return from Kinshasa in 1967, a steward came to tell us that someone was waiting for us on the quay. Looking over the rails, I saw a tall, distinguished-looking black gentleman. Who could this mysterious man be? And what did he want? It was Haley, who wanted to discuss his findings. Obviously, however, the hurly-burly of the wharf was not conducive to talking, and anyway, we had to rush with a mountain of luggage to catch a train. So we arranged for him to visit us in Madison.

On a crisp day in the fall, Friday, October 13, we met Haley at the airport. His main piece of luggage was a bulging briefcase. As soon as we arrived home, he began to talk and to ask questions, sometimes taping the dialogue, sometimes not. He was an excellent storyteller. He told us about his life and about the autobiography of Malcolm X. He narrated the whole outline of *Roots*, the book he was writing, at least from the landing of his ancestor onward.[50] He also told us anecdotes about his quest as he went from place to place in search of records. The funniest story was the description of his rebuff by a rural parish priest in Ireland when he was tracking down the Irish branch of the family. The priest seemed less shocked by the color of this Irishman than by the thought that Haley was about to glorify "the wrong side of the blanket."

The conversation returned to that earliest African, as we mulled over the words that had been handed down in the family and how they had been handed down. They sounded western West African all right, but the family name, Kante, bothered me. Did this American pronunciation stand for Kante, a famous clan, or Kente? At one point I checked with Phil Curtin by phone. *Kambi bolongo* as a putative "the River Gambia" did not conflict with the other remembrances. We talked until late in the night, and at breakfast the next morning I told him that his family saga in the States sounded convincing and suggested that he contact Gambians to check on the clan name of his ancestor. By then it was noon and time to drive him back to the airport. After that I heard nothing further from him. At that point I thought that he might be able to confirm the clan name and thus establish an African ancestry, even if a somewhat generalized one, given the size of such clans in West Africa. I heard no more about it, the episode faded, and I began to think that the book would never be written. I felt sorry about it, because I was well aware of the great significance which Haley's findings held for African Americans. I did not make a record of this marathon meeting, and I only vaguely remember the range of topics that we touched upon or discussed. Haley, however, taped much of the conversation and took some notes.

At that time my mind was on the Tio anyway. Barely a year after our stay at Mbe, out of the blue I received a letter from Henri Brunschwig, telling me that Pierre Savorgnan de Brazza's heirs had donated a number of trunks of his papers to the French archives. These included much about the Tio from 1878, and especially 1880 onward. Brunschwig asked me if I could contribute ethnographic notes for a set of text editions of these records. This was unexpected manna from heaven. By sheer serendipity it vindicated after the fact the choice I had made at Mbe to focus on the description of Tio life during the generation of de Brazza. Obviously I could contribute information to the texts. Equally obviously, they in turn yielded *contemporary* confirmation and elaborations of many oral assertions about Tio life at the time. Therefore, I now set to work arranging the much expanded information concerning the period.[51] Moreover, de Brazza was only one of those who visited the area and left records. During the next years I worked hard to identify and recover all the written data relating to the earliest colonial ventures around Malebo Pool, on which both Kinshasa and Brazzaville are located. This search also turned up a prize: the published notebooks of Attilio Pecile, an observant servant of de Brazza's.[52] Because of other commitments, however, the work was proceeding only very slowly, so I fled to Antwerp in 1969–70 and wrote the final monograph there.[53]

It became a large book. Its main goal still was to show that one could describe a society at a given period of the past in a way that matched the "thick description" of anthropological monographs about "the present," something which hitherto had been thought impossible. The work was structured in three parts, dealing with community, the larger society, and a temporal context for the 1880–1900 generation. Its main conclusions were that the more complex and large-scale institutions become, the more dynamic they are, the more susceptible to change, while the institutions of local communities are most stable and change mostly in reaction to the modifications that occur in a wider realm. Doing the research and writing for this book was one of the most deeply satisfying experiences in my professional life: it came out just as I wanted it to.[54] Yet although this monograph received some glowing reviews, some years later it was attacked in *Cahiers d'Etudes Africaines* as "ethnography in the imperfect tense," an assertion which provoked rejoinders.[55] My own rejoinder details some of the theoretical positions taken in the book. Yves Person, the author of the monumental *Samori*, regretted that the book was too concise. He was right. Yet I had to be concise for fear that no publisher would accept a longer work, for the very choice of English as a medium limited its audience to scholars who were not specialized in the historiography of equatorial Africa.[56] Despite the publicity of the polemic and letters of support from historians of Africa in France, the Tio book was not much used thereafter, because it dealt with a French-speaking territory. French or Congolese scholars do not read English easily, so most of them ignored it, while most anglophone historians are not interested in equatorial Africa. Moreover, by the time of the book's publication, anthropologists, except for Claudine Vidal, were tacitly abandoning the ethnographic present and their claim that only fieldwork in "the present" could yield satisfactory data. But vindication came almost fifteen years later. In 1987 Tio intellectuals contacted me with a plan to translate the book in French on their own and publish it in Brazzaville.[57]

Once the Tio work was finished, I had planned to return to the Kuba and write a book about Kuba religion and symbolism, to be followed by one on the Kuba arts. Both works would be designed to impress on outsiders the complexity of African cultures.[58] But I got caught up in the affairs of Lovanium until late 1971. Then I briefly envisioned a long monograph about precolonial Rwandan history, only to dismiss it.[59] The bitter experience with the Rundi book was still too fresh in my mind. Moreover, I was then solicited for a very different research project, the so-called Leonardo Seminar. I decided to have all the data from 1957–60 microfilmed— some six thousand pages—so that Rwandan or foreign researchers would have full access to them. Also, I would be freed from the task of publishing this material or making a study based on it while being far from the country.[60]

The Leonardo Seminar project was to be a study of how decisions are made about natural resources both in the United States and in the rest of the world. The group consisted of half a dozen persons: a nuclear physicist, a biologist, a lawyer, a political scientist, a journalist, and myself.[61] I joined them in the hope of finally getting a good grasp of the mainsprings of American society, as I planned then to leave the country "for good." We all learned a great deal from the business people, economists, political figures, and others whom we interviewed in person in Madison or by telephone, and also from each other. Soon a genuine atmosphere of collaboration sprang up within our group, and the research advanced so rapidly that by the summer we had jointly written the basic draft of the book that was to result from it. As for me, I had indeed learned a great deal about "the ethnography of a complex society," even though I realized that "the key" to "America" was still escaping me.

* * *

Although I was kept quite busy between 1965 and 1973 with teaching and research, I was still restless and felt out of place in Madison. How could I manage to find a position back in Africa and be in daily contact again with research, or back in Europe, where we belonged more than in the United States? And failing that, how could I secure more time for research? As it happened, a bewildering variety of opportunities did appear during those years. I was just back in the States when Northwestern made me another offer. Madison countered this. The University of Chicago followed suit in January 1966. By then I had made up my mind to spend perhaps two more years in the United States and then to move permanently to Lovanium, which had tendered a proposal at about the same time as the offer came from Chicago.[62] Madison met all my concerns, however, with an agreement whereby I would be on leave at an African university during one semester of each year, or for the whole of each alternate year as needed, and I was given a maximum of research assistance.[63] This was the best that could be achieved, short of leaving the United States. So when Yale put out a feeler in December 1967, I did not even properly listen to the invitation. The only point I had not foreseen in the agreement was the practical necessity of supervising large numbers of graduate students. No wonder that by 1969 I found myself teaching twice the usual load again, just to keep up.

Meanwhile, outside of the United States, there were two other possibilities of employment besides Lovanium: Leuven and ORSTOM in France. From 1964 to 1966 I angled for an appointment at ORSTOM because it meant research in Africa. Hubert Deschamps, the French historian of Africa who was one of its directors, encouraged me. But these plans foundered on the requirements of an edict by Napoleon III which restricted recruitment into all the branches of the civil service to French nationals. ORSTOM was a civil service.

After a first stay at Lovanium in 1966–67, the prospects there became very attractive. My task there would consist of training African history professors and hence my successors with all possible speed. Therefore it was but prudent to foresee what would happen to me after that. Because of my family responsibilities I could not leave it all to the luck of the draw, and the 1966 agreement with Madison foresaw just such a situation. Yet meanwhile, Jozef Desmet, my former mentor at Leuven, was still pursuing his campaign to have me return to my alma mater. According to Belgian ideas of loyalty at the time, it behooved an alumnus, when called upon to do so, to return to serve the university that had nurtured him. During these years Leuven was in the eye of a political hurricane in Belgium. This crisis over ethnicity was resolved in 1968, when the university split into a Dutch-speaking university, Leuven, and a new francophone university, Louvain-la-Neuve. This split resulted at once in a huge demand for faculty and in the opportunity for them to recruit me. For me it was easier to combine Lovanium and Leuven than Madison and Lovanium because of the structural links between them.

Moreover, this was also our chance to return to Belgium, the land of our families, although adapting to the country and its ethnic stress would not be automatic. While our families and backgrounds were Belgian, Claudine was Walloon, and I Flemish. She, moreover, was born in Rwanda and had lived there for longer than in Belgium. Bruno was born in Rwanda and raised wherever we had been. The scission of the university in Leuven led to bitter recriminations over the division of its assets; this process sometimes verged on chaos. That was the background to a tentative offer which I had received by June 1968. At first I accepted it and resigned from Madison, effective January 1969. We sold the house and prepared to move. But in the first days of September a passing visitor from Leuven painted such a scary image of the chaos there that I got cold feet. Nor was the appointment there really final. So I now requested that Madison annul my resignation, and I even bought the house back from the agents to whom it had been sold a few weeks earlier! At least for now I chose a combination of Madison and Lovanium. I returned for the second time to Lovanium in January 1971, but the spring semester there ended in disaster. President Mobutu conscripted the students into the army, closed the campus, abolished the university, and later in the summer replaced it with a new national university. I burned my bridges, resigned, and returned to Madison. As a result of this act of defiance, I was told that I could not return to Zaire anymore.[64]

Now my choices were stark: to stay in Madison or to return to Belgium. Leuven had not broken off discussions and was becoming a more definite option, but the proposed position kept changing shapes and departments as it was defined and redefined during academic power struggles about which I was kept ignorant. In the end I was offered a position in a department of anthropology to be housed in the faculty of psychology and education. I would help to set up this department, the first of its kind in Belgium. When the letter making the offer finally came, it was obvious that I would have to fight to establish a curriculum in African history, or even to develop African anthropology, because Africa was not intended to be a centerpiece of the department.[65] Nevertheless, by now I so yearned to return and was so confident that, once in Leuven, matters could be readjusted that I accepted. I was appointed, we sold the house, I resigned, effective May 1973, and we sailed away to Leuven, this time, we thought, for good.

"Chaos in the Congo" had been an almost permanent headline in the newspaper since the mutiny of the Congolese army in July 1960. One crisis followed another, and until the great rebellions of 1963–65, each one seemed worse than the previous one. Then the storm abated somewhat. Thus when General Mobutu overthrew the civilian regime in November 1965, everybody thought that this was just one more episode in a continuing saga: rebel secessionists and mercenaries were still roaming the land and had not abandoned their dreams.[66] Life in Congo-Kinshasa could be risky, as one might unexpectedly face dangerous and irrational situations. In 1964, when we were at Ngabe, on the border between Congo-Brazzaville and Congo-Kinshasa, sleeping in the annex of a shop on the Congo riverfront which constituted the border, we had once been awakened by a rabble of Congolese-Kinshasa soldiers who had crossed the river to loot the shop. But when they saw Claudine emerge like a ghost from a side door to ask the shopkeeper what was going on, they were frightened and fled. Yet despite such risks, we were so attached to the area that we kept trying to return to it. That was now possible because of Lovanium.

In the midst of the turmoil, Lovanium opened its doors each fall and graduated students each spring. Its unflappable rector, Luc Gillon, with his engineer's mind, found solutions for everything, from the production of electricity to the procurement of faculty. The place soon became a Belgian enclave tethered to its metropolis by its own airline, which carried food and supplies, books and teaching materials, building materials, and faculty back and forth as required. Meanwhile, Gillon carefully cultivated the successive leaders in Kinshasa and kept his university out of the turmoil. He was well briefed, especially by the political scientist Benoît Verhaegen, who had followed and documented the slightest twists and turns of the politicians since 1959, when he had joined the faculty. Verhaegen, a Fleming but a French speaker, belonged to the milieu of my former schoolfellows of abbatial school days and was thoroughly imbued with their sense of elitism. A historian by training, he developed "immediate history," the practice of gathering documents and witness accounts of ongoing events and publishing these. Theoretically he was then a Marxist Catholic, sympathetic to all "underdogs," whether they were unsuccessful nationalists or rebels. He soon became an idol to most students by excoriating the abuses of the regime in his lectures. Yet he remained on good terms with the regime and was an excellent source of advice for Gillon.[67]

In the first years after independence I had remained in sporadic contact with some of my former Kuba associates in Kasai but had lost sight of Lovanium until Verhaegen picked up the thread and filled me in when he met me in Brazzaville in 1964 to ask me to write the *Ethnographie*. A year later the authorities there asked me to join the university: Lovanium had finally decided to set up a curriculum in African history. Their offer was quite appealing to the whole family because it meant being back in Central Africa, where we felt most at home. I would finally help to develop a curriculum in the history of Africa and teach the subject to its "natural public." Here was an exciting opportunity to train indigenous historians, at least to the level of the proposed program of *licence*. Meanwhile, my craving for fieldwork and research could be satisfied by directing dissertations in Kinshasa, a form of research by proxy which suited my temperament. Indeed, some measure of personal research in the field would be possible, given the flexible arrangements for teaching common at Lovanium. And I knew precisely what to do: the original inhabitants of Kinshasa had been a group of Tio, and no one had studied them.

The agreement with Madison allowed me to go ahead, and so one day in October 1966, after a memorable trip by sea, the whole family arrived in Lovanium. In some ways the place was disturbingly familiar. Many of the professors we had known in the late fifties were still there and had been joined by new Belgians, all hoping one day for an appointment back home at Louvain or Leuven. On the whole they were still as ignorant of the Congolese as they had been earlier, and they had even fewer contacts in town and none with Congolese other than former students.

But there was change. Not all professors were Belgian. Others had been hired or brought in for temporary duty to the campus, and not just clergy from various Western European countries, but also civilians from Eastern European countries such as Romania, Poland, or Czechoslovakia. There were at least two Catholic Vietnamese. All of these people could be hired at low cost. There also was an annual Fulbright lecturer.[68] The faculty had thus acquired a discrete international flavor. There were even a few Congolese, evidence that Lovanium was slowly "Africanizing." Congolese held the highest administrative positions on campus, barring that of rector. Monseigneur Tharcisse Tshibangu, a theologian, was the vice rector; Albert Mpase Nselenge Mpeti, who was pursuing his doctorate in sociology, was the general secretary; and A. Pene Elungu, a philosopher, had arrived a few weeks before me and was slated to be yet another high official.[69] Among the professors there was a Congolese nuclear engineer, a well-known lawyer, and two linguists. Lovanium was realizing the kind of decolonization at a leisurely pace which had earlier been planned for the whole Belgian Congo, and the atmosphere certainly was "late colonial." Yet what would have been daring in 1959 now struck one as incongruous, if not wholly retrograde.

That was soon brought home to me when I went to the rectory to hear Mpase give a speech of welcome to the new faculty. In his diplomatic address he stressed that the Congo was not Europe and that daily life might not flow as smoothly as in Europe yet, because Congo was a developing country. He went on to explain why the task of training Congolese was a special mission, and he added that the Congolese expected their foreign professors to be guides, who would eschew personal attitudes of superiority in daily life. The innuendos in his speech puzzled me at first, but very soon they began to make sense. Most of the faculty were *coopérants*. That is, they were well paid by their national aid agencies, and their standard of living reflected it: it was much higher than it would have been back in Europe. They pampered themselves: most of their food and drink was imported by air from Europe, and much of it consisted of higher-priced luxuries. Their wives had developed a strict social hierarchy, signaled by deportment, affectations of speech, an appeal to supposedly noble origins of the "Madame la baronne!" variety, and the equivalent of tea parties. To our amazement, we discovered that the most decadent colonial mentality continued to flourish in the world of the *coopérants*.[70] The faculty shopped at a store on campus at a place called Livulu. To her surprise, Claudine soon saw how the Belgian lady at the counter would serve whites first, claim to have run out of choice cuts of meat when she served Congolese, and yet have them ready for the next white customer. A color bar in the Congo of 1966! At the same time the next shop in the row sold academic books and supplies imported and subsidized by Gillon at throwaway prices, while a little further down the hill a daily open-air market flourished, where students and Congolese staff and faculty shopped. Certainly Lovanium, in its attempt to Africanize, was a tale of two societies.

At first the teaching curriculum looked unchanged, except for political science, unaffected by the lessons of the last years. I found myself, once again, in the faculty of social sciences teaching anthropology to the future administrators who were trained there. It was all routine, only now the students were more advanced. Was that the reason that they were so distant, unlike former times? It was not: this reserve flowed from the power struggle between the student union and the authorities of the university which had broken out into the open two years earlier.[71] Thus the only two students I came to know well were the two I supervised for the *licence*, Lema Gwete from Lower Zaire, who later became director of the National Museum, and Barnabé Mulyumba wa Mamba from Kivu, who later became a professor at the National University.

It was routine—until the day I was accosted on campus by a thin, taut, abrupt but vivacious man who presented himself as Jean-Luc Vellut. He went on to tell me that the university had finally decided a year earlier to open a department of history, in which it was now accepted that African history would be the centerpiece. For that purpose they had recruited him and three other part-time Belgian faculty members: Annette Thuriaux, who had a *licence* and had studied colonial history, Canon Louis Jadin, a church historian from Wallony, who was a prolific writer and had achieved fame as the editor of many of the missionary reports concerning the former kingdom of Kongo, and Father François Bontinck, a Flemish missionary of Scheut who had been destined for China and was an expert in Chinese mission history. But the Communist victory in China intervened, and Bontinck was sent as a missionary to the Congo, where he turned to African history in the late fifties.[72] Vellut himself, scion of an internationally minded Brussels family, had arrived at Lovanium in 1964 from Australia. His knowledge of Africa was minimal, but he was acquainted with the British historians of Africa from SOAS, who encouraged him to become a historian of Africa. He soon became an expert on inland Angola and the Lunda Empire in the days of the slave trade. Yet because intellectual fashions in Paris or Brussels interested him less than those in London, he found himself rather a loner at Lovanium.[73]

No one in social sciences had bothered to tell me anything about this. This was excellent news. Now at least a serious beginning could be made with African history. In a way the proposed program for the department was typical. The Belgian university curriculum was still the template, but the place of Europe was now taken by Africa. The Catholic university had drawn on the only earlier group of historians of Africa available, church historians, and had hired Vellut to anchor the whole endeavor. This was the beginning of African history at the university colleges in British colonies from 1948 onward all over again. Given their conception of history, the elders in the department had not thought of me as a historian, but Vellut did. It was merely accidental that I happened to be there the first year that curriculum reform began.

To our mutual delight, Vellut and I soon found that we spoke the same language. We shared a vision of African history that no other faculty member then really understood, we were interested in each other's research, and we agreed on the pattern of advanced courses that would have to be created in the coming years as the *licence* in African history was developed. Lovanium was quite fortunate to have Vellut. In large measure his unwavering tenacity allied to diplomacy ensured the later success of the department.

Meanwhile, Claudine, Bruno, and I led the life of islanders at Lovanium, even though we went fairly often to Kinshasa. The mood in the city was cautiously hopeful. Most ordinary people thought that the turmoil of the past few years was over and renewed prosperity was around the corner, despite the lingering remnants of rebellions and the problems caused by European and South African mercenaries, some of whom were camped in Kinshasa. But at first we knew no one in town. Gradually that changed when our beach began to throw up visitors. Thus I saw Mikwepy Anaclet, my first Bushong assistant. He had just left the administration in Mweka to become a businessman in Kinshasa. So I caught up on all the local news and through him later met other Kuba living in Kinshasa. A former researcher at IRSAC also turned up, as did various visitors from Tervuren and one or two anthropologists passing through Kinshasa.

One day, out of the blue, I was hailed by two people from the road which ran high on the hillside above our house. Presentations were made. The visitors were Willy De Craemer and Renée Fox, both sociologists and former students of Talcott Parsons. De Craemer was a Flemish Jesuit, a quiet person who well knew that "to speak is silver, silence is gold." His specialty was the sociology of religion. He had come to the Congo in 1951 as an educator and had been posted first in Kivu and then in Lower Zaire, where many of the present intellectual elite of the republic had been students. He had carried out research on an urban African religious movement in Katanga, and he had just been involved in a study of the recent rebellion in Kwilu province. Now he headed a center for sociological research and a center of studies for social action. No scholar at this time knew the Congo and its contemporary affairs better than he did. Renée Fox, a voluble New Yorker, was one of founders of a sociology of medicine in the United States based on participant observation and fieldwork. She was studying the sociology of medical research in Belgium, which eventually led to a study of Belgian society as a whole. During this research she became intrigued by the astonishingly rapid creation of a community of Congolese physicians after 1960, and the exploration of this phenomenon became a product of her first fieldwork in the Congo in collaboration with

De Craemer.[74] They were both fascinated by the symbolic and religious roots of the then-recent Congo rebellion and had come to talk about the ethnography of Congolese religions.

They could not have chosen a subject in which I was more interested. Ever since my Kuba days I had been fascinated by the Kuba's lack of formal religious dogma allied to the fuzzy logic of their symbolism. To what extent was Kuba "religion" an artifact of Western scholars? Yet the religious movement sweeping Kuba country in the fifties certainly was "religious." The concept of religion itself left me in a quandary with which I had been struggling for years. My theoretical background up to then was primarily informed by Emile Durkheim, the standard source for anthropologists, and by historians of religion such as Mircea Eliade. As students of Talcott Parsons, Fox and De Craemer shared his approach and that of Max Weber. All of this could not be discussed at once, so we met again and again all year long. Our backgrounds clashed, but they were complementary. My sensitivity to the contingency in history made me distrust Parsons' attempts to find universal laws, while Fox and De Craemer wanted to get at the gist behind the concrete detail that historians love. They taught me much, especially how general sociological concepts do underlie much of the reasoning of historians and how sociology should be understood as a search not for laws but for concepts that help one to "understand." It was revealing to see how sensitive sociologists could open up new vistas and transform banal familiarities into intriguing phenomena begging for further exploration. In the end we resolved to write a theoretical article about Central African religion, an endeavor which helped to maintain close ties between us during the coming years.[75]

Through De Craemer I came to know several interesting Congolese. One of these was Mpase, who had been De Craemer's student and was now pursuing a doctorate in sociology dealing with the sociological underpinnings of solidarity among the inhabitants of two ethnic groups in the area of Lake Mayi Ndombe, from which he hailed. Mpase sought my help with this. And so it came about that around Easter 1967 I accompanied him to Inongo on Lake Mayi Ndombe. For several weeks I was back in the rainforests at Inongo, and in two villages inland. I spent much time in the compounds of Mpase's families, watching, helping with the chores, and asking questions.[76] One of the villages was Ngongo Mosengele, the capital of a major chief. Mpase arranged a formal session with the chief's council members, during which the chief gave us a summary of the history of his office and a list of his ancestors. But I noticed a doubtful face in the crowd and looked the man up the next day. He had a different list of chiefs, and to prove his point he produced a well-thumbed exercise book. One thing led to another, and it soon became clear that the content of all the oral performances here derived from various written accounts. Among these there was, they said, one "true" version, the record made in the twenties by a district commissioner who himself had acquired nearly mythical status. Here then was "feedback" from writings back to oral tradition on a scale I had never experienced before.

We left Kinshasa in 1967 but kept ties there. Mpase corresponded about the progress of his doctorate, and Vellut wrote irregularly with news of the department of history. Meanwhile, in 1968 the tensions at Lovanium between Congolese faculty, staff, and students, on the one hand, and foreigners, on the other, were finally spilling over into the political arena. The university was to be reformed. This episode ended when President Mobutu forced the appointment of Tshibangu as rector while Gillon was relegated to the role of technical adviser.[77] Then on June 4, 1969, the students, inspired both by student exploits elsewhere and by the teaching of Benoît Verhaegen, marched on the city to demand political reform. They were met by the army. Several protesters were killed, and thus the seeds for future confrontations were sown.

Meanwhile, the new program in history was advanced enough for the head of the department to inquire whether I could commit myself to teaching there full time.[78] This state of affairs gave me the idea that it would be good if the most promising history students to obtain the *licence* could go on straightaway to a doctoral program at Lovanium itself. A doctoral program was an exciting prospect because it would help to decolonize both African history and Lovanium, for as long as universities such as Lovanium were dependent on foreign institutions for such degrees, they were not intellectually independent. In 1970 I managed to convince Jim Coleman, who was acting for the Rockefeller Foundation, to support this initiative on the grounds that it would be much cheaper and of more lasting value than the practice of bringing the Congolese for doctoral training to the United States or elsewhere. The foundation agreed. Because the 1966 agreement with Madison made it possible for me to teach at Lovanium in alternate years, I could return to Kinshasa for eighteen months early in 1971. I had to leave Claudine and Bruno behind in Madison, however, in order not to disrupt Bruno's school year.

First came a stopover in Nigeria to meet Ebiegberi J. Alagoa and Babatunde Agiri, my former students, and to visit the universities of Lagos, Ibadan, and Ife with them.[79] Everywhere the majority of professors were Nigerian, and Ibadan, the seat of the then most influential department of history in tropical Africa, had a flourishing postgraduate program. I could see just how far Lovanium lagged behind. During this stay I also had the chance to visit the ruins of a nineteenth-century Yoruba town, now deep in a desolate bush, and the sites that yielded the world-famous naturalistic sculptures of Ife. I even toured an *oba's* (Yoruba king's) palace at Oyo, under the expert direction of a historian who later became an *oba* himself in another town. But for balance I also visited a dying cocoa plantation and the old sewage works at Lagos. The quality of the local infrastructure (especially the main road from Ife to Ibadan), the relative wealth of the middle class in Lagos, and the general dynamism of Nigerians made a deep impression.

Unfortunately I also came down with cholera, which delayed my departure. Still weak, I landed on February 17 in Kinshasa, where I was picked up by a strapping, highly efficient young man, Bogumił ("Jacek") Jewsiewicki. Jacek was a Polish historian of an adventurous disposition who had managed to be sent from the University of Lodz to the Congo a few years earlier. He claims that he was part of a deal about cabbages. He first taught a year at the high school of Mbandaka, the capital of Equator province, but was then recruited by the history department at Lovanium in the fall of 1968, when they needed more personnel to teach the *licence* level. He had abandoned Polish history for the history of Africa but had kept his convictions, which were historical materialist, although he maintains that they were and are not strictly Marxist.

The general climate of the university had changed, but not all that much. There were many more African faculty now, and Congolese were in command. Most of the older Belgian faculty had taken the opportunity provided by the split between the universities of Louvain and Leuven to join one or the other of these. Younger scholars had replaced them. The non-Belgian foreign contingent of teachers was on the whole neither more nor less important. But most Europeans at Lovanium were even more isolated than before. It was much more difficult to move around the city. Lawlessness and robberies were increasing, while soldiers and police resorted to harassment whenever possible in order to earn bribes. Standards of efficiency were declining everywhere, even at the hospitals, and even at the university hospitals.

The history department was doing splendidly. Its curriculum had become second to none. There were now eight faculty members who specialized in Africa (none were African), well over a hundred students in each of the beginning years, and the first *licence* theses then in progress promised to be exemplary. Most of the basic official published records of the colonial period and most of the journals of the period were available in the library, while Bontinck had gathered what even today probably still is the most complete private collection of publications anywhere about the late precolonial and colonial eras of the Congo. Vellut and Jewsiewicki were the leaders. They complemented each other very well. Vellut was the more cautious scholar, wary of leaping to grand conclusions from scanty evidence and never straying far from the sources.[80] It was he who had methodically built up the department and its resources. In contrast, Jewsiewicki was a fireworks display, always enthusiastic about something new, always immersed in grand philosophies of history, always ready to conjure up grand vistas which he brought to bear on concrete episodes of Africa's history. So while one was firing up the imagination of the students, the other was teaching them the rigor of the craft.

On arrival I jumped right in, teaching over three hundred students, taking over the direction of four *licence* theses in history, and advising one doctoral student.[81] The details for the final proposal to the Rockefeller Foundation were hammered out with the faculty, and the proposal was mailed off and approved by the foundation all during that semester. It foresaw the replacement of most of the faculty by Congolese Ph.D. graduates trained at Lovanium, after three years only. By the fall of 1975 the department and the doctoral program should be in the hands of the Congolese.[82] Everybody pitched in, and everything went like clockwork. Vellut, Jewsiewicki, and myself especially were in each other's hair at all hours of the day and evening. Many of my discussions with Jewsiewicki centered on the usefulness of historical materialism for a history of the Congo. We read voraciously in the records to expand our own knowledge about the colonial period, and we compared our findings, created outlines for the future doctoral program, and wrote articles. Over the Easter break I went to Paris to attend the first UNESCO conference about the *General History of Africa* and brought back information about books, ongoing research, and programs elsewhere in Africa. The winds were fair, and the sailing was swift. Suddenly the boat sank.

In early June the students had planned protest marches against the military regime of Mobutu to commemorate the martyrs of 1969 and to air grievances about their scholarships. These led to small clashes. Then somehow in the early morning of June 6, I heard that something was wrong. I went to campus and found a large crowd of staff and faculty at the edge of the campus proper, where they were held back by soldiers in battle gear. A rusty-looking machine gun in the grass on the edge of the road was trained on us to keep us from moving any further. Some soldiers were running in the yards as they pursued fleeing students, to round them up and then to disappear with them. Other soldiers were emerging from the dormitories, where they had rooted out larger numbers of students. They escorted the students away with guns held at the ready. This scene lasted the whole morning. I almost fainted in fury but, given the machine gun, was totally powerless to do anything. Bontinck, who had also arrived at the scene, noticing my anger, pulled me away and took me to his quarters to quiet me down.

Somewhat later someone came to tell us that no one outside the encircled university knew about its plight. Someone should warn the Jesuits at Kimuenza, the nearest locality away from the city. I volunteered to slip through the barricade with another person. I was given a small cross for my lapel and pretended to be an innocent Jesuit from Kimuenza who had been caught in the siege and wanted to return home. We were waved through. I told the people of Kimuenza our news and then a few hours later, at high noon, returned on my own. The problem now was to reenter the university. I did not dare slip under the barbed wire along the perimeter, for fear of being shot. So I boldly went to the main entrance and started to talk, and talk, and talk. I talked more than an hour, until the officer on duty finally let me slip in. Later that day we learned that all students had been drafted into the army and that the university was closed.

But that was just the beginning. Within days concerned and influential parents were pressuring Mobutu, while unrest flared up at night in all the townships of the capital, as rumors spread that all or at least many students had been killed. The situation became so tense that despite his martial displays on television Mobutu had to give in: he had at least to produce the students alive in public. By the second week of the crisis the public was invited to attend a large parade of the new soldiers. Afterward parents could talk to their sons and daughters to reassure themselves about their fate. When I arrived at the scene, there was bedlam. Thousands of people were running and milling around at first, and then craning in the crowds during the parade to identify students. A general rushing around of student-soldiers and their relatives trying to find each other or trying to find a soldier who might have news about so-and-so followed. One parade was not enough, so several similar parades followed. In the end all our students were accounted for except for three from the *licence*. None of their comrades or acquaintances had seen them anywhere. Had they been killed, or had they somehow escaped recognition by anyone?[83]

At first we all thought that this would pass. I was kept very busy preparing for the imminent arrival of my family, and we continued to work at the history program.[84] A lesson from the Second World War was that it is of the greatest importance to keep schools open in times of war. A few days after the first parade, my family arrived. A little later, when the situation had quieted down and it looked as if somehow Lovanium would open again in the fall, the whole history staff left the campus to spend four days in seclusion for a discussion of the proposed doctoral program.[85] A detailed program down to specific sets of M.A. topics was agreed to, Ph.D. responsibilities for various themes and periods were laid out, and graduate courses and seminars were assigned. Lists of public or private archives were compiled, and plans were made to microfilm these systematically. Moreover, Vellut, Jewsiewicki, and I discussed a plan to write three basic volumes on colonial Zaire. Jewsiewicki was to write on economic history, Vellut on political history, and I on cultural and social history. To prepare new courses was the most urgent task. Hence I spent the summer systematically going over all the available official records, newspapers, and journals to prepare a course on the most obscure period of the Belgian Congo: 1908–20.[86]

Meanwhile, the situation remained tense until the students were finally released on September 7 to take their examinations. They still remained in the army, however—for another twenty-one months—and were still housed in barracks. It then became quite clear that the three missing students had indeed vanished. I happened to know a personal friend of Mobutu's who also knew the senior officers in the army, so I asked him to find out what had happened to them. He could not discover—or would not divulge—anything. Meanwhile, the university had become a casualty in the wider struggle between state and church which had raged in the land since April. Mobutu had proclaimed a new state ideology of *authenticité* which had anti-Christian overtones, while Cardinal Malula was upholding an African Catholic ideology.[87] Lovanium had been brought under government control on June 8 and was later nationalized. Barely two months later, in August, the three universities in the country were first abolished and then merged into a single new official institution. A few weeks later the ax fell. Lovanium's faculties were to be dispersed, and most members were assigned to the former campuses of the two other universities, at Lubumbashi (formerly Elisabethville) and Kisangani. Because most of the student protesters had been enrolled in the faculties of letters and social science, these schools especially were to be removed from the capital, where their students' protest marches could destabilize the regime. They were sent to

Lubumbashi. Army planes were to carry students and faculty there by November 12–15.[88] This last decree stirred up a hornet's nest on campus. Faculty members were concerned both about the state of the facilities for teaching in Lubumbashi and about living conditions for themselves. A scouting party of deans reported back that things could be worked out, and after much hemming and hawing the professors accepted the "inevitable" and prepared to leave.

At Lubumbashi, despite all obstacles, Vellut, Jewsiewicki, and others would carry out the doctoral program. They trained a group of first-rate Zairian historians, who took over the department only a year later, than foreseen, in 1975.[89] Their task accomplished, Vellut and Jewsiewicki left in 1975, Vellut for Louvain-la-Neuve and Jewsiewicki for Canada, where he now teaches at Laval University in Quebec.

Ever since June I had been plagued by the parallel between this take-over of a university by a dictator and the Nazi takeover of the German universities after 1933. The university faculty then had given in with scarcely a whimper, and the same was occurring here. It also seemed to me that the doctoral program in history would be nearly impossible to realize, and I certainly did not feel ready to push it through "at all costs." The three missing students did not turn up, and my acquaintance could not account for them. I became convinced that they had been killed, and I wanted no part of an institution where teachers enjoyed a certain immunity to say what they pleased but where the students who trusted them were killed. That would not do. Hence a few days after the return of the other students to campus, I went to see the secretary general and declared that I would resign in protest if the three missing students did not turn up. Five weeks later I did.[90] Even though some of the university authorities were furious, they could not do anything about it: yet I knew that as long as Mobutu ruled I would not be allowed to return to Zaire, as the country was called beginning October 28, 1971.[91] Nor did I wish to return as long as Mobutu ruled. But who could foresee then that he would still be in charge today! Twenty years later two of the three students in question turned up. They had been sent to the Ekafera concentration camp deep in the rainforests. The third one has never been heard from or seen since that fateful day in June 1971.

The tragic events of 1971 were but a prologue. Over the years students protested again and again, and the regime crushed them ever more brutally. The students were the enemy, but an enemy necessary to the country. Hence the universities could not be abolished, but students could be, and they were terrorized. A climax of sorts occurred in 1990, when elite presidential troops crept onto the campus at Lubumbashi at night and murdered a score of people or more, while plundering everything in sight. As a result of this direct persecution and of the collapse of the formal economy in general, the universities have now practically ceased to exist.[92]

8

Betwixt and Between

I DIMLY recollect from an article by Jozef Desmet that the first mention of *Flandria nostra* ("Our Flanders") as an ethnonym occurs in a Latin poem vaunting the special qualities of butter in what is now West Flanders. No doubt the butter was good, yet the poem was really about the satisfaction of the familiar. It was about "home," the places and sights from childhood, where one was at ease, where people spoke one's own language, where they understood the unspoken as well as the words uttered, a place where one unquestionably belonged. Why did we return to Belgium in 1973, even though the position at Leuven was not congenial? We returned because of our outlook. During all these years both Claudine and I had seen our status in the United States as temporary: we were visitors, not immigrants. Now Bruno was about to finish high school, and this was our last chance to return. It had to be now so that Bruno could still enroll at a Belgian university. For Claudine Belgium, even Wallony, was still a foreign country in which she had spent only a few years, but her family was there and she was close to some of my sisters. I imagined that it was a return to a place where I felt at home, a society from which I had been partially estranged but into which I could reintegrate, returning to a family and a friend or two who warmly welcomed our plans. Also, I had come to detest our house in Madison. So we returned to Belgium because . . . the butter was better.[1]

The great accounting began. We threw out and sold belongings, packed the remainder, sorted out relationships, and said good-byes. Steven Feierman was upset and felt abandoned. So did one of the graduate students, who even managed to reach me by telephone when we were in transit at New York's Kennedy Airport for angry and bitter words. Soaring over Canada I read about oral traditions among the Dogrib Indians of northwestern Canada. It would come in handy for teaching. Then we were gone.

That summer was gorgeous. The woods and meadows around my parents' house had never looked more attractive. But there was no time to enjoy them. Claudine and I had to run to Leuven and find a house before our belongings arrived by sea. None of the Leuven faculty could be reached—they were all on their sacrosanct vacations—but we found an old, sound shell of a house that we could afford. We planned to install amenities such as plumbing, central heating, and appliances over the next year. Meanwhile, my aged mother found us a small apartment in Antwerp. We moved there and arranged for Bruno to attend the Antwerp International School, where he had been in 1969–70. The summer was gone. Claudine and Bruno stayed in Antwerp, and I went to the house in Leuven. At last I met the dean of the faculty of sociology and psychology. He received me for all of ten minutes and was at a loss for what to say, except that Eugeen Roosens would tell me all about the job. I felt like a cuckoo who had somehow stumbled into the wrong nest.

At last I saw Roosens. He had trained in applied sociology at the Institute for Development Studies in Leuven and never took a formal degree in anthropology. He joined the Jesuit order, which sent him to pursue research on social change among the Yaka people, southeast of Kinshasa. He wrote this up as a doctorate of development studies around 1964.[2] Clad in drab brown, he looked like a beetle. He told me much about his years of burrowing in the labyrinthine tunnels of academic politics, but little about teaching, students, or colleagues: he had the worldview of a beetle too, I thought. But this was not to deny that the position really was odd. Leuven was the only place in the world where anthropology was a subdivision of the department of psychology, itself half of a faculty of education and psychology. For Roosens, sociology and the faculty of the social sciences were deadly enemies, and he dismissed the faculty of letters and specifically the residents of the department of history as irrelevant meddlers. His, he claimed, was the only realistic vision of an anthropology program one could imagine. I had better not rock the boat for fear of upsetting what he had achieved at the cost of countless compromises.

Although I had been in Leuven for years, I had been there downstairs as a student and had no idea of life upstairs, among the professors. It did not take long to figure out that, whatever the structure on paper, the university consisted of a collection of fiefs run by powerful individuals. In our faculty the laird was the psychologist, Canon Nuttin. That much was evident at the first faculty meeting I attended. Everybody filed in, clad in dark brown or dark blue suits, white shirts, and matching subdued ties, the blue suits (education) on one side, the brown ones (psychology) on the other. The agenda was thick, but the speakers were few. Item after item was first presented by an underling, approved by Nuttin and his deputy on the education side, and then voted on, with those magnificent majorities which used to be common in totalitarian countries. When one item came up dealing with the publication of a Ph.D. dissertation, I was surprised to learn that only the major professor was allowed to decide where a dissertation could be published. As an uncouth fledgling, I raised my hand after Nuttin had spoken. There was a stunned silence, and looks of surprise were registered above all those subdued ties. After a moment of hesitation the presiding dean allowed me to speak. I merely pointed out that their position was illegal and cited the provisions of the relevant copyright law in Belgium. Nuttin oozed benevolence toward this misguided young fellow and proceeded to educate me: dissertations were really the fruit of the labors of major professors, those "who gave the best of themselves," who should therefore enjoy their rewards. That was that, and the ritual vote was called.

Apart from this situation, larger structural difficulties obstructed the possibility of setting up a solid program in anthropology. In Belgium all studies are divided into two groups: some lead to "legal degrees," and others to "scientific degrees." Any diploma that leads to entry into a recognized profession, including high school teaching—that is, recognized as a profession in the late nineteenth century—is "legal." The curricula for "legal degrees" are set by Parliament and enshrined in law. Psychology was too new to be a "legal" degree, and of course anthropology was brand-new and hence certainly "scientific"! Their curricula were not laid down by law and varied from university to university. In psychology the constraints of the marketplace and the existence of large numbers of professionals ensured that the curricula were well built. But in anthropology there were no experts. Our curriculum had in fact been cobbled together bit by bit from propositions which had been solicited by the big men of the university from various anthropologists. Thus in the early 1960s I had worked out one curriculum for a canon in the faculty of letters, and later Daniel Biebuyck wrote another one for yet another canon. But the existing curriculum now was not the product of a thorough comparison of these various proposals or of programs elsewhere, but the outcome of the negotiations between Roosens and Nuttin. Because Nuttin was not an anthropologist himself, the management of the program was totally left to the discretion of Roosens, working within the small budget that had been allotted to him. The deadly flaw of this setup was that it all hinged on the idiosyncrasies of a single person endowed with little scholarly imagination

Betwixt and Between

and without formal training in the discipline, but well versed in academic politics. Even though this was the first year of the program, my role was strictly to teach. I enjoyed that, especially a course in economic anthropology, and found some time for my own research.

Meanwhile, that first winter I camped in the chilly house where I acted as contractor. Claudine and Bruno visited every weekend. During the week I scouted around, and on Saturdays Claudine and I jointly hired workmen and suppliers, whose work I then supervised during the week. In this fashion we gradually remodeled the whole house, starting with basics such as electricity, water, heating (during the winter I lived off the heat of my neighbors which seeped through the wall), and even a kitchen, and ending with the final plastering and painting. By the summer of 1974 the house was in good shape, Bruno had finished high school, and we were all reunited. Life, we felt, was about to improve.

But it was not to be. Bruno had difficulty at the university, not so much with Dutch as a language of instruction as with the practice of learning by rote, which was still the expected norm there. My disagreements with Roosens about a decent curriculum in anthropology mounted and eventually produced a great clash. By the end of the second year, in which the students who had been there the year before had learned little that was new, things came to a head. Roosens now planned for students in the third and last year of the program simply to repeat the course they had taken during the second year. To me this was a sham which I could not countenance. The University of Leuven had established a program on the strength of which it had attracted students who could otherwise have obtained an excellent education at departments of anthropology nearby in the Netherlands, Britain, or France. They had trusted that they would be trained to a professional level. Now Roosens proposed to fudge the obligations inherent in the program and to fob the students off with a make-believe certificate. I made counterproposals; they were rejected. I alerted the academic authorities, but to little avail.

Outraged, I threatened to resign rather than to accept this situation, despite the great financial and emotional costs involved for me. True, I would not be out of work. For during this time the history department and the university administration in Madison had been pleading with me to return, at least as a visitor. When Philip Curtin resigned in April 1975, Steven Feierman urged me by telephone to return. I replied that I would consider returning to Madison, not as visitor, but "permanently," and I underlined the word.[3] I well knew that if I resigned I would have to leave Europe, where I felt at home, for good. A resignation would resonate

171

throughout the whole Belgian academic establishment in African studies. It eventually did.[4] Still, I put it to the authorities in Leuven that either Roosens' proposals would be dropped or I would leave. They did not budge, so I resigned with a bang.[5]

Yet despite "the brown beetle," the years in Leuven were enriching. Leuven was not an isolated outpost. Situated near Brussels, it lay at a geographic crossroads in Europe and halfway between Africa and the United States. It was within reach of the major capitals and centers of African studies in Western Europe, and by plane tropical Africa was not so far away either—and I could travel there without jet lag. I have never been kept as well up to date about African history and African studies as at Leuven. On September 7, 1974, I wrote to Willy De Craemer: "From Zaire I saw Mpase and briefly Bontinck, De Plaen, and Vanneste (after you passed through); from Nigeria the Alagoas, from the U.S. Curtin. We still expect Lovejoy from Toronto (on his way to Nigeria) and Agiri from Lagos before the month is out. And probably we will see Bontinck again and Vellut."[6]

Every summer my former colleagues at Lubumbashi and Kinshasa came to visit, full of news about the general conditions and about research in Zaire. During the same season colleagues from Madison, students, and former students on their way to and from Africa stopped over in Leuven. Those returning from Africa, still basking in the afterglow of their field-work, related detailed tales of successes, and those from North America kept me up to date on the Africanist goings-on there. As for Europe, during my stay in Leuven I visited and lectured at major African history programs in France, Britain, and West Germany and at an anthropology program in the Netherlands.

I even went back to New York for a single day to deliver a lecture titled "The Dynamics of Trade in Precolonial Zaire: The Role of the African Trader as Innovator." It was an innocuous enough topic, and yet suddenly it got entangled in contemporary Zairian politics. I had been talking about the traders in the great Congolese commerce of the nineteenth century and paid no particular attention to the presence of Zairian diplomats. Imagine my surprise when I learned that before the week was out Mobutu was citing this lecture on television in Kinshasa as a legitimation of his policy of "Zairization," that is, his forced nationalization of foreign businesses in Zaire, which ruined a good part of the economy of the country. How naive academics can be! I had never even dreamed of a connection.

At Leuven I had more direct relations with Africa than simply hearing travelers' reports, however valuable. There were more African students here, especially from Zaire and Rwanda, than there had been in Madison, but there were also some from other countries, such as Nigeria and Uganda. Many came or wrote to me to ask me to help them informally with their dissertations, and they told me much about their experiences in their own countries. Informally I was involved with six doctoral dissertations concerning Zaire, while formally I supervised one on Zaire and another on—surprise—Bolivia. In addition, I gained a wide range of new contacts with African and Africanist scholars as a result of my association with UNESCO.[7] This environment thus made "Africa" much closer and more a part of my daily reality than it had been in Madison. That was satisfying indeed.

When I went to Leuven I looked forward to working on the rich data housed at Tervuren and elsewhere in Belgium. I had not known how fruitful the proximity of Leuven to the centers of intellectual discourse in Europe could be. Meanwhile, teaching general anthropology also drove me to increase my familiarity with the major bodies of theory in social science. Even at the Catholic University of Leuven, Marxism was then all the rage. Although I had earlier learned some Marxist theory from Jewsiewicki at Lovanium, I now sat in on a seminar about *Das Kapital* at the Free University of Brussels.[8] Moreover, my understanding of the epistemology and methodology of history was strongly stimulated by the debates going on elsewhere, especially in Paris. I was kept abreast of these by the very well-informed Aimé Lecointre, the editor of the journal *Cultures et Développement*, who was somewhat of a maverick.[9]

As a result of these influences, I came to formulate a position on epistemology which I still believe is correct. I accepted the views of the philosopher Karl Popper, tempered by the exposition of the experimental method in the natural sciences as laid down by Claude Bernard in the late nineteenth century and by the recent work of Paul Veyne, whose insights seemed to find the right balance between old-fashioned positivists, doctrinaire Marxists, and those who seemed to deny the possibility of knowing the past, such as Michel Foucault, Jacques Derrida, and Michel de Certaux.[10] I finally wrote an article, "The Power of Systematic Doubt in Historical Enquiry," in which I set forth what I believed to be the foundations for reasoning and research in history and placed the "unusual" sources of African history in that context.[11] It may well be the single most significant piece I ever wrote. Yet its publication went by unnoticed, perhaps because it appeared in the first issue of a new journal. Whatever the reason for its obscurity, it still represents my basic attitude toward the craft of the historian today.

* * *

On August 21, 1975, we were back in Madison. To my colleagues it just looked like a return from an extended leave of absence. Yet the experience for us was totally different. We knew that we were at a major turning point in our lives. I was filled with forebodings about possible failures to adapt truly, because for the first time we were actually immigrating. We were coming with the intention that the whole family would stay permanently. The future, as we saw it now, was one in which Bruno would study and then settle in the United States, while I would teach and have further opportunities for research. Yet we promised ourselves that we would "visit" Belgium and Europe as often as possible.

Our assessment was right. In retrospect, 1975 was indeed a major turning point in our lives. From now on we were anchored to Madison. That resulted perhaps less from the move itself than from two subsequent developments. Fortune twice smiled on us. Barely a month after classes had started, I was in the office when Merrill Jensen, my now-elderly colleague who had rented his house to us when we arrived in 1960, dropped in to tell me that he was retiring. How, he asked, could he sell his house without going through a big hassle? He had barely finished speaking when I announced: "We will buy it." In all our years in Madison this was the house we had liked best, and we had always longed to find its equivalent. Now it was ours, even though we took a huge financial gamble: our house in Leuven was not yet sold, and the market was sluggish there. But the gamble paid off. The house in Leuven was sold a year later. The second development was the award of a Vilas research professorship.[12] A Vilas professor was allotted a sum of money for research annually. This allowed one to plan long-range research objectives. Moreover, the Vilas fund could be approached to fund unusual special expenses for "exploration," that is, fieldwork. The combination of the house we loved and the exceptionally good research conditions proved to be the cables which tied us to Madison ever after, despite the attractions of outside offers and the setbacks the African History Program would encounter.

After 1975 our lives became routine and highly predictable, as the round of academic years succeeded each other, even though different tasks in different places had to be reconciled with each other. Time had to be allotted betwixt teaching and research, and between being in Madison and being away. The continuity of teaching was punctuated from time to time by travels, at first every third academic year and in the eighties no more than a semester at a time, because of the requirements of the history program. In spite of this diminishing allotment of time for research, my conviction that research gave a full meaning to life had not diminished: I still saw the scholar as an explorer on the edge of the known universe. But I had matured. As late as 1983 I still stressed research: "I want to do research, whenever I can and to help promote research."[13] This statement, however, was written in a letter which explained why I had to stay in Madison to train students: the operative words had become "to promote research," that is, to train the scholars of tomorrow.

If the thrill of discovery was the reward of research, the thrill of teaching was to watch budding talents unfold themselves during their own explorations. Earlier this had been true as well, but then students had been almost coevals and our relationships had been marked by camaraderie: we were all in this together. Now the difference in age was more marked, the relationship had become more distant, perhaps more nurturing on my side, more demanding on the student side. Whatever the reason, teaching, and especially the training of graduate students, became an ever more absorbing task. Hence a realistic tale of my activities during the decade after 1975 should chronicle this betwixt and between—the almost daily intertwining of teaching and my own research—but that would be utterly confusing. The two strands are therefore presented as follows: first a story about my own research, then one about the African History Program, and later a return to my personal research.

As the reader has long since noticed, my pattern of research had always been to work on a major, substantive project and to study other issues as accompaniments on the side. In 1976 the major reexamination of Kuba history was drawing to a close. The book went to press and was published in 1978. At the same time the writing of a textbook in African history, which I had launched in 1966 and which had been a major collaborative effort with others, was finished by 1977.[14] An account of the writing of this book is too long to be told here. Both the editor and the collaborators changed over the years, yet the text reflects a common basic view of the field held by the original authors of 1967. This was not "state and trade," but the "ordinary person." Now the time had come to launch a new major project. Within months after the Vilas appointment in early 1977, I submitted a proposal for a research project in eastern Cameroon, which was approved.

But Cameroon was not to be. For on a sunny July 1 a former student of the department, Muhammad Jerary, came to visit us. Jerary was an easy person to remember. A Libyan from the Sahara, he had come to Madison to study ancient history. In order to do so, he had mastered both Greek and Latin in less than three years. At that time I had been an active member of his doctoral committee because his dissertation dealt with Libyan nomads in late Byzantine times, hence with "Africa." Now I saw him again, and he had a proposal. He had successfully convinced his head of state, Mu'ammar Gadhafi, to let him launch a center for historical research. This was eventually to cover all phases of Libyan history, but right now Gadhafi viewed it as an institute to celebrate the study of Libyan resistance to the Italian conquest (1911–32). Knowing about my previous experience at IRSAC, Jerary wanted me to come to Tripoli to help him to set up the institute and, in particular, to create a permanent program of oral history which would lie at its heart. To me this was a dream come true. Here was the chance to build the ideal center for oral research, because Libya's oil wealth removed the usual financial constraints on such an endeavor. Claudine was also thrilled. As a child she had once been in Cairo, and North Africa appealed to her. The main drawback was that I knew no Arabic at all. Even though Jerary thought that knowledge of Arabic was not necessary to this project, I thought that it was. Nevertheless, I accepted the challenge, and we proposed to be in Libya by January 1.

The very next week I began to study. That fall I used every spare minute to cram Arabic. While waiting near a garage as the car was being repaired, I was intoning Arabic verb tenses, and in the bathtub I was figuring out rules to remember irregular plurals of nouns. As luck had it, the language was taught that year by a visiting Egyptian philosopher, Gabr Asfour, assisted by one of my own students. Asfour mistook the teaching program for the whole year to be the program for one semester. This meant that, with additional coaching right up to my departure time, I was taught almost all of the grammar, I acquired a small basic vocabulary, and I began to have a feel for the language. Meanwhile, Claudine was also learning Arabic on her own by correspondence.

After a journey enlivened by a snowstorm in Chicago and a nearly missed rendezvous at Heathrow, we took our place in the queue of travelers that slowly wound its way to the immigration window in the peaceful, still warm early evening at the airport in the desert. Once at the window, my rudimentary Arabic barely sufficed to explain to a suspicious and apparently puritanical officer that the lady with me was indeed my wife, not a mistress, and we were allowed in. Then followed the bedlam of a small terminal overflowing with passengers, porters, and officials. Jerary found us and took charge, not a moment too soon. We were waved through customs by officials who did not even look at our heavy suitcases. Only later was I to learn that nearly all the books and teaching materials they contained were in fact prohibited imports!

Libya, a large desert country inhabited by two million people or so in 1978, was much talked about in those days. It had been the archetype of a poor underdeveloped country until oil was discovered there. Then on September 1, 1969, a Colonel Gadhafi toppled the monarchy which been established there after the Second World War. He set up a totalitarian regime based on populism and strident pan-Arabism. To the Western world Gadhafi was a black sheep. He had led the Organization of Petroleum Exporting Countries in its successful drive to impose a massive rise in the price of oil in 1973, and he did it again in 1978. This made the country wealthy, so wealthy that Libya in 1978 could be called a rentier state. The Western powers also accused him of financing and encouraging terrorists all over the world. Within the country, however, many people in 1978 admired Gadhafi, mainly for having raised the standard of living of everyone and for having made huge investments in an infrastructure which were transforming the country. He had provided the whole population with adequate housing, health services, good schools, and employment, and in doing so he sedentarized what had been, at least until 1945, an overwhelmingly nomadic population. Now nomads were the exception, and even camels were rare.

Tripoli itself was in a sense a typical Mediterranean city—lemon trees, laurel bushes, and all—but it was also an Arab city on the edge of the desert. It was a city of traders, and its shops and markets struck us as something out of the *Thousand and One Nights*. The range of products from all over the world (not just from Western Europe or North America) overwhelmed the senses, and the jewelry shops in the covered market streets took one's breath away. All that glittered here was indeed gold! Most foreigners were other North Africans or West Africans in menial jobs, but there were a few places where Eastern European military advisers and Western European or North American technicians lived.

Jerary's center was then housed in a villa at Hay Andalus, a suburb of Tripoli, right on the shore of the Mediterranean. It was still embryonic, consisting of the director, Jerary, a librarian, and an administrator, each with one or two supporting staff. The first week or so we lodged in a hotel downtown, busy with buying the furniture and utensils necessary to convert a small whitewashed empty servant's room on the roof terrace of the center into living quarters. It was an enchanted place far from the bustle of the floors below, with a view on the ever-changing sea and a low spit of land that arched into it—a small room with a huge open space next to it or a living room in open air! Living there immersed us totally in a Libyan way of life, and we had practically no contact with Europeans or North Americans. In a sense we were participant observers. We learned proper behavior in and out of the office, adjusted to the different daily rhythms of life, and were taught to look for the appropriate nuances of time and place which gave specific meaning to vague general utterances. For this was a culture where the mode of communication was often allusive, so allusive indeed that from time to time honest misunderstandings occurred even between Libyans working in the same office. It certainly was a fascinating learning experience.

That was the setting. The main task was first to find, then to train intensively a number of candidate researchers in oral research, initiating them in the general methodology as well as preparing them for the specific work ahead. The project was to be oral research about Libya's military resistance to Italian colonialism between 1911 and 1932. For this period there were no public archives at all in the country. There had been a small project organized by a national writers' union to collect reminiscences from veterans from the colonial wars, but it was rather desultory, more interested in *couleur locale* than in history. A similar small project in Libya's main eastern city, Benghazi, was not much more significant. We had to start from scratch, having only the major Italian accounts of the war supplemented by some published reports of British intelligence. It was also clear that a well-organized large-scale project had the potential to alter received knowledge about the period radically.

Jerary was able to obtain leave from the Ministry of Education to recruit seventeen high school teachers, all men, for the program. We ordered and obtained the necessary tape recorders and cameras, and I was teaching two weeks or so after my arrival. Although the students did not know much English, I taught mostly in English, with passages in Arabic. Sometimes the students and I were stuck, and we had to look up a particular word or expression. So the pace was slow. But it was steady, well over eight hours a day. Much of it was practical work, starting with the basics of how to operate a tape recorder and camera and moving to the practice of interviewing people without a questionnaire but with a well-memorized guide of topics to elucidate. By the end of February the students had learned to elicit reminiscences without questionnaires and yet to cover all the points of the guide, to make good-quality tape recordings, to make standardized abstracts of their tapes, to transcribe these well and within a given time, and to keep the requisite diary in a uniform way.[15] They had all practiced with informants in or around town until they were efficient, and all had learned how to evaluate the particular talents and blind spots of each interviewee.

At that stage Jerary placed announcements in the papers and on the radio to explain the project to the general public, negotiated with the ministry to obtain a permanent transfer for fourteen of the students to his center, and also obtained import licenses for a fleet of cars and jeeps and for a stock of five thousand cassettes. Meanwhile, I set up a formal research design. The country was divided into fourteen areas according to historical and geographic discreteness, but also according to our estimate of how long it would take a researcher to find and interview all the veterans in the area assigned to him. The topics to be researched included questions about recruitment, training, actual battles, army (also on the Italian side) and guerilla life, intelligence, logistics (weapons, ammunition, food, and other supplies), medical services, treatment of information about casualties, morale issues, religious issues, propaganda, including the reception of various calls to *jihad*, or "holy war," issued by Istanbul and by local leaders, population flight and reception in neighboring countries, concentration camps, famines, women's participation in the war and war effort, and the impact of the war on children and the fight for control over their education.

The students had internalized the relevant issues for all of these topics. Moreover, they had learned to dissociate questions about the informant from the interview proper so as to avoid the impression of being tax collectors or bureaucrats. But they did record identities, data on literacy, geographic mobility, and prior experience with interviewers (especially for the radio services) from questions interspersed throughout the meeting. Everyone was to be seen twice, so that the follow-up and more directed second interview could fill in gaps. Given the widespread use of tape recorders in Libya, it was also decided to give every informant a copy of his or her own testimony to keep.[16]

The first task of each researcher in his area was to locate all veterans. Every researcher had to keep careful track of who exactly informed him about which persons were veterans (to avoid being subtly guided by local authorities into interviewing only selected veterans). Later this device was found to be quite useful. It helped us to show that indeed our youngest researcher was being manipulated in this way. In another case it appeared that all the villages strung out along a very long wadi were divided into two hostile sets, with villages of one faction alternating with those of the other. The researcher was only given information by people in the set in which he had started. Once the problem was clear, an entry into the rival set was found, and interviews were completed there as well. The researchers also had to interview a valid sample of women. That, we knew, was going to be a major problem, because in Libyan society communication between men and women who were not close kin was severely restricted. Some researchers found ways around this particular difficulty, and we did collect very interesting reminiscences by women. Yet in the end we did not obtain a statistically valid sample. Most researchers were motivated mainly by genuine intellectual curiosity, although another motive was the lure of travel to remote parts of the desert, and all hoped that the data from their regions would allow them to gain at least an M.A. at the University of Tripoli.

There was a slight delay in this program during March, caused mainly by difficulties of finding transport. But soon the researchers were all in the field. About a month later they were called back for a three-day seminar to evaluate the results, check the tapes, abstracts, diaries, and journals they were keeping, and in general to make certain that we were obtaining comparable data on the research topics from nearly the whole of the country. The researchers also exchanged experiences and learned about the progress of the whole project. Thus as early as April we all learned that our researchers regularly stumbled on informants who had some papers which they did not want to surrender to any archive. We could easily borrow the documents to photocopy or even bring the people to the center to copy the documents and ask questions about them there. Once we recognized this possibility, we easily devised proper procedures to cope with such a situation.

At the second seminar, held in June, it became clear that some informa-tion was redundant, while big gaps remained in other areas. From now on researchers could soft-pedal some topics to emphasize others. By then we had also begun to experiment with photographs. The center had set up a photographic laboratory which reproduced and enlarged photographs from Turkish and later Italian newspapers of the period. The memory of many veterans was triggered by viewing these. This feature was later systematically used, by bringing the informant to the center whenever the researcher thought it appropriate. Today I am still amazed that the system worked so well from the beginning and that it needed so little procedural revision later on.

Meanwhile, from March onward I began with the next phase of the operation: to recruit and train a second crew to fully transcribe the tapes in Arabic. These were people without much formal training. To begin with, everyone at the center was invited for a friendly competition: to see who could transcribe one hour of tape well in the shortest possible time. Thus we established that the average time needed was around seven hours. I could then foresee how many workers would be needed to transcribe and file the number of interviews generated by the researchers and how often the latter should transmit their tapes. New personnel were then trained as transcribers as well as indexers, along with two "quality inspectors." Machinery was also needed. With the help of a Japanese engineer from Sony, we set up a laboratory for dubbing tapes, five copies at a time. The master tape and a spare, for use by library patrons, were cataloged and stored, one tape went back to the person interviewed, and two served as working copies for transcribing and indexing.

By July all of this was operating. The next task was to create a general integrated index in collaboration with the head of the library of the center. This was to be a cross-index to tapes, written documents, and photographs. Work on this was begun during the summer, but I never saw the result. At the same time I began to train one of our researchers, Mabruk, to replace me. Jerary and I had carefully followed all of the researchers and had agreed that Mabruk was the best prepared to take over from me. I began to involve him in every facet of the operation and the decision making. Together, for instance, we decided to pick out the eighty most promising informants for more in-depth interviews. Up to that time each person had been interviewed on average about one hour and a half. We foresaw that by September 1 the general survey would be finished. Then the eighty chosen persons would be interviewed, each for a full life history, for about forty hours per person. I also foresaw that the focus of the overall research projects pursued by the center should be altered every six months, starting in January 1979, and worked out with Mabruk why this should be so and how to choose new topics. A new project, say, on the history of land tenure or on social history in the late Turkish period would become the focus of activity for the six months to follow. By the end of Ramadan in the first week of August, the job was done.

It had all worked well. Abundant, detailed, and often totally unexpected information on all aspects and all periods of these complex wars, except for the practical operation of Turkish, British, and Italian intelligence services, was flowing in. But what was to be done with all this information? Jerary and I agreed that the center would not sponsor any official history. The sources were a history by the people that should be for the people.[17] Anyone interested should be encouraged and free to consult the material and interpret it, each according to his or her own historical consciousness. Still, the center would encourage specialists to consult its holdings.

By the time of our departure the center itself had grown far beyond its limited beginnings. Its library, its burgeoning archive (much of its material on microfilm), and its photo laboratory were all expanding. Researchers were beginning to consult our holdings, and Jerary could project an official opening to the general public for later that fall. Anyone could come in and ask for information and would be directed (via the cross-index) to the relevant materials. I did not see the completion of that operation, however, and so I do not know how well this worked. I only heard later that many ordinary people really stop by to use the facilities in search of information about family or local history. From then until now the center has continued with its oral history projects. The value of these records is now fully recognized, even in Italy. In 1990 the center began the publication of the first out of over a hundred projected volumes of testimony relating to Libya from late Turkish times through the colonial period. By most criteria the project has been a resounding success. To me the one that matters most is the length of time that elapsed between recording the testimony and giving the public access to it. By this measure this oral history center seems to be the most efficient in the world. Of course, this result could only be obtained with the unstinting financial support the center has enjoyed over the years. Nevertheless, the results are still mainly due to the dedication of the researchers and staff. I still am proud of having been the first architect of this endeavor.

Our time in Libya provided Claudine and me with a host of happy memories. Perched on our roof, we surveyed each day's work, every day we swam out to the coral reefs, and we enjoyed the sea. We were happy tourists on Fridays and holidays, first in Tripoli itself. Later, as the occasion presented itself, we visited Roman sites further away, even though we were not allowed to drive ourselves or to visit sites inland: Libya, after all, was a country which kept a close watch on every move made by everyone. Still, we remember sandstorms, mirages, wells on farms so deep that one no longer heard any "plock" when a pebble hit the water far below where it had been stored ever since it fell as rainwater around 3000 B.C. or so, and many other happenings. Perhaps the funniest event occurred when a researcher living near the Tunisian border invited me for dinner (without Claudine, because of the strict segregation of the sexes in all Libyan households). One of his "informants" would fetch me. At the appointed hour came a distinguished and portly gentleman with a Mercedes. During the long drive, mostly on a superhighway, he regaled me with stories about his visit to Minnesota and other places! He had circled the globe twice, once completely and once "almost." It turned out that he had been a minister in one of the previous governments. He, like other Libyans, loved to travel. (Chauffeurs would nonchalantly tell us that they were off for their fortnight of vacation in Paris or in Bulgaria.) Here was a man only more recently successful than some others among the veterans we interviewed. Later in the evening I was thinking how different such "informants" were from those in Central African villages when my reverie was interrupted. Said someone proudly: "Is this not just like Paris?" I looked around the sitting room, where an all-male company reposed like ancient Romans on cushions and mats, all sipping tea and watching television. The only thing female we saw that evening was a pair of arms passing food through a hole in the wall. Yet I understood what he meant. I answered, "Maybe it is."

There were great contrasts between the African History Program in Madison before and after my return in 1975. Before 1972 the program was expanding; after 1975 it almost collapsed at first and then held steady. Before 1972 it was mainly a graduate program; by 1985 it had become mainly an undergraduate program. Earlier a comparative approach dominated; later social science theories, especially Marxism, held sway. The cohesion and parallel interests of the graduate student cohort of 1965–73 had been exceptional. Later the community of students became qualitatively different, and the interests of individual students diverged more from each other. The relative unity of theoretical points of view among the staff before the departure of Philip Curtin was later replaced by some disagreement. Yet the continuities in the program were scarcely less obvious. The size of the staff remained the same. Despite innovation in the curriculum, the role of language training and fieldwork remained as central as ever, while the links between social or cultural anthropology and history were stressed even more than before and the seminars continued in the old style. As a result, a graduate of Wisconsin of the early eighties was still similar to one of the early seventies and easily distinguished from graduates of other institutions.

Nevertheless, I returned to a program which "felt" very different in 1975 from the one I had left, despite the fact that I had only been away for two years and had kept in touch with faculty and students. The most obvious contrast with Leuven was my own role in the setup: I was now the senior person and as such was expected to bear overall responsibility for the program even though I was not a chairman. I called meetings to admit students and to set the curriculum for the coming year, or meetings to write and evaluate preliminary examinations. It was my lot to find positions for freshly minted doctoral graduates, to keep track of financial aid for students, to monitor our relations with the African Studies Program, and to defend the interests of both the program and my junior colleagues within the department.

The smooth operation of the program depended very much on good relations between its three staff members, William Brown, Steven Feierman, and myself. Until 1980 all went well, and the usual minor disagreements over this or that point were easily settled by give and take. All three of us taught graduate and undergraduate students, and as "major professor" each of us took special responsibility for those students who wanted to work with us. Later the situation changed in such a way that I became much more responsible for following the regular progress of all the graduate students. As a result, I could no longer leave Madison for more than roughly one semester at a time. Moreover, financial support for the students continued to deteriorate, and that required increasing efforts on my part to find what remedies I could.

The major intellectual innovation in the program following 1975 was the growing importance given to the formal teaching of social science theory. Historians in the United States had discovered grand sociological theories and the statistical methodologies of the social sciences and believed that these would make the discipline more accurate and more scientific. With each passing year more and more historians became enamored by the application of various social science methodologies to their research.[18] The enthusiasm for theory was especially great among historians of Latin America, Africa, and Asia who espoused "radical" points of view and were beguiled by various versions of Marxism or dependency theory.[19] Soon the graduate students enrolled in programs affiliated with the "Third World" caucus, the African History Program among them, were required to take a new course, History and Theory, in which most teachers expounded a mixture of Marxism and dependency theory.[20]

Steven Feierman had always been fascinated by grand theories in social science and was an ardent promotor of this new course. When he taught it, first he focused on the relevance to African history of symbolic, cognitive, and structural anthropology, while later he focused more on Marxist theories. I stood betwixt and between theory and practice. Certainly the use of concepts drawn from the social sciences by historians could be very fruitful when relevant to the question at hand. But the formal exposition of grand theories was an error, because most students in history were not sophisticated enough to realize how reductionist and antihistorical many of these theories were.[21] Hence I tended to introduce and apply concepts drawn from the social sciences during discussions of concrete historical situations. The effects of our joint endeavor were well caught by a graduate student who commented in 1976 that the students learned "theory" with Mr. Feierman and then applied it during my history lectures.

Before 1975 the program had been mostly concerned to teach graduate students: undergraduate enrollments in the introductory courses stood steady at sixty to seventy.[22] New enrollments in the program had reached their peak in 1972, when twelve new students entered the program, and most students were well funded. But over the next two years this inflow dropped abruptly to four each year and then stabilized until 1981, when it dropped again by half and then remained steady at an average of two newcomers a year. At the same time new academic positions for historians of Africa also collapsed, while funding for graduate students shrank even faster than enrollments did. Undergraduate enrollments dropped after 1972 but only by about a third. They gradually began to recover from 1975 onward. Since then they kept growing. By 1980 they exceeded the levels of 1972, and by 1985 demand had become so great that we had to limit enrollment in all African history courses. This situation impelled us to invest more and more of our efforts in undergraduate teaching.[23] Our graduate program now became justified in the public eye by undergraduate demand, although for us its raison d'être still remained the training of graduate students.

Despite the drop in numbers of applicants, the quality of graduate students remained excellent, as measured by their continued success both in national competitions for grants to do fieldwork and in finding employment in spite of a more and more competitive situation. The reduction in their numbers after 1972 was accompanied, however, by a shift in the social composition of the graduate student community. Starting in 1977 the proportion of women rose to rival that of men, while that of African American students also rose slightly. The proportion of Africans remained fairly constant. This feature, as much as the drop in absolute numbers, accounts for the appearance of new patterns of internal coherence, new interests, and new concerns in the graduate student community.

Indeed, after an overlap with students of the "Wisconsin Mafia" during the mid-1970s, a new distinctive cohort appeared in 1977. This community was both smaller and looser than the previous one. It revolved around a tiny but tightly knit core group of coevals surrounded by a relatively larger number of loners. The core group set the tone. Its members believed, often uncritically, in the power of neo-Marxist theories to "explain" history and to be a guide toward a better future in Africa. They asked questions about gender, labor relations, peasantry, the social impact on health issues, and race discrimination. Given the fact that both Feierman and I were also anthropologists, it was no accident that the aspirations of most students gradually focused more and more on "social history," that is, a kind of diachronic social anthropology about the social groups they were studying. Many students of the core group carefully kept their distance from me. They seemed to believe that I was too demanding. I do not really know why this situation developed. My insistence on applying theory critically to concrete evidence, my age, the fact that I had been in Africa during the colonial period, my status as a foreigner still—all may have played a role, according to snippets I picked up here and there. Yet I enjoyed the confidence of others. As for me, I missed the ebullient intellectual daredevil attitude of the students in earlier times. Many students now were far too serious, far too passive, and far too career-oriented for my taste.

Around 1983 a new cohort took over. The internal cohesion of the community as a whole, now half the size of what it had been before 1981, increased. There were almost no loners, because every year the one or two newcomers forged bonds with senior students. The new community was thus much less linked to a particular group entering in any given year. Therefore it has lasted longer than its predecessors: indeed it is only beginning to wane now. Intellectually this group shared the concrete interests of their predecessors, but they were much more critical about underlying grand theories as "truth," while their search for meaning in history shifted to an understanding of mindsets *(mentalités)* and away from an explanation of abstract "social forces" such as capital or class. The obduracy of the concrete began to fascinate them. They rejected elegant but superficial demonstrations of the "all other things being equal" variety. The students in this cohort drew closer to me than their predecessors, I guess in part because their interests tallied more with mine but in part because the gap in our ages had now grown to a comfortable generation or more. They could relate to me as a person of their parents' generation to whom they could turn for advice. Whatever the reasons, the result was that I came to know them much better as persons. Their numbers now were so small that I could closely follow their progress and tutor them individually as needed. Given such close relations, I do perhaps overrate their potential as scholars. Yet some among them carried out superlative fieldwork as a consequence of their fascination with the concrete and the contingent, and their dissertations do stand out for the rigor and the originality of their discourse and contributions. I don't believe, therefore, that "all the greats" were among our earliest students.[24]

Do teachers become bored as they teach the same subject year after year? This is a question one may well ask. The answer differs from person to person. I did not for several reasons. First, I enjoyed slipping in accounts of new discoveries in the survey courses every year, and every time I taught them I tended to rework them. Thanks to my work with the UNESCO project, some information and insights taught in the general courses on African history were years ahead of publication. The students had no inkling that on some points they were now ahead of most of the professors in the field, but I savored the irony of the situation. To teach the general courses remained a pleasure, as I more and more relished the fresh, untutored enthusiasm brought to the subject by undergraduate students, who were not jaded and who encountered "Africa" for the first time. And how could one be bored when one taught a new course or seminar topic almost every year? The secret fun in the seventies was to discuss aspects of history such as religion, art, or the evolution of concrete complex cultures and societies which did not fit easily in the prevailing materialist theories of history. Later, however, several of these courses had to drop into oblivion because their number had grown to the point that I had to stick to those which were most needed.

Moreover, I always have had a particular inclination toward certain topics. Thus at first I adored teaching the methodologies of African, or general, history, and the one time I taught History and Theory, methodology was the core of the course. I liked to take the students on a mental sight-seeing trip and let them discover the traces of the past in language, the traps set by archaeology, the lures of ethnography. I enjoyed seeing them sleuthing to decipher the origin myth of the Japanese emperors, to cope with Winnebago ethnography or history in Wisconsin, to discover the dynamics of borrowing between the ancient Germans and classical Rome or the archaeological traces of the Christian conversion movement in early Great Britain. Moreover, I was no longer teaching anthropology, and this was the place where one could show how history and anthropology interacted. That course taught students how to deal with evidence and hence was at the core of the program. Yet it was not required, and I abandoned it after the spring semester of 1979. The last time I taught it was in 1982 as a seminar in "ethnohistory" for graduate students at the University of Pennsylvania. Still, even today I think of it as perhaps the most mature course I ever taught.

But the course had to give way. It was being crowded out by African History and Art. For many years we had attempted to hire a historian of African art. Then, while in Tripoli, I resolved to develop a course in this area myself and to teach it in the department of art history in order to demonstrate that there was a genuine student demand for this field. Anyway, it was a nice thing for me to do because it was a means to honor my late father: he had been an excellent art historian. From my youth onward I had learned a good deal about the methods of art history in general, and I knew that history was sorely slighted in African art studies, while African historians seemed to have no idea how often art objects were relevant sources for topics they were studying. Moreover, it was also a subject in which Claudine was quite interested. As soon as I was back in Madison I started building up a slide collection for it. The department of art history allowed me to teach this course as an "overload," and history cross-listed it. It was offered for the first time in the fall of 1979. Not without stage fright did I clamber onto the podium of a large, well-appointed theater filled with students and most of the faculty of the art history department and prepare to cope with the controls of two slide projectors as I spoke. It all went well, and the course eventually attracted a hundred or so students each time it was offered. The subject also attracted the attention of a publisher, and I agreed to write a book on the topic.

So in the spring of 1982 I accepted an offer to teach at the University of Pennsylvania, in order to have a relatively quiet time for writing the book while Claudine drew its many illustrations. The work appeared in 1984.[25] To the uninitiated it was just another textbook. To the informed it contained a general critique of the way studies in African art history were being conducted. Most reviewers were polite, I received some enthusiastic letters of support from well-known authorities in the field (especially from museum curators), and several younger art historians accepted my positions. But the book also generated further involvement. Ever since, I have been solicited to give advice about exhibitions or to write for their catalogs. Yet this course was crowded out in 1985, this time to make way for a demanding administrative commitment: the direction of the African Studies Program. By then the direct goal of the course was achieved. The demand for African art history eventually led the art history department to appoint a distinguished scholar of African art, who is now fully developing the subject.

But teaching in Madison lacked one feature: there were too few African students. Meanwhile in Paris, there were many students from equatorial Africa but no specialist to take care of them. By 1983 my colleague there, Jean Devisse, convinced me to teach in Paris as a visitor. And so I did in the fall of 1985. The general course was not very lively. The classroom was as old as the Sorbonne building itself, and the organization of teaching was as magisterial and distant as it had been in my youth: no discussion sections, no series of tests, no required reading, and no regular audiovisual presentations. But the Centre de Recherches Africaines in Paris was different. Here there was intensive interaction between faculty and graduate students, all squeezed into cramped quarters, and here there were up-to-date seminar rooms and long discussions. A score or so of Gabonese and Congolese students needed some help with their dissertations, and I spent most of my days discussing their topics with them, going over their notes, evaluating their results, and generally trading stories about the past and the present in the region. But I could only spare a few months before resuming the direction of African studies in Madison. Still, we were now in contact. During the following years and until recently, we corresponded about the doctorates, and whenever I could go, I was in Paris to confer with the students and to sit on their dissertation juries. They have been a breath of fresh air for me, a renewal with the concrete realities of life in equatorial Africa, affecting both the milieux to which these students belong and the rural or urban people they studied. Besides, it was exhilarating to see the new evidence they were uncovering. It was almost like conducting research myself by proxy between Paris and Madison. From then onward teaching became even more fulfilling than I could ever have hoped.

The story of the African art book shows just how intertwined teaching and research can become. In some ways that case was unusual. In general I kept my own major research projects well out of teaching, especially graduate teaching, for I had always believed that graduate students are young scholars who have to find their own way. The role of the teacher is to encourage them to do so, not to foist some pet project on them, as so often happens. Still, several of the side issues which accompanied the major projects I was interested in had an impact on teaching, and none more so than the general "state of the art" publications for which a new demand always seemed to crop up as soon as I had written one. But on the whole my research odyssey diverged considerably from my task as a teacher, and hence it became a respite from being a "professor."

The main task at Leuven and later (until 1976) had been the writing of the revised Kuba history. In order to concentrate on this question, I had finally dropped all thought of publishing a large annotated set of traditions from Rwanda, and I also pushed aside, for the time being (in fact forever), further work on religious history in colonial Zaire. The Kuba project, I felt, was more urgent. I now clearly saw that in my previous book on Kuba history I had merely rendered the historical consciousness of the Bushong elite and other Kuba about their own past, without evaluating this view. How could such an evaluation be done? What valid outside materials could be used? In the sixties I had realized that to trace the history of words was to trace the history of their meanings and that the vocabulary of a language encompassed "ethnography." One can trace the history of the *form* of a word by the tried-and-true comparative method: one could establish what was a loan and what was ancestral. Thus the English word *king* is ancestral western Germanic, while *monarch* is a loan word.

As I was applying this to Bushong, I found that there was more to it. One could also show how certain terms were innovations, either newly minted forms, such as *word processor,* or old forms acquiring new meanings, such as *computer,* which once designated a person who calculates and is now used to designate a particular machine. These are internal innovations in the language, innovations that occur only because a novel situation has arisen which requires new vocabulary. Such traces of internal innovation are absolutely crucial for the historian, because they allow one to break out of the old straitjacket of documenting only outside influence (loan) or an unchanging heritage (ancestral form). Because much, perhaps most, historical change is not imposed from the outside but is internal to a society, the realization that Words and Things could also trace such changes was significant. The application of the method did allow me to develop a view of the Kuba past which differed from conscious Kuba oral traditions and yet still was testimony "in their own words." But it was testimony of which they were not conscious or, as historians put it, testimony despite themselves. The book nevertheless still opened with an exposé of Kuba historical consciousness before turning to my reconstruction, on the basis of "additional evidence," much of which was based on the Words and Things technique.

The Children of Woot was well received.[26] But once again the language in which it was written cut off its most interested audience: few Kuba could read English. Still, as in the Tio case, many years later there was a Bushong reaction and a predictable one. Bushong historians accepted the exposition of Kuba historical consciousness as developed in the traditions, published in earlier work and summarized in *The Children of Woot,* while they rejected the critique of this vision and the historical reconstruction based on other data.[27]

By 1977 my main research project was finished, and I was free to start another one. I had prepared for fieldwork in Cameroon, and in 1976 I had further developed the plan to write a collective history of colonial Zaire. Jean-Luc Vellut agreed to write a volume on social history, Bogumił Jewsiewicki would write one on economic history, and I would write one on intellectual and cultural history.[28] At first this and the Cameroonian project were delayed by the Libyan interlude. Then they were pushed aside by another project. One Tripolitanian afternoon in our white-washed room by the sea, I was musing about major research projects: at forty-eight, I was really becoming too old for fieldwork and roughing it in unhealthy places, so perhaps Cameroon might not be a good idea. Would it not be better for Zairian historians to write their own history than for us expatriates to do it?

I mused about this and that until it suddenly flashed through my mind that I should try to write a history of all the peoples in the rainforests. It had been said that this huge area was "ahistorical": one would never be able to know anything about its early history.[29] That was a genuine challenge. Maybe it could not be done, but maybe it could be by using the possibilities inherent in Words and Things. I might try to provide an overall reconstruction of the past of this vast area. As it stood, everyone, even at the universities in the countries involved, seemed to be stymied into inaction. The project would be a splendid opportunity for a full-scale test of the Words and Things technique; I would make more use of internal innovations than I had hitherto done. I could do it because, thanks to the Vilas stipend, I could count on student help semester after semester to track down all the relevant published literature about this vast area. The risk was that there would not be enough linguistic information to do it, but I thought that by using the terms cited, however badly, in ethnographies, supplemented perhaps by short spells of fieldwork, that might be overcome. Anyway, it was worth a try. Somehow, between the crash of two lines of rollers on the beach nearby, this wisp of an idea became a firm goal. As soon as I returned to Madison I began to work at it.

During the following academic year information from the scholarly literature began to be collected. It soon became apparent that, with the exception of the coasts, no scholar had given much thought to history here, except for accounts of migration. It was also evident that most ethnographies were couched in standardized terminologies. Most of these populations were described in suspiciously similar ways. Yet when one read the accounts of other European residents it became clear that they were not similar at all. Something was wrong with the standard accounts, especially their terminology. By 1979 I realized that the common acceptance of a series of basic concepts and general ideas by authors in the past had in effect blocked any possibility of thinking historically about these peoples. They had imagined such societies as mere collections of kin groups, who

191

had "always" lived in this way and who barely survived in the green hell of a rainforest environment, people without any government at all who had known no change for millennia in their rustic and simple institutions. This rubbish had to be cleared first. As this whole attitude was condensed in the concept of "lineage," the first task was to understand what the fundamental units of society actually were. I soon realized that these were not "lineages," but it did take a whole summer to grasp the characteristics of what such units actually were and to find an appropriate label for them.[30] Once this mental block was removed, an incredibly varied panoply of social and political organizations suddenly replaced the former dull uniformity, a fascinating variety which both testified to a complex history and was its product. At a conference in July 1980 at Canterbury on Central African history, I could at least propose a preliminary view of the kind of history which one could expect to find in these regions.[31]

From the fall of 1980 to May 1981 Claudine and I were on research leave in Belgium and France looking for published and archival materials.[32] Gaps in the linguistic record brought us to Libreville, Gabon, for a long month. That was my last bit of fieldwork. Thanks to local help and to the local center of ORSTOM, we were set up a few hours after the plane banked over the misty, wooded expanse of the estuary, and early the next morning we were at work.[33] Both of us took notes from rare publications or manuscripts in libraries and collections, visited academics at the university, and met knowledgeable missionaries and officials. Soon speakers of "rare" languages turned up, and I was straining my ears to write down correctly the standard basic vocabularies which the linguists at Tervuren needed for the lexicostatistics of the Bantu languages.

We even found a kind soul to take us on a lengthy day trip by jeep over muddy and sandy lanes through the forests all the way to Cocobeach at the border with Equatorial Guinea. It was the complete bush trip, including the car giving up the ghost in the bush. It reminded me of other rainforests in Zaire or around Yaounde. But these were very different. None of these forests were primary forest, and none were in very good condition. Yes, the vegetation looked luxuriant, but most trees belonged to the few fast-growing species that spring up like weeds on deforested soils. Nature shrieked her protest everywhere we went. The state of knowledge about the history of Gabon before 1800 was also in poor shape, this time for lack of exploitation! The local historians believed that their ancestors settled in Gabon only six or seven centuries before, and they reduced history to a tale of migrations.[34] When I gave a talk at the university and explained that historical linguistics suggested a time depth of four thousand years ago or so for the settlement of Bantu speakers, rather than the presumed six hundred, there were gasps of disbelief in the audience. And yet they all knew about abundant archaeological evidence even in the area of Libreville. A few years later archaeological research would confirm the time depths I had put forward.[35]

The whole trip was very satisfying. By the time we left we had quite a harvest of data, and not even one day had been lost. Yet the trip was also a failure. My purpose had been to obtain a research permit to carry out from six to nine months of fieldwork in an area of complex ethnicity, well suited to studying the impact of different environments on local life. The bureaucrat responsible, a haughty Gabonese Harvard graduate, dismissed us out of hand and even refused to give us the necessary forms. He was in an unresponsive mood because that very day he had been lampooned in the local newspaper for his uncooperative ways! Meanwhile, even during this short stay we became fully aware of how oppressive and exploitative the Gabonese regime was, and we shied away. After all, when a minister tells you that he would like you to visit region X so you can advise him how he can make the lazy good-for-nothings start to grow cash crops, there is a sense of colonial déjà vu. Later I was to learn exactly how the authorities managed to control researchers in the field, down to the last "spontaneous" informant. I am glad that we were not sucked into this trap. Still, the lack of fieldwork was a setback. This eventually turned out to be only a minor inconvenience, because I found several Gabonese among the students I taught in Paris in 1985 who had worked in their own rural communities. They and their dissertations supplied me with many of the data—if not the experience—I had wished to acquire.

Despite the mass of information acquired during this trip, progress on the project turned out to be much slower than forecast. In part this flowed from my determination to find all accessible published materials about the area and to use archival data as a complement where published sources were inadequate.[36] The going was slow. Moreover, as of the summer of 1981 the project also began to be interrupted by other research on side issues. Some of these were merely necessary extensions of the main research topic: I wrote a few articles, for example, which dealt with demonstrations of the uses of Words and Things or with other types of evidence.[37]

Not surprisingly, the "Bantu question" was one of these side issues. In order to fully interpret lexical data, I needed as much information as possible about the history and the "genealogical tree" of the languages involved, so that I could distinguish between items which were ancestral to all Bantu languages and items which were later innovations only in certain branches of the family. A tree might also allow one to trace the path taken and roughly date Bantu expansion, while the concomitant study of truly ancestral lexical items would also help one to understand both how farmers had settled this huge region and what their societies and cultures had been like.

Oliver's synthesis of 1966 was now obsolete. Linguists had known for a long time that the best way to arrive "rapidly" at a valid family tree was to use lexicostatistics, a technique based on the comparison of basic vocabulary: the more words two languages have in common in both form and meaning on the standard list, the closer they are. The linguists at Tervuren had been gathering data since 1953, and I had been involved from the outset.[38] Despite this early start, the first to propose a genealogical tree based on lexicostatistics, taken from dictionaries, was Bernd Heine in 1973. His article broke a logjam and became the foundation for a new overall interpretation of the Bantu expansion by David W. Phillipson.[39] But Heine's database was very small, and its quality could be disputed. Nevertheless, his achievement prompted the group at Tervuren to publish its lists as well. In the later seventies it became apparent that the trees varied according to the number of languages sampled. Definitive results required data from almost all the languages. Hence several scholars, including me at Libreville, continued to gather lists.

A linguistic conference on the Bantu expansion at Viviers in 1977 emphasized the difficulties and drawbacks of the technique to the point that that even some linguists such as Hélène Pastoors were discouraged.[40] By then most historians and archaeologists faced with conflicting claims either stuck to Phillipson or were thoroughly disoriented. Indeed, an editor of the *Journal of African History* referred in a letter to the question as "the hoary Bantu origin problem." Still, the group at Tervuren persevered, and I could use an unpublished but fairly full set of data to reconstruct the expansion of western Bantu speakers in 1983, and later as a tool for the study of Words and Things.[41] Nevertheless, one still had to wait for definitive results until enough data were collected and processed for nearly all Bantu languages. Only in January 1992 did the computer at SOAS finally produce new trees based on over 90 percent of the six hundred Bantu languages.

Meanwhile, other side issues demanded larger investments of my time. The art history project was one of these, oral traditions another. It was as if I had once grasped a tiger by the tail and it would not let me go! The debates about oral traditions raged for years, and I reluctantly realized that I would have to write a new book to replace my original work about the topic. I did this in Frankfurt, when the opportunity arose for me to spend a semester in residence at the Frobenius Institut there.[42] Claudine's and my arrival there lacked somewhat in panache. At the airport in Frankfurt we were asked to identify our suitcases and then were almost arrested as smugglers when I mistook a case identical to mine for my suitcase. But rather than fifty pounds of books and papers, it contained fifty pounds of pure heroin! If it were not for the tags which showed which suitcase came from Madison and which one from Karachi, we would have landed in jail rather than at the institute. After this little incident, however, Claudine and I spent a marvelous time there. She was happily discovering and drawing old and striking art objects of Zaire, mainly from photographs of objects collected by Frobenius and others, while I worked hard at the new book and discussed moot points with the two first-rate historians in residence, Adam Jones and Beatrix Heintze.[43] We also found the time for excursions to various German cities and their museums of African art.

Perhaps the most time-consuming side issue of all was the UNESCO project. UNESCO's ambition to write a general encyclopedic work, encompassing the history of the whole African continent, to be used as a foundation for scholars and schoolbooks alike, taught all those involved with it more about African history and the currents and eddies of its historiography than we could ever have learned otherwise. I loved it, because it was a vicarious way of being in "Africa" over all these years, even though I fully realized that it was an "Africa" of intellectuals. After the initial meeting in 1971, the project was slow to start up until the mid-1970s. From then onward we often met and kept up a continous and voluminous flow of correspondence with each other. An exceptional esprit de corps developed among those who were fully involved in the project, and we came to know and appreciate each other more and more. Among these colleagues were scholars from various parts of the world, including nearly all the African leaders in the field, and they all had much to say about the present as well as about the past. Whether they realized it or not, the African scholars brought with them a kaleidoscope of information and impressions of daily life in Africa. One felt as if one had a finger on the pulse of Africa's people! Soon every new meeting turned into a reunion of sorts for us, and sometimes the intellectual debate grew to be so engrossing that horrified practical UNESCO officials accused us of turning meetings into research seminars. But precisely that quality made meetings, especially of the bureau, a challenge. All of this more than compensated for the huge amount of work that was involved. The critical evaluation of each of nearly 250 chapters and special editorial work on two volumes took up more time than the writing of a book would have involved. After all, the seven chapters which I authored by themselves were already equivalent to a book. They all required some original research, and one among them dealing with modern African art was in effect a totally new research project.[44]

No wonder that such activities slowed down work on my major research project to almost a snail's crawl between 1981 and 1986. But in the end it was well worth the delay. Most important, the continuing contacts with African scholars and students kept my feet firmly on the ground. I was not working just with an image of "Africa," a faded reminiscence of yore, nor just with the pretty snapshots which a brief visit to one or another capital in tropical Africa provided. "Africa" remained concrete and refused to be reduced to either a memory or an image. So perhaps many of the byways which distracted me from my main goal were not byways at all. Certainly on Christmas Day 1985 at Niamey, Niger, I did not feel any regrets about time lost when the archaeologist Boube Gado unpacked for me, almost one by one, a large collection of terra-cotta sculptures from a remote barren site, sculpted in the most diverse, unfamiliar, and forceful styles. These figures seemed to gaze at me across a thousand years of time, while I stared back at them in awe.

9

Professionals and Doctrines

WHILE most foreign Africanists in January 1971 still celebrated contemporary "Africa" as a continent where nations were being built and where peoples were still locked in heroic liberation struggles, especially in southern Africa, Idi Amin took power in Uganda, and Walter Rodney was writing his book *How Europe Underdeveloped Africa*.[1] If in the eyes of most foreign Africanists such events as the tyranny of an Amin coup were merely unfortunate accidents, to Rodney and some East African historians the strident trumpets of nationalist historiography grated ever more out of tune. To them the underlying axioms of this historiography were proven false by the unfolding of contemporary events.[2]

Rodney was the first to strike a rather different note. He was then teaching at Dar es Salaam, where political pressure for a view of history more in line with the official socialist ideology was becoming stronger by the day. In his book he claimed that the character of African history had been misunderstood because it had been studied in isolation from that of the rest of the world. Over the last centuries Europeans had gradually subjugated other parts of the world in a single global web of exploitation. That was the relevant framework for the study of African history. Even though this "dependency theory" was by then a household article to students of Latin American affairs, and Rodney was a Guyanan, and although the Egyptian social scientist Samir Amin had espoused the same position earlier, the book still came as a thunderbolt out of the blue to English-speaking historians of Africa.[3] To them Rodney's argument was so unusual that many practitioners at first dismissed it as an imaginative eccentricity. That indeed was how the book was described to me when I first heard about it in Leuven. But far from being eccentric, the book signaled a sudden, profound, and momentous shift in the orthodoxy of

African historiography. Dr. Abdul Sheriff, recalling Dar es Salaam about 1970, writes: "My encounter with this new trend during that first year at Dar es Salaam was of too short a duration to allow me to digest it, and yet long enough to impress on me the need to come to grips with the fundamental philosophical questions in the debate."[4] He goes on to explain how this shift in paradigm delayed for many years the publication of the dissertation which he was then writing at SOAS in the "empiricist" style. The suddenness of the shift and its success can be shown by the fact that barely two years later Terence Ranger, who had left Dar es Salaam in 1969, felt compelled to defend the nationalist position because it created a "usable past" against those whom he dubbed the "radical pessimists."[5]

In hindsight this sudden appearance of a fundamentally new outlook is not surprising, but one would have expected a Marxist outlook to emerge rather than one focused on dependency. In some ways, dependency theory was a red herring, and most historians of Africa soon abandoned it for Marxism when it became evident that the two theories were incompatible.[6] Marxist interpretations of African history, which soon became dominant, were almost as old as the field itself and had enjoyed a following in France, where many academics professed socialist leanings.[7] But the mainstream in African history had ignored such interpretations, until the students of 1968 adopted historical materialism and clung to this doctrine when they became teachers. Thus one of two new appointments made at Parisian universities in 1971 went to Cathérine Coquery-Vidrovitch. As a student in 1968 she had actively participated in the "events of May." A year later she wrote a seminal article on the development of a specific Marxist interpretation of African history.[8] Now she became a pivot for the propagation of a specifically neo-Marxist view of history. Moreover, the student rebellions of 1968 transformed historical consciousness in academic circles in other ways. They convinced many historians that they should be *engagé*, that is, "involved," in contemporary affairs. Hence Ranger appealed to a "usable past." In the United States the generation of 1968 also convinced many historians for the first time of the crucial relevance to history of the methodologies and the findings of social science theories.[9]

Within four or five years the new trend had become dominant in the whole field, and it was to remain so for well over a decade. Coquery-Vidrovitch's department was its main fountainhead in France. In the English-speaking world, the new historians coalesced around the *Journal of Southern African Studies*, founded in 1974.[10] The first major monographs in the new style appeared in 1976 and 1977.[11] The speed with which a sizable coherent English-speaking community of Marxist historians of Africa took shape owed much to developments in the historiography of South Africa. There a community of "radical" historians had been growing for years. They reacted to the preceding "liberal" historiographers, who themselves were revisionists rebelling against both the contemporary Afrikaner and earlier imperial historiographers.[12]

The new historiography advertised its virtues by damning the old trend, now labeled "Africanist." Its adherents charged that their elders had erred by being blatantly nationalist, a stance betrayed by such favorite slogans as "African activity," "African adaptation," "African choice," and Ranger's cherished "African initiative." In precolonial history, these Africanists were charged with obfuscation: the creation of a mystique of method to cover up their theoretical poverty. They had promiscuously borrowed from social and cultural anthropology, a field tainted by its colonial associations. They had artificially separated the economy from political and social life, and they had focused on trade at the expense of political economy. Their emphasis on state formation was an idealist and "moralist" justification for the elites of modern African states. The track record of the "Africanists" was no better for recent African history. They used the slogan "African initiative" to sidestep embarrassing questions about imperialism, to provide an ancestry for the later nationalist movements, and to legitimate the petty bourgeoisie which took power at independence. In general, the older historiography had ignored the insights provided by Marxism.[13] This indictment was far more severe than Ranger's position in 1974, which defended the older historiography. Ranger had conceded two weaknesses: an uncritical acceptance of the authority of "culture heroes" who had overextended themselves and a certain "flabbiness" stemming from the overeager readiness of a public to believe.[14]

The charges now made were exaggerated, sometimes to the point of caricature, but as the counter to the new sophisticated enlightenment proposed by the revisionists, that was only to be expected. Still, they convinced many younger scholars, who accepted the need for theoretical underpinnings to any history and the appropriateness of Marxist theory. Yet not all scholars were won over. As a result, the broad consensus which had hitherto reigned in African history soon lay irremediably shattered. While by itself that was a rather welcome development, because a lack of controversy too easily leads to mentally lazy routines, the intransigence which accompanied this process all too often was not.

Now that the days of the pioneers had ended, the field was becoming more like other established specialties in charge of professionals. For the new generation of historians of Africa were truly professionals, explicitly trained as such. They began to be active in significant numbers during the early seventies. Their numbers were finally satisfying the demand that existed for the specialty, at least outside of tropical Africa itself. Yet that very success exacted its price. Now that the demand was satisfied, the numbers of positions available to newcomers fell dramatically, and the overall rate of growth in the field of African history slowed considerably.[15] The number of specialists in the world now took twenty years to double. This effect resulted not just from the growth of the specialty itself, but also from the abrupt end to the general university expansion which had characterized the sixties in all of the North American, Western European, and African countries. Moreover, by 1970 tropical Africa rated less and less attention by the media in the Western countries, except for France. As a result, the number of historians of Africa and enrollments fell sharply in Great Britain after about 1980, and the influence of its leading historians also began to decline.[16] In France the number of faculty appointments grew a little during the seventies but then stabilized, while enrollments of French students remained weak.[17] The number of historians of Africa continued to grow only in Africa and in the United States. In Africa the need for historians to teach in high schools and a further expansion of universities, especially in the seventies, underlay the continuing demand, while in the United States African history continued to be linked to the early past of a sizable African American population.

Nevertheless, in France African history also blossomed, especially during the seventies. That was mainly due to Yves Person. He dominated the scene from the time of his appointment in 1971 at Paris until his untimely death in 1982.[18] His African students adored him, other academics respected him, and as an influential publicist in the newspapers he was a tireless advocate for the cultural values and the rights of nationalities, whether his own Breton or African. Whether addressing precolonial or recent history, he continued to espouse and teach the same principles. While Person directed the only department of African history labeled as such, Cathérine Coquery-Vidrovitch was appointed in 1971 to a department of Third World studies at the University of Paris VII, which she would later head. As a more orthodox neo-Marxist, she pursued and directed research on recent African history from this angle. After Person's death, the study of African history eventually became split between Paris I, where the department focused on precolonial history, and Paris VII, which specialized in the more recent past, while elsewhere few new scholars were trained. As she became a *mandarine*, Coquery-Vidrovitch came to have such influence that she was celebrated as the outstanding figure of the field in France and francophone Africa.[19]

Around 1970 many observers, myself included, believed that soon the mass of historians of Africa would be Africans working at universities on the continent itself. They would set the agenda and lead future developments in the field. But it did not happen. The numbers did increase, but tropical African universities were prevented from taking over the expected leadership role. With the exception of a few countries, especially ones rich in oil, standards of living deteriorated in tropical Africa after 1970. Only in Nigeria, Kenya, Senegal, and the Ivory Coast did universities continue to flourish for a while.[20] But even there the deteriorating economic situation stunted further growth during the eighties and made the life of historians and history departments increasingly difficult.

During the seventies and eighties a handful of families of rulers and traders in tropical Africa became increasingly wealthy, while everyone else became progressively poorer. Clashes between the military and students protesting the abuses of the ruling regimes grew in lockstep with these disparities, and the repression of such protests became ever harsher. The intellectuals at the universities became more and more disaffected and hostile, while direct government interference in the affairs of the universities grew apace.[21] Budgets for higher education were continually cut, until in many cases only the outer rind of the universities survived, the fruit itself having withered away. Salaries and scholarships became a mere pittance, research and publication an impossible dream, books an unattainable luxury, and in the worst cases, as in Zaire, teaching turned into the telling of tattered tales, buildings into ruins, programs and academic calendars into fiction, and morale into elegiac despair. As a result, most African history departments could not lead the field, despite the valiant efforts of some in Senegal, Nigeria, Tanzania, Kenya, and Zimbabwe after 1980.

The situation would have been worse were it not for UNESCO and especially the *General History of Africa* project. Not only were African scholars such as Jacob Ajayi, Adu Boahen, Bethwell A. Ogot, and Joseph Ki Zerbo leading figures in the activities, and not only did meetings of the committee or its bureau provide regular occasions for such leaders to meet and confer, but the project spawned the realization of smaller projects.

201

Twelve symposia were organized to debate particular issues pertaining to the history of Africa in the decade after 1974. African scholars dominated all of them, and many of the meetings took place in Africa itself, providing an opportunity for local African scholars to attend as well.[22] Some of the general meetings and most of the meetings of the bureau were also held in Africa until 1983, providing further occasions for contacts and opportunities for African historians to lobby government agencies for the maintenance or expansion of history programs. The activities of the *General History* project did enable scholars from the major African universities to exercise leadership and to influence the development of the field until the middle eighties. The UNESCO project has therefore been a major catalyst in the historiography of the field, despite the fact that its activities attracted little notice (and some suspicion) in the United States and project leaders met on occasion with outright hostility in Great Britain. But the project activities declined sharply in the mid-eighties, as the main work began to reach completion and UNESCO itself ran into major budget problems. It is unfortunate that its role in providing a forum for African leadership in the field has been curtailed and even more that it has not been taken over by other agencies.

Thus by default the leadership in African historiography fell more and more to the programs in the United States, even though there too public support for universities and research programs shrunk in the seventies and more severely in the eighties. As a result, North Americans began to set the agenda for research and publication according to the significance of issues in their own society, whether or not they were held to be significant in the societies of tropical Africa itself. Yet at the same time the political situation in tropical Africa still exerted great influence on research, particularly because of its impact on opportunities to do fieldwork. Most North Americans flocked to English-speaking countries or to Senegal, the nearest one. As living conditions deteriorated and/or as governments increasingly regulated and often discouraged fieldwork, larger numbers of scholars traveled to the same few countries where conditions for research were better. Thus in the seventies a host of researchers congregated in Tanzania and Kenya, while later Botswana, Zimbabwe, and then South Africa and Namibia became the favorites. In West Africa similar forces favored Nigeria and Senegal. In addition, teachers focused in their lectures on the parts of Africa where they had worked and encouraged students to conduct research there. Therefore, leading journals carried more articles about such countries than about others, thus amplifying the effects of the hazards of access to research opportunities. The result has been a shriveling of the mental map of "Africa" in the minds of many North American students to a few English-speaking countries in tropical Africa.

Good conditions for fieldwork have become more and more difficult to find over the last twenty years for researchers, whether expatriates or nationals. Harsher living conditions, greater health risks, and increasing government intervention are the most obvious culprits. The activities of researchers, nationals and foreigners alike, came under increasing scrutiny by various government agencies. In many countries governments screened topics for research more and more efficiently, while in some cases they discouraged research in history or in the social sciences away from major cities altogether. In reaction, researchers, anxious to maintain future access to their fields, began to practice more and more self-censure. Just as relevant and often overlooked are the stress and the risks which internal economic, social, and political conditions can create for individuals and communities who assist the researcher or are the subject of the research. In the best of cases, it takes a special effort on the part of a person to set aside pressing concerns and become an "informant"; in the worst of cases, simply allowing oneself to be interviewed is already an act of defiance. So far no one seems to have studied the precise impact of these factors on the directions in which knowledge about African history grew, but I am convinced that they have been just as important in the historiography of Africa as the appearance of new doctrines has been.

Dependency theory or various Marxist theories seemed to offer a fresh point of view with a much greater explanatory power than the previous nationalist and functionalist stance had ever reached, especially with regard to studies about the impact of Europe on Africa and about the colonial period.[23] But there were problems. Dependency theory could not easily explain the differences between local reactions in different places to European exploitation or the widely different outcomes that resulted. The grand view obliterated most of the historical substance of tropical Africa and could not be reconciled with Marxism. This trend soon waned, in part for these reasons. Yet historical materialism had its own problems. Although claiming to be universally valid, the original doctrines of Marx and Engels were nevertheless mainly a distillation of their conclusions about the European experience and especially about the effects of capitalism in the nineteenth century. With the exception of Algeria, the founders had never been concerned with Africa. Their theories about capitalism and class conflict could easily be applied to the twentieth century, but what about earlier times? In orthodox Marxism, capitalism had grown out of a feudal order.[24] Yet even the founders had perceived that the feudal stage was not universal and had toyed with an alternative model, "the Asiatic Mode of Production."[25] In order to apply the doctrine to Africa, one had to know whether precolonial Africa fit into that scheme or not.

The question was hotly debated by Marxists in France during the sixties. That was the background to Coquery-Vidrovitch's article about an African mode of production in 1969. She claimed that there was a specific African mode of production unforeseen by Marx, Engels, or even Lenin. The expression *mode of production* refers not to the technology of production but to the relations obtaining between producers and the owners of the means of production. These have been relations of exploitation ever since the times of a mythical "primitive community," and they give rise to the formation of antagonistic classes. Coquery-Vidrovitch claimed that classes were unknown in precolonial Africa because private ownership of the land did not exist. But there was exploitation by elites, whose power ultimately rested on their control of trade.[26] Other historians of Africa accepted her view that the question of "mode of production" was crucial and neglected the more conventional focus on the dynamics of class struggle. But they disagreed about the specific features of a "African mode of production" or, indeed, whether there was only one or only one at any time. Could there not be several? Could several not coexist side by side, and if so, how were they then "articulated" to each other? This debate raged for nearly two decades and finally bogged down in an unmanageable welter of different and competing modes of production.[27]

Meanwhile, other historical materialists debated the definitions of capitalism and class back and forth. They applied various doctrines of Marxist inspiration to the study of industrial labor in colonial Africa and to the rise of a peasant class.[28] The results were impressive, as the works of Charles Van Onselen and Frederic Cooper show. But in my opinion, at the time such views, like all other grand social science theories, were reductionist. In this case they erased the African character of workers and peasants, to retain only their role as laborers. That was an oversimplification. It was also bound to provoke protests from those who felt that their Africanness was inextricably bound up with the colonial situation. After all, what became of racism in this scheme? Eventually it became evident that class consciousness among wage laborers did not develop in the same fashion as it had done in Europe and that the cultural makeup of Africans could simply not be ignored. Considerations about consciousness later led many researchers to the work of Antonio Gramsci, especially his Prison Notebooks.[29] Gramsci and his followers hold that the ruling classes succeed in imposing a cultural hegemony on the whole of society and thus eventually achieve the acquiescence even of the oppressed. Hence culture is relevant. African nationalists also loudly resisted this erasure of "Africanness." They complained that Marxism was just another European import and a trick to deny any specificity to Africans. In the end this criticism won the day. Although doctrinaire nationals at Dar es Salaam and later at the University of Maputo in Mozambique fully subscribed to historical materialist views, many among them felt queasy about its abolition of Africanness and gradually abandoned this reductionism during the eighties.

A large number of historians who espoused Marxist-inspired views were, by that very fact, attracted to certain topics rather than others. They profoundly modified the profile of the field by their practice. To them colonial rather than precolonial history was the most relevant. That was also a boon for foreign graduate students, because to a large extent they could now investigate issues by relying on archives. Many of these topics did not seem to require fieldwork (although they really do), and most documents were written in easily accessible European languages. One rather suspects that this easing of requirements attracted more than one young scholar to work on this period. Moreover, these abundant archival documents seemed not to pose any technical problems, so that most of these scholars foolishly dismissed methodological discussions as a smokescreen hiding the absence of theory.[30] Now researchers liked to focus on southern or eastern Africa rather than on West Africa, which "has remained remarkably self-satisfied within the Africanist paradigm" because, as Bill Freund puts it, of "the shakier situation of the new ruling classes and the potential for social revolution" in East and Central Africa.[31] He also alludes to the fascination of the struggle for majority rule in South Africa. One might add to this the greater industrialization of southern Africa compared with West Africa, the greater numerical importance of "workers" in southern Africa, and the fact that labor movements in southern Africa had played a much more visible role than elsewhere. As for relevant issues, social classes, capitalism, labor, and peasantries were all obvious topics for historical materialists.

Thus, much of what I had been interested in—precolonial history, political history, and methodology—was now becoming distinctly unfashionable. It would have been easy to shift my research interests to agree

205

better with the climate of the times. After all, I was considering a major research project on colonial Zaire, and the work in Libya dealt with the twentieth century. Yet I resisted the trend for a simple reason: so many scholars were now involved in the study of the recent past that I was more useful to the field by keeping precolonial issues alive. Moreover, I continued to be intrigued by issues of religion and art as a reaction to the summary dismissal of these issues as mere curlicues or epiphenomena by historical materialists, and also because I had begun to sense how essential ideologies and worldviews are to the construction and maintenance of social and cultural life.[32]

In any case, I mistrusted and rejected orthodox Marxist doctrine itself. It promoted a false, rigid evolutionary view of history.[33] It falsely asserted the existence of general historical laws; it was teleological because it saw history as a process in which the present was the preordained and inexorable outcome of the past; it denied the relevance of anything specifically African—in that regard it returned to colonial historiography; and the jargon of this historiography rendered it inaccessible to any audience other than that of converted colleagues.[34] My fundamental objection, however, remained that strict Marxism clung to an irrational belief in the inherent goodness of human nature, a view which clashed with experience in general and in particular with the experience of totalitarian oppression in socialist countries. Rather than being just unfortunate accidents in the construction of an egalitarian society, such totalitarian realities pointed to fundamental errors in the orthodox Marxist conception of society and humanity. Finally, on a practical level, the theories were of little use to those who were grappling with many issues in precolonial history. Nevertheless, I also appreciated that historical materialism did raise a series of thoughtful and fruitful questions about issues such as the creation and maintenance of inequality, exploitation, and social stratification. So like most other scholars, I became deeply influenced by the general discourse about Marxism, even though I rejected its doctrinaire underpinnings.[35]

I was not alone in rejecting historical materialism. As the record of publications for the seventies and eighties shows, the various variants of doctrine did not convince everyone. The well-known time lag between writing and publication explains in part why the masterpieces of the earlier "Africanist" school appeared during the seventies. But there was more to it. Some scholars actively rejected Marxism altogether and adhered to other points of view. Thus the monumental *Asante in the Nineteenth Century* of Ivor Wilks is not just an effect of "lag." Wilks, a philosopher by training, had always been an ardent adherent of the general social science theory promoted by Max Weber, and he stuck to his guns. Among the younger scholars, some tested the new doctrines and found them wanting. Gwyn Prins is perhaps typical of those who did carefully examine materialist positions, only to conclude that the evidence did not support them.[36]

Another group of scholars was less concerned with the application of social science theories to African history than with the job of handling the evidence itself. As the years went by they became more and more disturbed by what they saw as the prevalence of unsound technical practices. They accused the "Africanists" of reconstructing a history for Africa in such haste that the rules of historical evidence went by the board, and of proposing interpretations that went far beyond the evidence at hand. David Henige, one of the former Wisconsin students, endowed with a sceptical eye, a practical hand, and good humor, was one of them.[37] David crystallized the concern of this group of scholars by founding *History in Africa: A Journal of Method* in 1974, an annual which rapidly became one of the leading journals in the field. Most of its contents deal with the examination of specific types or bodies of evidence, whether the sources are written, oral, or other, but some contributions tackle general issues of methodology or theory in history, as well as historiographical questions. The journal drew and still draws its contributors from across the whole spectrum of opinion among historians of Africa. Paradoxically perhaps, because it welcomed contradictory debate, it did promote the unity of the field, despite the divisions created by differences of opinion.

My sympathies lay with these scholars because the laxity of the treatment of sources and especially of their interpretation was disturbing me more and more. After all, a concern for method had been at the core of my own training in Leuven, and the flaws of the current historiography were painfully visible. For instance, I had been surprised about the way in which *Kingdoms of the Savanna,* which was specifically introduced as a provisional "state of the question," had been turned by its readers, even by Ranger at the time, into a "definitive" and authoritative account, but I had not reacted.

Yet another body of theory began to influence African historiography during the early 1970s: structuralism. It entered the field by way of the debate about oral traditions. The doctrine holds that oral traditions are myths which themselves merely are the expression of the human mind when it is idling, that is, thinking about itself. According to structuralists, the study of such myths therefore allows one to discover the universal processes of symbolic logic operating in the "untutored" mind.[38] The

207

emergence of structuralism dates from the late forties. Twenty years later it became one of major currents in anthropology. It burst on the scene like unexpected fireworks during a calm night in African history with the publication of *Le roi ivre*, by my former colleague at IRSAC, Luc de Heusch. The doctrine was familiar to me, as it had been ever since my salad days in London, when I read Claude Lévi-Strauss's *Structures élémentaires de la parenté*.[39] In his book de Heusch compares the various traditions about the origin of the kingdoms in southeastern Zaire and demonstrates that they were but variants of a single body of "myth." He decodes this corpus by using symbolic logic and claims to have uncovered the perceptions of its carriers about fundamentals of society and human nature. This was, he concluded, "the ideological legacy of proto Bantu society."[40] In 1973 he summarized his argument in English and stated: "I think that ethno-historians, particularly Jan Vansina, have too readily believed themselves able to interpret the legendary chronicle of the Luba kingdom as a historical text."[41]

Thus the gauntlet was laid down. If structuralism was correct, then traditions, especially traditions of origin, could no longer be considered as sources for history.[42] In the following years structural analysis became quite fashionable and convinced not a few historians. It also acquired a new twist. Thus the English anthropologist Roy G. Willis, who, unlike de Heusch, was also a convinced historical materialist, used symbolic logic to "decode" a body of traditions and to conclude that they "really" express the tenets of a local theory about the nature of the local society. It turned out that this homemade social science had uncovered a number of tenets dear to historical materialists. Was this a genuine surprise? Did it not merely reflect that this "symbolic logic" was merely a rhetorical device which allows the analyst to reach any desired conclusion?[43]

Structuralism has been quite influential in African history. Its effect was immediate on those historians of Africa who were still concerned with precolonial history and who were struggling with the "correct" interpretations of oral traditions. This group of historians, however, was rapidly dwindling as a percentage of the whole, because precolonial history was no longer fashionable. But the use of "symbolic logic" also opened the eyes of these and others to the relevance of literary issues in general, so that by the late eighties structuralism facilitated the entry of postmodernist literary theories into the historiography of Africa. It is for that reason (and not because it often involved my own work) that I paid special attention to the debates about oral tradition between 1970 and 1985.

After Tom Beidelman's rejection of the validity of oral tradition as a source, historians began once more to debate the value of oral traditions and the ways in which they could be correctly interpreted. In 1970 also, Joseph Miller, then one of my students, who had done research on the early history of the old kingdom of Kasanje in Angola (founded in the 1620s), began to analyze the traditions which he had recorded in partial conjunction with contemporary writings. He argued that traditions should not be interpreted literally. Rather, one should make use of the insights gained from a study of the social organization and the imagery current in the society studied, to "decode" the narrative clichés of these traditions. For such clichés were created to provide a sort of personalized shorthand that was easily memorized.[44] He applied these insights and used what seemed to me and to some other specialists at the time to be a daring and perhaps too imaginative interpretation of the traditions to reconstruct the origins of this kingdom.[45] De Heusch published his work barely a year after the defense of Miller's dissertation. And yet other claims that oral tradition did not faithfully report past events were in the air. Scholars of tradition as art had gradually discovered how deeply both narrative and poetic traditions were interwoven with their "performance."[46] Soon they would claim that the whole contents of traditions were but a product of contemporary performance, not a heritage of the past. They were fiction, not fact.

Historians reacted in various ways to this onslaught.[47] One group, the "literalists," shrugged it all off and continued to handle traditions as if they were a literal record from the past.[48] Others took the stand that traditions reflect both the present and the past. These scholars proposed literary techniques of interpretation, usually inspired by structuralist practice. Some "symbolists" followed the lead of Joseph Miller and were more upbeat.[49] Others became ever more critical.[50] Some historians became convinced that some or all types of oral traditions were totally untrustworthy. Thus David W. Cohen, in *Womunafu's Bunafu: A Study of Authority in a Nineteenth-Century African Community*, rejected the notion of a transmission, and Terence Ranger believed that oral traditions were of no use outside of states.[51] Literalists, structuralists, symbolists, performers, and sceptics all debated each other with gusto, without coming to consensus.[52] Meanwhile, Alex Haley published *Roots* in 1976. A year later the book made history in television as the first miniseries. Thus, just when many historians had growing reservations about oral traditions, the book and even more the miniseries convinced millions of their value as history.[53] The search for one's roots became so popular that for a while genealogical societies found themselves overwhelmed by new customers.

Having written the first book on the question, I could not avoid being drawn into all this turmoil, but I attempted to limit my own involvement. By 1973 further research on the Kuba had shown that traditions of origins are more statements about the nature of the world than historical recollection, so I reported this.[54] When in 1974 I read the first accounts by Haley in *Playboy* and the *Reader's Digest* about how he had obtained the tale of the kidnapping of his ancestor in the Gambian village of Juffure, I thought that the story could well be a fabrication foisted on him by local entrepreneurs, for Haley had been imprudent enough to let it be known what it was that he wanted to discover. But I kept out of it.[55] The fallout of the publication and airing of *Roots* for me was a bit of correspondence and telephone calls from hopeful people—not just African Americans—in search of their ancestors. They submitted clues ranging from odd words to six-fingered ancestors, and even Gog and Magog! Then research in Libya greatly enriched my experience about the processes of remembering, and I reported on the results.[56]

Even though scholars now found fault with this or that statement in my *De la tradition orale* or interpreted its passages in unintended ways, I had no desire to plunge into the debate. Yet eventually I was provoked into polemics against an extreme Marxist position and later against structuralism, which de Heusch had represented so elegantly that he was convincing many historians.[57] I had long been familiar with the techniques involved and with the fundamental arbitrary character of "symbolic logic." The patterns of symbolic and poetic reasoning among the Kuba, as taught especially during initiation and used in everyday life and ritual, had intrigued me so much that I had wished to devote a major study to establish which rules of logic, if any, prevented such lines of thought from being totally arbitrary. I found that in generating "poetic logic," anything goes as long as metaphors can be linked to each other. So when Luc de Heusch once again challenged me directly in his *Rois nés d'un coeur de vache* and further silence would only be construed as assent by other historians, I did react and wrote a detailed rebuttal.[58] Nevertheless, it was clear that the original handbook would no longer be very useful and that it could not simply be "updated." Thus I came to write *Oral Tradition as History*.[59] The work did not have much impact, for soon after its publication a new fashion in literary criticism began to transform the whole debate about oral traditions.

The first half of the 1970s constituted a turning point in the historiography of Africa, not only because the earlier consensus among scholars concerning the ideological premises underlying the history of Africa was being shattered but also because the field began to fragment into an ever-increasing number of subspecialties, to the point of balkanization. Certainly specialties, such as economic history, the history of the slave trade, and the Bantu question, were by then flourishing, but most researchers had been involved in several of these specialties simultaneously. In the seventies, however, the number of specialties sharply increased, while more individual scholars tended to conduct research in only one chosen specialty, such as labor or gender studies, and thus became less and less aware of new findings in other specialties. Both the advent of professionalization and the increase in the numbers of scholars involved are to blame for this.

Yet those causes do not explain why some subfields were established and flourished while others remained undeveloped. An examination of the choices made indicates that they were in part dictated by the emergence of new ideological premises, as is evident from the emergence of such specialties as political economy, labor, or peasantry. But the appearance of other new subfields was inspired more by specific questions of general contemporary interest in the societies to which the historians belonged and should be linked to parallel developments in other domains of history, such as American history in the United States, for instance, or to parallel developments in other disciplines of African studies. Thus the appearance of a field of women's studies in the early seventies is connected both to the women's movement in North America and Europe and to its rise in American history.[60] The droughts which plagued Africa after 1973 and the nearly contemporary concerns about the environment and ecology in North America and Europe both prompted the rise of a specialty in the history of climate and ecology, while the history of demography can be linked to concerns about "population explosion." Finally, the vigorous growth of national or regional historiographies in various African countries, which had begun (e.g., in Nigeria) during the previous period, was linked to questions of national identity. Moreover, especially for foreign researchers but also for nationals, some research topics required such a high degree of specialization because of the language skills required, the types of data involved, or the vast amounts of extant documentation that they naturally gave rise to specialties. This is obvious, for instance, in the precolonial historiography of the Gold Coast or of "Kongo and Angola."

Yet such explanations do not account for everything. Thus the history of production, agriculture, technology, or material culture did not attract many scholars, despite the relevance of such studies to issues in contemporary Africa.[61] Perhaps this was due to an ideological blindness that emphasized relations of production at the expense of production itself. But one suspects that it also resulted from the generally poor background in natural and physical science of students attracted to the history of Africa. The lack of development of a genuine art history may be due in part to ideological distastes for what seemed to be an epiphenomenon or just an irrelevancy, but art studies have also been quite strongly influenced by the attitudes prevalent in the market for art objects in North America and Europe, and until fairly recently history has been irrelevant to that market.[62]

Conversely, how does one explain the early growth of an interest in a subfield such as the social history of health? This specialty emerged on the scene in the early to mid-seventies when a number of anthropologists and historians, such as John M. Janzen, Steven Feierman, Gerald Hartwig, and, somewhat later, Gwyn Prins, discovered a topic which hitherto had been confined to conventional accounts of biomedicine or relegated to the lands of "religion and magic."[63] The sensitivity of these fieldworkers to social factors in health care certainly played a role. Nevertheless, the clash between the practice of traditional medicine and biomedicine in African countries after independence forcefully called attention to this issue. Already by the mid-sixties the practice of the Kongo people had thrust the issue on John Janzen and a physician of his acquaintance in Zaire.[64] In this case, then, the new specialty was primarily a response to new conditions in Africa.

The link between anthropology and history helps to explain the rise of "social history," a fairly vague but vast field in the historiography of Africa which came to be recognized as distinct during the late seventies and early eighties.[65] By then the older functional or structural styles of ethnography were almost universally rejected. More and more fieldworkers began to search for the past which underlay the contemporary precipitation of ethnography. In this fashion much of the earlier corpus of ethnography, along with anthropological theories about small-scale societies, was appropriated by historians. Contrary to some assertions, anthropology was now influencing African history more deeply than ever before.[66] An ethnography conscious of time and wary of sweeping generalization cannot be anything but a social history.[67] Hence, for instance, my own Tio book had been a social history *avant la lettre*. The label itself crystallized only later, to gather the experience of any and all aspects of ordinary life in one sheaf of subfields. Subjects as diverse as ecology, local peasant issues, health, gender, and more all belong here because they all focus on ordinary people.

Yet by itself the practice of fieldwork does not explain the rise of "social history." The term was old in European history, where it had undergone a revival when historians of a leftist persuasion adopted it during the early seventies.[68] This renaissance of the term certainly stimulated its emergence in the historiography of Africa.[69] Thus "social history" in African historiography arose from a brew involving the example in European historiography, the impact of leftist ideologies, and the recuperation of ethnography by historians.

This example shows that future historiographers will need to invoke a variety of factors to explain the rise of each of these subfields: just an appeal to an overall "paradigm" will not do. Moreover, once a subfield exists, it develops its own dynamics, even though changes in paradigm often have affected the historiography of particular subfields: thus the specialty "slave trade" turned to the study of slavery as a form of exploitation and labor in Africa—or a mode of production—under the influence of the new ideologies.[70] Likewise, the effects of historical materialism or structuralism can easily be discerned in Islamic studies. But sometimes that did not happen. A small specialty could remain totally impervious to the main trends. A good example of this is the issue of the Bantu expansion. Perhaps the technical nature of the question, allied to a lack of interest by many historians, accounts for the indifference of the literature about "Bantu origins" toward the dominant "paradigms" of the day. After all, from the seventies until recently, no historians, with one or two exceptions, have been engaged in further research on the issue. One can attribute this precisely to the impact of the reigning doctrines: the question was simply not congenial to them. But in all instances, one finds also that the historiography of specialties, regional or topical, developed a discourse of its own: later authors worked for the most part within the axiomatic parameters set by the founders of the specialty, added to the hitherto extant knowledge, and acted as revisionists rather than revolutionaries.

By the eighties several specialties had developed their own general body of theory, which often was not particularly tied to the discipline of history. Indeed, specialists invoked fellow specialists in other disciplines (usually of the social sciences) more often than they referred to historians outside the specialty. A particular body of theory in turn used distinctive slogans or expressions as a shorthand and thus elaborated a distinctive jargon. Wittingly or not, the authors in such a field thus tended to isolate it from the historiographical mainstream, or what remains of it. That in turn promoted tunnel vision and a relative isolation from the major cross-currents flowing through the historiography at large. Moreover, as they became more and more professional, scholars no longer dared or wished to contribute to research in several areas. In part this resulted from an ever-increasing flood of publications. No one could even hope to follow the whole output of African historiography any longer, and keeping up with one's own subfield soon became a full-time task. For even though the number of scholars in the field grew only slowly after 1970, the rate of publications still accelerated. The dynamics favoring the appearance and growth of new subfields often tied as much to other disciplines as to history meant that by the mid-eighties African historiography was in danger of fragmenting into a collection of insular specialties. The mainstream was fast becoming a trickle like any other in the braided stream of an ill-defined and generalized social science.

Nor were all specialties equal in the numbers of scholars involved or the amount of research required. Some were popular, some esoteric: Bantu was quite esoteric, the slave trade and slavery moderately popular, women's history and social history exceedingly popular. The subject of women's history, for instance, attracted women historians of Africa from the early seventies onward, at a time when affirmative action and a general interest in the specialty were developing, especially in the United States.[71] At that time more women historians of Africa were entering the profession, and the subject attracted many of them.[72] The specialty grew slowly at first, no doubt in part because only a handful of scholars were involved and in part because women had so rarely been the focus of archival reports, ethnographies, or reports by community historians that finding the relevant evidence and interpreting it was an arduous task. But in part the indifference of formal women's studies programs toward Africanists and the inchoate character of early feminist theories must also be blamed.[73] Despite this slow growth, the specialty did catch on among some women scholars in Africa as well.[74]

The contrast of this specialty with the other highly successful one, social history, is instructive. Many historians flocked to the banner of social history, but that amounts to saying that the banner itself was a hit. The label provided respectability for the pursuit of a potentially infinite variety of topics. Hence the expansion of social history was propelled by the very process of fission active in African historiography as a whole. And yet the label was useful, for it maintained a common link between an ever-growing number of researchers in spite of the fact that their underlying points of view often diverged considerably. In particular it included

214

the work both of those who stressed the study of social groups and of those who stressed the cultural effects of cognition and symbolism. In part because of the common label, these scholars felt that the research all social historians conducted was of mutual interest, and moreover, the language they used in writing was common to them all.

Why in the last instance, then, were some specialties more popular than others? In part they were more closely linked to issues of great moment in the society in which the historians worked, in part there was more resonance between the specialty and the dominant paradigms in the field itself. Thus social history and women's history resonate well with the general attitude of scholars who want to champion the cause of "the ordinary person" or of "the grassroots," just as the Bantu expansion had appealed to an earlier generation because it showed that "Africans had a history". Now the Bantu topic seemed splendidly irrelevant to issues of concern to a wider public. At least it did not resonate with general attitudes. No wonder that it does not attract the scholarly crowds—at least outside of Africa. On the continent itself, the very foundation in 1983 of the Centre International des Civilisations Bantu (CICIBA) by the governments of ten African countries proves the continuing contemporary cultural and political relevance of the topic to Africans in the area.[75] Relevance is relative. Hence a historiography which is only the sum of relevant specialties may well acquire a different physiognomy inside and outside of tropical Africa. That is worrisome, because if the history of Africa written by outsiders becomes meaningless to Africans themselves, then the whole endeavor becomes pointless, in my opinion. I for one am not interested in an alienated history of Africa for exclusive consumption overseas.

A whimsical chronicler in an imaginary monastery might record for 1986 that Mikhail Gorbachev started his reforms and that Roland Oliver retired. Both these events portended the end of an era. Gorbachev heralded the collapse of communism in Europe, the end of the cold war, and the devaluation of Marxist ideologies, while Oliver signaled the retirement of a generation of academic pioneers in African history and the advent of a new one, the third since the field was founded as an academic endeavor.[76] A fortune-teller could safely have predicted in 1986 that a new phase was about to begin in African history.

There was unrest in the tribe of historians. Their intellectual mood was shifting. The mode of production debate was becoming a surrealistic absurdity: African modes of production multiplied, and attempts to save the concept by focusing on "modes of reproduction" did not reprieve it for

215

long.[77] After Gramsci, historical materialists discovered Michel Foucault, whose oeuvre dealt with the notion of ideology as the main tool by which power is imposed. Thus what had earlier been dismissed as "superstructure," "epiphenomenon," or indeed "false consciousness" now became the central focus of research. At the same time an introspective mood took hold and expressed itself in essays and books about the writing of history. In 1981 the *African Studies Review* began to publish a series of papers, commissioned by the American Council of Learned Societies and the Social Science Research Council, about the state of African studies, an effort designed to counteract the increasing fragmentation in the field. The series began with essays by Frederic Cooper on economy and John Lonsdale on states and social processes. Historians later contributed essays on many other topics, including Ralph Austen and Rita Headrick on technology (1983), Bill Freund on labor (1984), Sara Berry on agriculture (1984), Terence Ranger on religion (1985), Steven Feierman on health (1986), Bogumił Jewsiewicki on African historical studies in general (1989) Allen Isaacman on peasants (1991), and Cathérine Coquery-Vidrovitch on urbanization (1991).[78] Such "state of the question" papers were not new. What was novel was the introspective mood of most of those contributions.[79] This mood was widespread and was expressed in book-length historiographies published from 1983 onward.[80] Indeed, the tribe was growing restless!

Another sign that the general atmosphere in the field was changing was the halfhearted rebellion by some against the anonymity of isms which recounted the deeds of faceless forces rather than those of "real people." Historians of Africa had always been quite allergic to the notion that "great men" or "great persons" had shaped history, and as a consequence genuine biographies had remained quite rare in the field.[81] Now even some historical materialists were feeling unhappy with this state of affairs. By the mid-seventies Jewsiewicki was promoting the collection of biographies in Zaire, and a decade later biography and autobiography became more acceptable.[82]

Yet another break with the past came with the publication of books that were a joy to read! They deliberately aimed at literary quality. One might have expected this from Landeg White, who wrote *Magomero: Portrait of an African Village,* because he was a professional writer, but not from Jeffrey Peires, who wrote *The Dead Will Arise,* or from David W. Cohen and Atiene Odhiambo, who wrote *Siaya: The Historical Anthropology of an African Landscape.*[83] They were all academics. The choice to write books in this way meant that these authors rejected earlier theoretical trends along with

216

their sometimes turgid jargon and reaffirmed the ties between historiography and literature.

The combination of introspection with the awareness that ideology was linked to power, that historiography was ideology, and that it was therefore also involved in plays for power relations, allied to a new sensitivity about the role of literature in historiography, has led over the past few years to the emergence of "postmodernism" or "deconstructionism," which espouses these stands. The concepts designated by these labels were originally developed by literary critics, from whom anthropologists first and historians later have borrowed them.[84] Postmodernism in history asserts, first, that all historical consciousness is an ideological product of the present and only reflects power relations in the present: "The past does not exist." Second, it maintains that even had it existed, the past cannot be known, because its direct traces (written texts or archaeology) are interpreted and hence "invented" by readers in the present ("deconstruction"). Third, it insists that objectivity is not only impossible to attain but that it is wrong to strive for it because the main point of interest in historiography is the subjective interpretation of a given author.[85] Fourth, there is no genuine divide between fact and fiction.[86] Finally, to strive for a consensus is hypocrisy because that is tantamount to imposing the relative view of one person or of an oligarchy on all others.[87]

Postmodernism was well established in anthropology and hotly debated by historians of Europe and North America years before it entered into the historiography of Africa. It appeared there in two specific ways. One of these was the debate about oral tradition, a debate that had long been influenced by theories of literary criticism. In the late eighties most historians still stuck to their guns, while anthropologists studied oral traditions more and more as expressions of historical consciousness in present-day societies.[88] Recently this trend has culminated in an elegant book about historical consciousness by Elizabeth R. Tonkin, titled *Narrating Our Pasts.*[89]

Meanwhile, however, a few historians abandoned the view that oral traditions can be sources. Donald R. Wright entitled a final article about the data he gathered in the field "Requiem for the Use of Oral Tradition to Reconstruct the Precolonial History of the Lower Gambia," but he did not generalize from his experience.[90] Two others, though, bitterly attacked all uses of these traditions to reconstruct the past with the zeal of new converts. Thus Edward I. Steinhart writing in *Ethnohistory* dismissed earlier work as the product of "retread documentary historians or anthropologists manqué." He naively believes in history as "science" and in "factual truth." From this he deduces that the "factualness" of an event will flow from documentary, archaeological, and ethnographic sources and not from oral traditions.[91]

Steinhart defers to David W. Cohen, the historian turned anthropologist who wrote "The Undefining of Oral Tradition" in the same issue of *Ethnohistory*. Cohen argues that historical consciousness in present-day societies stems from "everyday critical, lively intelligence" born from the practice of daily life, not from oral tradition. Thus "the production of historical knowledge" derives from everyday communication and interaction, rather than from a distinctive series of historical texts transmitted from generation to generation.[92] For him both culture and the historical traditions it produces are only products of the present. A study of oral traditions therefore teaches how people today produce historical consciousness and does not reveal anything whatsoever about the past that was.[93] These critics have thrown out the baby with the bathwater. They have come to overlook the obvious, namely that traditions often do reflect the past and remain useful as historical sources, especially for the last century and sometimes for a few centuries preceding the date of their recording. Yes, such sources, like all others, require careful scrutiny, and one must be on one's guard to detect recent fabrications. For instance, the early parts of Alex Haley's *Roots* are now alleged to be just that: a willful fabrication for personal and collective advantage.[94] But all that teaches us is the need to apply faithfully the standard rules of evidence to such sources.

In *Siaya* Cohen and Odhiambo study "the ways in which people—in ordinary, common place activities—have produced society and culture not only through social practice but also through the formation of histories and anthropologies."[95] This statement more clearly, although still implicitly, denies the existence of any knowable social and cultural history, a position which I hold to be totally false. This sweeping stance simply overlooks that much of what a community now interiorizes as history and culture is in effect information and practice which really does stem from earlier times when that past was a present. Every generation does not reinvent everything all the way back to how one lights a fire!

In the early nineties, as chair of the Northwestern Program of African Studies, David W. Cohen used his position to assiduously promote this thesis and the broader message of postmodernism.[96] He seems to have abandoned history altogether as an impossible enterprise and to have adopted the views of the circle of the postmodern anthropologists and sociologists of the University of Chicago without any reservation.[97]

Postmodernism also entered into the field under the influence of a trio of scholars, all trained in philosophy, who had met at Lubumbashi during the early seventies: the philologist and philosopher Valentin Y. Mudimbe, the anthropologist Johannes Fabian, and Bogumil Jewsiewicki. Mudimbe, a willowy, unassuming Zairian, was the most articulate of the three. Forced into exile by Mobutu in 1981, he immigrated to the United States. By that time he had written *L'odeur du père*, in which he showed that the very ideas and interpretations of "Africa" and African culture held by African intellectuals were the product of European and North American social science and humanities, that these disciplines lacked universally "scientific" validity, and that they were but the expression of particular cultural axioms and values. In other words, these disciplines were totally ethnocentric, and even the minds of Africans had been colonized. In his later work *The Invention of Africa: Gnosis, Philosophy, and the Order of Knowledge* he developed these themes further.[98] This book became an instant success among Africanists in North America. They had been prepared for such argumentation, especially by earlier publications.[99] To his readers, who hitherto had paid scant attention to the philosophy of history, Mudimbe seemed at one stroke to demolish the basis for an "objective" science of history in general and for historical materialism in particular. In actuality he did not argue against the possibility of attaining objectivity but merely denounced the biases of existing social sciences and humanities. Many historians of Africa suddenly discovered for the first time that history is not a "science" and that absolute "truth" does not exist. The postmodernist premises listed above now seemed to make sense, and some were ready for Fabian's appeal to go "from rigor to vigor."[100] Unfortunately, such scholars did not realize that no bridge exists between the statement that history cannot be true in the philosophical absolute and the postmodernist premises.

It is too early to evaluate how deeply postmodernist trends are affecting the field. So far such ideas seem to have brought the dominance of both structuralist and historical materialist doctrines to an end, and questions raised by some postmodernist ideas have affected concrete research to various degrees. They are quite evident in recent doctoral dissertations, such as those defended at Madison from about 1990. Some of these ideas fascinate some historians, yet few accept the whole package, and many, probably most, other historians resist the core message. One must reject the triumph of subjectivity as a goal or the erasure of the boundary between fact and fiction.[101]

Postmodernist tendencies so far have not affected historians in Africa to any extent. Some ask whether there exists a connection between this armchair introspection of African history overseas and the decreasing amount of longer-term residence and fieldwork by foreign scholars in tropical Africa itself. Yet even if such a connection should be shown to be valid, the fact still remains that African history is not the only field affected by postmodernism. No consensus exists today in any field of history about what the discipline is and how history should be written. How that situation will evolve is for a futurologist to say, not for a historiographer.

In the last few years spectacular developments have been occurring in tropical Africa. In South Africa the racist policy of apartheid was abandoned in 1989, and a process of building a more representative government began a year later with the liberation of Nelson Mandela. Despite outbreaks of violence, that process continues. Most historians had not foreseen this development, and events are provoking wrenching revisions. Afrikaners have repudiated their whole historiography, and those historians who had interpreted the past as a prologue to a socialist revolution "like 1917 in Russia" will also have to revise theirs.[102]

Meanwhile, in Liberia and Somalia political chaos and civil war have reached unprecedented and unforeseen heights, ostensibly brought on by the politics of ethnicity. Other countries also are threatened by such chaos. Although some African historians had long since been interested in the creation of tribalism, the tenacity of ethnicity and its protean transformations still took Africanists by surprise, especially in the case of Somalia.[103] As a country inhabited by a single ethnic group, Somalia had always been cited as one of the few true nations in the region. These developments, coupled with the resurgence of nationalism in both Western and Eastern Europe, certainly have contributed to the recent emergence of ethnicity as a major specialty in African history.

Moreover, the immiserization of tropical Africa, relative to the evolution of standards of living elsewhere in the world, steadily continued. Its effects on the academic establishments are still severe and affect more countries than before. Therefore, the contribution of African historians to the historiography of Africa continues to decline in relative terms. In addition, one gains the impression that some students of African history abroad are so discouraged by the experience of tropical Africans today that they have turned their backs on the present realities there to take refuge in "nice topics" which block out the unpleasantness and provide an escape into a fantasy world. This situation, combined with the fact that postmodernist fashion encourages the fragmentation within "social history" into ever more esoteric subspecialties, is responsible for the growing chasm which I sense between a historiography which feeds on such themes and one that resonates with African experiences today. Most African scholars, like the general public in their countries, continue to focus on topics that can illuminate the contemporary problems they face or on themes which are relevant to the ideological debates in their countries. So are some foreigners: thus the renewed debate about the significance of the Mau Mau revolt in Kenya against British rule involves mostly Kenyans, but also some foreigners. Yet other foreigners choose "nice topics" and write for each other.[104] Such a chasm between the writing of African history by Africans and by outsiders would blight the field as a whole and should be averted: we should all be writing our major works for an African public.

Today the historiography of Africa is in flux. Old habits and doctrines are crumbling, a great variety of new approaches is being tried out, and many novel imaginative topics are being broached. Intellectually this is a fascinating time for those who maintain a wide-open curiosity about the reconstruction of various pasts in Africa. For this is a rare moment of transition, both between paradigms and between academic generations, one fraught with great dangers of failure but also with great promise. The greatest danger now is a professional attitude which leads scholars to write for each other, rather than for the African populations which should be their preferred audience. If professional reflexes of this sort can be overcome, the next generation may well construct a vision of Africa's past richer and more detailed than their elders could ever have hoped for.

10

Transitions

I WAS a contented child, as I was sauntering along the lane next to the pond in the shade of the gnarled plane trees and passing by the rustic iron park benches. Parents with their toddlers passed by, the air was fragrant with the tinkling of children's voices on the merry-go-round or on rafts on the pond—such a nice familiar outing. Yet the pond was Bei Hai, and Claudine and I were in Beijing. It was a childhood dream come true. When I was a child, China had intrigued me more than any other place: it was on the reverse of the world and therefore an inverted Europe as different as anything could possibly be, and its people were sages because they were so far away. The Chinese herbalist's shop in Antwerp was proof of that. In my schoolbook for the fifth grade a picture of the goddess Ku'an Yin (Guan Yin) followed one of Egyptian fields inundated by the Nile (That is why Egyptians invented geometry!). I daydreamed then that had I been Chinese she would have been a genuine goddess. I wondered how that felt. Not much later at the monastery I had met Dom Pierre-Célestin Lou, the Chinese monk, once a famous and controversial Chinese prime minister, who burned joss sticks, showed me silks, and told Confucian aphorisms.[1]

Now we really were in China, and I was smitten not by the utter strangeness I had expected but by the sense of coming home. It was very much like Belgium before the Second World War: the bicycles, the strollers, the pace of work and leisure, the daily scenes on the streets, the horses and the carts on the rural roads.[2] The pace of life here was more like Europe than the United States. That was wholly unexpected. I was prepared for a maximum degree of difference, not for this uncanny similarity in homely detail. The strangest experience of all was the sudden recognition of individual faces in the crowds. Some people looked the spitting image of others I knew back in Europe or in the United States. The utter fascination

222

of China was its sameness underneath the gaudy exotic raiment of land-scapes, buildings, roofs, rock gardens, and bold script. The wonder was that I instinctively understood so much, that only three weeks later I could ask my way around the city and began to recognize a character or two of the foreign script. The wonder was in this summer of 1986 that I was teaching Central African history and felt that the audience understood me well. The teaching dealt with one cultural world, the teacher came from another, and the public came from a third. Certainly I had carefully "trans-lated" all my similes in parallels taken from Chinese history and clothed my argument in the language of Chinese ideology, but it was still a wonder to find that beyond this language barrier Chinese experts on Tanzania, for instance, saw exactly the same problems I saw and worried about the very same issues concerning its future.

But why was this such a revelation? After all, had I not been in the field, had I not recognized the similarities between the Kuba, who had partly socialized me, and the people at home? Yes I had, but here the parallels were more directly and intimately linked to my own childhood and to my childish construction of the perfectly exotic. This trip was the closure of a quest I had not known I was engaged in. Its effect was an ineffable contentedness and peace.

Visiting China was the first of three omens heralding transitions. The second was a telephone call from New York. A year earlier I had assumed the chair of the African Studies Program in preparation for a meeting of the African Studies Association in Madison and the concomitant celebra-tions of its twenty-fifth anniversary. The program was in poor financial shape. In real terms, student fellowships had declined to one-fourth of what they had been around 1970 and to one-third of what they had been less than a decade earlier. General funding was also slowly shrinking from year to year. It was evident that business as usual would in due course completely hollow out the substance of the program. Hence I prepared a new collective project and had hopes for substantial funding to reinvigo-rate the program. But morale was so low among the members of the program that nothing came of this. Then in 1986 Donald Easum, who was active in relations between Africa and the United States, called me on behalf of Francis X. Sutton, a sociologist with East African experience and a former vice president of the Ford Foundation, to tell me that, as part of a major reorganization, the major foundations were proposing to cut all assistance to African studies programs in the United States.[3] They be-lieved that these programs were adequately supported by the federal Department of Education and that they had drifted into routine to the point that they were now estranged from and irrelevant to the pressing contemporary problems of tropical Africa. Something had to be done, and Sutton enrolled the help of a few colleagues to reverse these proposals. Sutton's campaign bore fruit, and funding for the programs in the United States was saved.

Meanwhile, I found myself one day in early October discussing the situation with a vice president and some of his officers at the Rockefeller Foundation in New York. Evidently African studies programs needed to change in order to survive: this was a problem of transition and renewal. The major question debated was whether the existing programs could be salvaged or not. I argued that they could be and proposed several measures to encourage radical change in order to make research in the social sciences and the humanities more directly relevant to the major issues of the day in tropical Africa. In the end the foundation adopted this view and put some of the ideas we had discussed into practice. Since then some programs have changed, but unfortunately many others still run on and on in the same old rut.

The third sign of transition came in late October during the convention of the African Studies Association in Madison. The former students in history had prepared a celebration to honor Philip Curtin. There was a day-long academic presentation on "Research Trends and Perspectives for African History," followed by the presentation of a Festschrift at a dinner in the evening.[4] But colleagues and former students had schemed behind my back. They had successfully nominated me for a "distinguished Africanist" award by the association. The award was given in recognition of a "lifelong" contribution to African studies. Was it a subtle signal that no more was expected of me, that my useful life was over at age fifty-seven, that the profession was ready to retire me to the portrait gallery of dusty ancestors?[5] They also organized a dinner in my honor to celebrate the award. The atmosphere there was aglow with camaraderie, and I was quite touched by the warm feelings of the former students toward me. Yet I was a little melancholy. The eminence and dynamism of so many of the alumni and alumnae struck me forcefully when I saw so many of them together. I rejoiced in it, yet this occasion, like the festivities for Philip Curtin, signaled a changing of the guard. It was now up to the next generation to tend the garden of African history.

The omens of 1986 were not an illusion. Managing transitions has been the leitmotif ever since. First came the need to manage my own gradual transition into retirement. Because graduate students need at least five years between their admission and their doctorate, the first step to take was to set a date after which I would no longer accept new students for the doctoral degree. Starting in the fall of 1990 I began to supervise new students only as a provisional caretaker. The next step was to phase out formal classroom teaching and to concentrate on tutoring the graduate students I supervised. That step was taken in the fall of 1991.

In 1987 Michael G. Smith, my former tutor at University College, had drawn my attention to the fact that I had never trained anyone in the practice of reconstructing history by using lines of evidence drawn from various disciplines, and especially not in the application of the technique of Words and Things. But those questions were too advanced for an already crowded graduate curriculum. A grant in 1987 made it possible to remedy the situation somewhat.[6] I could now sponsor postgraduate research and initiate one scholar at least into the technique of Words and Things, and provide an opportunity for concrete research in the field combining various techniques. The grant entailed support for a full-scale research project, including fieldwork in tropical Africa. This plan was carried out. Between 1991 and 1993 I supervised one postgraduate scholar throughout the whole process. In addition, a second postgraduate found funding herself, so in 1992–93 I was able to teach her Words and Things as it applied to her research project. It was none too soon for me to take such steps toward managing transition, because personal circumstances were also changing. A death in my large family of origin led to a major reorganization there beginning in 1990, while Claudine and I began to be plagued by bouts of ill health from early 1989 onward. The time had come to enter a different phase of life.

Still one big task remained: to ensure the future of the African History Program at Madison. A transition between generations began on the Madison campus of the university with the appointment of a new chancellor in 1988. In the following years the senior academic administrators who had run the campus for two decades retired from office, while the chancellor instituted major new policies and restructured the administration to reflect the changes. Among these came an ever-higher stress on undergraduate education, education being understood in the sense of "training for life" rather than as a transmission of knowledge. As the dean of students put it: "Our search is far more important than the quest for fusion, the secrets of DNA in cells, or perhaps even the cure for cancer. Why? Because our democracy will not survive unless we succeed."[7] As the quotation shows, this emphasis was sometimes accompanied by a downgrading of research and the acquisition of knowledge. For a program such as

African history, whose justification lay in its contribution to graduate training and research, such pronouncements were disquieting, all the more so because the state of Wisconsin's budgetary support for the university and especially for the Madison campus continued to weaken. Meanwhile, I had also played a role in fashioning a transition within the history department itself at a time when many of its older members were retiring and new teachers were taking their places. The department completely reorganized its administrative structures and began rethinking its mission. In such a climate of change, the rock-solid support which the African History Program had hitherto enjoyed could no longer be taken for granted.

Transition in that program itself began in 1987, when the dean of letters and science unexpectedly called me to authorize the hiring of an additional historian of West Africa. During the next academic year I chaired a search committee, and we hired a woman candidate. But an African scholar, who had been in charge of our outreach program in African studies and had not been chosen, was so offended that he launched a lawsuit against the university, initially on the grounds of racial discrimination. Discrimination on the grounds of age was added later. Following nearly a year of legal proceedings, the case came to trial in federal court and was settled a few months later by mutual agreement. As chair of the committee I was most involved in the proceedings and was the one most under stress as a result.[8] By then it was the summer of 1989, and Steven Feierman was leaving to assume a position at the University of Florida. The department immediately began another search for a senior person to replace him. This became a frustrating effort which lasted three years before we were able to appoint Tom Spear, a well-known senior East Africanist. But when he accepted the position in 1992 it became clear that our new West Africanist would leave Madison and that I would retire in the not so distant future. Hence the transition of staff remains unfinished, and the program's future is still not completely safeguarded.

Teaching was not in transition. It continued as before. Indeed, I enjoyed one course in particular. Steven Feierman, who had taught the history of South Africa, left at a time when that country was undergoing a dramatic change, a situation which was closely followed by public opinion in the United States. This roused interest in a solid course on the subject. I created a brand-new lecture course with a set of over five hundred slides as a backbone.[9] The class was large, and the students were so keen that the lectures became like installments in a weekly television series that was working toward a climax in the last week of the spring of 1991. Indeed, I prepared the final lectures at the last minute to keep pace with the denouement of apartheid after the takeover by F. W. De Klerk and the release of Nelson Mandela.

At the same time a number of exceptionally gifted graduate students were developing research projects which took some of them in wholly uncharted directions. They worked much more closely with me than their counterparts had even a few years earlier. Intellectually they were influenced by the new introspective trends which sought to explain historical developments, not by the work of anonymous and hidden social forces, but by the interaction of people's conceptions, images, and aspirations with the situations in which they found themselves. Yet in order to achieve this deeper level of understanding, the students had to achieve a greater command of the language of research than had hitherto been necessary. Some of them achieved it. These same projects also needed a longer time in the field, and the students managed that too. Thus for me these years were particularly exciting, as I closely followed the progress of these innovative projects.

All this was quite gratifying, yet at the same time also depressing. This closer collaboration between us was imposed by the increasing difficulties encountered by the students. These were financial, connected with field-work, and linked to the hardships of finding employment. Nineteen eighty-six was the first year in which prospective candidates arrived and were accepted in the program already burdened with sizable debts, at a time when the opportunities for financial support were still dwindling. Indeed, we lost some students because we could not find enough support for them. So students spent increasing amounts of time working for a daily living, which slowed down their progress through the curriculum. Because field-work was becoming increasingly difficult, students also needed more guidance in connection with their doctoral research than had been the case previously. Once back from the field, they needed further encouragement and advice, because, contrary to earlier projections, there were few new openings for employment. This created a situation which led recruiters to escalate their expectations of applicants. It was no longer enough for candidates to be writing up a doctorate and perhaps have some experience as teaching assistants. Some recruiters now expected a doctorate in hand, published articles, and evidence that applicants had taught whole courses by themselves. How could our students meet such high expectations? How could they find opportunities to teach, find time for writing articles, and find the strength to suddenly translate their fascination with the complexities of ongoing research into a tight schedule to write up a doctorate? It was my task to help them through the transition from field researcher to dissertator and from dissertator to teaching faculty.

Of all these problems, fieldwork has lately been the major worry for me. Students are not aware of the extent of the breakdown of public health and internal security in many countries of tropical Africa, and the professional associations do not publicize these for fear of creating a negative impression about "Africa." Nevertheless, the dangers are genuine. In addition, because of their youth and inexperience, most students are not very impressed by such issues. I felt responsible for them, though, and I was quite concerned. I would not let them go to places which were reputed to be too dangerous or too unhealthy. Even so, some students contracted serious diseases in the field but, thank God, overcame them without major disaster. At the same time the fear of government officials in many African countries that foreign researchers would witness and report on the extent of misrule and oppression increased, and consequently research activities were more and more distrusted. Research permits came to be hedged about by increasingly severe restrictions or were simply refused.

To my surprise, I found China in 1986 to be far more open to research than a clutch of tropical African countries. In some of the latter, researchers were confined to the capital, while a few countries went so far as to refuse a research permit to anyone who knew the dominant local language well. Everywhere government officials monitored the activities of all researchers, nationals as well as foreigners, and in a few cases even made sure that researchers only met "approved" informants.[10] In all countries, research on "sensitive topics" was impossible, and there were more of these than met the eye. The upshot was that research in many countries became more difficult, that in countries such as Angola, racked by civil war, it became nearly impossible, and that the person overseeing a research project always had to be reasonably well informed about health, security, and government clearance in every single case. Indeed, I once found myself carefully negotiating the conditions for the fieldwork of one of my students with the national authorities in charge.

In the later eighties my contacts with Africa, especially Africans living there, became less intense. Given my increased responsibilities in Madison and creeping age, extended fieldwork was no longer possible. UNESCO's project and the collaboration with Paris were winding down, and it made no sense any longer for me to teach at African universities: they had all the staff they needed or were in such a state of disorganization that it would be an empty gesture. Did I not miss "Africa"? Claudine and I both did, but we both found vicarious solace in reading the often long and enthralling letters which some of the graduate students kept writing from the field, so that we could still keep abreast with the ups and downs, the twists and the turns, of their research experiences and with various aspects of daily life in the communities where they worked. The letters told us how communities in Africa were changing and how far daily life there diverged from the conditions we had experienced even a decade earlier. In addition, friends and visitors from Africa prevented us from becoming totally estranged and helped me to keep a somewhat realistic view of the tie between my own research and the interests of African intellectuals. The question of a common core of culture seemed to be a central issue there, whereas Africanists outside of the continent, finding it too romantic or too ethereal, did not pay much attention to it. Thus the creation of CICIBA in 1983 caused little comment overseas. Yet as it happened, the creation of an organization devoted to the study of "Bantu culture" made my project on the peoples of the forests still relevant and timely.

Work on my major research topic continued. It was both an exhilarating experience and a somewhat unsettling one. On the one hand, it was exciting to sail into totally uncharted waters, but on the other the questions I dealt with became so different from those with which other scholars were grappling that this quest left me almost totally isolated from what was going on in African historiography. I had, therefore, no idea how these scholars would receive this kind of work. Moreover, Words and Things had become the pivot for the whole historical reconstruction research, and I did not even know how convincing this methodology would be to others. I planned to write a large work in three volumes in French. But as I began to compose it, I soon realized that it was totally unrealistic to expect that a French publisher would produce such a book at a time when academic publications were in crisis in France. So early in 1988 I changed course and decided to write a short work in English and have it translated into French. In this way at least something could go into print. As I was ruthlessly condensing the results of the research, an overall thesis began to stand out in bolder and bolder relief. The peoples in the rainforests had inherited a single ancestral way of living and thinking some four thousand years ago or more. They had elaborated and transformed these ancestral patterns in a huge variety of ways through the ages but had preserved its basic principles as late as 1900.

This book recounted the history of a single Central African tradition, for the only appropriate concept for this sort of phenomenon was the term *tradition*. And yet ever since the beginning of my career that term had been anathema. I loathed expressions such as "traditional life" or "traditional times" because they implied that before the arrival of the Europeans nothing had ever changed. The term had often been used as a screen to hide prejudice and ignorance. Ever since the days of Hitler, historians of Europe had been very much aware that many "traditions" were invented.[11] In the eighties historians of Africa began to apply this knowledge as a means to understand the rise of tribalism, that is, the "invention" of new ethnicities in colonial times. In the process they denied that genuine "tradition" in the older sense of the word existed.[12] But these historians seemed to imply that all "traditions" are spurious and by implication to deny the very existence of the type of phenomenon which now emerged: a very old and yet dynamic heritage of a complex of worldview and behavior, something comparable, for instance, to the use of *tradition* in the expressions "Judeo-Christian tradition" or "Confucian tradition." I found myself defending the notion of "tradition" as a genuine phenomenon.[13] The point is important, because such traditions seen at any given moment are called "civilization." In other words, the use of the term *tradition* underlined the fact that there had been a genuine Central African civilization.

The manuscript was finished in 1989 and published a year later.[14] That had by no means been a foregone conclusion. After all, the work was very condensed, and hence not easy to read. It contained an unusual methodology and communicated less familiar reflections about history. I was all the more eager to see how it would be received. The reviews were good, and some were even glowing, although David W. Cohen in *Current Anthropology* took a postmodernist stance. Some reviewers regretted excessive condensation, while all of them looked at the book from the point of view of their own specialties. Thus an economic anthropologist regretted the lack of emphasis on the concept of wealth, a feminist the lack of prominence of women, and the *Times Literary Supplement* regretted that so much effort had been spent on a less important part of Africa.[15] The reviewers did not dispute the phenomenon of tradition, and the methodology elicited no negative comments. It was especially gratifying to receive the support of various professional linguists, even though they naturally found some fault with points of detail here or there.[16] It was equally reassuring to hear from various African scholars in the region that they agreed with the reconstructions proposed for their areas of specialty.

My greatest satisfaction, however, came from the reception of a long and glowing letter of approval by a hitherto unknown reader in Kinshasa, C. Inogwabini Bila-Isia, a student of physics and a "native Zairian of the true Equatorial Forest," because it showed both that I was reaching the intended audience and that the book made sense to those who actually live in equatorial Africa. He argued that most publications dealt with the "Africa" of Africanists, and the "Africa" of romantics, and then claimed that "this is one of the rare cases in which 'the true Africa' can be read, can be felt in writing, whether these are from the hand of African Africanists or others."[17]

Still the book had not yet reached the public I had most aimed at: the scholars and students at the universities in the region itself. Inogwabini's first request was to have a French translation "for all those other young people who cannot read English." The translation had been made and the search for a publisher in Paris was already under way in 1989. But eventually, just as had happened with my earlier books, none could be found there. Yet the translation did appear in 1991 as a copublication from the French-speaking University of Louvain and a research center at Mbandaka in Zaire.[18] Still, even though the book is now available, at least in Kinshasa and Mbandaka, my aim to bring it to its natural audience is still being thwarted. In the present circumstances no one in Zaire can afford to buy it, even at the most nominal price.

Meanwhile, as this "main project" was being finished, the ancillary project dealing with the genetic classification of Bantu languages was also coming to fruition. After thirty years of data-collecting and countless delays, the computer performed some twenty million operations and finally spewed out a nearly definitive set of trees for Bantu languages in January 1992.[19] While this involves 542 languages, the result can only be called nearly definitive because data for perhaps 25 languages, mostly from southern Tanzania and southwestern Angola and nearby Zambia, are still lacking. Yet these cannot significantly affect the overall results. The time has come for a historical interpretation of the data, even though the addition of the missing languages will require some revisions of detail later on. The computer has produced five trees according to different statistical assumptions. Collectively these document the main outlines of the linguistic history of every language involved: its genetic ties and the major linguistic influences to which it was later subjected. Moreover, the computer also produced spatial distributions of every form and every single meaning of the basic words involved. The historical implications of all this information need to be worked out. This certainly will be an issue that will occupy scholars for some time to come.

When the book went to press, the time had come either to start on a new "main project" of long duration or to decide whether I should restrict my future research activities to less ambitious goals. On reflection, it seemed better to realize a final contribution first. I had always imagined that at the end of a career any researcher should leave a work that distilled the essentials of his or her experience. I had also imagined that this would take the form of a "last word" book, in which one would sum up all of one's views about Central African history. I now was faced with the realization that this was silly. The pace of research would soon overtake whatever was a "last word," and besides, my views were already available to anyone who was interested enough to follow the trickle of my publications. Was it not more useful, as a legacy to the profession, to speak about my own experience in the framework of the general historiography of African history, and to do so now, at a time when a fashionable collective introspection is creating sometimes spurious and often paralyzing uncertainties?

11

Living with Africa

A T T H E end of our journey, we are in the present. We have seen that the development of academic African history was incapsulated in an overall social background. The reconstruction of a new world after 1945, the collapse of colonialism around 1960, the student protests from 1968 to 1970—these general turning points exercised a deep impact on this field. The collapse of apartheid after 1989, a more local event in world history, initially has had a more immediate impact on African history than the collapse of communism in Eastern Europe and the Soviet Union.

Against this background, a sociologist could tell the following story and correlate it reasonably well with these turning points. In a first "phase movement" after 1945, the first academic posts are created in the colonial capitals and in some of their dependencies. By 1960 massive growth in the recruitment and training of historians occurs both in the United States and in tropical Africa itself, more modest growth elsewhere in Europe. During a second phase movement after 1970, this growth slows down considerably in the United States. In tropical Africa the adversary relationships between universities and governments as well as an increasingly rapid economic decline begin to disable universities and their programs in African history. Meanwhile, recruitment to the field first stagnates, then drops, in Europe, especially in Great Britain. Yet at the same time, through the effect of the lag in academic recruitment combined with the lag between research and publication, the number of publications continues to grow very rapidly. By 1970 a new generation of scholars, the first to be especially trained as professional historians of Africa, enters the field. An unintended consequence of the rise of professionalism is the fragmentation of the field into subfields led by separate networks of specialists, as well as the blurring of the boundaries between history and the other social sciences.[1] By the later

233

1980s the issues and agendas for research generated in North America totally dominate the field, while historians in tropical Africa itself (except for southern Africa) have gradually lost the means to publish and even to pursue new research.

A historian of ideas would tell a different tale, which also articulates well with the major turning points. The first historians believed that a universal truth exists and that it can be found by correctly interpreting the relevant sources. The history of Africa could be recovered "as it had actually been," or nearly so. Their approach was "positivist" and followed the "hypothetico-deductive" method as proposed by Karl Popper, an approach they shared with most historians elsewhere.[2] In reaction to the former imperial history prevailing before 1960, they held that the history of Africans could be reconstructed and that Africans could not be reduced to the role of supporting cast for the deeds of Europeans in Africa. That was their "paradigm."[3] This first generation of African historians was deeply marked by the ideologies propagated among the Western allies during the Second World War, a war which had been fought against racism and for self-determination. They expected that the independent countries in tropical Africa, once liberated from the chains of colonialism, would flourish. They celebrated Africanness and nationalism. In their struggle with imperial historians—and many of them had been trained as historians of empire—they borrowed much of the conceptual framework and the general point of view of their adversaries: for instance, they shared with them a thematic predilection for states and trade. Under outside pressure to publish new histories of Africa in a hurry, they produced these far too quickly, often at the expense of a full and careful study of their sources. During the fifties the focus remained almost entirely on precolonial African history, with the slogan "Africans have a history!" Later, in the sixties, the focus shifted to the colonial period, and the terms "African resistance" and "African initiative" allowed writers to integrate the record of this period into a partisan nationalist history.

After 1970 the rise of the first professional generation of historians generated a new revisionist "paradigm" which soon became dominant. Many among them had been student protesters in 1968–70, and they were disenchanted with the established order everywhere. These scholars held that there is a universal truth, that there exist universal laws of history, and that the truth can be found, but not by working from sources. The laws can only be discovered by inference from theoretical premises, and laws are then used to interpret sources, never vice versa. Hence these scholars were at least as positivist as their predecessors had been, but they rejected the hypothetico-deductive method in favor of what they saw as a more "scientific" Kuhnian interpretation. As a result of their belief in universal laws, they stressed the similarities between historical developments in Africa and elsewhere and dismissed any specific "Africanness" as irrelevant. Ironically, they thus shared the stand of imperial history that in the end there was no specific African history, but only one "world history." Marxist theories were the most successful among the various social science theories and induced researchers to focus on classes and exploitation, especially as revealed in the history of capitalism, relations of production, workers, and peasants. The theme of exploitation was also extended, however, to other groups, such as women. This type of theory was clearly influenced by the general rise of socialist ideologies during the period. Most historians of this generation expected that socialist rule, as practiced, for example, in Tanzania or Guinea, would lead to prosperity and stability in the countries that had adopted it. They were convinced that apartheid in South Africa would be violently overthrown by a class-based revolution. But by itself the stress on theory was perhaps even more a product of the desire to turn African history into something more "scientific," and hence more professional. As a result, theories bred jargon, which in turn limited the audience for such writings, while theoretical disputes took precedence over quarrels about empirical evidence. These two developments strongly encouraged subspecialization.

In the late 1980s the new generation of revisionist historians appeared at the very time when the oldest academic historians of Africa were beginning to retire. Once again the Young Turks proclaimed another new "paradigm." They denied the existence of a universal truth. Neither sources nor theory can find what does not exist. Hence the writing of history merely expresses present-day beliefs about the past. Therefore, historians should be content to investigate what, how, why, by whom, and for whom historical consciousness is produced and written down. These scholars thus rejected any variant of positivism—extremists among them rejected the possibility of any kind of history—but they continued to cling to a professional theory, this time literary theory. These young historians were disillusioned by the discouraging economic and political developments in Africa and by a dwindling interest in the history of Africa elsewhere. As a result, they turned to introspection. Deconstruction and postmodernism fitted their disenchanted mood perfectly, while expressing it in a new jargon and endowing it with new theories and a professional aura. Yet as a result of their stress on consciousness, these scholars, like their ancestors of the fifties and sixties, have reintroduced a specific African dimension to the history of Africa. Even though they violently rejected sociological theory in favor of literary theory, they stressed "theory" even more than their predecessors. This paradigm as a whole is therefore even more conducive to increased fragmentation and particularism in historical studies. These have now progressed to such an extent that one may well ask what a general history of Africa still consists of. Meanwhile in Africa itself, few historians have embraced this trend. Ironically, it once again robs them of a past, and anyway most among them cannot afford to ignore the difficulties of daily life in order to indulge in the luxury of intense introspection. As a result, an intellectual chasm threatens to open up between the historiography of Africa in Africa and outside.

These two sorts of tales about the historiography of African history are plausible and compatible with each other. Yet they are flawed: they erase nuances, reify sociological generations; they homogenize attitudes toward professionalism or toward the impact of contemporary events on the minds of scholars, and they exaggerate tendencies by turning them into concrete successive dogmas called "paradigms" and by implying mass conversions from one set of convictions to another. In reality, a whole gamut of "paradigms" can be found at any given time and at all times. To be sure, African historiography has gone through several phases, but not from one orthodox dogma to another. Yes, the social milieu and the intellectual style in the fifties and sixties was demonstrably different from that of the seventies and eighties and is now becoming different again, but there are no iron-clad paradigms, and the periodization of these tendencies is not nearly as sharp as I have presented it for the sake of exposition. Indeed, the sometimes stark contrast between the general account of how the field developed and the story of my own experience shows how untidy the rise and development of intellectual tendencies in African history has been. Rather than a dynamic of Kuhnian crystallization and recrystallization, its development is more similar to the uneven flow of a plasma in which nearly random differences in the trajectory of single molecules affect the whole. The study of historiography is like the study of the weather. Only a theory of chaos can fully account for it!

At journey's end it is easy to see that this present we find ourselves in is not the preordained conclusion of things past. It could have been otherwise. It is easy to perceive how accounts about the "state of the question" subtly distort the record and how essays which advocate present practice either by contrasting it to the errors of the past or by claiming the authority of enlightened precursors distort even more. Those sorts of accounts

are the bane of historiography. Yet they are frequent because the legitimation of the present and the tyranny of hindsight make them so attractive. It
is therefore unfortunate that they still represent most of the easily accessible historiographies of African history.[4]

If partiality is the most obvious among the flaws of these sorts of
accounts, their most insidious impact lies elsewhere and unfortunately
often remains undetected. These tales are such tidy and satisfying narratives and the itinerary they lay out is so straightforward, leading up to
such an attractive climax in the present, that they are utterly persuasive.
By starting from the present, such accounts of the writing of history
become tales of a quest in which pilgrim historians travel from one paradigm to the next and better paradigm, coming ever closer to the Holy Grail
of an immanent "truth." That is their mistake. In contrast, the itinerary
described in this book was anything but tidy. We traveled along one mean-
dering trail among many, from one fork in the road to another, now going
here and then there, seemingly going nowhere and everywhere. This is a
bad story line, and therefore our tale is not nearly as persuasive. Yet it is
more authentic, because the Grail is not an immanent truth, which does
not exist.

No historiographer can ignore the current debates about the notion of
truth, because the meaning of his or her whole practice is at stake here.
Hence a digression on that issue becomes necessary. In one sense truth
stands for being genuine, as in "This document is not faked; rather, it is
true." In a second sense, truth is opposed to fiction. It is defined as "reality."[5] Either Alex Haley had an ancestor Kunta Kinte or he did not; Kunta
Kinte came from the village of Juffure in Gambia or he did not. Even if
some scholars today advocate that this distinction should be blurred,
because historians, like creative writers, convince their audiences, the general public everywhere in the world knows better. There is an opposition
between true and false: it is the difference between telling the truth and
lying and also between "real happening" and dreaming.[6] In practice
events do happen or they do not.[7] When it comes to the present, no one
denies this. Yet is the present not merely the most recent past? Hence one
cannot deny this for the past either.

But truth is also usually defined as "what really happened."[8] To historians, that immediately recalls Leopold von Ranke's "Wie es eigentlich
gewesen" ("as it really happened"), the determination of which he supposedly claimed to be the task of history.[9] Historians, by long-standing
custom, love to cite and to damn this expression. Never mind that it does
not mean what they say it does. Ranke used the expression twice, once to

237

plead for dispassionate study in contrast to those who saw the task of history as teaching and/or judging, and once in contrast to a teleological presentation. Moreover, it is evident that later readers have attributed far too much esoteric meaning to this "as it really happened"; *eigentlich* ("really") does not have a metaphysical sense here, but signals a contrast. "As it really happened" can never be achieved, because we will never have all the evidence needed to reconstruct a past perfectly in all its details. Hence history is never totally true. But no one who makes a statement about the present is in possession of all the data either. Yet we distinguish between true and false statements about the present. The point surely is that although a statement is never true in the "absolute" sense because of the lacunae in the information and the subjectivity of the speaker, it is true or false as far as the available evidence goes. It is unwarranted to claim that there is no truth unless it is total truth. The available evidence then is true or false, and statements are false when they are contradicted by evidence. Historians can truthfully reconstruct the past, and they can do this better and better from generation to generation as more evidence accumulates. Old Ranke is not as out of date as it seems when he writes on the next page that his ideal was to have his exposition come as close as possible to the event itself in its human intelligibility, in its unity, and in its fullness, but that he failed. This is far from an obtuse positivism![10]

But there is more, because evidence does not exist by itself. A history is an *interpretation* of the past, and historians select the evidence that is germane to the issue they study. Evidence thus flows from an interpretation, and in this sense there are no facts out there. It was the error of the extreme positivists to think that there are facts out there and that their assembly automatically yields "the" correct reconstruction of the past by itself.[11] The word *interpretation* refers to the way a person understands or conceives of a situation or event, and the activity is therefore eminently subjective. Even interpretations of present events or situations are not "real" events or "real" situations, but subjective ones. Interpretations themselves are neither true nor false. In historical practice, one requires therefore that interpretations be "truthful to the evidence," that is, that they not be contradicted by any known germane evidence. That is the reason for all those footnotes! When interpretations are called "true," "truth" must refer to something else. Indeed it does: In this sense, and in this sense only, "truth" refers to *conviction*, a consensus shared by audience and writer or narrator that "it was so."[12] Hence truth in this sense is conferred by the audience upon the author, and its quality hinges on the competence of the audience.

The task of the historian consists in selecting an "issue" to be studied, assembling the relevant evidence, interpreting it, and publishing the results as an argument or as a narrative. Thus when one assesses history writing over time, one deals, from the point of view of "truth," with apples and oranges. The bits of evidence are true or false. A hypothesis about "what happened" is true for the moment (but given the lacunae, not totally true) if all the data conform but is shown to be false (falsified) as soon as contradictory evidence turns up. An interpretation—which is neither true nor false in itself—is true when it convinces a given audience. It follows that while historians can make "truer and truer" reconstructions as more evidence is uncovered over time, there can be no growth toward an immanent absolute and universal truth when it comes to interpretations, including theories. Hence these two developments in the historiography must be considered separately. It is ironic that the humble activity of constructing low-level hypotheses around evidence to show *what* happened is usually given short shrift in histories of history writing, as compared with the attention lavished on the successive theoretical interpretations about *why* it happened. Such is the glamor of grand theories that their succession delineates the very phases of historiography. And yet theories cannot become truer over time, while low-level hypotheses about evidence can.

The history of academic African history has been exceptional in two ways. In no other case has European-style higher education, and academic historiography with it, been transplanted at such speed and on such a continentwide scale (if portions of North Africa are excepted). This transplantation was a part of the planned "decolonization" process and therefore affected all colonies where this process took place. Second, the activity of writing African history is the only case on such a scale dominated by outsiders even today.[13] This is a continuing anomaly. In all other major parts of the world, and that includes the major so-called Third World areas, the writing of history, academic history included, has primarily been conducted in the area itself, by authors of the area, in the languages of the area, and for audiences in the area. But in tropical Africa the writing of academic history was organized by "outsiders," and ever since, the epicenters of this activity have remained outside Africa, despite all efforts to alter the situation. It is a crucial anomaly. Reviewing this book in manuscript, John O. Hunwick put it as follows: "Imagine how it would be if French historiography had been pioneered by Indians or British history by Egyptians!"[14]

Outsiders initiated academic history here. They created the university departments, and they wrote the first substantive histories. They set up the framework within which African historians later worked, and they "trained" them how to write academic history. The pioneers wrote for an outside audience which shared their worldviews and social practice, not for an audience in Africa itself, except for African historians of Africa and a few others who had absorbed Euro-American academic culture. When African scholars began to take their destinies into their own hands, they unwittingly continued to write their major works to a large extent for the same academic audience rather than for their own national populations. This occurred despite the fact that in many countries concerted efforts were made to bring the results of historical research to the attention of a national public, mostly teachers and students in high schools.[15] While these authors attacked imperial history and promoted national history, they continued to write in English or in French, thus limiting access of their local audiences. Implicitly they still looked for approval of their work in Europe or North America as a guarantee of its high technical standard. In the early seventies, it seemed for a moment that African institutions and scholars were taking the lead in the field worldwide, but new economic and political trends prevented this from happening. As a result, the intellectual epicenters of the field, even today, still lie primarily in North America and to a lesser degree in Europe. This situation has resulted despite the crucial role Africans have played in shaping the field and despite the fact that most readers are in Africa. Only there is this history of general interest to the whole population, and only there is it a core subject taught to millions in schools and at universities.[16]

This anomaly goes to the heart of this historiography because it affects the fundamental relationship between author and audience. The usual "natural" situation in history writing occurs when an author and audience share the same worldviews and basic social norms and when the history itself deals with their forebears, whose worldviews and social norms were the antecedents of those prevailing now. Then history is written and evaluated within a single cultural framework, and both author and audience are best placed to understand the motivations of their forebears whose history they tell.[17] Where there is no shared common culture between author, historical actors, and audience, a somewhat artificial history results. In African history the most common situations are either that author and audience share a common culture which is not African or that the model audience African authors have in mind is foreign rather than the actual African audience who reads their work and for whom they may intend to write. Such a situation adds the risk of cultural distortion to any historical reconstruction.[18]

Outside historians of Africa, including some westernized Africans themselves, are pushing the limits of what historians can achieve because they are coming perilously close to a situation in which consensus between author and audience about the "truth" of an interpretation as it is conferred by the audience becomes meaningless. Local audiences are much more knowledgeable about the nature of the evidence, the context surrounding the historical actors described, and their motivations than foreign audiences. For the latter, authors must translate the cultural specificity of African situations, even down to simple statements about geography, into terms understandable to their audience. Hence comparative statements are necessary, such as "Central Africa is the size of the United States east of the Mississipi" or "Central Africa is slightly larger than West and Central Europe." These assertions are both right and wrong, for apart from size in square kilometers, Central Africa is quite different from either Europe or the United States. More important, such statements cannot be evaluated by any single audience either in Africa or abroad, because they transcend cultural experience. Hence foreign audiences evaluating the believability of a historical reconstruction about Africa remain ill informed, and their approval of a particular work means little.

While most foreign historians of Africa have avoided the exuberant excesses Hollywood commits when it portrays ancient times or tells of remote civilizations, they are still highly vulnerable to yawning traps of cultural misinterpretation.[19] To avoid these, they should therefore seek the opinion of a "natural" audience. Problems of cultural mistranslation would soon be pointed out to them. It follows that, wherever possible, detailed historical reconstructions should be written for the best-qualified African audience, whether academic or popular. On the other hand, "natural" audiences anywhere are poor judges of technical issues (e.g., dating, discussions of authenticity, and the like) and often ill informed about comparative material. Hence the ideal audience to address such issues consists of fellow specialists. Nevertheless, in the end, our justification as historians is to write full-fledged historical reconstructions, not technical comments or metahistory. Therefore, historians of Africa should write at least their major works for those communities in Africa who are the descendants of those whose history is being told and hence are the most valid "natural" audiences. Unfortunately this is easier said than done. Outsiders find it very difficult, if not impossible, to do so, because the practical difficulties seem insurmountable. The language in which history is being written, the availability of a publisher, the distribution and the cost to the readers, are all major hurdles. Another significant consideration is the prevailing practice in academic life to judge an author's quality, standing, and reputation by the opinion of his or her peers. Hence academic authors tend to write for each other.

Yet the question of the audience is, I believe, the most serious challenge facing the writing of African history, and it should be addressed. As a young scholar I used to believe in a single universal truth accessible to collective academic endeavor: one wrote for one's peers. My "Kuba history" was not even written in a language accessible to Kuba intellectuals. But by the sixties I understood that history was to be written for those whose identities were most concerned in it. I therefore attempted to publish the *Tio Kingdom* in French, the European language in use in the area. I was incapable of writing it in Tio, and even if I could do so, who would publish it? But even French turned out not to be possible. So I published in English, a language unknown to the Tio at the time. As a result, it took almost a generation before some Tio had access to it. Once they did, they began of their own accord to translate it into French. When I began to work on *Paths in the Rainforests,* my specific goal had become to write for African academics and other intellectuals in equatorial Africa. Yet once again, the book had to be published in English first, although in this case a French version speedily followed. Now the book exists in French and is available in two cities in equatorial Africa, but no one in Zaire can afford to buy it! In the case of *Kingdoms of the Savanna,* the French translation was published even before the original in English, and it reached a sizable number of readers. Some among them reported their reactions to me. So there has been a "natural" audience. Recently a summary of the book was published in Kikongo, which is read by people who are among the descendants of those whose history is told in the book. However difficult to achieve, authors, insiders and outsiders alike, must strive to reach "natural" audiences and thus end this anomaly of African historiography.

Some may reassure themselves by the observation that after all the historiography of African history has run parallel to the successive intellectual movements which have unfolded in the historiographies of Europe and North America. Even the stress on "African history for Africans" has its parallel in that stream of historiography which set out to document the history of the common folk and to give a voice to those who were silent in the official record.[20] That, of course, is to be expected from a transplant! True, by the mid-sixties some divergences with a general Western historiography appeared. The commitment to nationalism by some authors in African history did contrast with the positions espoused by the most influential writers of European or North American history. Even so, many historians, especially those who, like Yves Person, hailed from smaller European ethnicities, wrote in a vein similar to nationalist African historians. But such divergences are small and only underline how deep the parallel runs. Even the conviction still held by some proud historians of Africa that they are special because they were in the vanguard of the historiography in Europe or North America is unjustified. Almost always historians of Africa have followed their siblings rather than preceded them: it was not just African history but history in general which discovered oral history and was influenced by the social sciences in the seventies and by postmodernism after 1985. Indeed, usually these tendencies appeared just as early or a little earlier in the historiographies of Europe and North America. In the end, the parallelism between the historiographies remains overwhelming and still points to a certain degree of alienation of African history from its natural audiences.

In contrast to the picture just painted, when one looks at forty years of historiography from the angle of substantive content, these have been years of undeniable achievements. Researchers in African history have accumulated more and more evidence about more and more facets of the past. They have been reconstructing the past in ever-greater detail. To appreciate this, consider what we knew about Central Africa half a century ago. Its precolonial history was almost totally unknown. With the exception of the coastal areas of Kongo and Angola, an opaque mist covered the past of the whole region until the late nineteenth century. For earlier times there were conjectures about migrations, but they were like geometric figures, tied neither to a chronology nor to geography. Nothing was concrete, nothing merited the term *reconstruction*. Here and there some local reconstructions were based on oral tradition, but they were so few and so isolated that little meaning could be derived from them: only the occasional dot of feeble light trembled in the mists. By the 1990s the fog had lifted. The major features of a detailed history have been reconstructed for the whole area over the last half millennium, and the outlines of a political history are appearing for at least a half millennium before that. A somewhat vaguer outline of economic history is emerging for that period as well, and a tentative but realistic chronology now covers the whole area from the times when farmers first settled there, between two and four millennia ago. In this sense obvious progress has been made. More precise hypotheses about what happened have succeeded each other, and every year still brings a new crop of them.

A similar story obtains for other parts of the continent. The gains of substance are easily appreciated, for instance, by comparing the detail of concrete contents in Basil Davidson's *Old Africa Rediscovered* of 1959 with the eight volumes of the *Cambridge History of Africa*, which give an SOAS view from the mid-sixties to the mid-seventies, and then moving on to the *General History of Africa*, written from various point of views mostly between the mid-seventies and the mid-eighties. Decade after decade, and generation after generation, irrespective of dominant phases, African history is being reconstructed in a more and more detailed and plausible way.

This accumulation of knowledge obviously has affected overall interpretations of why all this happened, because this accumulation forces overall views to account for more data, to become more concrete and more precise. Richer data and debates about more precise interpretations eventually lead to challenging even old, established verities. For instance, it has always been accepted that around the turn of the last millennium a kingdom of Ghana flourished in West Africa and that it was succeeded by a different kingdom or kingdoms called Mali. But in 1992 one author could propose a general reevaluation of this view. For him Ghana and the earliest kingdom of Mali were one and the same.[21] Whatever the merit of this new proposition, it certainly will lead to a renewed evaluation of all the pertinent evidence and thus to a better-grounded hypothesis. Thus the succession of interpretations contributes to a continuing accumulation of knowledge and improvements in the understanding of Africa's history.

Greater understanding has been fostered either by proving that some earlier explanations are untenable because they are contradicted by the relevant evidence, by pointing to some fatal contradiction in the logic of the argument itself, or by pointing out lacunae of research. Thus the Marxist paradigm pointed to the lack of research on a set of topics related to exploitation, and the recent postmodern paradigm has provoked research on such topics as childbirth, hygiene, or the effects of alcoholism. Hence, even though the concurrence or succession of paradigms by itself cannot lead to a closer approximation of a nonexistent immanent truth, successive or competing paradigms can eventually lead to more informed or truer reconstructions. Looking back, one cannot but conclude that genuine progress has occurred in African historiography.[22]

Finally, what does the confrontation of my personal experiences and a more conventional account of the historiography of Africa in general tell us about historiography? Clearly I, like more than a few others, especially in the early days, unwittingly stumbled into this field. Yet soon my research and publications were quite in line with general developments in African

244

history. I had become just another fish in the shoal. It is easy to see how this occurred. I joined a community which collectively had set for itself a common topic, an agenda, and a goal. In some ways this is similar to playing soccer. The field is laid out, one plays by the rules, and the aim is to score goals. But it is a strange kind of soccer. The posts are shifted, the rules keep changing, and there is only one team.

But was I just a fish in the shoal? What about personal quirks, such as my refusal during the second phase of African historiography to take up the fashionable subjects of the day? Quirks are not unusual. After all, historians like everyone else do have personal inclinations. Personal inclination and some serendipity explain how Bogumił Jewsiewicki, a self-avowed "historical materialist," became interested in modern Zairian art and introduced the subject into the historiography of Zaire, which in turn contributed to the formulation of the general postmodernist trend.[23] In this case a quirk of personality has influenced the whole field. It is therefore legitimate to ask how one's own work has contributed to the historiography in general. In a practical way one can distinguish four sets of activities here: contributions to the body of knowledge about the past, contributions to the way in which knowledge about the past can be acquired (methods), contributions to a body of theory, and contributions to the training of historians.[24]

Many of my activities have aimed at increasing the body of knowledge about the past. Many of the topics of substance discussed in my publications, including the studies about Burundi, Rwanda, and to a certain extent the Kuba, have been developed by later researchers and hence have proved fruitful. I hope that this will also be the case for *Paths in the Rainforests*. Among my books, one or perhaps two, the Tio book and some of the Kuba studies, may be of more permanent value, even generations from now, because they contain the record of a mass of oral data and observations which can no longer be obtained.

Most other scholars seem of the opinion that my most useful contribution has been in the development of methods. They mention oral traditions in particular, perhaps because my contribution came at such a propitious time in the development of the field.[25] In my own view, that contribution, like the book about the methods of art history in Africa, merely consisted of thinking through the application of general historical method to particular fields. The more original contribution lies in the concrete applications of the Words and Things approach, which has, I believe, even greater potential. Again, the principles were well known earlier, but the connection with ethnography had not been made, and I did develop the methodology more consistently and systematically than before. Its potential to test the results of most other available sources leads to more convincing reconstructions and produces the framework for a general method of inquiry that can be applied to all societies without writing anywhere in the world. Whether this method will be used in this fashion and used with sufficient rigor remains to be seen. After all, the single most important article on method I ever wrote was "The Power of Systematic Doubt in Historical Enquiry," and yet, as far as I know, only the editor of the journal in which it was published ever read it![26]

As for theory, writers of letters on my behalf have praised me as an ethnographer, I suspect in order to sidestep that question.[27] Ever since my youthful days at University College, I have kept up with general social science theory, and I have used concepts and lines of reasoning derived from one or another theory for the historical interpretation of particular cases, but I have never believed that any single body of theory is "truer" than all others, and today I remain as sceptical as ever. I watched some theories grow and admired their ingenuity, and I accept the usefulness of theory in challenging one's own unspoken assumptions. Yet the contingent is as important as the general to the historian in me, and much social science theory is outrageously reductionist: "All other things being equal," it grandly says, when "all other things" are most of the substance studied. As a sceptic I see all too well that the word *theory* often merely stands for a body of unsubstantiated propositions and understand all too well why philosophers define theory as opinion.[28] Hence I have exhibited a relative lack of curiosity about and interest in theoretical novelties that showed no immediate promise for the better understanding of a practical problem I was working on. That in turn explains why I seem to have been less affected by the succession of grand paradigms in the historiography of Africa than have many other historians.

Effective teaching is based on personal interaction and must be a collaborative effort between a set of teachers and students as well as between each teacher and each student. This is especially true for teaching at the more advanced levels.[29] It is therefore difficult to disentangle what one's own contribution has been in that regard, all the more so because an evaluation of this type of impact tends to remain so subjective. Still, I was a part of the team at Madison. Today well over eighty scholars educated there are themselves teaching, many at major universities in the United States. Because half or more of all the positions at major U.S. institutions of higher learning went to our graduates between about 1965 and 1980, Wisconsin has exercised a definite impact. Many of the intellectual leaders in the field today studied in Madison. A number of African students and others from Madison are teaching at universities in tropical Africa. Scholars whose dissertations I supervised are now professing in Botswana, Burundi, Kenya, Nigeria, South Africa, Zaire, and Zambia. Indeed, some of them have become founding fathers in their own countries. At a less advanced level, the training of Libyan oral historians has proved more successful than I could ever have hoped. Also, individual students, often from Central Africa and often in fields other than history, have sought me out for unofficial advice and support. Official and unofficial students have given much meaning to my life, yet I do not really know how much our interactions have contributed to the historiography of Africa.

To establish a balance sheet, as I have just done, is, however, quite misleading. It gives the impression of a person calculating "contributions" in a strictly rational way. It does not work like that at all! Many scholars do not allow their own research to be dominated by an obsession with career considerations. Thus one cannot explain the existence of general intellectual trends in a historiography by the observation that scholars rationally jump on a bandwagon because it furthers their careers. I became a researcher out of curiosity, without much worry about what career this could lead to. I stayed with it because of the satisfactions derived from this kind of work: the emotional satisfaction of interacting with "ordinary" people in different cultures, the intellectual satisfaction of finding out how bits of data come together to form meaningful wholes, the satisfaction to the imagination, that much abused "historical imagination" of recent writers, in creating grand reconstructions to account for a myriad of patiently collected data. That gave most meaning to my professional life at first. My choices were then entirely made on the basis of which position offered the most research opportunities. Later, however, training scholars in my own field acquired just as much meaning for me and became a major consideration.

In any case, an evaluation made by considering personal satisfaction and a sense of achievement often differs from what a balance sheet approach concerned with a whole field shows. For instance, the books I enjoyed writing most were the *Art and History* study, the Tio book, and *Paths,* especially the last two, not my best-known work on oral tradition. The one which was the least challenging was the *Ethnographie du Congo,* and the one that required the most dogged determination in the face of indifference to write was the *Légendes du passé* about Burundi, even though the research in Burundi itself had been quite pleasurable and was informed by perhaps the best field design I ever developed. No doubt the quality of

247

any publication must be influenced by the state of mind and the degree of enthusiasm which underlies its writing, yet when one reads one's own books years later, that is not self-evident. Certainly reviewers do not often seem to pick up such signals. I am surprised myself at the strengths of books I struggled to produce and at the weaknesses in works that were quite inspired and with which I was well pleased at the time. There is no direct correlation between the state of a writer's mind and his or her emotions and the quality or the impact of the work, nor is there a correlation between the amount of work involved and the impact of a book on the field. Yet a state of mind and emotions are important in two ways at least. They give the lie to the notion of a dispassionate and "objective" scholar who rationally digs his or her quota at the coalface of the mine of knowledge, and they help to destroy the common view that the dynamics of historiography in history consist of a rational, calculated progression of data, ideas, and insights, even within the "normality" of one of the Kuhnian paradigms. There is no such thing as "normal science" in history.

The inextricable link between personality and scholarly writing or teaching naturally leads to further questions. For instance, I have been asked why methods have always fascinated me. And what was it that tied me so strongly to tropical Africans and to the study of their past in the first place? It would be disingenuous and conceited for anyone to claim that he or she could in fact be so objective and informed about his or her own personality as to give fully satisfactory answers to personal questions such as these. Yet others cannot do so either, because they always lack much of the necessary information. Because fully authoritative answers cannot be forthcoming to such questions, historiographers often erase all references to personality or personal experience. Yet if one is to account fully for all the factors which condition the creation of a historiography, such answers are needed: to omit any consideration of them constitutes a serious distortion of the dynamics of historiography and creates the spurious image that these dynamics follow strictly disembodied logical processes.

And yet individual quirks are crucial indeed. In order, then, to grasp the intellectual richness of a historiographical tradition, one must capture the continuing tension between them and the resulting general trends. An account of the succession of phases in a historiography and their correlation with general contemporary events traces the movement of the shoal. But it cannot explain how the trends change, how the shoal changes direction, or how it dissolves to form new shoals. To do that, one must follow the quirks of individual fish. Change is only possible because individuals differ. In their idiosyncracies, they harbor the potential for change. Hence, along with an account of the tensions between the cultures of author, audience, and the community studied, the tension between the individual and the collective should be at the heart of any historiography. This book is one attempt to do so. Others certainly will approach the historiography about Africa from different angles. Yet whatever the specific angle, these two types of tensions, which regulate the heartbeat of African history, must be addressed.

In the end, one must recognize that it is impossible ever to write a complete and definitive historiography. There are just too many factors to account for: differences in the personalities and the cultural heritage of the historians involved, differences in the milieux in which they work, the accidents of clusterings among them by acquaintance and friendship rather than by similarities of theoretical views, the accidents of the general political, economic, religious, and ideological trends which are always sweeping the world and making certain topics more "interesting" than others, sheer luck, the serendipity that comes from stumbling over something when the time is ripe for that issue. And yet the panoramic overviews do show that beyond the Brownian motion of individual accident, genuine patterns exist. There are academic communities and academic cohorts and generations, there are overall financial trends, and general intellectual trajectories do exist. "Paradigms" do influence research, there are trends, often influenced by the expectations of institutions which provide career positions and by those who decide about publication, and there does exist a genuine and common enterprise: the exploration of a historical academic consciousness which underpins the debates in which all of us are involved. Hence it would be as much mistaken to rely solely on the experience of individual historians as it would be to rely only on the grand panorama of historiographical reconstruction. Only a combination of the two, I believe, will do.

When I am asked what the effects of this almost lifelong quest for the history of "Africa" have been on myself, the honest reply is that it has made me "live with Africa." No doubt that has also been the effect of this endeavor on many others. But what did this "living with Africa" actually entail? For me it began with an education in Kuba country. The experience of fieldwork is very different from that which usually confronts historians. I used to imagine at that time that I preferred it because it was a lively interaction with "real" people rather than the poring over the written remains of ghosts who could not answer any queries. But when I went out to Kuba country, I had no idea of the long-term effects which this and similar experiences later were to have on me, precisely because the "object" of study consisted of very lively subjects! My teachers in London had left me with the impression that the dispassionate researcher stayed in the field and mocked its hardships (Remember the "stiff upper lip"?) solely in order to observe the behavior of the subjects. Then the researcher returned, never to see or hear from the subjects again. He or she developed a scholarly analysis of all this behavior in splendid seclusion, an analysis which later was called *etic*, that is, universally valid, as opposed to the inferior quality called *emic*, that is, the colorful but parochial and naive sense the subjects themselves made out of their own behavior.

None of these assumptions were correct. There was nothing dispassionate to the interaction (rather than aloof observation) between the Kuba and myself. I arrived in Kuba lands still young enough to be malleable, and Kuba elders imparted much wisdom to me. When engaged in this, they were the active subject, and I the passive object! Then there were the hardships. I had been used to rural wartime conditions, and on the whole Kuba conditions were a shade better. Yet the place had its share of hardgoing: this was outdoor life in the tropics, with its heat and mosquitoes, its monotonous and often inadequate staple foods, sometimes endless hikes, and above all its ill health. After the first two or three months I never really felt well, and twice disease nearly killed me. The effects of that experience were subtle. I valued the evidence I gathered all the more for the hardships necessary for obtaining it: such data had to be quite valuable and "rare" to be so difficult to collect. I also developed strong bonds of fellowship with my Kuba collaborators, who went through similar experiences themselves. And when I left the field, such social relationships endured. Some among my associates continued to work for me, and we later corresponded for years. Indeed, some twenty-odd years after I left Kuba country, the mail brought me a little statuette one day, carved by one whom I had forgotten but with whom I had shared a common initiation. He remembered me. Instead of being an interlude, then, fieldwork became an experience that endured for life and wove a web of lasting social ties. I became a part of a Bushong network which only faded away twenty years later. Even then, young Kuba academics, the sons of my contemporaries, were beginning to seek me out. Some still do.

Later experiences in Rwanda, Burundi, the Tio country, and to some extent Libya, in a less intense way, have been similar. Moreover, as I came to be known as an "Africanist," I met and worked with Africans from many other regions and countries, usually students. Once again, to varying extents, we became part of a mutual personal network. From the late

250

seventies onward, as I was rubbing shoulders with a number of African colleagues on the UNESCO project, we developed a mutual familiarity and appreciation for each other. Given the family's involvement with African people and issues, it was and is but natural to follow the news of what happens on the continent day by day, year by year, and to gossip about it, because the places mentioned recall the fate of persons Claudine and I know. In this way, even following current events by itself ties me ever more to the continent. When I speak of "living with Africa," that expression stands for all of these personal ties, all of the ways in which "Africa" has become a part of my self.

But what is this "Africa" we live with? It is the sum total of the places on the continent which Claudine and I have known, frozen at the time we were there or altered through updates. It also is the sum total of all the persons we know who are in the continent or from the continent. It is in part constructed of all that reading and study as well. This adds up to a continent definitely other than the one that appears on a standard map, where every part is shown at a single scale. I could draw my Africa: in a distorted mental geography, Tanzania is not much bigger than Rwanda-Burundi, and Nigeria dwarfs all the rest of West Africa. This distortion happens to every Africanist, to everyone who speaks of "Africa." I suspect from glancing at a number of syllabi and from reading a content analysis in the *African Studies Review* that for many students in North America, the continent is composed of West, East, and Southern Africa, and in this map Nigeria borders Kenya, Zambia, and the beaches of the Mediterranean.[30] Moreover, a mental map grows and alters with its beholder. My mental map at first showed a continent shaped like a medallion, with Zaire as the picture in it. Now it has become an embroidered scarf of many patterns and colors. The dangers of distortion created by such a mental "Africa" are obvious, especially when one generalizes about "Africa." One must therefore realize how one's view diverges from the Africa out there and avoid generalizing from one or two well-known cases. Being aware of the distortion helps one to overcome it, although no one can totally avoid the effects of personal experience on an overall understanding of African history—regardless of whether the historians are Africans themselves or not.

In the case of Claudine and myself, "living with Africa" has also created some degree of alienation from other identities. Already in 1956 in Belgium, acquaintances would comment about how funny my accent had become. I thought at the time that they merely referred to the impact of Bantu tones on Dutch speech, but there was clearly more to it. They saw some cultural estrangement: I was beginning to think "differently," and I sometimes did things "differently," often in unexpected ways. Certainly cultural disharmony was involved in the failure of the attempt to teach at Leuven in the mid-seventies. Indeed, when I left, the dean sighed: "And just as you are beginning to catch on . . ." Similarly, in Wisconsin we always were somewhat alien, and as late as the eighties one of my less charitable colleagues apparently was recommending that students not choose me as a major adviser, because I was foreign and did not understand the unspoken verities which rule American society.

"Living with Africa," together with the fact that we did not settle in our country of origin, did alienate us to a certain degree from the various societies in which we have lived. That sometimes makes for some loneliness. But it also has had a certain advantage. It has kept Claudine and me just far enough out of the mainstream not to be swayed by intellectual or emotional fashions which course through every community. It has allowed me to perceive more clearly how the revelation of almost every new topic which crops up in the writing of African history is actually tied to questions of interest in contemporary Western Europe or North America. It also allows me to perceive more easily that the pursuit of certain topics by historians rooted in this or that culture is hampered by severe social and cultural handicaps, due to the inherent biases of their culture of origin.[31] In particular, my own experience of belonging in part to three different worlds has made me ever more sensitive to the questions of the cultural milieux of authors, historical actors, and audiences.

This account of my own experience does not claim that all those studying the history of Africa necessarily must become alienated from their communities of origin. Nor does it imply that history written by one who is in that situation is more plausible than any other. It means merely that the cultural and social makeup of an author matters, because it significantly affects the relationship between author and audience and the sort of interpretations preferred by an author. It may be a little easier for partly acculturated authors to address various audiences in the parts of Africa with which they are connected than for others, but then partly acculturated authors may also be more confusing to an audience, because their expositions always sound just a little unfamiliar.

Studying the history of Africa evidently has given me a profound satisfaction. One may well ask, Precisely why? That certainly has something to do with the thrill of discovery. It occurs when a flash of insight suddenly opens up new avenues of knowledge. This happened when Mbop Louis made me realize the potential historical value of oral tradition. More commonly, the thrill occurs when hitherto disjointed pieces

252

suddenly pop into place to form a harmonious whole. It does not matter much whether the discoverer is oneself or someone else. The thrill is still there. Thus the discovery of the remains of old Jenne, a city in West Africa, by the archaeologists Roderick and Susan McIntosh in 1977 sent a current of excitement throughout the community of African historians.[32] This find suddenly made clear that such cities are not just the product of North African influence. Now one could perceive how a network of such cities, spanning most of West Africa by the end of the first millennium, had been the transmission belt for all manner of people, objects, values, and ideas. This discovery taught us in a flash why the standard anthropological ethnographic focus on small rural communities in West Africa had been misguided. Sometimes outsiders may find all the excitement slightly ridiculous. The enthusiasm displayed by scholars about the discovery that vitrified dung deposits can show up on aerial photographs seems farcical. Yet that discovery allowed archaeologists to find almost all the sites of human settlement covering a span of a thousand years over a huge area of southern Africa at one stroke.[33] Only those who know how crucial and how rare such an occurrence in archaeology is can fully appreciate the discovery.

Yet such revelations are uncommon in a researcher's life. Most of the time the work consists of plodding on, overcoming an obstacle here, finding one more piece of a puzzle there, until finally, often after years of work, the overall pattern gradually takes shape or is confirmed. Thus the evidence for the domestication of millet and sorghum around 6000 B.C. in southern Egypt found early in 1993 finally validates more than a generation of work in this area.[34] My own book *Paths* arrived at a totally new tale about the history of the peoples living in the rainforests, without any single spectacular breakthrough. The picture resulted from steady work. But just as steady water drops hollow out granite, so steady work finally amounted to a breakthrough. This daily work, with the goals and hopes that are embedded in it, is accompanied by a sort of serene satisfaction as the task slowly moves forward.

Neither momentary thrills nor the satisfaction of doing one's daily rounds can account for the fascination which has tied me to African history for so many years. My sense of fulfillment must have other roots. Indeed, it stems from something else, something similar to contemplation. Perhaps I can best convey this by describing my most memorable experience in 1992. It occurred in a windowless room of an ethnographic museum, and it lasted over three hours. That day the curator showed me about five hundred bits and pieces of textiles which had been recovered from some caves in West Africa and dated from the eleventh to the seventeenth centuries.[35] There was nothing fancy about them to the lay person: they were all woven in a straightforward way, almost all of them exhibited a pattern of checks or twill, and the eye could discern only two or three different dyes in the whole collection. They were simple objects of daily wear. Yet as I carefully stared at one piece after another, I was overcome by increasing awe, because I gradually discovered their infinite variety. They were all the same, they were all simple, yet every check, every twill, was a little different. Together and in sequence these rags revealed the grandeur of human ingenuity. Century after century humble weavers using the same type of loom in this West African backwater had defeated an uniformity that seemed inherent in their technology. They refused repetition, and they engineered novel decorative solutions every time they wove a piece of cloth. That collection of textiles thus becomes a great monument to the endless ingeniousness of the human mind.

That ingenuity has been deployed anew, generation after generation, in every human community everywhere in the world, always to cope with the same challenge: to survive physically, to survive as a community, to give meaning to living, to express that meaning, and to celebrate or lament it. Like the ebb and flow of the ocean tide, the same challenge endlessly recurs to confront every successive generation. Each time, in every culture, in every community, human inventiveness finds new solutions to the eternal riddle of living. To contemplate that ingenuity at work in the history of Africa is what enriches the meaning of my own life. Ultimately the study of African history becomes for me a meditation on the African incarnations of the grandeur and the misery of the human condition itself. Thus any one of us, African or foreigner, author or audience, the meek or the mighty, can recognize an image of self in the mirror of African history. To gaze in that mirror is also to live with Africa.

Notes

Index

Notes

AMRAC   Annales du Musée Royal de l'Afrique Centrale, Sciences
         Humaines
ARSOM   Académie Royale des Sciences d'Outre-Mer
ASR   *African Studies Review*
BARSOM   *Bulletin* of ARSOM
CEA   *Cahiers d'Etudes Africaines*
CICIBA   Centre International des Civilisations Bantu
CNRS   Centre National de la Recherche Scientifique
CRISP   Centre de Recherches et d'Information Socio–Politiques
Folia   *Folia Scientifica Africae Centralis* (Lwiro)
HA   *History in Africa*
IAI   International African Institute
IJAHS   *International Journal of African Historical Studies*
JAH   *Journal of African History*
PF   Personnel file, Jan Vansina, Department of History, University
         of Wisconsin–Madison
SOAS   School of Oriental and African Studies, London

CHAPTER 1. BEFORE

1. In English, Leuven is usually known as Louvain. I use Leuven to distinguish this university from its francophone namesake *Université Catholique de Louvain*. Before 1968, when they formally separated, they were in effect two parallel universities, one operating in French and one in Dutch (the language of Flanders), sharing common facilities.

2. Ernst Bernheim (1950–1942) published the first edition of the influential *Lehrbuch der historischen Methode* in Leipzig in 1889. The sixth and last edition, much augmented, appeared in 1908. The standard formulation of the rules of evidence is best known from Bernheim's work, although he derived it from the exposition by Johann Gustav Droysen (1808–84) in *Grundriss der Historik* (1858).

3. M. Bloch, *Apologie pour l'histoire; ou, Métier d'historien* (Paris: Colin, 1949); P. Gheyl, *Napoleon: For and Against* (London: Cape, 1949); J. Romein, *De eeuw van Azië* (Leiden: Brill, 1956).

4. F. Olbrechts, *Ethnologie* (Antwerp: Standaard, 1936). Olbrechts had been a student of the famous American anthropologist Franz Boas and had done fieldwork among the Cherokee. Later he specialized in folklore and in African art history. His lasting contribution was a method of stylistic analysis contained in *Plastiek van Kongo* (Antwerp: Standaard, 1946). See his obituary in *BARSOM* 5 (1959): 136–45.

5. E. E. Evans Pritchard, *Witchcraft, Oracles and Magic among the Azande* (Oxford: Clarendon Press, 1937). For an overview of his work by an admirer, see M. Douglas, *Evans Pritchard* (London: Fontana Books, 1980).

Maesen was trained by Olbrechts in art history. He did fieldwork among the Senufo of the Ivory Coast in 1938–39. He achieved reknown for his expertise in African art. See his obituary in *BARSOM*, forthcoming.

6. On Forde, see M. G. Smith, foreword to *Man in Africa*, edited by M. Douglas and P. Kaberry (London: Tavistock, 1969), xv–xxvi; see also Forde's obituary in *Africa* 43, no. 4 (1973): 281–87, and *Africa* 44, no. 1 (1974): 1–10.

7. A. Kuper, *Anthropologists and Anthropology: The British School, 1922–1972* (London: Allen Lane, 1973).

8. See Kaberry's obituaries in the *London Times*, November 18, 1977, and *Africa* 48, no. 3 (1978): 296–97. Her books on New Guinea, *Aboriginal Women, Sacred and Profane* (London: Routledge and Son, 1939), and the Cameroons, *Women of the Grassfields* (London: HMSO, 1952), were pioneering studies of women.

9. Michael G. Smith was an unusual anthropologist then because he worked with complex societies and sought to tease out their structure by a study of historical regularities. He studied Jamaica, his native land, and the Caribbean, as well as northern Nigeria. His major works about Africa are *Government in Zazzau* (London: IAI, 1960) and *The Affairs of Daura* (Berkeley: University of California Press, 1978). For an obituary, see the *New York Times*, January 7, 1993, section D, p. 19.

10. In the 1960s Mary Douglas became one of the foremost anthropologists in Britain with her *Purity and Danger* (London: Routledge and Kegan Paul, 1966). See S. Hargreaves Heap and A. Ross, eds., *Understanding of the Enterprise Culture: Themes in the Work of Mary Douglas* (Edinburgh: Edinburgh University Press, 1992), 1–18; U. Gacs et al., eds., *Women Anthropologists: A Biographical Dictionary* (Westport, Conn.: Greenwood Press, 1988), 65–71.

11. See A. R. Radcliffe Brown, "The Comparative Method in Social Anthropology," *Journal of the Royal Anthropological Institute of Great Britain and Ireland* 81, nos. 1–2 (1951): 15–22.

12. See obituaries of Guthrie by D. W. Arnott in *Bulletin of the School of Oriental and African Studies* 36 (1973): 629–37, and H. Carter in *Proceedings of the*

British Academy 59 (1973): 473–98. See also G. Atkins, "Writings of Malcolm Guthrie," *African Language Studies* 11 (1970): 2–4.

13. It was A. Brown Edmiston, *Grammar and Dictionary of the Bushonga or Bukuba Language* . . . (Luebo, Zaire: J. Leighton Wilson Press, [c. 1929]).

14. On Fagg, see F. Willett, "William Fagg: A Memoir," in *William B. Fagg: One Hundred Notes on Nigerian Art from Christie's Catalogues, 1974–1990*, ed. E. Bassani (Milan: Quaderni Poro 7 Sipiel, 1991), 13–53.

15. For a sympathetic portrait, see J. Mack, *Emil Torday and the Art of the Congo: 1900–1909* (London: British Museum, 1990).

16. J. Vansina, *Les tribus Bakuba et les peuplades apparentées* (Tervuren: AMRAC, 1954).

17. For an obituary, see A. Coupez in *Africa Tervuren* 233, no. 4 (1977): 57–63.

18. Maquet came to anthropology from a specialty in the sociology of knowledge at the University of Louvain. He studied with Daryll Forde at University College in 1948–49 and then went to Rwanda. In 1957 he joined the staff of the official university in Lubumbashi. He transferred in 1960 to the institute of the sociologist George Balandier at the University of Paris. Around 1970 he moved to the University of California, Los Angeles. The best known of his works is *Le système des relations sociales dans le Ruanda ancien* (Tervuren: AMRAC, 1954).

19. Harroy, a specialist in conservation, taught at the University of Brussels. He was governor from 1955 to December 31, 1961, and oversaw the decolonization of Rwanda and Burundi. On his experiences, see J. P. Harroy, *Rwanda: Souvenirs* . . . (Brussels: Hayez, 1984), and *Burundi, 1955–1962: Souvenirs* (Brussels: Hayez, 1987).

CHAPTER 2. IN THE FIELD: KUBA COUNTRY

1. For a chronological account of the fieldwork among the Bushong, see J. Vansina, "History in the Field," in *Anthropologists in the Field*, ed. D. Jongmans and P. C. W. Gutkind (Assen: Van Gorcum, 1967), 102–15.

2. J. Vansina, "Miko mi Yool, une association religieuse kuba," *Aequatoria* 22, nos. 2–3 (1959): 7–20, 81–92.

3. Field notebook 14: 90.

4. The records of this fieldwork are available on microfilm at the Chicago Research Libraries and the Memorial Library of the University of Wisconsin—Madison.

5. J. Vansina, *De la tradition orale* (Tervuren: AMRAC, 1961), 159. Later the contribution of such "encyclopedic informants," or, better, "community historians," would provoke a lively debate. See J. Vansina, *Oral Tradition as History* (Madison: University of Wisconsin Press, 1985), 39, 210 n. 19.

6. Regardless of the accuracy of this allegation, the fact that this piece of

gossip circulated shows how *bulaam* played with fire: knowledge was power, and the *bulaam* easily could overstep the limits of what was deemed proper by the king to divulge. By the same token, this piece of gossip also shows the presence of a vigorous antiroyal faction in town.

7. It was published in Bushong with a Dutch translation: J. Jacobs and J. Vansina, "Nshoong atoot: Het koninklijk epos der Bushoong," *Kongo Overzee* 22, no. 1 (1956): 1–39.

8. Field notebook 16: 73–75, August 9, 1953.

9. This is a reference to Europeans, who were said to have lived at the beginning of time together with the Bushong on a primeval beach.

10. The details of this story can now be revealed, as most Bushong are well aware of them.

11. René Schillings was the territorial officer active since 1920 in Kasai. In 1955 he was the administrator for Mweka, and in 1956 he was interim district commissioner for Kasai. His nickname refers to *makup*, "abandoned capital," the term which also gave rise to the ethnonym Bakuba. As this shows, he was perceived as a wholehearted supporter of the Kuba monarchy and its king.

12. J. Vansina, "Initiation Rituals of the Bushong," *Africa* 25, no. 1 (1955): 138–55. In 1981 David Aaron Binkley also attended initiation in the area. See Binkley, "A View from the Forest: The Power of Southern Kuba Initiation Masks," Ph.D. diss., University of Indiana, 1987.

13. This was a legal fig leaf invented in 1917 to impose cash-crop cultivation by forced labor.

14. After independence, he became administrator of the territory of Mweka. By 1966 he had left the service to set himself up as a wholesale exporter of palm products and maize for the industrial belt of Shaba. By the early eighties he was embroiled in commercial disputes, and since then I have not heard from or about him.

15. I was able to arrange for Evariste to collect research materials until about 1962. Later he became a schoolteacher. After the mid-1970s he found himself more and more isolated from Bushong and modern regional leadership.

16. For a map, see J. Vansina, *Geschiedenis van de Kuba van ongeveer 1500 tot 1904* (Tervuren: AMRAC, 1963), kaart 2. I could not double check their work in all the 138 villages and well over 1,000 clan sections myself, but eventually I managed to check about 20 percent of them in all parts of the country.

17. Script of the television documentary "Als de wereld zo groot, zo is Kongo," aired October 13, 1957, by the Belgische Radio Televisie, p. 3.

18. See Binkley, "View from the Forest."

19. Much later Mary Douglas passed on a notebook of his to me which lists amounts paid by taxpayers.

20. L. van den Berghe, "La recherche scientifique," in *Livre blanc* (Brussels: ARSOM, 1962), 27–30.

21. See van den Berghe's obituary in *BARSOM* 26 (1980): 59–61.

22. Its model seems to have been the famous Institut Français de l'Afrique Noire, created in 1938 and directed from Dakar by Théodore Monod, rather than the Rhodes Livingstone Institute, founded a year earlier in Northern Rhodesia, whose mission was limited to the social sciences.

23. Local seminars were held twice a year at Astrida. See *Folia* 1, no. 1 (March 30, 1955): 19.

24. In 1957 Hiernaux left IRSAC for the official university at Lubumbashi, where he became the rector. In 1961 he returned to teach in Brussels and Paris. His book *The People of Africa* (New York: Charles Scribner's, 1974) is still the standard work on the subject today. See his entry in *International Who's Who in Science in Europe* (London: Francis Hodgson, 1978). He died around 1980.

25. See P. de Maret, "Un interview avec Luc de Heusch," *Current Anthropology* 34 (1993): 289–98.

26. In 1957 Coupez also joined the university at Lubumbashi part time and then in 1961 went to Brussels, while still working in Rwanda and at Tervuren. He is now retired.

27. He achieved it. Jacobs left IRSAC for Ghent in 1957 and taught there until his recent retirement. His main publications deal with the Tetela language and oral art.

28. See *Folia* 1, no. 1 (March 30, 1955): 27–31.

29. Vansina, "Initiation Rituals of the Bushong," 138–55.

30. For an account by John Jacobs, see *Kongo Overzee* 20 (1954): 78–80.

31. Victor Turner, in contrast, was then developing these subjects in works such as *The Forest of Symbols: Aspects of Ndembu Ritual* (Ithaca, N.Y.: Cornell University Press, 1967).

32. J. L. Vellut, "La peinture du Congo-Zaire et la recherche de l'Afrique innocente," *BARSOM* 36, no. 4 (1990): 633–59, especially 643–44.

33. J. Vansina, *Esquisse de grammaire Bushong* (Tervuren: AMRAC, 1959).

34. Later Evariste told me how frightened he had been in the isolated railway station of Kalemie deep in unknown Katanga when he saw a small light moving toward him. He was sure that this was a *mutumbula,* a man-spirit who had come to snatch his soul for some European ghoul. It turned out to be just a fellow traveler! The episode shows how high colonial tensions were already running in 1954.

35. After his military service Biebuyck taught at Lovanium and briefly worked on land tenure for the colonial government. He immigrated to the United States in 1961. See entry in J. Duffy, M. Frey, and M. Sims, eds., *International Directory of Scholars and Specialists in African Studies* (Waltham, Mass.: Cross Roads Press, 1978), 22–23.

36. See *Folia* 1, no. 1 (March 30, 1955). The theme on that occasion was migrations.

37. Reported in *Folia* 1, no. 3 (September 30, 1955): 14–15.

38. See J. D. Fage, "Reflections on the Genesis of Anglophone African History after World War II," *HA* 20 (1993): 15–26.

39. It belonged to the Kisale culture and dated probably between A.D. 1000 and A.D. 1350.

40. *Annales Aequatoria* will publish an article by Bope Nyim-a-Nkwem, a Bushong scholar, about my work there in its 1993 issue.

41. See Van Bulck's obituary in *BARSOM* 13 (1967): 143–55.

CHAPTER 3. OLD AFRICA REDISCOVERED

1. B. Davidson, *Old Africa Rediscovered* (London: Gollancz, 1959). On the early role played by Davidson, see C. Fyfe, ed., *African Studies since 1945: A Tribute to Basil Davidson* (London: Longman, 1976), 1–16.

2. See, for instance, a text by Hegel dating from 1830 as quoted in T. Hodgkin, "Where the Paths Began," in *African Studies*, ed. Fyfe, 8. One could also cite Immanuel Kant. Among British historians, A. P. Newton repeated the charge in "Africa and Historical Research," *Journal of the African Society* 22 (1922–23): 267.

3. M. Perham, "The British Problem in Africa," *Foreign Affairs* 29, no. 4 (July 1951): 638, my italics. The words in italics enumerate most of the false prejudices held by imperialists, although Perham rejected by omission the most crucial one, the clause about racial inferiority. Even in 1963 Hugh Trevor Roper would still make similar charges. For a reply to Perham, see K. O. Dike, "History and Politics," *West Africa* nos. 1879 (February 28, 1953): 169–70, 177–78, 225–26, 251.

4. Davidson, *Old Africa*, 267, 268.

5. On K. O. Dike, see R. July, *An African Voice* (Durham, N.C.: Duke University Press, 1987), 141–45; obituary in *Journal of the Historical Society of Nigeria* 12, nos. 3–4 (1984–85): 5–8; and references in J. F. A. Ajayi and T. N. Tamuno, eds., *The University of Ibadan, 1948–1973* (Ibadan: Ibadan University Press, 1973).

6. See, for instance, from Timbuktu, the *Tarikh Es-Soudan*, edited by O. Houdas and M. Delafosse (Paris: Leroux, 1913), or *Tarik- El-Fettach*, edited by O. Houdas (Paris: Leroux, 1900), and *Tedzkiret en Nizian*, edited by O. Houdas (Paris: Leroux, 1901). Others are known from Hausaland, Bornu, and Gonja. Ethiopia has had a written and oral historiography since at least the thirteenth century.

7. S. Crowther, *A Vocabulary of the Yoruba Language* (London, 1843). I am grateful to Dr. Carolyn Keyes Adenaike for the reference to this work and to nine other histories of Yorubaland published between 1852 and 1900.

8. Listed by A. Delivré, *L'Histoire des rois d'Imerina* (Paris: Klinksieck, 1974), 423–24.

9. On East Africa, see A. H. J. Prins, "On Swahili Historiography," *Journal of the East African Swahili Committee* 28 (1958): 26–41. On Xhosa historical writing,

see J. B. Peires, *The House of Phalo* (Johannesburg: Ravan Press, 1981), 175–79. The earliest articles on history appeared in *Ikhwezi* (The Morning Star) in 1844–45.

10. John O. Hunwick was kind to call my attention to J. Marquart, *Die Benin-Sammlung des Reichsmuseums für Völkerkunde in Leiden beschrieben und mit ausführlichen Prolegomena zur Geschichte der Handelswege und Völkerbewegungen in Nordafrika* (Leiden: Brill, 1913).

11. For an introductory bibliography concerning West Africa, see N. Levtzion, *Ancient Ghana and Mali* (London: Methuen, 1973), 255–59.

12. Cf. F. Pigafetta and D. Lopes, *Relatione del reame di Congo e delle circonvicine contrade* (Rome: Grassi, 1591).

13. F. Bontinck and J. Castro Segovia, eds. and trans., *Histoire du royaume du Congo (c. 1624)*, in *Etudes d'histoire africaine IV* (Louvain: /Paris: Nauwelaerts, 1972), 1–45. This is an annotated translation of the text.

14. See, for example, A. Dalzel, *The History of Dahomey* (London, 1793), or W. Ellis, *History of Madagascar*, 2 vols. (London: Fisher and Son, 1838). For a general overview of European historiography of Africa before 1945, see T. Filesi, *Realtà e prospettive della storiografia africana* (Naples: Giannini Editor, 1978), 95–153.

15. See the special issue of *Revue Française d'Histoire d'Outre-Mer* 66, nos. 242–43 (1979): 5–14; C. A. Julien, "Hubert Deschamps: L'homme et l'ami," in *Perspectives nouvelles sur le passé de l'Afrique noire et de Madagascar: Mélanges offerts à Hubert Deschamps* (Paris: Publications Sorbonne, 1974), 11–16, esp. 13–14.

16. See A. B. Aderibigbe, "Biobaku the Scholar and His Works," in *Studies in Yoruba History and Culture*, edited by G. O. Olusanya (Ibadan: Ibadan University Press, 1983), 4–25; "My Time at Ibadan, 1953–1957," in *Ibadan Voices: Ibadan University in Transition*, edited by T. N. Tamuno (Ibadan: Ibadan University Press, 1981), 160–68; and Ajayi and Tamuno, *University of Ibadan*.

17. See J. W. Blake in the preface to his book *European Beginnings in West Africa, 1454–1578* (London: Hakluyt Society, 1977), and P. E. H. Hair, "J. W. Blake: A Tribute," *HA* 16 (1989): 413–14. Blake made a plea in 1949 to see the history of Africa "through African eyes."

18. In elementary and secondary school, colonial history was shown as a heroic fight against Arab slave traders. This was personified in the figures of Lieutenant Joseph Lippens and Sergeant Henry Debruyne, who gave their lives to free the Congolese from the Arab yoke. This was also the dominant message of most monuments glorifying the colonial conquest.

19. See *The Autobiography of W. E. B. Du Bois: A Soliloquy on Viewing My Life from the Last Decade of Its First Century* (New York: International Publishers, 1968). On Du Bois, see also Filesi, *Realtà* 127–134.

20. But this was not the case in France, or in Britain after 1914. See F. W. Voget, *A History of Ethnology* (New York: Holt, 1975), 317–59.

21. The standard handbook after the Second World War was H. Baumann

and D. Westermann, *Les peuples et les civilisations de l'Afrique,* translated by L. Homburger (Paris: Payot, 1948). The original text was completed in 1940.

22. D. Westermann, *Geschichte Afrikas: Staatenbildungen südlich der Sahara* (Cologne: D. Reimer, 1952). The text was completed in 1940.

23. See, for example, A. P. Newton, E. A. Benians, and E. A. Walker, *South Africa, Rhodesia and the Protectorates,* vol. 8 of *The Cambridge History of the British Empire* (Cambridge: Cambridge University Press, 1936). Newton is the same one who thought Africa had no history. Blake, *European Beginnings;* J. W. Blake, *Europeans in West Africa: 1450–1560,* 2 vols. (London: Hakluyt Society, 1941–42).

24. For instance, Jean Cuvelier and Louis Jadin in Belgium, and Alfredo de Albuquerque Felner and especially António Brasio in Portugal.

25. On the Rhodes Livingstone Institute, see Mwelwa Musambachime, "The University of Zambia's Institute for African Studies and Social Science Research in Central Africa, 1938–1988," *HA* 20 (1993): 237–48. On IFAN's creation and history until its incorporation into the University of Dakar, see "Historique de l'Institut Français d'Afrique Noire," *Notes africaines* 90 (April 1961): 34–44. The Algerian, Moroccan, Indochinese, and Malagasy examples were an inspiration here.

26. On Mauny, see G. Brasseur, "Raymond Mauny," in *Le sol, la parole et l'écrit,* edited by J. Devisse, 2 vols. (Paris: Société Française d'Outre-Mer, 1991), 1: 1–20.

27. E. Ashby, *Universities, British, Indian, African* (Cambridge, Mass.: Harvard University Press, 1966), 212, 428–29, 162.

28. Ibid., 214, 219–20. There had been a split in the Elliot Commission between the African members and the others over the question of whether there should be one college or three, nor Counting Khartoum.

29. Ibid., 233, 320, 441 n. 50, 352.

30. Ibid., 221, 430 n. 68.

31. C. H. Philips, foreword to *History and Archeology in Africa,* edited by R. A. Hamilton (London: SOAS, 1955), 1.

32. In 1992 Philips shared these reminiscences with R. Frykenberg, who graciously informed me of them.

33. On R. Oliver, see *JAH* 29, no. 1 (1988): 1–4, and J. Vansina, "Lessons of Forty Years of African History," *IJAHS* 25, no. 2 (1992): 391–98; on J. Fage, see *JAH* 27, no. 2 (1986): 193–201. It would be a boon to historiographers if Oliver and Fage published memoirs.

34. Personal communication from one of the social anthropologists he contacted.

35. He defended his doctoral dissertation in 1951–52 at Cambridge University. See R. Oliver, *The Missionary Factor in East Africa* (London: Longmans, Green, 1952).

36. This was a typical imperial history for Cambridge: "The Achievement of Self-Government in Southern Rhodesia, 1898–1923."

37. After the return of Fage from Africa in 1959 and after Oliver's influence over the history departments of the university colleges faded away after 1960, their joint intellectual leadership in Europe was preserved by their activity as editors of the *Journal of African History* (1960–   ) and of the eight volumes of the *Cambridge History of Africa* (1975–86).

38. For a full statement of the doctrine, see J. D. Fage, *On the Nature of African History* (Birmingham: Birmingham University Press, 1965), 1–20. In his inaugural lecture, R. Oliver expressed his view about the description of the SOAS curriculum; see Oliver, *African History for the Outside World* (London: SOAS, 1964), 11–22.

39. Ashby, *Universities*, 428 n. 40.

40. M. Delafosse, *Haut-Sénégal-Niger (Soudan français)* (Paris: Larose, 1912).

41. C. A. Diop, *Nations nègres et culture* (1954; Paris: Présence Africaine, 1955). See July, *African Voice*, 137–40.

42. This deep difference between British- and French-inspired scholarship is well illustrated in M. Fortes and G. Dieterlen, eds., *African Systems of Thought* (London: IAI, 1965). The editors contrast French interest in *connaissance* with the British concern for social and political relations (3–4).

43. Compare *Présence Africaine* 24–25 (1959) and 27–28 (1959) with articles by C. A. Diop, S. Biobaku, and M. Achufusi.

44. See Ashby, *Universities*, 369, on the manner in which the French transplanted higher education to tropical Africa.

45. Both were entitled *History and Archaeology in Africa* and published by SOAS. R. A. Hamilton edited the first report in 1955, and D. H. Jones the second one in 1959.

46. Jones, *History and Archaeology*, 11.

47. C. Flight, "The Bantu Expansion and the SOAS Network," *HA* 15 (1988): 273.

48. Jones, *History and Archaeology*, 35–41.

49. J. Stengers, "La IIe conférence d'histoire et d'archéologie africaine (Londres juillet 1957)," *BARSOM*, n.s. 3 (1957): 1071–77.

50. Ashby, *Universities*, 222.

51. J. D. Fage, "The Writing of West African History," *African Affairs* 70, no. 280 (1971): 236–38.

52. J. D. Fage, *An Introduction to the History of West Africa* (Cambridge: Cambridge University Press, 1955); idem, *An Atlas of African History*, maps by M. Verity (London: Edward Arnold, 1958).

53. July, *African Voice*, 140–41. On Ibadan until 1962, see Ajayi and Tamuno, *University of Ibadan*, 22–68. On the archives, see Paul E. H. Hair, "The Nigerian Records Survey Remembered" *HA* 20 (1993): 391–94.

54. See July, *African Voice*, 145–47. The major textbooks produced for schools at Ibadan between 1961 and 1965 are listed there.

55. K. Ingham, *A History of East Africa* (London: Longmans, 1962). Ingham left Makerere in 1962.

56. B. A. Ogot, "Trois décennies historiques en Afrique de l'est," in *Le processus d'éducation et l'historiographie en Afrique* (Paris: UNESCO, 1986), 65–81.

57. See R. Oliver's main articles, "The Historical Traditions of Buganda, Bunyoro and Ankole," *Man* 54 (1954): 43, and "The Traditional Histories of Buganda, Bunyoro and Ankole," *Journal of the Royal Anthropological Institute* 85 (1955): 111–17. Note that these were the leading journals in British social anthropology. See also Hamilton, *History and Archaeology*, 11–13.

58. K. O. Dike, "History and Politics," *West Africa*, February 28, 1953, p. 225. S. O. Biobaku demurred in "The Wells of West African History," *West African Review* 29 (1953): 18–19, and later in "Myths and Oral History," *Odu* 1 (1955): 12–17. Cf. Aderibigbe, "Biobaku," 7.

59. Hamilton, *History and Archaeology*, 35–41.

60. Cf. T. O. Ranger, "Towards a Usable African Past," in *African Studies*, ed. Fyfe, 18–19.

61. On the founder of African history in East Africa, see W. K. Ochieng, ed., *A Modern History of Kenya: In Honour of B. A. Ogot* (London: Evans, 1989), 1–5, 245–55.

62. July, *African Voice*, 148–53; B. A. Ogot, *A History of the Southern Luo* (Nairobi: East African Publishing House, 1967). I had collected some traditions from hunter-gatherers in Kuba lands, but these mimicked the genre of traditions prevalent in the chiefdoms.

63. Hamilton, *History and Archaeology*, 2–3; Jones, *History and Archaeology*, 51–52.

64. Dike, "History and Politics," 251; July, *African Voice*, 177–97.

65. Jones, *History and Archaeology*, 7, 10, 40–41, 51; R. Oliver and G. Mathew, *History of East Africa*, vol. 1 (Oxford: Clarendon Press, 1963).

66. The most infamous example of this disregard for the quality of evidence was the repeated use of Olfert Dapper's compilation of translations known for their inaccuracies: *Naukeurige beschrijvinghe der afrikaensche gewesten* (Amsterdam, 1668).

67. Jones, *History and Archaeology*, 52.

68. In this regard, July, *African Voice*, 134–40, discusses G. Padmore, *The Gold Coast Revolution* (London: Dobson, 1953), J. C. deGraft-Johnson, *African Glory* (London: Watts, 1954), and Diop, *Nations nègres et culture* (1954).

69. Jones, *History and Archaeology*, 8.

70. A. J. Hanna, *The Story of the Rhodesias and Nyasaland* (London: Faber and Faber, 1960), 40, cited in Ogot, "Trois décennies," 69.

71. J. Huxley, the much-admired first director general of UNESCO, unfortunately excluded Africa from his notion of "civilization."

72. Dike, "History and Politics," 178, 225.

CHAPTER 4.
TOWARD THE MILLENNIUM OF INDEPENDENCE

1. G. Van der Schueren, "La naissance de l'université Lovanium," in *Problèmes de l'enseignement supérieur. . . . Receuil d'études en l'honneur de Guy Malengreau*, (Paris: Pichon et Durand-Auzias, 1975), 13–35.

2. C. Young, *Politics in the Congo* (Princeton, N.J.: Princeton University Press, 1965), 143. All of this developed against the background of a major "school war" in Belgium itself.

3. A. J. J. Van Bilsen published a "Thirty-Year Plan for the Political Emancipation of Belgian Africa" in December 1955. See R. Lemarchand, *Political Awakening in the Belgian Congo* (Berkeley: University of California Press, 1964), 153–57.

4. Young, *Politics*, 106, 294–95; Lemarchand, *Political Awakening*, 206.

5. Lemarchand, *Political Awakening*, 158–63.

6. On Malengreau, see *Problèmes*, 7–12.

7. He referred to Yves Urvoy, a French administrator in Niger who had published *Histoire de l'Empire du Bornou* (Paris: Larose, 1949).

8. G. Balandier, *Afrique ambigüe* (Paris: Plon, 1957).

9. *Folia 4, no.* 3 (1958): 66.

10. They were activated by a spring unwinding at a standard speed, guided by a gyroscope. After various repairs, the recording speed of each machine became so unique that one could listen to a tape only on the machine on which it was recorded or on a rare gadget that allowed the user to set variable speeds.

11. A. Borsboom, J. Kommers, and C. Remie, eds., *Liber amicorum: A. A. Trouwborst* (Nijmegen: Instituut voor Culturele en Sociale Antropologie der Katolieke Universiteit, 1989), 1–2, 451–58.

12. He died in 1981. For a succinct curriculum vitae, see UNESCO, ed., *Histoire et diversité des cultures* (Paris: UNESCO, 1984), 349–50.

13. J. J. Maquet, *Le système des relations sociales dans le Ruanda ancien* (Tervuren: AMRAC, 1954), 14–15.

14. These groups were not castes, ethnic groups, or hierarchical "strata," although they shared some of the characteristics of all of these. Hence I use the less specific term "ranked social category."

15. J. J. Maquet and M. d'Hertefelt, *Elections en société féodale: Une étude sur l'introduction du vote populaire au Ruanda Urundi* (Brussels: ARSOM, 1959).

16. R. Lemarchand, *Rwanda and Burundi* (London: Pall Mall, 1970), 139. Note that the date in note 28 on page 517 is incorrect.

17. M. d'Hertefelt, "Mythes et idéologies dans le Rwanda ancien et contemporain," in *The Historian in Tropical Africa,* edited by J. Vansina, R. Mauny, and L. V. Thomas (London: IAI, 1964), 219–38.

18. This book was published for the administration in 1956 and printed at Kabgayi.

19. Marcel d'Hertefelt, a graduate in Germanic languages, joined IRSAC in 1957 to assist Maquet. He became a self-trained social scientist specializing in government and remained in Rwanda until he was appointed to a post at the museum in Tervuren during the middle sixties. He stayed there until his retirement in 1993. He also taught anthropology part time at the universities of Antwerp, Leuven, and Liège.

20. M. d'Hertefelt, "Huwelijk, familie en aanverwantschap bij de Réera (Noordwestelijk Rwaanda)," *Zaire* 13, no. 2 (1959): 115–48, and no. 3: 243–85.

21. On these differences and their social causes, see J. Vansina, *De la tradition orale* (Tervuren: AMRAC, 1961), 138–41.

22. J. Vansina, *La légende du passé* (Tervuren: AMRAC, 1972), 16–18.

23. On *umuganuro,* see E. Mworoha, ed., *Histoire du Burundi* (Paris: Hatier, 1987), 213–15, 223–25.

24. *Folia* 4, no. 3 (September 1958): 69–70; J. Hiernaux and E. Maquet, *Cultures préhistoriques de l'âge des métaux au Ruanda-Urundi et au Kivu (Congo Belge): Deuxième partie* (Brussels: ARSOM, 1960), 66–68.

25. *Folia* 4, no. 3 (September 1958): 70; *Folia* 5, no. 2, (June 1959): 36.

26. See J. Nenquin, *Contributions to the Prehistoric Cultures of Rwanda and Burundi* (Tervuren: AMRAC, 1967). Nenquin was then head of the new archaeology section at the museum in Tervuren.

27. *Folia* 4, no. 1 (March 1958): 13.

28. *Folia* 4, no. 3 (September 1958): 66; R. Oliver, *Sir Harry Johnston and the Scramble for Africa* (London: Chatto and Windus, 1957).

29. In its breadth IRSAC was similar to the French institute Office de la Recherche Scientifique et Technique d'Outre-Mer, which was devoted to the study of practical problems. Yet unlike ORSTROM, but like some research centers in Europe and North America, IRSAC dealt with fundamental research.

30. On Lovanium, see B. Lacroix, *Pouvoirs et structures de l'Université Lovanium* (Brussels: Centre d'Etude et de Documentation Africaines, 1972).

31. Biebuyck was then also in government service, in charge of a general inquiry into the existing land tenure systems in the country.

32. I did not have access to John Fage's textbook on West African history, nor even to R. Cornevin, *Histoire de l'Afrique des origines à nos jours* (Paris: Payot, 1956), the latest text then available.

33. Hendrik was a Scheutist missionary of Dutch origin, who had been in Kinshasa since 1933 and was to continue to work there until the eve of his death in 1974. He had become a self-taught archaeologist of genuine merit. On

his research and his museum collection, see H. Van Moorsel, *Atlas de préhistoire de la plaine de Kinshasa* (Kinshasa: Université Lovanium, 1968).

34. Young, *Politics*, 290.

35. J. G. Libois, ed., *Congo, 1959* (Brussels: CRISP, 1960), 9–16.

36. At the end there were a total of 103 oral examinations, averaging seventeen hours a day.

37. On fund-raising activities in general, see L. Gillon, "Aspects financiers de la réalisation et du fonctionnement de l'Université Lovanium (1954–1969)," in *Problèmes*, 37–65.

38. Lemarchand, *Political Awakening*, 206–9.

39. "Situation au Kasai: L'affaire d'empoisonnement à Mweka," *Courrier d'Afrique*, January 6, 1960, p. 4. See also J. Vansina (based on eyewitness information mostly by Evariste Shyaam aNce), "The Bushong Poison Ordeal," in *Man in Africa*, edited by M. Douglas and P. Kaberry (London: Tavistock, 1969), 245–60.

40. J. G. Libois and B. Verhaegen, *Congo, 1960*, 2 vols. (Brussels: CRISP, 1961), 1: 9–69. On the seminar, see D. Biebuyck, ed., *African Agrarian Systems*, (London: IAI, 1963).

41. See Lemarchand, *Rwanda and Burundi*, 80–85, 145–88.

42. *Folia* for July 1959–July 1960.

43. Lemarchand, *Rwanda and Burundi*, 156–57; the poem of H. Codère, "Le roi est mort, vive le roi," *Antioch Review* (Fall 1961): 181–92.

44. A. Kagame, "Le code ésotérique de la dynastie du Rwanda *Zaire* 1, no. 4 (1947): 364–86.

45. He survived. In November 1960 I received a letter from him asking for back pay covering the whole period.

46. See Lemarchand, *Rwanda and Burundi*, on events up to 1969.

47. Helen Codère was then an experienced and highly regarded American anthropologist who had previously studied Kwakiutl society on the northwest coast of North America.

48. H. Codère, *The Biography of an African Society: Rwanda, 1900–1960* (Tervuren: AMRAC, 1973). This is based on forty-eight biographies.

49. J. Vansina, comp., *Ibiteekerezo: Historical Narratives from Rwanda* (Chicago: Department of Photo Duplication, University of Chicago Library, 1973), microfilm, MF 2739 (6 reels).

50. J. P. Chrétien, "Du hirsu au hamite: Les variations du cycle de Ntare Rushatsi, fondateur du royaume du Burundi," *HA* 8 (1981): 3–41.

51. Etienne van de Walle, a demographer, was one of the IRSAC researchers in my care. He later joined the University of Pennsylvania and is now a leading scholar in his field.

52. For a synopsis of Ranger's career, see R. Hodder-Williams, ed., *Directory of Africanists in Britain* (Bristol: Royal African Society, 1986), 61.

53. See the entry on Thompson in J. Duffy, M. Frey, and M. Sims, eds.,

International Directory of Scholars and Specialists in African Studies (Waltham, Mass.: Cross Roads Press, 1978), 288.

CHAPTER 5. ON WISCONSIN!

1. At my parents' house at Gooreind, in the woods, water came from a well, there was no heating beyond wood-fed stoves and a huge hearth, and electricity was unreliable.

2. They were Virginia and John Emlen, to whom we remain deeply indebted.

3. Letter to my parents, July 21, 1962.

4. The Institute for the Humanities at the university began to function in the fall of 1959.

5. L. De Lacger, *Ruanda*, 2 vols. (Namur: Grands Lacs, 1939).

6. J. Vansina, *L'évolution du royaume rwanda des origines à 1900* (Brussels: ARSOM, 1962).

7. In 1957 John Fage, then visiting professor in Madison, had delivered these lectures. They were published as *Ghana: An Historical Interpretation* (Madison: University of Wisconsin Press, 1959). The introduction (pp. vii–viii) contains Curtin's earliest statement about the place of African history.

8. J. Vansina, *Le royaume Kuba* (Tervuren: AMRAC, 1964). The study was finished by October 1, 1961.

9. As can be seen from the comments by Bope Nyim-a-Nkwem, "La perception Kuba de leur histoire à travers l'oeuvre de J. Vansina," *Annales Aequatoria* (1993), forthcoming.

10. On such works, see W. Van Binsbergen, *Tears of Rain: Ethnicity and History in Western Zambia* (London: Kegan Paul, 1992).

11. For instance, I simply forgot to incorporate Manoel Correia Leitão's report of 1755 about the lands beyond the kingdom of Kasanje, although I had read it. Cf. Gastão Sousa Dias, ed., "Um viagem a Cassange nos meados do século XVIII," *Boletim da Sociedade de Geografia de Lisboa* 56 nos. 1–2 (1938): 3–30.

12. J. Vansina, *Kingdoms of the Savanna* (Madison: University of Wisconsin Press, 1966), 3–4.

13. For instance, it was summarized without further reflection in T. O. Ranger, ed., *Aspects of Central African History* (Evanston, Ill.: Northwestern University Press, 1968), v.

14. It led directly to four articles about trade, chronology, and the origins of the kingdom of Kongo that were published in the *Journal of African History* in 1962 and 1963.

15. G. P. Murdock, *Africa: Its Peoples and Their Culture History* (New York: McGraw-Hill, 1959).

16. J. H. Steward, *Theory of Culture Change* (Urbana: University of Illinois Press, 1955).

17. M. G. Smith, *Government in Zazzau (1800–1950)* (London: IAI, 1960). Zazzau is one of the Hausa emirates in Nigeria.

18. J. Vansina, "The Use of Process-Models in African History," in *The Historian in Tropical Africa*, edited by J. Vansina, R. Mauny, and L. V. Thomas (London: IAI, 1964), 375–89.

19. Vansina, Mauny, and Thomas, *Historian*, 51–53. The numbers are thirteen anthropologists, fourteen historians (six from the network of SOAS and five from the network of French historians), four linguists, and eight others.

20. Even Cheikh Anta Diop, who lived in Dakar, was absent. Did he boycott the meeting, or was he excluded? Yet Bakari Kamian from the *lycée* of Bamako was there.

21. The interest of UNESCO meant little to me at the time, yet it is significant in view of the central role that the agency was to play later in the development of African historiography.

22. Vansina, Mauny, and Thomas, *Historian*, 76–83, esp. 76–77.

23. P. D. Curtin, *Two Jamaicas: The Role of Ideas in a Tropical Colony* (New York: Atheneum, 1959).

24. On African studies programs, see chapter 6.

25. These were Crawford Young in political science, Herb Lewis in anthropology, and A. C. ("Joe") Jordan in South African languages and literature. On Jordan, see P. Ntantala, *A Life's Mosaic* (Berkeley: University of California Press, 1993), 194–98. In addition, Fred Simoons was in the department of geography before 1960.

26. At that time only reports based on fleeting visits by two anthropologists and a geographer were available about Tio society and culture. In linguistics, both Malcolm Guthrie and Emiel Meeussen had recorded unpublished notes based on the speech of the "Bateke" in Kinshasa.

27. Marcel Soret worked in Brazzaville as an officer of ORSTOM from 1950 to 1970. See his doctoral dissertation, "Les Teke de l'est: Essai d'adaptation d'une population à son milieu," Université de Lille, 1973, pp. 1–4.

28. See R. Boutet, *Les Trois Glorieuses; ou, La chute de Fulbert Youlou* (Dakar: Chaka, 1990).

29. That experience supports the view sketched in J. F. Bayart, *L'état en Afrique* (Paris: Fayard, 1989).

30. Coleman was then the leading political scientist studying Africa in the United States.

CHAPTER 6. THE ROARING SIXTIES

1. M. Klein, "Back to Democracy," *ASR* 35, no. 2 (1992): 1–12, esp. 1–3.

2. V. V. Matveyev, "Al-Djakhiz sur les Zindjs de l'Afrique orientale," paper presented at the Second International Africanist Congress, Moscow, 1967.

3. For December 1961 I can easily trace eighty-two specialists by name;

estimates for 1970 come from P. D. Curtin, "Recent Trends in African Historiography and Their Contribution to History in General," in *Methodology and African Prehistory*, edited by J. Ki Zerbo, volume 1 of UNESCO's *General History of Africa* (London: Heinemann, 1981), 64, 70. He adds that more than three hundred doctorates were awarded at institutions in North America and offers other quantified estimates. He maintains these estimates in Curtin, "African History and World History," in *Colóquio sobre Educação e Ciências Humanas na Africa de Língua Portuguesa, 20–22 de Janeiro de 1975* (Lisbon: Gulbenkian, 1979), 276.

4. For 1960, two issues of *JAH* comprised 345 pages. For 1970, four issues of *JAH* were 624 pages, and two issues of *African Historical Studies* comprised 514 pages. A similar estimate for writing in French cannot be made, since a specialized journal did not exist.

5. E. Sik, *Histoire de l'Afrique noire*, 4 vols., translated from the Hungarian by F. Léderer (Budapest: Akademiai Kiadó, 1961–79). Volumes 1 and 2 were available by 1964. Because the translation was in French, the work did not stir much interest in English-speaking milieus. It was known among French speakers. See J. Vansina, R. Mauny, and L. V. Thomas, eds., *The Historian in Tropical Africa* (London: IAI, 1964), 27 n. 10.

6. *JAH* 3 (1962): 192, 193. The statement then calls for preservation of archives and archaeological remains and for freedom of research, teaching, and publication.

7. Curtin, "Recent Trends," 65, 68. One should add Warsaw and Prague to Moscow and Leningrad, which Curtin mentions.

8. R. July, *An African Voice* (Durham, N. C.: Duke University Press, 1987), 145–47; J. F. A. Ajayi and T. N. Tamuno, *The University of Ibadan, 1948–1973* (Ibadan: Ibadan University Press, 1973), 62–63, 181–82.

9. J. F. A. Ajayi and I. Espie, eds., *A Thousand Years of West African History* (Ibadan: Ibadan University Press, 1965), vii–viii. Only Fourah Bay College did not accept the new curriculum.

10. Texts for high schools were Ajayi and Espie, *Thousand Years,* and J. C. Anene and G. N. Brown, eds., *African History in the Nineteenth and Twentieth Centuries* (Ibadan: Ibadan University Press, 1965). The first textbook for universities was written by the head of the department at the University of Ghana and by a teacher at Ibadan (later at Makerere); see J. B. Webster and A. A. Boahen with H. O. Idowu, *The Revolutionary Years: West Africa since 1800* (London: Longman, 1967). After 1971 a large, detailed *History of West Africa* in two volumes, edited by J. F. A. Ajayi and Michael Crowder (London: Longman, 1971–74), became the standard textbook at universities. All these works include contributions by West African and European scholars.

11. Contra C. Neale, *Writing "Independent" History: African Historiography, 1960–1980* (Westport, Conn.: Greenwood Press, 1985), 103–24. She claims that the major differences lay between historians of East and West Africa, not

between Africans and whites (103, 120). This is correct, especially after 1970. She did not contrast British historians of the SOAS network in Britain with West African historians, including European and American expatriates.

12. In L. H. Gann and P. Duignan, eds., *Colonialism in Africa: 1870–1960*, vol. 1 (Stanford, Calif.: Stanford University Press, 1969). Note that Ajayi was the only African contributor. The editors were the two best-known scholars who favored a balance sheet approach, in which the ledger showed a profit from the European intervention.

Jacob Ajayi became assistant vice chancellor at the University of Ibadan, vice chancellor at the University of Lagos, director of the IAI in London, and a leading scholar in the UNESCO project. He also has continued to edit and write publications of major importance.

13. See Kenneth Dike's intervention at the SOAS conference in 1957 in D. H. Jones, ed., *History and Archaeology in Africa* (London: SOAS, 1959), 8.

14. Curtin, "Recent Trends," 69. Citing an unpublished paper by Roland Oliver for SOAS, he mentions that 58 percent of the people receiving doctorates between 1963 and 1973 took up initial posts in Africa; fewer than 20 percent were British. In Paris the programs developed somewhat later, and the proportions of Africans among the students may have been even higher.

15. H. F. C. Smith taught Islamic history at Ibadan beginning in 1959 and became the head of department at Ahmadu Bello University in Zaria in 1963 or 1964. J. Bertin Webster taught at Ibadan until 1967; he then exported the spirit to Makerere, and in 1972 went to Malawi. On Michael Crowder, see J. F. A. Ajayi and J. D. Y. Peel, eds., *Peoples and Empires in African History: Essays in Memory of Michael Crowder* (London: Longman, 1992), x–xxv. Webster and Crowder assisted in the publication of texts for schools and universities.

16. By 1963 universities had been set up in Lagos, Nsukka (on the U.S. model), Zaria, and Ife, and colleges depending on them soon followed.

17. This was true only because the newly independent countries established their own universities: Addis Ababa in Ethiopia (1960), Mogadishu in Somalia (1961), Dar es Salaam in Tanzania (1963), Nairobi in Kenya (1964).

18. B. A. Ogot, "Trois décennies historiques en Afrique de l'est," in *Le processus d'éducation et l'historiographie en Afrique* (Paris: UNESCO, 1986), 67–74; B. A. Ogot and J. A. Kieran, eds., *Zamani: A Survey of East African History* (Nairobi, 1968); B. A. Ogot, ed., *Hadith*, vol. 1 (Nairobi, 1968).

19. On the team, see T. O. Ranger, "History at the University College, Dar es Salaam," July 26, 1967, mimeo, pp. 3–6. Kimambo obtained a doctorate from Northwestern University in 1967 and succeeded Ranger as head of the department in 1969. Later he was to become vice chancellor of the university. Arnold Temu, who held a Ph.D. from the University of Alberta, became well known a few years later when he espoused a Marxist interpretation of African history.

20. T. O. Ranger, ed., *Emerging Themes of African History* (Dar es Salaam: East African Publishing House, 1968).

21. D. Denoon and A. Kuper, "Nationalist Historians in Search of a Nation: The New 'Historiography' in Dar es Salaam," *African Affairs* 69, no. 277 (1970): 329. Ranger's rebuttal and a counterrebuttal followed: *African Affairs* 70, no. 278 (1971): 50–61, and 70, no. 280 (1971): 287–88.

22. T. O. Ranger, ed., *Aspects of Central African History* (Evanston, Ill.: Northwestern University Press, 1968); I. N. Kimambo and A. Temu, eds., *A History of Tanzania* (Nairobi: East African Publishing House, 1969); Andrew Roberts, ed., *Tanzania before 1900* (Nairobi: East African Publishing House, 1968).

23. Webster was head at Makerere from 1967 to 1972. He left for Malawi after the takeover in Uganda by the dictator Idi Amin. Chancellor College itself was founded in 1964.

24. The University of Botswana, Lesotho and Swaziland was founded in 1964. Lesotho split off in 1975.

25. Curtin, "Recent Trends," 70. The basis for these quantitative assertions by Curtin remains unclear. My own feeling is that the figure for new doctorates is inflated.

26. The journal was an initiative of Norman Bennett of the African Studies Center at Boston University. Its first issue appeared in 1968. In 1972 it became the *International Journal of African Historical Studies*.

27. See, for instance, Robert Rotberg, *The Rise of Nationalism in Central Africa: The Making of Malawi and Zambia, 1873–1964* (Cambridge, Mass.: Harvard University Press, 1965); idem, *A Political History of Tropical Africa* (New York: Harcourt, Brace and World, 1965). In the latter, Rotberg gave prominence to "the stirrings of discontent" by new churches and nationalists and to "the triumph of nationalism" (337–71). In contrast, Oliver and Fage's textbook of 1962 stressed administration and economic development.

28. J. Rowe's report on the "The History of Africa" text for Little, Brown and Co., dated October 10, 1967, p. 1, summarizing the results of our meetings in 1966 and 1967.

29. P. Novick, *That Noble Dream: The "Objectivity Question" and the American Historical Profession* (Cambridge: Cambridge University Press, 1988), 415–68; Klein, "Back to Democracy," 1.

30. These developments in Harlem have not yet been studied with the attention they deserve. I am only aware of them through chance contacts at the time.

31. R. Oliver, *African History for the Outside World* (London: SOAS, 1964), 10–17.

32. Ibid., 8–9.

33. *Perspectives nouvelles sur le passé de l'Afrique noire et de Madagascar: Mélanges offerts à Hubert Deschamps* (Paris: Publications Sorbonne 1974), 11–16. See J. Vansina et al., *Etudes africaines offertes à Henri Brunschwig* (Paris: Ecole des Hautes Etudes en Sciences Sociales, 1982), v–xi. Brunschwig had been a

colleague of Léopold S. Senghor's and a fellow prisoner of Braudel's in a German camp.

34. C. Coquery-Vidrovitch and B. Jewsiewicki, "African Historiography in France and Belgium," in *African Historiographies: What History for Which Africa?* edited by B. Jewsiewicki and D. Newbury (Beverly Hills, Calif.: Sage, 1985), 139–50; on CNRS, see p. 149. Only Jean-Pierre Chrétien and, for a few years, Yves Person held a CNRS mandate.

35. Coquery-Vidrovitch and Jewsiewicki, "Africanist Historiography," 147. Three-quarters of all doctorates awarded between 1960 and 1980 went to Africans.

36. J. D. Fage, "The Writing of West African History," *African Affairs* 70, no. 280 (1971): 251 and n. 59. The new universities were Abidjan, Tananarive, and Yaounde.

37. *Histoire de l'Afrique à l'usage du Sénégal* (Paris: Hachette, 1968), written mostly by Raymond Mauny and Vincent Monteil; J. Ki Zerbo, *Le monde africain noir: Histoire et civilisation* (Paris: Hatier, 1963). On Ki Zerbo, see the entry in D. M. McFarland, *Historical Dictionary of Upper Volta (Haute Volta)* (Metuchen, N.J.: Scarecrow Press, 1978).

38. J. Ki Zerbo, *Histoire de l'Afrique noire* (Paris: Hatier, 1972). On this work, see T. Filesi, *Realtà e prospettive della storiografia africana* (Naples: Giannini Editor, 1978), 178–85.

39. Curtin, "Recent Trends," 68; *1967 Programme officiel: Conférence des ministres africains et malgache de l'éducation*.

40. Much of the credit for this success belongs to Amadou-Mahtar M'Bow, later director general of UNESCO, and the historians Joseph Ki Zerbo and Jean Devisse.

41. H. Brunschwig, "Pour une histoire de l'Afrique noire," *CEA* 7 (1962): 337–38. This was the first issue of this leading journal in African studies that was devoted to the history of Africa.

42. The debate about *ethnohistoire* was raging in France at the time. See S. Krech III, "The State of Ethnohistory," *Annual Review of Anthropology* 20 (1991): 364. At first Hubert Deschamps was the main defender of the concept, but he abandoned it in 1968. See Deschamps, *Traditions orales et archives au Gabon* (Paris: 1962), 1–2, for his early views.

43. Coquery-Vidrovitch and Jewsiewicki, "Africanist Historiography," 148–49. To this day no journal of African history exists in France.

44. He even published a history of the kingdom of Kongo: G. Balandier, *La vie quotidienne au royaume de Kongo du XVIe au XVIIIe siècle* (Paris: Hachette, 1965), which unfortunately was blind to chronology and contingency alike. I pointed this out in "Anthropologists and the Third Dimension," *Africa* 39, no. 1 (1969): 64–68. This review in turn antagonized both him and some among his epigones for nearly two decades.

45. A. Coupez, "Etudes africaines en Belgique," *Africa Tervuren* 29, no. 2 (1983): 17.

46. For instance, many insisted that African independent religious movements "were" an expression of political resistance. Perceived function was turned into a hidden goal in such a case.

47. See A. Richards, ed., "Feudalism in the Interlacustrine Kingdoms," in *East African Chiefs* (London: Faber and Faber, 1959), 378–93. Feudalism was also the topic of a social science faculty research seminar in Madison during the summer of 1961. R. Coulborn, ed., *Feudalism in History* (Princeton, N.J.: Princeton University Press, 1956), a comparative study across the Old World, was analyzed by specialists in the areas concerned.

48. J. J. Maquet, *Le système des relations sociales dans le Ruanda ancien* (Tervuren: AMRAC, 1954). The literature about Rwanda and Burundi had always presented them as feudal states. H. Meyer, *Die Barundi* (Leipzig: Otto Spamer, 1916), 86–92, speaks of *Lehnswesen*. For a recent statement, still in an evolutionary mold, see P. De Maret, "Un interview avec Luc de Heusch," *Current Anthropology* 34 (1993): 293.

49. J. J. Maquet, "Une hypothèse pour l'études des féodalités africaines," *CEA* 6 (1961): 297, 307, 313. For a classic Marxist view, see I. I. Potekhin as cited by J. Goody, "Feudalism in Africa?" *JAH* 4, no. 1 (1963): 10, and Neale, *Writing*, 160–61.

50. Goody, "Feudalism," 1–18, esp. 13.

51. Certainly African historians believed in progress and held a teleological view of history, but not an evolutionary one. See Neale, *Writing*, 3–23. One suspects that the reason the *Journal of African History* published Goody's article was that it provided a summary of anthropological thought about African "states."

52. *Listener,* November 28, 1963, P. 871, as cited in J. D. Fage, *On the Nature of African History* (Birmingham: Birmingham University Press, 1965), 1–2.

53. Oliver, *African History;* Fage, *On the Nature.*

54. Neale, *Writing*, 3–23.

55. E. V. Walter, *Terror and Resistance: A Study of Political Violence* (New York: Oxford University Press, 1969). The reviews roundly denounced him for his negative spirit. It is significant that neither the *Journal of African History* nor *African Historical Studies* reviewed the book.

56. Neale, *Writing*, 15–16, citing Shula Marks.

57. See T. O. Ranger, *The Inglorious Age: The Navy and Commerce under the Early Stuarts* (Salisbury, Rhodesia: Central Africa Historical Association, 1961).

58. T. O. Ranger, *State and Church in Southern Rhodesia, 1919–1939* (Salisbury, Rhodesia: Central Africa Historical Association, 1962); idem, *Revolt in Southern Rhodesia, 1896–1897* (Evanston, Ill.: Northwestern University Press, 1967).

59. Ranger, *Emerging Themes*, ix–x, xi–xiv. His discussion of oral tradition is in part inspired by this (xi–xii), but he was also impressed by the British historians E. Paul Thompson and Eric Hobsbawm.

60. Ranger, *Emerging Themes*, xv–xvii, xviii–xix. Ranger denied that there

was a school in his reply to Donald Denoon and Adam Kuper. See T. O. Ranger, "The New Historiography in Dar es Salaam: An Answer," *African Affairs* 70, no. 278 (1971): 50–61. See also the rejoinder in *African Affairs* 70, no. 280 (1971): 287–88.

61. His inaugural lecture in 1969 was entitled "The Recovery of African Initiative in Tanzanian History."

62. Many first learned about them from Ranger's celebrated article "Connections between 'Primary Resistance' Movements and Modern Mass Nationalism in East and Central Africa," *JAH* 9 (1968): 437–53, 631–42.

63. R. Mauny, *Tableau géographique de l'ouest africain au moyen âge* (Dakar: IFAN, 1961). Conferences were held at SOAS and Dakar in 1961, at Northwestern University in 1962, at Dar es Salaam in 1965, at Farnham in 1966, and at Chicago in 1968.

64. Henri Brunschwig challenged this claim in his "Pour une histoire," 337.

65. G. P. Murdock, *Africa: Its Peoples and Their Culture History* (New York: McGraw-Hill, 1959). For an account of the North American school of culture history, see F. W. Voget, *A History of Ethnology* (New York: Holt, 1975), 317–59.

66. D. McCall, *Africa in Time-Perspective* (Boston: Boston University Press, 1964). In 1968 he wrote an unpublished essay, "The Methodology of History," which discussed written sources and developed an analysis of the relative historical validity of the various types of sources.

67. McCall, *Africa*, 150. W. MacGaffey, "History, Anthropology and Rationality" *HA* 5 (1978): 108. See 101–20.

68. July, *African Voice*, 177–97; personal communication from John O. Hunwick, June 15, 1993.

69. J. Vansina, "Recording the Oral History of the Bakuba, I. Methods," *JAH* 1 (1960): 43–51; idem, *De la tradition orale* (Tervuren: AMRAC, 1961). The book became commonly known only in the English translation, *Oral Tradition* (London: Kegan Paul, 1965).

70. Fage, *On the Nature*, 5 n. 10; idem, "Writing," 245. He claimed that in West Africa anthropologists had made a more successful use of oral traditions than historians had.

71. Even though publication of his research was delayed until 1967, its results became known in 1961.

72. P. D. Curtin, "Field Techniques for Collecting and Processing Oral Data," *JAH* 9 (1968): 367–85, and, much later, D. Henige, *Oral Historiography* (London: Longman, 1982), with a valuable bibliography.

73. D. K. Dunaway and W. K. Baum, *Oral History: An Interdisciplinary Anthology* (Nashville: American Association for State and Local History, 1984), esp. the graphs (10–11) showing the success of oral history in the sixties.

74. Ranger, *Emerging Themes*, xii. On research activities in Tanzania, see Ranger, "History at the University College," 3–8, and the first issue of *Tanzania Zamani*, cyclostyled.

75. Thus, for instance, Tio oral traditions did not allow them to reconstruct their political history much before 1880, but no one concluded that my use of them to reconstruct Tio life around 1880 was invalid.

76. T. Beidelman, "Myth, Legend, and Oral History: A Kaguru Traditional Text," *Anthropos* 65 (1970): 74–97. By the end of the sixties other social anthropologists were beginning to study oral traditions as literature. See R. Finnegan, *Oral Literature in Africa* (Oxford: Clarendon Press, 1970).

77. The publication of the proceedings was delayed until 1970. See D. H. Jones, "Problems of African Chronology," *JAH* 11 (1970): 161–268.

78. Ibid., 161–76; D. Henige, *The Chronology of Oral Tradition: Quest for a Chimera* (Oxford: Clarendon Press, 1974).

79. For a general overview of the historiography of the issue, see J. Vansina, "Bantu in the Crystal Ball," *HA* 6 (1979): 287–333, and 7 (1980): 294–325.

80. R. Oliver, "The Problem of the Bantu Expansion," *JAH* 7, no. 3 (1966): 361–76.

81. M. Guthrie, *Comparative Bantu*, 4 vols. (Farnborough, Eng.: Gregg Press, 1967–71).

82. B. M. Fagan, "Wenner-Gren Research Conference on Bantu Origins in Sub-Saharan Africa: Chicago, March 24–29, 1968," *African Studies Bulletin* 11, no. 2 (September 1968): 225–31.

83. Colin Flight has detailed these issues in "Malcolm Guthrie and the Reconstruction of Bantu Prehistory," *HA* 7 (1980): 81–118, "Trees and Traps: Strategies for the Classification of African Languages and Their Historical Significance," *HA* 8 (1981): 43–74, and "The Bantu Expansion and the SOAS Network," *HA* 15 (1988): 261–301.

84. E.g., B. Davidson's *Black Mother* (Boston: Little, Brown, 1962).

85. P. D. Curtin, *The Atlantic Slave Trade: A Census* (Madison: University of Wisconsin Press, 1969).

86. R. A. Austen, "Economic History," *ASR* 19, no. 3 (1971): 426–28; C. Coquery-Vidrovitch, "Recherches sur un mode de production africain," *La Pensée* 144 (1969): 61–68.

87. On economic history, see Austen, "Economic History," 425–38; Curtin, "Recent Trends," 62–63. For a typical work of the time, see R. Gray and D. Birmingham, eds., *Pre-colonial African Trade: Essays on Trade in Central and Eastern Africa before 1900* (London: Oxford University Press, 1990). On substantivism, see G. Dalton, ed., *Tribal and Peasant Economies* (New York: Natural History Press, 1968).

88. A. G. Hopkins, *An Economic History of West Africa* (London: Longman, 1973).

89. This opinion culminated in the 1274 pages of R. Rotberg and A. Mazrui, eds., *Protest and Power in Black Africa* (New York: Oxford University Press, 1970). The dedication to the memory of E. Chivambo Mondlane, the leader of the movement for the liberation of Mozambique, assassinated in 1969, is significant.

90. M. Wright, "African History in the 1960's: Religion," *ASR* 14, no. 3 (1971): 439–45.

91. T. O. Ranger and I. N. Kimambo, eds., *The Historical Study of African Religion* (Berkeley: University of California Press, 1972). See also my rather disappointed reaction in *IJAHS* 3 (1972): 178–80. Later I was rebuked for this by J. Matthew Schoffeleers, a leading historian of religion in Central Africa, on the grounds that the book was a beginning and the subject should be encouraged.

92. Philip Curtin was too optimistic in his assessment of this point in "Recent Trends" (62).

93. J. S. Trimingham, *Islam in West Africa* (Oxford: Clarendon Press, 1959), 30, 40, 46. Trimingham's *History of Islam in West Africa* (Oxford: Clarendon Press, 1962) and later volumes were not much better.

94. See J. C. Froelich, *Les musulmans d'Afrique noire* (Paris: Editions de l'Orante, 1962), 11; V. Monteil, *L'Islam noir* (Paris: Editions du Seuil, 1964), 40–41. Monteil was the first to denounce such views.

95. J. Humphrey Fisher, *Ahmadiyyah: A Study in Contemporary Islam on the West African Coast* (London: Oxford University Press, 1963); J. Abun-Nasr, *The Tijaniya* (London: Oxford University Press, 1965). See Fage, "Writing," 246–47. John O. Hunwick and H. F. C. Smith also opposed Trimingham's views.

96. I. M. Lewis, ed., *Islam in Tropical Africa* (London: IAI, 1966), 4–96, esp. 58–75; N. Levtzion, *Muslims and Chiefs in West Africa* (Oxford: Clarendon Press, 1968).

97. See Fage, "Writing," 244–51, for the situation in West Africa. Art historians held their first triennial conference at Hampton College, Virginia, in 1968, but apart from Frank Willett and myself, the conferees were little concerned with the history of art. The discussions there dealt with anthropological context or with styles.

98. *Tanzania Zamani* 1; T. O. Ranger, "The Historical Association of Tanzania," 1967, mimeo.

99. J. B. Webster, ed. "Leadership in Nineteenth-Century Africa," *Tarikh* 1, no. 1 (1965). On West Africa in general, see Fage, "Writing," 249 n. 52.

100. Y. Person, *Samori, une révolution dyula*, 3 vols. (Dakar: IFAN, 1968–75). Person had started work on this subject about 1960. On Person, see obituaries in *Africa* 53 (1983): 74, and *Journal des Africanistes* 52 (1983): 181–92.

101. See P. D. Curtin, "Field Techniques for Collecting and Processing Oral Data," *JAH* 9, no. 3 (1970): 367–85.

102. R. Oliver and J. D. Fage, *A Short History of Africa* (London: Penguin, 1962).

103. For an overview, see J. Vansina, "UNESCO and African Historiography," *HA* 20 (1993): 337–52. See a different appreciation in Filesi, *Realtà*, 186–225.

104. These goals were hammered out during the general discussion of the project at the first meeting, on March 24–April 1, 1971, in Paris, which I attended.

105. "Third Conference in African History and Archaeology," *JAH* 2 (1961): 192 n. 1.

106. D. Laya, *La tradition orale: Problématique et méthodologie des sources de l'histoire africaine* (Niamey: Centre Régional de la Documentation Orale, 1972), 11–16.

107. See Vansina, "UNESCO," for more detail.

CHAPTER 7. A RESTLESS TEMPERAMENT

1. The title of this chapter comes from a letter from R. Oliver to T. Hamerow, October 1975, characterizing me (PF).

2. The Voting Rights Act dates from 1965. Martin Luther King, Jr., died in April 1968. The Gulf of Tonkin resolution was passed in 1964, legitimating a military buildup, which reached a peak during 1968–73.

3. On W. A. Williams and the "Wisconsin school" in American history, see P. Novick, *That Noble Dream: The "Objectivity Question" and the American Historical Profession* (Cambridge: Cambridge University Press, 1988), 446–57; on the impact of civil rights on the history profession, see pp. 472–91.

4. A fund to appoint a woman professor in history became available in the fall of 1969, and Philip Curtin saw it as an opportunity to gain a further position in African history. PF: my letter to Mort Rothstein, November 15, 1969.

5. PF: planning committee memo to chair, February 27, 1969.

6. On the impact on the historical profession, see Novick, *That Noble Dream*, 427–38; on the atmosphere in Madison, see T. Robbins, *Still Life with a Woodpecker* (New York: Bantam Books, 1970).

7. M. Klein, "Back to Democracy," *ASR* 35, no. 2 (1992): 3. Klein claims that "both right and left bought Lenin without Marx." That was not really so, either among the students or, according to Novick, among faculty.

8. This was Emile Snyder, who joined us in the fall of 1967.

9. Crawford Young published *Politics in the Congo* (Princeton, N.J.: Princeton University Press, 1965), which became and still is the authoritative study on the topic. He later became one of the foremost political scientists concerned with cultural pluralism, including ethnicity, especially in Africa. He still teaches at Madison.

10. Phil Curtin had been its first chair, and I replaced him in 1962–63 and 1965–66 when he was on leave.

11. Anne Curtin for the African Studies Program, 1966 report to the Ford Foundation.

12. J. Vansina, "How the Kingdom of the Great Makoko and Certain Clapperless Bells Became Topics of Research," in *The Historian's Workshop*, edited by L. P. Curtis, Jr. (New York: Knopf, 1970), 237.

13. PF: chair to vice president, February 1.

14. PF: memo from me to the Comparative Tropical History Program, February 2, 1965, point C1.

15. The matter came up during the discussions surrounding my decision to join the University of Leuven.

16. PF: my memo to the Comparative Tropical History Program, September 22, 1967; my "Proposal Major Field in AH," [December 24, 1969]; minutes, Comparative Tropical History Program, January 15, 1969; and my letter to Curtin about students, November 2, 1968. More "fine tuning" occurred in 1969–70. See PF, my draft "proposals" of December 24, 1969.

17. R. Oliver, *African History for the Outside World* (London: SOAS, 1964), recalls a similar struggle in West Africa and retraces Oliver's efforts to shift from an optional subject in colonial history to an undergraduate degree in African history at SOAS.

18. PF: November 23, 1965; on student numbers, October 15, 1970; and "Activities [Kinshasa] 70–71." By the fall of 1972 there were twenty-three graduate students in the seminar, according to the student roster.

19. PF: my letter to Curtin, November 2, 1968. After the arrival of Steven Feierman in the fall of 1969, the Africa seminar began to rotate among the three of us.

20. PF: e.g., my letters of February 1, 1965, and November 2, 1968, to Phil.

21. It would be invidious to list the most brilliant scholars among them here. Suffice it to say that around 1974 about ten of them were considered by others as "stars" in the profession.

22. PF: Curtin to me, December 27, 1973; student's personal letter to me, December 23, 1992.

23. This includes one person who had not followed the standard program.

24. When I left Madison in 1973, he also took over the direction of four doctoral candidates who had been working with me.

25. PF: my letter to Curtin, November 2, 1968.

26. PF: Curtin's letter to me, November 2, 1968.

27. Seminar notes: fall 1972, introductory comments. This was accompanied by a warning that more rigorous research in African history was needed.

28. Larry Yarak, the future specialist on the history of the Gold Coast, recalls that he visited me in Leuven a year later to ask my opinion about the prospects in the field. I vigorously attempted to dissuade him from embarking on a field which held no chance for gainful employment. Personal communication, May 1992.

29. Data from M. Harries, *Africa-Related Doctoral Dissertations and Masters Theses Completed at the University of Wisconsin through 1986* (Madison: African Studies Program, 1986). The data on doctorates were used. The topics for M.A.'s were similar except for one thesis on art and history by Robert A. Rohde (1969).

30. This is the interpretation of one former student, but hints from many others seem to bear it out.

31. The few students who had entered earlier did not really belong to this network or "family," as their later associations and careers make clear.

32. J. Maes, *Volkenkunde van Belgisch Kongo* (Antwerp: Kompas, 1935); N. De Cleene, *Introduction à l'ethnographie congolaise* (Antwerp: Zaire, 1944; Antwerp: De Sikkel, 1956; French translation, Antwerp: De Sikkel, 1957); and G. Van der Kerken, *De Afrikaanse bevolking van Belgisch-Kongo en Ruanda-Urundi* (Ghent: Fecheyr, 1952).

33. R. M. Underhill, *Red Man's America: A History of Indians in the United States* (Chicago: University of Chicago Press, 1953).

34. PF: chits of 1964–65 for Ross Dunn and William O. Brown.

35. J. Vansina, *Introduction à l'ethnographie du Congo* (Kinshasa: Editions Universitaires du Congo, 1965), 223.

36. Letter, May 13, 1963. I had applied for and received summer funding from the Wisconsin Alumni Research Foundation, an institution unique to Madison which has been a godsend for many researchers.

37. R. Anttila, *An Introduction to Historical and Comparative Linguistics* (New York: Macmillan, 1972), 137, 291–92.

38. J. Vansina, "Probing the Past of the Lower Kwilu Peoples (Zaire)," *Paideuma* 19–20 (1974): 332–64; idem, "Vocabulaire politique et histoire des Basaa du Bas-Kasai," in *Forschungen in Memoriam Erika Sulzmann*, edited by E. W. Müller and A-M. Brandstetter, vol. 1 of *Mainzer Beiträge zur Afrika-Forschung* (Mainz: Reimer, 1992), 455–80.

39. J. Vansina, "The Use of Ethnographic Data as Sources for History," in *Emerging Themes of African History*, edited by T. O. Ranger (Dar es Salaam: East African Publishing House, 1968), 97–124.

40. J. Vansina, "Cultures through Time," in *A Handbook of Method in Cultural Anthropology*, edited by R. Naroll and R. Cohen (Garden City, N.Y.: Natural History Press, 1970), 165–82.

41. J. Vansina, "The Bells of Kings," *JAH* 10 (1969): 187–97; see also Vansina, "How the Kingdom of the Great Makoko," 223–43.

42. J. Vansina, *La légende du passé* (Tervuren: AMRAC, 1972), 219.

43. Correspondence with L. Cahen and E. Meeussen. Meeussen, who had "written the book" about Kirundi, found about one tonal mistake per page and therefore vetoed any publication of the original texts.

44. There were few reviews, some quite late. A rather ill-informed and patronizing review by Aylward Shorter, in *Azania* 11: 185–86, appeared only in 1976.

45. L. Ndoricimpa and C. Guillet, eds., *L'arbre-mémoire: Traditions orales du Burundi* (Paris: Khartala, 1984). The editors did not feel it necessary to point this out, however.

46. Despite dismissive reviews in *Aequatoria* and the *Times Literary Supplement*, the review by Daniel McCall in the *American Anthropologist* led to the English translation of 1965.

47. T. O. Ranger, "Towards a Usable African Past," in *African Studies since 1945: A Tribute to Basil Davidson*, edited by C. Fyfe (London: Longman, 1976), 18. "If he had not existed we should have had to invent him."

48. In 1961 at the seminar in Dakar, I had been horrified to learn that one researcher, who will remain anonymous, had derived his "authentic" eyewitness accounts through interviews with the ancestral actors themselves as they spoke through the mouths of their mediums!

49. Given the present interest in this matter, it is unfortunate that no record of this correspondence seems to have survived.

50. A. Haley, *Roots* (New York: Doubleday, 1976).

51. H. Brunschwig, "La négotiation du traité Makoko," *CEA* 17 (1965): 5–56; idem, "Les cahiers de Brazza: 1880–1882," *CEA* 22 (1966): 157–227; idem, ed., *Brazza explorateur* (Paris: Mouton, 1966); and C. Coquery-Vidrovitch, ed. *Brazza et la prise de possession du Congo*, (Paris: Mouton, 1969).

52. E. Zorzi, *Al Congo con Brazza: Viaggio di due esploratori italiani nel carteggio et nel "giornali" inediti di Attilio Pecile (1883–1886)* (Milan: Instituto pergli Studi, di Politicá Internazionale, 1940).

53. I had hoped to have it finished earlier and had planned to reserve that year to write up the results of my research about Kuba religion. That was put on the back burner and never published.

54. J. Vansina, *The Tio Kingdom of the Middle Congo: 1880–1892* (London: IAI, 1973).

55. C. Vidal, "L'ethnologie à l'imparfait: Un cas d'ethno-histoire," *CEA* 16, nos. 61–62 (1976): 397–404; rejoinders by J. P. Chrétien, C. H. Perrot, and myself, as "Histoire africaine, constations, contestations," *CEA* 16, nos. 66–67 (1977): 369–80. Letters from various historians in France in the spring of 1977 to me linked the negative tone of Vidal's review to my critique of Balandier's book on Kongo in *Africa* 39, no. 1 (1969): 64–68. Later writings by Vidal confirm this.

56. Yet James Fernandes, in *Bwiti* (Princeton, N.J.: Princeton University Press, 1982), writing on a Fang cult in Gabon, did manage it: his book is 721 pages long, but then much of it provides background information well known to specialists in the area and to local audiences, but not to his academic and English-speaking audience.

57. As far as I know, however, this project has not been completed. In the meantime a number of Tio scholars have access to the book and use approximate translations.

58. PF: proposal to the Guggenheim Foundation, October 1968.

59. PF: dean's office to me, January 17, 1972.

60. J. Vansina, comp., *Ibiteekerezo: Historical Narratives from Rwanda* (Chicago: Department of Photo Duplication, University of Chicago Library, 1973), microfilm, MF 2739 (6 reels).

61. Leonardo Scholars, *Resources and Decisions* (North Scituate, Mass.:

Duxbury Press, 1975). The research was conducted between January and June 1973.

62. PF: February 1965; January 1966; Robert de Borghgraef, December 1965.

63. PF: letter from our chairman to the dean, January 13; letter from the dean to me, January 25; and general memo from the chairman, January 25, 1966.

64. PF: my letters to Mort Rothstein, October 27 and 29, 1971.

65. PF: letter from Eugeen Roosens, January 15, 1973, p. 2. For Roosens, "Africa" was equated with "the former colony"!

66. A huge literature exists about the various episodes of this period, and CRISP published annual volumes from 1959 to 1968 which chronicle and document the events year by year, yet no one so far has written a general narrative of these years.

67. On Verhaegen as a historian, see J. Stengers, "Belgian Historiography since 1945," in *Reappraisals in Overseas University,* edited by P. C. Emmer and H. L. Wesseling (Leiden: Leiden University Press, 1979), 168. Background entry in J. Duffy, M. Frey, and M. Sims, eds., *International Directory of Scholars and Specialists in African Studies* (Waltham, Mass.: Cross Roads Press, 1978), 302.

68. No doubt the selection committee in Washington had not given much attention to the names of Fulbright scholars, but the Congolese students were bemused by these: "Miracle" was followed by "Leopard" and then even better by "Hymans, Immense," all evocative and promising wonders.

69. The history of power at Lovanium is related by B. Lacroix, *Pouvoirs et structures de l'Université Lovanium* (Brussels: Centre d'Etude et de Documentation Africaines, 1972).

70. It apparently still does in such expatriate milieux today.

71. Lacroix, *Pouvoirs,* 65–78.

72. See Jadin's obituary notice in *BARSOM* (1973): 70–101. He taught at Lovanium until 1970. François Bontinck later taught full time at the university and then at the school of theology in Kinshasa. Like Jadin, he edited numerous first-rate text editions but also wrote many articles on African leaders in the Congo Independent State.

73. Personal communication, January 29, 1993. See also the brief entry in Duffy, Frey, and Sims, *International Directory,* 301.

74. W. De Craemer and R. Fox, *The Emerging Physician* (Stanford, Calif.: Hoover Institution, 1968).

75. W. De Craemer, J. Vansina, and R. Fox, "Religious Movements in Central Africa: A Theoretical Study," *Comparative Studies in Society and History* 18, no. 4 (October 1976): 458–75.

76. On this region, see A. Mpase Nselenge Mpeti, *L'évolution de la solidarité traditionelle en milieu rural et urbain au Zaire: Le cas des Ntomba et des Basengele du lac Mai-Ndombe* (Kinshasa: Kinshasa University Press, 1974).

77. Lacroix, *Pouvoirs,* 72–78.

78. Letter from Hubert Silvestre to me, June 13, 1968, with a list of courses.

79. PF: January 1972; activities report, January 31–February 17, 1971. A specialist on the early history of the Niger Delta who has published much on the subject, E. J. Alagoa was then teaching at Ibadan. Later he created a flourishing department of history at Port Harcourt in the Delta. He has become one of the most revered history teachers in Nigeria. Babatunde Agiri was then, as he is now, teaching at the university in Lagos.

80. On his approach, see J. L. Vellut, *Guide de l'étudiant en histoire du Zaire* (Kinshasa: Editions du Mont Noir, 1974).

81. PF: my letter to Mort Rothstein, March 20, 1971.

82. PF: my letter to Bertram Hill, May 12, 1971.

83. On this experience, see J. Vansina, "Mwasi's Trials," *Daedalus* (Spring 1982): 49–70; also PF: June 12, September 12, 1971.

84. Letter to my mother, July 2.

85. We met at Mayidi in Lower Zaire on July 9–12. Letters to my mother, July 5, 16, 17; PF: my "Activity Report," January 20, 1972.

86. Correspondence file: "Histoire du Zaire." Today a good overall study of the colonial era and especially of this transitional period is still lacking.

87. C. Young and T. Turner, *The Rise and Decline of the Zairian State* (Madison: University of Wisconsin Press, 1985), 65–69, 198.

88. PF: my letters to Mort Rothstein, August 16, September 12. The school of education went to Kisangani, and Benoît Verhaegen switched from social science to education in order to move there.

89. Ndaywel e Nziem, "La formation des historiens africains à la Faculté de Lettres au Zaire," *Likundoli*, série C, 1, no. 2 (1976): 1–42; Stengers, "Belgian Historiography," 169, 178–80. The first ones among them were Sikitele Gize, Mumbanza wa Bamwele, and Ndua Solol. Some of the first dissertations are truly remarkable achievements. It is deplorable that so far no publishers have been found even for a single one of them.

90. PF: my letters to Mort Rothstein, September 12, October 12, and October 29. I took a "leave of undetermined length."

91. The new name was a symbol of *authenticité* and its adoption an occasion for yet another major currency devaluation.

92. On Zaire to 1987, see Young and Turner, *Rise and Decline*; Nzongola-Ntalaja, *The Crisis in Zaire: Myths and Realities* (Trenton, N.J.: Africa World Press, 1986); and Michael Schatzberg, *The Dialectics of Oppression in Zaire* (Bloomington: Indiana University Press, 1988). Since then the situation has become even worse. On the clashes of Lubumbashi, Victor Digesika Pibuka, *Le Massacre de Lubumbashi, Zaire, 11–12 mai 1990: Dossier d'un témoin accusé* (Paris: Harmattan, 1993).

CHAPTER 8. BETWIXT AND BETWEEN

1. Or, as I stated in my letter of resignation to the chairman of the department in Madison: "I yearned to rejoin my homeland." PF: March 14, 1973.

2. Later published as E. Roosens, *Socio-culturele verandering in midden-afrika: Een gevalstudie, de Yaka van Kwaango* (Antwerp: Standaard, 1971). He left the order before ordination, stayed in Leuven, and set about to find a niche for himself at the university, first in the faculty of medicine and then in psychology.

3. PF: my letter to Theodore Hamerow, April 12.

4. J. Stengers, "Belgian Historiography since 1945," in *Reappraisals in Overseas University,* edited by P. C. Emmer and H. L. Wesseling (Leiden: Leiden University Press, 1979), 170 n. 18; M. Van Spaandonk, "Afrika Boe?" *Trends* 8 (October 1992): 59.

5. Nuttin pressured me heavily not to resign. He even claimed that I would be a traitor to Flanders if I did. Roosens heads the program at Leuven today and is still very involved in its academic politics. The year after I left he made an unsuccessful bid to become rector.

6. Letter of September 7, 1974, to Willy De Craemer.

7. For example, in December 1973 I attended a UNESCO conference in Cameroon for a few days and flew back in a single day from a bush post there all the way to Leuven. There I had experienced the setting of forests and the open landscapes of Bamum, conducted some tests on language, and met people as diverse as Zimbabwean guerillas and Alexis Kagame.

8. This was doubly taboo, because I was a professor and because that university was the archrival of the Catholic universities!

9. The journal, founded in 1968, succeeded the older colonial journal *Zaire,* which folded in 1961.

10. P. Veyne, *Comment on écrit l'histoire: Essai d'épistémologie* (Paris: Editions du Seuil, 1971).

11. *HA* 1 (1974): 109–27.

12. PF: letter to me from the dean, September 20, 1976.

13. Letter to Muhammad Jerary, June 19, 1983.

14. P. D. Curtin, L. Thompson, S. Feierman, and J. Vansina, *African History* (Boston: Little, Brown, 1978). Correspondence in the files labeled "Textbook."

15. Writing a standardized abstract is a technique for transcribing the gist of a conversation. For every sentence, one notes subject, action, object, circumstance, and all personal names or place-names, rather similar to the way in which telegrams are written. Such abstracts are necessary because full transcriptions take a long time, and they are sufficient because one can easily go from them to any passage on the tape for which one wants precise wording.

16. Although this practice could easily lead to contamination of testimony by comparison between informants, we still went ahead. Informants talked

about these interviews to each other anyway, and they prized a concrete record of what they had said. Moreover, this dispersal of the research record enhanced the chances that all would not be lost if some disaster hit the center.

17. When the project was presented to the public in the fall of that year, the center projected a series of slides showing every one of the interviewees in succession. This gallery of portraits was labeled the "author."

18. R. Fogel and S. Engerman, *Time on the Cross: Evidence and Methods* (Boston: Little, Brown, 1974), was the first major work to use rigorously quantitative reasoning derived from economics.

19. According to the latter, the "West" had reduced the "Third World" to its present peripheral and increasingly dependent place in the world economy. Instead of altruistically promoting genuine "development," the capitalist West exploited the Third World for its own purposes. Thus, seeming economic growth hid growing "underdevelopment."

20. The department was internally divided into three caucuses: American, European, and Third World. The journal *History and Theory*, from which the course took its title, had been founded in the 1960s. It was edited by philosophers and shunned by most historians as mere "navel gazing." See P. Novick, *That Noble Dream: The "Objectivity Question" and the American Historical Profession* (Cambridge: Cambridge University Press, 1988), 593.

21. Most theories were reductionist in the sense that they dismissed the unique and contingent with the phrase "all other things being equal" in an argument striving to discover general laws. But all other things were never equal; moreover, because only history dealt with concrete situations, all other things were crucial to it.

22. All the statistical information was compiled from my files labeled "Students." Departmental records tend to be discarded after a few years. Matriculation records are kept but are organized by student name and number, not by department or specialty.

23. For instance, by 1977 I began to use large amounts of time, and some of the Vilas research funding, to create visual aids that were precisely tailored to each course. This is yet another instance of juggling time between two goals: graduate and undergraduate teaching.

24. The expression comes in an "of course" comment made by a recent doctoral graduate. This erroneous belief is widespread among the students themselves, as well as others. Those who subscribe to it tend to compare apples and oranges, that is, scholars who have fully realized their potential and newly minted Ph.D.'s. My own remarks are strictly based on comparing doctoral students.

25. J. Vansina, *African Art and History* (London: Longman, 1984).

26. J. Vansina, *The Children of Woot: A History of the Kuba Peoples* (Madison: University of Wisconsin Press, 1975).

27. See Bope Nyim-a-Nkwem, "La perception Kuba de leur histoire à travers l'oeuvre de J. Vansina," *Annales Aequatoria* (1993), forthcoming.

28. "Histoire du Zaire" file.

29. R. Cornevin, *Histoire de l'Afrique,* 2 vols. (Paris: Payot, 1962–66), 2: 26.

30. J. Vansina, "Lignage, idéologie et histoire en Afrique Centrale," *Enquêtes et documents d'histoire africaine* 4 (1980): 133–55.

31. See J. Vansina, "The Peoples of the Forests," in *History of Central Africa,* vol. 1, edited by D. Birmingham and P. Martin (London: Longman, 1983), 75–117.

32. I am grateful for a Guggenheim Foundation grant.

33. Claudine and I arrived on January 2, and we left on February 4, 1981. We are indebted to the linguist Madame Nasse for her efficient help.

34. A. Avaro, "Les migrations historiques," in *Géographie et cartographie du Gabon: Atlas illustré,* ed. J. Barret (Paris: EDICEF, 1983), 43–45.

35. See R. Lanfranchi and B. Clist, eds., *Aux origines de l'Afrique Centrale* (Libreville: Sépia, 1991).

36. I refused to use ethnic groups as units of observation. Hence, "the Fang do this or that" was of little use unless I could find out when and where the observer actually lived. The research design required that comparable data be found in spots not more than fifty kilometers apart, taking into account the mobility of the local populations around 1900. Hence I often needed more information than the published literature provided.

37. For instance, J. Vansina, "The History of God among the Kuba," *Africa* (Rome) 38, no. 1 (1983): 17–40.

38. Originally Emiel Meeussen and André Coupez, later also Yvonne Bastin, were involved.

39. B. Heine, "Zur genetischen Gliederung der Bantu-Sprachen," *Afrika und Uebersee* 56 (1973): 164–85; D. W. Phillipson, *The Later Prehistory of Eastern and Southern Africa* (New York: African Publishing, 1977), 210–30.

40. L. Bouquiaux, ed., *L'expansion bantoue: Actes du Colloque International du CNRS, Viviers, 4–16 avril 1977,* 3 vols. (Paris: SELAF, 1980); letter from Hélène Van Leynseele, June 7, 1977.

41. Andrew Roberts to me, October 11, 1977; J. Vansina, "Western Bantu Expansion," *JAH* 25, no. 2 (1984): 129–45.

42. I am grateful to the institute and to the late Eike Haberland for their support.

43. Beatrix Heintze was an old acquaintance. Trained as a culture historian–anthropologist by Hermann Baumann, she became the foremost historian of Angola for the sixteenth and seventeenth centuries.

44. This chapter, for volume 8, was completed in 1985 but was only published in 1993.

CHAPTER 9. PROFESSIONALS AND DOCTRINES

1. W. Rodney, *How Europe Underdeveloped Africa* (London: Tanzania Publishing House, 1972). Walter Rodney, a Guyanan, had obtained his Ph.D. at

SOAS in 1966 and was then appointed at Dar es Salaam, where he stayed until 1971, with a short interlude at Mona University of the West Indies in Jamaica, from which he was expelled as a radical. He returned to Guyana but was prevented from taking up a position at the university there. He became politically active and was killed by a bomb on June 16, 1980.

2. W. K. Ochieng, "Undercivilisation in Black Africa," *Kenya Historical Review* 2, no. 1 (1974): 45–57. Ochieng stressed Africa's "technological backwardness" and attributed that in turn to the abundance of land.

3. A. G. Frank, *Capitalism and Underdevelopment in Latin America* (Harmondsworth, Eng.: Penguin, 1971); S. Amin, *L'accumulation à l'échelle mondiale* (Paris: Anthropos, 1970); and, on a global scale, E. Wallerstein, *The Modern World System* (New York: Academic Press, 1974).

4. A. Sheriff, *Slaves, Spices and Ivory in Zanzibar* (London: Currey, 1987), x.

5. T. O. Ranger, "Towards a Usable African Past," in *African Studies since 1945: A Tribute to Basil Davidson*, edited by C. Fyfe (London: Longman, 1976), 17–30. Note that the conference was held in 1974. See also S. J. Hildebrand, "A New Paradigm in African Studies," *Ufahamu* 5, no. 2 (1974): 3–19.

6. R. Law, "In Search of a Marxist Perspective on Pre-Colonial Africa," *JAH* 19 (1978): 441. In addition to the arguments advanced there, the profoundly evolutionary character of Marxism contradicts the premises of dependency theory.

7. J. Suret-Canale, *Afrique noire*, 3 vols. (Paris: Editions Sociales, 1961–72), and the attention paid to Sik's *Histoire.*

8. C. Coquery-Vidrovitch, "Recherches sur un mode de production africain," *La Pensée* 144 (1969): 61–68.

9. Historians in France had been convinced of this much earlier, ever since the second foundation of the journal *Annales: Economies, Sociétés, Civilisations* in 1945.

10. Even though Ranger was the journal's editor, the board was solidly "radical pessimist."

11. They were C. Van Onselen's *Chibaro: African Mine Labour in Southern Rhodesia, 1900–1933* (New York: Pluto Press, 1976); F. Cooper's *Plantation Slavery on the East Coast of Africa* (New Haven, Conn.: Yale University Press, 1977); and R. Palmer and N. Parsons, eds., *The Roots of Rural Poverty in Central and Southern Africa* (London: Heinemann, 1977). G. Arrighi, *The Political Economy of Rhodesia* (The Hague: Mouton, 1967), was a precursor.

12. F. A. Van Jaarsveld, *The Afrikaner Interpretation of South African Society* (Cape Town: Ravan, 1964); L. M. Thompson, "The Historiography of South Africa," in *The Historiography of the British Empire and Commonwealth: Trends, Interpretations and Resources*, edited by R. Wink (Durham, N.C.: Duke University Press, 1965). The South African "radical" historians soon established links with members of the new school of Dar es Salaam and other East Africanists to form a single intellectual network. They succeeded better than Leonard M.

Thompson had in integrating a significant number of South African historians into the mainstream of African historiography.

13. The charges are summarized best in D. O'Meara, "Problèmes posés par la 'décolonisation' de l'histoire de l'Afrique," in *Histoire et diversité des cultures*, ed. UNESCO (Paris: UNESCO, 1984), 233–48, and B. Freund, *The Making of Contemporary Africa* (Bloomington: Indiana University Press, 1984), 5–15. See also the references cited in both.

14. Ranger, "Towards a Usable African Past," 18–20. But Ranger himself had belonged to that public. Cf. T. O. Ranger, ed., *Aspects of Central African History* (Evanston, Ill.: Northwestern University Press, 1968), v.

15. Compare the fivefold rate of increase during the sixties with the twofold increase during the next two decades.

16. By 1990 even that flagship of African history in Great Britain, the *Journal of African History*, recruited two North American editors.

17. See J. Devisse, "Recherches sur l'histoire," in *Etudes africaines en Europe I* (Paris: Khartala, 1981), 630–47.

18. He replaced H. Deschamps. See Y. Person, "Hubert Deschamps et l'histoire africaine," *Revue Française d'Histoire d'Outre-Mer* 66, nos. 242–43 (1979): 11–14.

19. Coquery-Vidrovitch is now regarded as the foremost historian of colonial and recent history in France.

20. B. O. Oloruntimehin, "The University in the Era of the Civil War and Reconstruction," in *The University of Ibadan, 1948–1975*, edited by J. F. A. Ajayi and T. N. Tamuno (Ibadan: Ibadan University Press, 1973), 99–126. For the situation in history, see E. J. Alagoa, ed., "The Teaching of History at African Universities" (Port Harcourt, Nigeria, n.d.), mimeo, the proceedings of a conference held at the University of Lagos in September 1977, with reports from almost all African universities.

21. The events at Lovanium in 1971 were extreme at the time, but not unique. Since then the closure of universities for longer or shorter periods has become common, and even the drafting of students into the army has occurred elsewhere.

22. The proceedings of the symposia were published by UNESCO as *Studies and Documents*. See also J. Vansina, "UNESCO and African Historiography," *HA* 20 (1993): 337–52.

23. Historians left postcolonial history to the political scientists and are still criticized for it. At a conference in Leiden, in June 1992, the Dutch anthropologist Kees van Dongen argued that such a policy of total discretion amounted to the co-optation of historians by the ruling regimes.

24. Hence the lack of interest by historians in the debate about feudalism in Africa during the early sixties was significant.

25. See L. Krader, *The Asiatic Mode of Production* (Assen: Van Gorcum, 1975), for the relevant texts.

26. Coquery-Vidrovitch, "Recherches," 61–78.

27. B. Jewsiewicki, *Marx, Afrique et Occident: Les pratiques africanistes de l'histoire marxiste* (Montreal: University Center for Developing Areas, McGill University, 1985); idem, "African Historical Studies: Academic Knowledge as 'Usable Past' and Radical Scholarship," *ASR* 32, no. 3 (1989): 1–76; B. Jewsiewicki and J. LeFourneau, eds., *Mode of Production: The Challenge of Africa* (Quebec: Safi, 1985).

28. Palmer and Parsons, *Roots of Rural Poverty;* C. Bundy, *The Rise and Fall of the South African Peasantry* (London: Heinemann, 1979).

29. Q. Hoare and G. N. Smith, eds. and trans., *Selections from the Prison Notebooks* (New York: International Publishers, 1971).

30. Freund, *Making*, 9. In fact, many of these documents pose serious technical problems, such as the question of authorship.

31. Ibid.

32. This was a reversal of the classic theses of Emile Durkheim. Wauthier de Mahieu demonstrated this in his dissertation, which I was supervising at Leuven in 1975. The text was later published as *Les structures sociales du groupe Komo du Zaire dans leur élaboration symbolique* (London: IAI, 1980).

33. A glance at the table of contents of B. Hindess and P. Q. Hirst, *Pre-Capitalist Modes of Production* (London: Routledge, 1975), the most famous doctrinaire text of the time, suffices to prove this.

34. Once again, Hindess and Hirst, *Pre-Capitalist Modes*, is a paragon of this.

35. See J. Vansina, "I stati precoloniali," in *Storia dell'Africa*, edited by A. Triulzi (Florence: La Nuova Italia, 1979), 15–37, which was strongly influenced by Friedrich Engels.

36. I. Wilks, *Asante in the Nineteenth Century* (Cambridge: Cambridge University Press, 1975); G. Prins, *The Hidden Hippopotamus* (Cambridge: Cambridge University Press, 1980).

37. His views are set forth in his letters to me from 1973 and 1974.

38. For a succinct exposition and a critique, see B. Nathhorst, *Formal or Structural Studies of Traditional Tales* (Bromma, Sweden: University of Stockholm, 1969).

39. L. de Heusch, *Le roi ivre; ou, L'origine de l'état* (Paris: Gallimard, 1972); C. Lévi-Strauss, *Structures élémentaires de la parenté* (Paris: Presses Universitaires de France, 1949).

40. De Heusch, *Le roi ivre*, 10, 298. Note the influence of Georges Dumézil, who attempted to reconstruct the original corpus of Indo-European myths from a study of their variants.

41. L. de Heusch, lecture, University College, London, 1973, published as "What Shall We Do with the Drunken King," *Africa* 45, no. 4 (1975): 363–72, quote on 363.

42. For my own position in 1973, see the summary in J. Vansina, "Comment: Traditions of Genesis," *JAH* 15 (1974): 317–22.

43. R. G. Willis, *On Historical Reconstruction from Oral-Traditional Sources: A Structuralist Approach* (Evanston, Ill.: Northwestern University Press, 1976); idem, *The Making of the State* (Bloomington: Indiana University Press, 1981). On the nature of this logic in Central Africa, see F. De Boeck, "Of Trees and Kings: Politics and Metaphor among the Aluund of South-Western Zaire," *American Ethnologist*, forthcoming.

44. This is another example of functionalist thought, this time confusing cause and effect.

45. J. Miller, "Kings and Kingsmen: The Imbangala Impact on the Mbundu of Angola," Ph.D. diss., University of Wisconsin, 1971, p. 553, later revised and published as *Kings and Kingsmen* (Oxford: Clarendon Press, 1976). As his adviser I was worried about the proper boundaries which should be put to imaginative interpretations. The same question also worried Beatrix Heintze of the Frobenius Institut in Frankfurt at the time.

46. The central role of "performance" in the creation of oral narrative was the thesis of Harold Scheub in his dissertation in 1969, published as *The Xhosa Ntsomi* (Oxford: Oxford University Press, 1976).

47. *History in Africa* has published articles on this subject in almost every issue since 1974.

48. J. B. Webster, ed., *Chronology, Migration and Drought in Interlacustrine Africa* (New York: Holmes and Meier, 1979), is a typical product of this tendency.

49. See, for instance, most of the contributions to B. Bernardi, C. Poni, and A. Triulzi, eds., *Fonti orali: Antropologia e storia* (Milan: Franco Angeli, 1978), and those in J. Miller, ed., *The African Past Speaks: Essays on Oral Tradition and History* (London: Dawson, 1980).

50. For instance, D. Henige, *The Chronology of Oral Tradition: Quest for a Chimera* (Oxford: Clarendon Press, 1974); idem, *Oral Historiography* (London: Longman, 1982); and four thoughtful articles by D. R. Wright in *HA* 5 (1978): 257–72, *HA* 9 (1982): 303–23, *HA* 12 (1985): 335–48, and *HA* 14 (1987): 287–309.

51. D. W. Cohen, *Womunafu's Bunafu: A Study of Authority in a Nineteenth-Century African Community* (Princeton, N.J.: Princeton University Press, 1977), 8–9, 188–89; T. O. Ranger, *Emerging Themes of African History* (Dar es Salaam: East African Publishing House, 1968), xi–xii.

52. See, for instance, C. H. Perrot, ed., *Sources orales de l'histoire de l'Afrique* (Paris: CNRS, 1989).

53. A. Haley, *Roots* (New York: Doubleday, 1976). Almost a hundred million people watched the miniseries when it was first shown. Since then perhaps as many as a billion people all over the world have seen it.

54. Vansina, "Comment."

55. Philip Nobile, in "Uncovering Roots," *Village Voice*, February 23, 1973, now alleges that the early parts of *Roots* were a fabrication engineered by Haley himself.

56. J. Vansina, "Memory and Oral Tradition," in *The African Past Speaks,* edited by J. Miller (Folkestone, Eng.: Dawson, 1980), 262–79.

57. Even some of the "bad faith" critical assessments of my book in K. Brown and M. Roberts, eds., "Using Oral Sources: Vansina and Beyond," a special issue of *Social Analysis* published in 1980, had not provoked me into a polemic. But I did reply to C. G. Smith, "For Braudel: A Note on the 'Ecole des Annales' and the Historiography of Africa," *HA* 4 (1977): 275–82, with J. Vansina, "For Oral Tradition (But Not Against Braudel)," *HA* 5 (1978): 341–56.

58. L. de Heusch, *Rois nés d'un coeur de vache* (Paris: Gallimard, 1982), esp. 354–55; J. Vansina, "Is Elegance Proof?: Structuralism and African History," *HA* 10 (1983): 317–48. For the reaction by de Heusch, see P. De Maret, "Un interview avec Luc de Heusch," *Current Anthropology* 34 (1993): 292–93.

59. J. Vansina, *Oral Tradition as History* (Madison: University of Wisconsin Press, 1985).

60. P. Novick, *That Noble Dream: The "Objectivity Question" and the American Historical Profession* (Cambridge: Cambridge University Press, 1988), 467–521. The *African Studies Review* documents the evolution in African studies.

61. For instance, Bogumił Jewsiewicki edited an issue of *African Economic History* entitled "Contributions to the History of Agriculture and Fishing in Central Africa" in 1979, which was not followed up. John E. G. Sutton was so struck by the neglect of agriculture in African archaeology and history when he attended a conference called Prehistoric Intensive Agriculture in the Tropics in 1981 that he vowed to redress this situation. Five years later he organized a conference in Oxford. Its proceedings were published in a special issue of *Azania* in 1989 entitled "History of African Agricultural Technology and Field Systems." It is striking that only two historians were among the contributors.

62. For the commercial links, see especially *Arts d'Afrique Noire,* but also the juxtaposition of texts, advertisements, and editorials in *African Arts,* the flagship in the field.

63. I am grateful to Renée Fox for this observation.

64. J. M. Janzen, *The Quest for Therapy in Lower Zaire* (Berkeley: University of California Press, 1978), xvii–xx. On the field in general, see S. Feierman and J. M. Janzen, eds., *The Social Basis of Health and Healing in Africa* (Berkeley: University of California Press, 1992).

65. For a later survey, see O. Zunz, ed., *Reliving the Past: The Worlds of Social History* (Chapel Hill: University of North Carolina Press, 1985).

66. See Freund, *Making,* 6.

67. See S. Krech III, "The State of Ethnohistory," *Annual Review of Anthropology* 20 (1991): 345–75, on the influence of history on anthropology, which has been especially strong since about 1980. On *ethnohistory* as a synonym for "social history," see pages 348, 357.

68. See E. J. Hobsbawm, "From Social History to the History of Society," *Daedalus* (1971): 20–45, for a short overview on the beginnings of the field. For

a different understanding of the term, see G. Duby, "Histoire sociale et idéologies des sociétés," in *Faire de l'histoire,* edited by J. Le Goff and P. Nora (Paris: Gallimard, 1974), 147–68.

69. E. le Roy Ladurie, *Montaillou* (Paris: Gallimard, 1975; English translation, New York: Braziller, 1978), and, later, the writings of Natalie Zemon Davis were favorite models for some dissertators, in Madison at least.

70. Contrast, for instance, P. Lovejoy, ed., *The Ideology of Slavery in Africa* (Beverly Hills, Calif.: Sage, 1981), and S. Miers and I. Kopytoff, eds., *Slavery in Africa: Historical and Anthropological Perspectives* (Madison: University of Wisconsin Press, 1977).

71. See Novick, *That Noble Dream,* 491–510, on developments in American historiography.

72. Just in Madison, there were Jean M. Hay (Ph.D., 1972) Iris Berger (Ph.D., 1973), and Claire Robertson (Ph.D., 1974). All three were interested in this specialty. (See letter of January 3, 1975, from Claire Robertson to me.) Later all three edited or wrote books on women's history.

73. N. Hunt, "Bibliographical Essay: Placing African Women's History and Locating Gender," *Social History* 14, no. 3 (October 1989): 359–79.

74. For instance, see A. P. Pala and M. Ly, *La femme africaine dans la société précoloniale* (Paris: UNESCO, 1979), a characteristic effort for an early stage of the writing of history in an ethnographic mold.

75. J. E. Mbot, introduction to *Racines Bantu—Bantu Roots,* edited by T. Obenga and S. Sovindoula (Libreville: CICIBA, 1991), 7–12.

76. John Fage retired in 1984.

77. Jewsiewicki, "African Historical Studies," 16–26.

78. Jewsiewicki, *Marx,* is almost identical to his contribution to this series.

79. Cf., for instance, R. A. Lystad, *The African World: A Survey of Social Research* (New York: Praeger, 1965).

80. D. P. Ursu, *Sovremennaya istoriographia ctran tropitcheskoi Afriki: 1960–1980* (Moscow: Nayka, 1983); C. Neale, *Writing "Independent" History: African Historiography, 1960–1980* (Westport, Conn.: Greenwood Press, 1985); and B. Jewsiewicki and D. Newbury, eds., *African Historiographies: What History for Which Africa?* (Beverly Hills, Calif.: Sage, 1987). T. Filesi's *Realtà,* however, was published in 1978.

81. For a long time, M. Hiskett, *The Sword of Truth: The Life and Times of the Shehu Usuman dan Fodio* (Oxford: Oxford University Press, 1973), had been the exception that proves the rule, and even this focused more on the times and the ideas than on the person.

82. See Jewsiewicki's letter of December 20, 1979, to me. See B. Jewsiewicki, *Naître et mourir au Zaire: Un demi-siècle au quotidien* (Paris: Khartala, 1993); A. Isaacman, ed., *The Life History of Raúl Honwana* (Boulder, Colo.: Lynn Rienner, 1988); and J. Boyd, *The Caliph's Sister, Nana Asma'u, 1793–1865: Teacher, Poet, and Islamic Leader* (London: F. Cass, 1988).

83. L. White, *Magomero: Portrait of an African Village* (Cambridge: Cambridge University Press, 1987); J. Peires, *The Dead Will Arise* (London: Currey, 1989); D. W. Cohen and E. S. A. Odhiambo, *Siaya: The Historical Anthropology of an African Landscape* (London: Currey, 1989).

84. Deconstructionism has been a movement in literary criticism ever since the sixties. For a delightful satire, see D. Lodge, *Small World* (New York: Warner, 1984).

85. Novick, *That Noble Dream*, esp. 523–629.

86. For a scathing rebuttal, see G. Himmelfarb, "Telling It as You Like It," *Times Literary Supplement*, October 16, 1992.

87. See the opinion of Peter Burke in *New Perspectives on Historical Writing*, (University Park: Pennsylvania State University Press, 1992), which Burke edited.

88. See Neale, *Writing*, 185–96.

89. E. R. Tonkin, *Narrating Our Pasts: The Social Construction of Oral History* (Cambridge: Cambridge University Press, 1992); see also R. Finnegan, *Oral Traditions and the Verbal Arts: A Guide to Research Practices* (London: Routledge, 1992), for a summary of all the views presently held about oral tradition.

90. *HA* 18 (1991): 399–408.

91. E. I. Steinhart, "Introduction," *Ethnohistory* 36, no. 1 (1989): 4, 5. Note that the anachronism inherent in ethnography is not even considered.

92. He coined the expression "production of history," perhaps as a last avatar of the modes of production and reproduction.

93. D. W. Cohen, "The Undefining of Oral Tradition," *Ethnohistory* 36, no. 1 (1989): 9–18. Cohen began as a very positivist historian. Cf. his "A Survey of Interlacustrine Chronology," *JAH* 11 (1970): 177–202. In his later works he has retreated more and more from this position.

94. Nobile, "Uncovering Roots."

95. Cohen and Odhiambo, *Siaya*, 3.

96. For instance, in the newsletter *Passages* and in the proposed "field of inquiry" for the specialized seminar planned for 1992–93: "The Constitution of Knowledge: The Production of History and Culture."

97. The Chicago group was formed from 1980 onward and includes scholars like Bernard Cohn for India, John and Jean Comaroff for Africa, and Wendy Griswold in sociology.

98. V. Y. Mudimbe, *L'odeur du père* (Paris: Harmattan, 1982); idem, *The Invention of Africa: Gnosis, Philosophy, and the Order of Knowledge* (Bloomington: Indiana University Press, 1988).

99. E. Said, *Orientalism* (New York: Pantheon Books, 1978); J. Fabian, *Time and the Other: How Anthropology Makes Its Object* (New York: Columbia University Press, 1983); idem, *Language and Colonial Power: The Appropriation of Swahili in the Former Belgian Congo, 1880–1938* (Cambridge: Cambridge University Press, 1986); and Fabian's subsequent works.

100. J. Fabian, "Ethnographic Objectivity Revisited: From Rigor to Vigor," *Annals of Scholarship* 10 (1993): 381–408.

101. If history and fiction were identical, why would the *Village Voice* and other newspapers that reprinted their conclusions think it so important to denounce Alex Haley's *Roots?*

102. In May 1992, at a symposium in Leiden, F. A. Van Jaarsveld, the dean of Afrikaner historians, formally acknowledged the failure of Afrikaner historiography. See Van Jaarsveld, "Recent Afrikaner Historiography," *Itinerario* 16, no. 1 (1992): 93–106.

103. L. Vail, ed., *The Creation of Tribalism in Southern Africa* (London: Currey, 1989), is the result of a conference held in 1983. In 1984 Jean Loup Amselle and Elikia Mbokolo organized a conference in Paris to discuss how recent the present ethnic groups are; see Amselle and Mbokolo, eds., *Au coeur de l'ethnie* (Paris: Découverte, 1985). Jean-Pierre Chrétien and Gérard Prunier of Paris followed this up with another one, entitled "Ethnic Groups Have a History"; see J. P. Chrétien and G. Prunier, eds., *Les ethnies ont une histoire* (Paris: Khartala, 1989).

104. A recent cultural history of soap in Zimbabwe certainly is imaginative, but how does it help the historiography of a country where so many other more pressing and more weighty topics remain to be studied?

CHAPTER 10. TRANSITIONS

1. P. C. Lou Tseng Tsiang, *Souvenirs et pensées* (Bruges: Desclee de Brouwer, 1945).

2. We arrived during an internal detente. China in 1986 was still a one-party totalitarian state, but the extreme harshness and terror of the Cultural Revolution was fading, while living standards were rising. Daily life was becoming more secure, and both intellectuals and the rural peasantry on the North Chinese plain felt confidence in the future.

3. On Donald Easum, see *International Who's Who* (London: Europa Publications, 1992), 456–57. On Francis X. Sutton, see *Who's Who in America* (New York: Reed Reference, 1992), 2: 3287.

4. Program, October 29–30; *ASR* 30, no. 2 (1987); P. E. Lovejoy, ed., *Africans in Bondage: Studies in Slavery and the Slave Trade* (Madison: African Studies Program, 1986).

5. I had felt a little bit scared during the standing ovation by a faceless crowd as I sat there to receive it. Somehow I felt as if I were in the path of a stampeding herd of hippopotamuses and could not hide.

6. I was granted a five-year John D. and Catherine T. MacArthur Foundation fellowship, administered by the University of Wisconsin.

7. M. Rouse, "Observations," *On Wisconsin* 93, no. 2 (January–February 1992), 4.

8. Even before my ethnographic excursion into American society—the Leonardo Seminar in 1973—I had been searching for the structuring core of American society and culture. I had joined the seminar in the hope of finding out what this was. The trial confirmed that this core lies in the federal court system. This system not only creates and enforces the rules which hold society together, but in it the most central rituals and beliefs which create society are enacted.

9. I was also lucky. The *Reader's Digest*, no less, had just published an *Illustrated History of South Africa: The Real Story* (Pleasantville, N.Y., 1988), compiled with the assistance of Colin Bundy, a senior South African historian. It was a large, thorough, and well-illustrated textbook.

10. Sources on concrete policies are confidential. Scholars should be aware that in several countries national researchers are even more restricted than foreigners.

11. In his book *The Past Is a Foreign Country* (Cambridge: Cambridge University Press, 1985), David Lowenthal vividly demonstrates for more recent times how this occurs.

12. E. J. Hobsbawm and T. O. Ranger, eds., *The Invention of Tradition* (Cambridge: Cambridge University Press, 1983).

13. J. Vansina, "Western Bantu Tradition and the Notion of Tradition," *Paideuma* 35 (1989): 289–300.

14. J. Vansina, *Paths in the Rainforests: Toward a History of Political Tradition in Equatorial Africa* (Madison: University of Wisconsin Press, 1990).

15. Reviewers expressed different opinions: D. W. Cohen, *Current Anthropology* 32 (1991): 363–64; C. Ehret, *American Historical Review* 98, no. 2 (April 1992); J. Guyer, *Ethnohistory* 39, no. 4 (1992): 510–11; C. Keim, *ASR* 36, no. 1 (April 1993): 131–35; R. Law, *African Affairs* 91 (1992): 631–33; R. Oliver, *Times Literary Supplement*, February 22, 1991; C. Wrigley, *JAH* 33 (1992): 129–34; M-C. Dupré, *Revue Française d'Histoire d'Outre-Mer* 79, no. 296 (1992); M. Douglas, *Anthropos* 88 (1993): 625–27.

16. Thus the Tervuren group sent me detailed comments but did me the honor of integrating my results into their database.

17. Undated letter from C. Inogwabini Bila-Isia (1991).

18. J. Vansina, *Sur les sentiers du passé en forêt* (Louvain-la-Neuve: Centre de l'Histoire de l'Afrique, 1991).

19. The gathering and the preparation of the data occurred at Tervuren, the computation at SOAS.

CHAPTER 11. LIVING WITH AFRICA

1. John O. Hunwick brought this point to my attention.

2. K. Popper, *The Poverty of Historicism* (London: Routledge and Kegan Paul, 1957). P. Novick, *That Noble Dream: The "Objectivity Question" and the*

American Historical Profession (Cambridge: Cambridge University Press, 1988), recounts the history of the objectivity debate in North America.

3. See T. S. Kuhn, *The Structure of Scientific Revolution* (Chicago: University of Chicago Press, 1962), for the current notion of "paradigm."

4. E.g., the series of articles published in the *ASR*, or A. J. Temu and B. Swai, *Historians and Africanist History: A Critique* (London: Zed Press, 1981), or B. Freund, *The Making of Contemporary Africa* (Bloomington: Indiana University Press, 1984), 1–15.

5. A. Lalande, *Vocabulaire technique et critique de la philosophie*, 11th ed. (Paris: Presses Universitaires de France, 1972), 1124.

6. A philosopher can deny this in principle and argue that the only certain reality is a sense of self, or not even that. In practice, this position is so extreme that it renders terms such as *reality* and *truth* devoid of meaning. After all, if true, such a statement itself shows that truth exists; if false, then truth can exist.

7. The notion of truth in courts of law derives from this axiom.

8. Lalande, *Vocabulaire*, 1223. About notions of truth, see also J. Searle, "Rationality and Realism, What Is at Stake," *Daedalus* (1993): 55–83, especially 62–66.

9. L. von Ranke, *Geschichten der romanischen und germanischen Völker von 1494 bis 1514* (Leipzig: Duncker and Humblot, 1824), preface, October 1824 (in the third edition of 1885, p. vii).

10. Von Ranke, *Geschichten*, viii.

11. C. Langlois and C. V. Seignobos, *Introduction aux études historiques* (Paris: Hachette, 1898).

12. P. Veyne, *Les Grecs ont-ils crus à leurs mythes?* (Paris: Editions du Seuil, 1983).

13. This situation also holds for Melanesia but on a much more modest scale.

14. Personal communication from John O. Hunwick, June 15, 1993.

15. The publication of pamphlet series such as *Tarikh, Odu, Hadith,* or the papers of historical associations destined for high schools shows this.

16. Indeed, one can argue that only the flow of African students to France and Britain has provided the enrollments necessary to keep departments of African history in operation there.

17. The more remote the periods being studied, the less close the cultural connection, yet as long as no massive cultural transformations have taken place between the culture of the forebears and the culture of its interpreters, "insiders" still remain privileged interpreters of the sources from that past.

18. The most extreme situation occurs when author, audience, and subject belong to three different cultures. I experienced this when I was teaching Central African history to a Chinese audience in Beijing. Even though I felt that the audience correctly understood my meaning and that this was close to that

of Central Africans today, despite the fact that it had gone through a double "cultural translation," there is no assurance that this was the case.

19. It is a point worthy of further reflection that in such movies the worst distortions do not occur in scenery or props but in the dialogue and in the general posture and demeanor of the actors.

20. E.g., E. P. Thompson, *The Voice of the Past* (London: Oxford University Press, 1978), on his "Problems of Method in Oral History," *Oral History* 4 (1973): 1–55.

21. D. Lange, "Das alte Mali und Ghana: Der Beitrag der Oraltraditionen zur Kritik einer historiographischen Fiktion," *Historisches Zeitschrift* 255 (1992): 587–623.

22. Historiography should not be confused with its substance, historical change itself. There is no progress or even a "purposive movement" toward a future in history. Historical dynamics are chaotic; that is, small causes can have large and unforeseeable consequences. Even using an "ebb and flow" metaphor to describe these dynamics, as espoused by Finn Fuglestad in "The Trevor-Roper Trap; or, The Imperialism of History: An Essay," *HA* 19 (1992): 309–26, implies too much regularity.

23. B. Jewsiewicki's letter to me, December 20, 1977; B. Jewsiewicki, ed., *Art pictural Zairois* (Quebec: Selat, 1992), and works cited therein.

24. In this evaluation I am guided by the opinions other scholars have expressed about me in book reviews or in letters to others.

25. T. O. Ranger, "Towards a Usable African Past," in *African Studies since 1945: A Tribute to Basil Davidson,* edited by C. Fyfe (London: Longman, 1976), 18–20, and, more scathingly, K. Brown and M. Roberts, "Introduction," *Social Analysis* 4 (1980): 3–12.

26. *HA* 1 (1974): 139–52.

27. PF: Mary Douglas in the fall of 1986.

28. Lalande, *Vocabulaire,* 1127–28.

29. This is not the place to discuss the appropriate character of various systems of teaching in use in different university systems. Suffice it to say that experience has convinced me that graduate and undergraduate training should be quite different, that tutoring and hands-on work is the only efficient way to train graduates, and that whatever scholars may want, universities will always reflect the ways of the larger societies to which they belong, with significant effects on the procedures and content of teaching.

30. R. Sanders, "The Last Decade: A Content Analysis of the *African Studies Review,*" *ASR* (April 1993): 115–26, esp. table 3.

31. Ethnicity is one of these. To scholars belonging to centralizing great powers, such as the United Kingdom, France, and the United States, ethnicity is a sort of irrational malady to be explained away by the action of economic or social forces. Belgians have lived all their lives with ethnicity and understand

its claims, justifications, and ramifications in exquisite detail. But they are so involved that to them ethnicity seems so natural and permanent that they can hardly understand that this is not so and therefore that ethnicity must be explained.

32. For a popular account, see "Finding West Africa's Oldest City," *National Geographic* 162, no. 3 (September 1982): 396–417.

33. J. R. Denbow, "*Cenchrus ciliaris:* An Ecological Indicator of Iron Age Middens Using Aerial Photography in Eastern Botswana," *South African Journal of Science* 75 (1979): 405–8.

34. F. Wendorf et al., "Saharan Exploitation of Plants, 8,000 Years B.P.," *Nature*, no. 6397 (February 13, 1993): 721–24.

35. R. Bolland, *Tellem Textiles: Archaeological Finds from Burial Caves in Mali's Bandiagara Cliffs,* translated by P. Wardle (Amsterdam: Tropenmuseum, 1991).

Index

Abili Ndiõ, 108
Abun-Nasr, Jamil, 132
Académie malgache, 45
Accra, International Congress of Africanists (1962), 136
Achimota College, 46, 53
Addis Ababa, University of, 46
Africa, 31, 45
Africa imagined, 12, 14, 195, 202–3, 219, 228–29, 251
African Americans, 43–44, 117–18, 143, 185, 200
African American Studies, department of, 137–38
African Arts, 293n62
African Economic History, 293n61
African Heritage Association, 118
African Historians of Africa, 43, 44, 58, 99, 112–16, 119, 226, 234, 240; and fieldwork, 203, 228; and UNESCO, 195–96, 201–2, 251. *See also* Africanization
African Historical Studies, 117
African History Program (Madison), 100–103, 139–46, 174–75, 225–28, 246–47; graduates of, 117, 175, 183–88, 219; Seminar in African History, 90, 102, 111, 140, 142–46, 183, 187
"African Initiative" doctrine, 116, 125, 199, 234
Africanist, doctrine, 48–49, 124–25, 199
Africanization: of departments of

history, 113–16; at Lovanium, 153, 156–57, 161–63, 166, 228
African Studies Association of the United States, 71, 118, 224
African Studies Programs, 45, 71, 111; in Africa, 55, 126–27; in Europe, 37, 89, 104, 172; in Madison, 100–103, 183, 188, 189, 223–24, 226; in the United States, 93, 117, 211, 216, 223–24
African Studies Review, 216, 251
Afrikaner historiography, 199, 200
Afrocentrism, 50, 118
Agiri, Babatunde, 161, 172
Ajayi, Jacob, 53, 99–100, 113, 114, 201
Alagoa, Ebiegberi J., 55, 161, 172
American Council of Learned Societies, 216
American History, 133, 134, 214
Amin, Idi, 197
Amin, Samir, 197
Anene, Joseph, 53, 113
Angola, 42, 158, 209, 211, 231, 243; civil war, 228
apartheid, 41, 116, 220, 233, 226–27, 235
Arabic, 42, 136, 176, 178, 180
Arabs, 43, 132, 177
archaeology, 44, 56, 58, 126, 127; and the Bantu question, 129–30; museums, 69, 74; research in, 55, 105–6, 110, 147, 193; sites, 29, 35–36, 68–69, 70, 110, 112, 135, 235. *See also*

expatriates: at African universities, 73–74, 113–16, 155–56, 157, 161, 162, 239–40, 272n14; and fieldwork, 203; and publication, 191

Fabian, Johannes, 219
Fage, John, 35, 40, 47–48, 58, 118, 123, 135; and curriculum, 53, 55, 57; and historiography, 48–49, 112, 124
Fagg, Wiliam, 11
Farnham conference on chronology, 121, 128
Feierman, Steven, 127, 226; and history of health, 212, 216; at Madison, 143, 168, 171, 184–86
feudalism, 95, 122, 204
fiction, 209, 217, 218, 237
fieldwork: effects of 249–51; financing, 27, 94, 174, 185; among the Kuba, 15–27, 31–34, 36–37, 56; in Libya 177–78; in Madison, 92, 152, 297n8; in medical sociology, 159; recent conditions for, 193, 220, 228; required, 56, 104, 134, 202, 205; in Ruanda-Urundi, 32, 63, 67, 84–85; and social history, 213; by students in Madison, 172, 183, 186, 227; among the Tio, 105–10; for "words and things", 191, 192. *See also* sampling and fieldwork
Florida, University of, 226
Ford Foundation, 139, 223
Forde, Daryll, 9–10, 37, 40, 103, 146; at conferences, 35, 52, 77, 99
Foucault, Michel, 173, 216
Fourah Bay College, 45
Fox, Renée, 159–60, 293n63
Fragmentation in African historiography, 211, 213–15, 216, 221, 233, 236
French Central Africa (alias AEF), 105–6
Freund, William, 205, 206
Frobenius Institut, 195, 292n45
functionalism, 10, 12, 17, 97, 99, 121, 203
Fyfe, Christopher, 47, 55

Gabon, 189, 192–93
Gadhafi, Mu'ammar, 176, 177
Gado, Boube, 196
gender, 144, 185, 211
Ghana, ancient kingdom, 73, 244
Ghana (formerly Gold Coast): independence of; 51, 56, 61, 101; University of, 47, 53, 58, 118, 126
Ghent, state university of, 30, 35
Gheyl, Pieter, 7
Gillon, Luc, 74, 75, 76, 155, 156, 157, 161
Gold Coast (now Ghana), University College of, 35, 46, 47, 55, 211
Goody, Jack, 122
Gramsci, Antonio, 205, 216
Gravel, Pierre, 83
great man view of history, 111, 133, 199, 216
Griaule, Marcel, 35
Guggenheim Foundation, 283n58, 288n32
Guthrie, Malcolm, 11, 129–30, 271n26
Gwete, Lema, 158

Haberland, Eike, 288n42
Haley, Alex, 149–50, 209, 210, 218, 237
Hamitic theory, 64
Hanna, A. J., 53, 57
Hargreaves, John, 47
Harlow, Vincent, 47
Harrington, Fred H., 89, 101, 139
Harroy, Jean-Paul, 13, 15, 28, 60, 62, 79, 81, 104
Hartwig, Gerald, 212
Headrick, Rita, 216
Heine, Bernd, 194
Heintze, Beatrix, 195, 292n45
Henige, David, 128, 145, 207
Herskovits, Melville, 35, 44, 92
Hiernaux, Jean, 29, 60, 68
Hill, Bertram, 102, 103
Hill, Polly, 131
historical consciousness, 17, 25, 41, 189, 190, 217, 218, 235, 249
historical imagination, 29, 100, 163,

305

Index

UNESCO, 99; and *General history of Africa*, 135–36, 163, 173, 187, 195–96, 201–2, 228, 244, 251
United Nations, 45, 78
Urvoy, Yves, 62
"usable past" doctrine, 116, 125, 198, 215
Usumbura (now Bujumbura), 32, 62, 78, 81, 83, 85

Vail, Leroy, 127
Van Bulck, Vaast (alias Gaston), 34, 37, 39
van den Berghe, Louis, 28, 62, 68–69, 70, 76
Van den Nieuwenhuizen, Jos, 7
van de Walle, Etienne, 85
Van Moorsel, Hendrik, 74
Vanneste, 172
Van Onselen, Charles, 204
Vellut, Jean-Luc, 158–59, 161, 163, 165–66, 172, 190
Verhaegen, Benoît, 110, 146, 155–56, 161
Veyne, Paul, 173
Vidal, Claudine, 152
Vietnam war, 137
Vilas Trust Fund, William F., xiii, 174, 175, 191, 287n23
Viviers, colloquium on the Bantu expansion, 194
Von Ranke, Leopold, 53, 237–38

Weber, Max, 122, 160, 207
Webster, J. Bertin, 114, 116
Wenner Gren Foundation, 129
West Africa: clans in, 150; historiography of, 42, 48, 49, 50, 53, 113–15, 125, 133, 134; history of, 131, 244, 253, 254; and independence, 57; intellectuals in, 58; Islam in, 131–32; 143; mental map of, 251; research about, 113, 115, 202, 205; teaching about, 145, 226; UNESCO and, 136; universities in, 46, 113, 118, 119; West African historians, 51; West Africans in Tripoli, 177

Westermann, Dietrich, 44
White, Landeg, 216
Wilk, Ivor, 121–22, 206–7
Willett, Frank, 279n97
Williams, William Appleman, 137
Willis, John Ralph, 143
Willis, Roy G., 208
Wisconsin, history of, 187
Wisconsin, University of (at Madison), 71, 88–103, 137–55, 156, 161, 168, 171–75, 183–89, 191, 223–28, 252
Wisconsin Alumni Research Foundation, 282n36
Wisconsin school, 144–46, 207
women at universities: as professors, 10, 226, 280n4; as students, 141–42, 185
women's studies, 211, 214–15, 230, 235
Woodson Carter, G., 43–44
words and things, 147, 148, 190, 191, 193–94, 223, 229, 245
World War II, 4, 43, 46–47, 49, 58, 177, 222, 234
Wright, Donald R., 217

Yale University, 153
Yarak, Larry, 281n28
Youlou, 109, 110
Young, M. Crawford, 139

Zaire: art in, 195, 245, ethnography, 146, 172, mental map of, 251, monographs about, 146, 231, 242; rainforests in, 192; researchers about, 71, 208, 212, 216; scholars from, 126, 219, 230; universities in, 126, 201; university students in, 110, 166–67, 173, 247. *See also* Congo, Belgian; Congo, Democratic Republic of; Lovanium
Zambia (formerly northern Rhodesia), 61, 116, 231, 247
Zimbabwe (formerly Rhodesia, Southern Rhodesia), 61, 201, 202